CW00921255

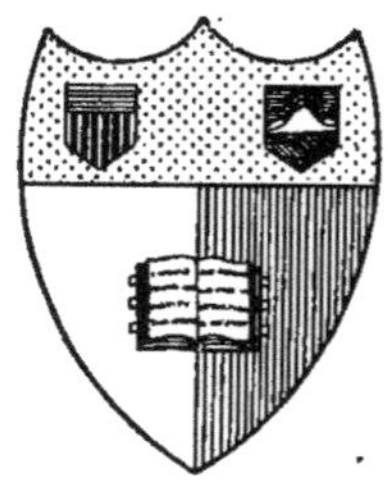

Date Due

SEP 8 19[illegible]			
[illegible] 1950			
JAN [illegible] 19[illegible] M P			
[illegible] D			
APR [illegible] 1980 F			

Lefco

THE HEART OF ARABIA

FAISAL IBN ABDULAZIZ IBN SA'UD, SECOND SURVIVING SON OF IBN SA'UD.
From a portrait by Miss Janet Robertson in the possession of Mr. J. Conway Davies.

THE HEART OF ARABIA

A RECORD OF TRAVEL & EXPLORATION

BY H. ST.J. B. PHILBY C.I.E. I.C.S.
B.A. (Cantab.), F.R.G.S., M.R.A.S.
FOUNDER'S MEDALLIST (1920) OF THE ROYAL GEOGRAPHICAL SOCIETY
CHIEF BRITISH REPRESENTATIVE, TRANS-JORDANIA
FORMERLY ADVISER TO THE MINISTRY OF THE INTERIOR, MESOPOTAMIA

IN TWO VOLUMES

VOL. I

ILLUSTRATED

CONSTABLE AND COMPANY LTD
LONDON · BOMBAY · SYDNEY
1922

TO THE MEMORY OF

MY BROTHERS

MAJOR H. P. PHILBY, D.S.O.

COMMANDING 2ND BATT. YORK AND LANCASTER REGIMENT

AND

LIEUTENANT D. D. PHILBY

1ST BATT. ROYAL DUBLIN FUSILIERS, ATTACHED 2ND BATT.
ROYAL MUNSTER FUSILIERS

WHO FELL IN FLANDERS DURING THE GREAT WAR

I DEDICATE THIS WORK

PREFACE

Of the pleasant year I spent sojourning and wandering amid the deserts and oases of Arabia I have endeavoured to compile a record, at once fully descriptive of my own experiences and designed to serve my successors as a faithful guide in their wanderings, when in their turn they take up the torch which has been held in the past by so many distinguished hands—Niebuhr and Burckhardt, Sadlier and Burton, Doughty and the Blunts, Wallin and Wellsted, Huber and Halévy, Euting and Guarmani, and, in modern times, Shakespear and Gertrude Bell, to name but a few of those whose names are writ large on the scroll of Arabian explorers.

It was with little fitness to undertake geographical or scientific work of any kind that I entered Arabia, but chance led me far afield from the tracks of those who had been in that country before me ; and natural curiosity, fortified by a sense of duty, impelled me to record day by day and almost hour by hour everything I saw or heard in the course of my wanderings in the hope that some day, the grain being separated from the chaff, there might remain a residue of useful matter worthy of presentation to the world. The few scientific instruments I carried with me, with a limited knowledge of their proper uses, have enabled the experts of the Royal Geographical Society to use the detailed itineraries of my journeys in the preparation of reasonable maps of a country hitherto in great part conventionally charted on the basis of second-hand information. To their unsparing efforts are due the two maps, which, with the Society's permission, I am able to publish with these volumes ; and it is but fitting that I should place on record my gratitude both for their work and for the generous encouragement I have received from the Royal Geographical Society itself since my return from Arabia.

Circumstances have necessitated the limitation of these volumes to a record of the first part only of my sojourn in Arabia, ending with my return to the *Wahhabi* capital after an excursion in the summer of 1918 to the provinces of Southern Najd. Circumstances alone will determine whether the record of the latter part of my wanderings and of the *Wahhabi* campaign against Haïl in the autumn of the same year shall ever see the light of day. But for the moment I have deemed it better to set forth in full the details of a portion of my experiences than to deal more summarily with the whole period of my residence in Arabia. And, finally, circumstances alone—circumstances over which I have unfortunately no control—will decide whether I shall ever return to the deserts of Arabia to resume a task which, I am fully conscious, I have left unfinished.

A few words of explanation on the vexed subject of the transliteration of Arabic names. In view of the lack of uniformity among the various official and unofficial bodies, who have occasion in the course of their work to consider this problem, the Royal Geographical Society has during the past year taken the lead and set to work to discover whether existing differences of practice can be reconciled by the adoption of any uniform system based on the elimination of all diacritical marks and accents. After much discussion of the subject by the assembled champions of all the systems in the field, a final decision has recently been arrived at in favour of a system based on and but little differing from that in general use by the General Staff of the Army in India. That system was used during the war in Mesopotamia for survey purposes; and there can be little doubt that the modification of it now accepted by the Royal Geographical Society represents as near an approach to the ideal as it is possible to arrive at in the circumstances.

Unfortunately that decision was arrived at after this work was completed in manuscript, and I have not thought it necessary to undertake the considerable labour which would be involved in making the requisite corrections, albeit such corrections would only be required in respect of two points. The ل of the Arabic definite article should be assimilated under the new system to the first letter of the following word in all cases, in which such assimilation takes place in the pronunciation of the Arabic, while I have transliterated it by its literal equivalent—L—in all cases;[1] and I have adopted -IYYA as the transliteration of the common termination ـيّة, while the new system prescribes the simpler -IYA.

With these two exceptions the system I had already adopted conforms with that now recommended by the Royal Geographical Society, which, needless to say, I shall adopt in future. But in the text of this work I have here and there deliberately adopted the vernacular pronunciation as the basis of my transliteration, with the sole object of indicating the character of such pronunciation; and furthermore, I have marked all long vowels *in the index only* for the information of those who are sufficiently curious to refer to it. The place-names on the map of Southern Najd have been transliterated in accordance with the system formerly accepted by the Royal Geographical Society and now discarded, but, the map having already been published, it has been found impossible to bring it into line with the new system.

I am much indebted for many suggestions for the improvement of these volumes to the Hon. Sir Percy Z. Cox, G.C.I.E., K.C.S.I., K.C.M.G., H.B.M.'s High Commissioner for Mesopotamia, and Miss Gertrude L. Bell, C.B.E., who have been kind enough to read them through in proof; and my especial thanks are due to my publishers for their unfailing patience and indulgence.

BAGHDAD, *December* 1920.

[1] In Central Arabia assimilation of the ل is often dispensed with.

CONTENTS

CHAPTER V

CHAPTER VI

CHAPTER VII

ILLUSTRATIONS

FACE PAGE

PLAN

INTRODUCTION

"Depuis quelques années il s'est élevé dans la province d'*el Âred* une nouvelle secte ou plutôt une nouvelle religion, laquelle causera peut-être avec le temps des changemens considérables et dans la croyance et dans le gouvernement des Arabes."[1] So wrote Carsten Niebuhr, the father of Arabian exploration, in his record of an expedition to Arabia undertaken at the instance of the Danish Government about the middle of the eighteenth century.

The information collected by him from prejudiced sources at a considerable distance from the scene of the events which he briefly recorded was far from being as full as we might desire; but to him belongs the credit of having been the first to bring to Europe news of the first beginnings of a movement, which not only justified his prediction of its import within half-a-century of its utterance, but has persisted through all vicissitudes of fortune with little change of form or substance to our own days, and may yet under the changed conditions of the modern world attain the goal marked out for it by its originators.

In those days Desert Arabia, inhabited by nomad tribes eking out a precarious existence under conditions differing little if at all from those obtaining in patriarchal times, was, politically speaking, parcelled out into a number of independent principalities, some of which at any rate owned a vague allegiance to 'Arair, the principal Bani Khalid *Shaikh* of the Hasa province. Strife reigned supreme until the birth of the "new religion," and since then peace and war have alternated in Arabia according as that religion was in the ascendant or in abeyance.

[1] Niebuhr, *Voyage en Arabie*, 1774, vol. iii. p. 298.

"Quelques-uns des *Schechs* indépendans nouveaux-convertis,"[1] wrote Niebuhr, "qui se faisaient auparavant une guerre continuelle, devinrent amis par l'entremise d'*Abd ul wáhheb* et s'accordèrent à ne rien entreprendre d'important sans avoir auparavant consulté leur nouvel Apôtre. Par-là la balance politique fut détruite entre les petits Princes d'*El Áred*, parce que plusieurs *Schechs*, qui pouvaient auparavant tenir tête à leurs voisins, ne furent plus en état de se soutenir contre tant de *Schechs* réunis ; et les guerres devenaient toujours plus meurtrières et plus vives, en ce que les peuples des deux côtés s'imaginaient, qu'on ne les poursuivait que pour la cause de leur religion, et qu'ils étaient obligés d'user de force contre les hérétiques obstinés, ou les incrédules qui persévéraient dans leurs anciennes erreurs." It would be impossible to summarise more concisely the character and methods of a militant policy whose goal was peace. The chosen instrument of that policy was a petty baron of the noble clan of ʿAnaza, who held his court after the *Badawin* fashion in a castle built by his ancestors on the rock of Daraʿiyya amid the torrent strands of Wadi Hanifa. Like his contemporary in the Scottish Highlands, Rob Roy of Clan MacGregor, whose struggles with the Dukes of Argyll and Montrose on either side of him were but the death throes of the tribal system in our own islands, Muhammad the third or fourth chieftain in the direct line of descent from Saʿud I., the eponymous ancestor of the dynasty of Ibn Saʿud, found himself in the middle of the eighteenth century surrounded by powerful and ambitious neighbours, of whom the most formidable were the principalities of ʿAyaina and Manfuha, ever contending with each other over the ruins created by their perpetual warfare for supremacy in Central Arabia.

But the prince of ʿAyaina was blind to his opportunity when it came, and it was to the court of Daraʿiyya, where the ʿAnaza tradition of lavish hospitality filled the halls of Muhammad with *Badawin* guests, that there came about the year 1759 a prophet who had found no honour in his own country. Born of Tamimi parents at Huraimala in the district of Mahmal about the third decade of the eighteenth

[1] Niebuhr, *Voyage en Arabie*, vol. iii. p. 299.

century, Muhammad ibn ʿAbdulwahhab had spent his youth studying at the Universities of Baghdad and Damascus, and now returned with a message calculated to electrify his fellow-citizens of ʿAyaina, but was driven forth from that city as one likely to disturb the peace of a court content with its own ways.

But the baron of Daraʿiyya and after him his successor Saʿud II. hailed the seer as a proper instrument for the furtherance of their secular ambitions, and the *Wahhabi* creed came into being as the result of their earnest collaboration. For all their backsliding from the true faith of *Islam* the Arabs were still at heart staunch to the principles of the puritan school of Ahmad ibn Hanbal, and it required but little effort to stir the embers of fanaticism ever latent among the desert folk of Arabia. The true faith was purged of the dross of ecclesiastical pedantry, and the salient facts of a moribund creed were made to shine forth again as beacons to every wanderer in the wilderness of doubt. The unity and jealousy of God, the vital necessity of belief and the certainty of reward to all believers—these [1] were the corner-stones of the edifice, which prince and priest set to work to erect upon the shifting sands of nomad society; and the edifice that grew out of those foundations was an Arabian Empire.

Before Saʿud II. and Muhammad, the priest, were gathered to their fathers at the end of the eighteenth century their dreams had been realised. ʿAyaina and Manfuha had fallen before the onslaught of their inspired armies, the Hasa had succumbed to them, lesser states had vanished from the scene and the Ottoman Empire itself had been rudely awakened to a sense of impending danger.

ʿAbdulʿaziz II., the son and successor of Saʿud, followed in the footsteps of his father with such success that the *Shiaʿ* shrine of Karbala, on the borders of Mesopotamia, experienced the terrors of a *Wahhabi* incursion in 1801, and two years later Mecca itself was annexed to the growing empire. But the desecration of Karbala was a crime for

[1] The principles of the *Wahhabi* creed were embodied by its founder in a pamphlet entitled "The Three Principles and the Proofs Thereof," which Ibn Saʿud has recently (1918) had reprinted at Bombay in connection with the *Ikhwan* movement.

which there could be no pardon, and the year that had witnessed his triumphal entry into Mecca saw 'Abdul'aziz bow down before his God in the great mosque of Dara'iyya for the last time—with an assassin's dagger between his shoulder-blades.

His son and successor, 'Abdullah, having completed his father's last campaign by the capture of Madina in 1804, turned his attention without delay to provinces farther afield, and made himself master of 'Uman and the Yaman before he had been long on the throne; but the apprehensions of Turkey had now been fairly aroused, and in 1805 Muhammad 'Ali Pasha became Viceroy of Egypt, with instructions to bring the *Wahhabi* Emperor to his knees. In 1810 the campaign, for which elaborate preparations had been made, was launched under the command of his son, Tussun, who, in 1812, suffered a signal defeat in the mountain passes between the Red Sea coast and Madina, but later in the same year recovered the latter town without much difficulty. Simultaneously success attended the Turkish cause in the south, and Jidda, Mecca and Taïf were occupied in rapid succession; but in the winter of 1813–14 Tussun was defeated at Turaba, and Burkhardt, who visited the Hijaz in the following summer and has left us an admirable summary of the events of this period, records that despondency was rife in the Turkish army owing to a variety of causes arising out of the rapacity and incapacity of the higher command.

The *Wahhabis* meanwhile carried on a guerrilla warfare with great success against the scattered forces of the enemy, and it was not until the spring of 1815 that the tide turned once more in favour of the Turks, whose victory at Busal, between Taïf and Turaba, put an end to 'Abdullah's influence in the south, while Tussun actually reached the Qasim on a flying raid into the interior from Madina and forced the *Wahhabi* monarch to agree to a truce, whose terms were certainly favourable to the Turks.

'Abdullah seems at this stage to have lost much of the ardour which had inspired his ancestors and his own earlier operations, and the initiative now passed definitely to Muhammad 'Ali, who, having spent two years in active preparations for the resumption of hostilities, sent another son, Ibrahim Pasha, in 1818, in charge of an expedition destined to achieve the end for which he had worked for thirteen years.

Dara'iyya was besieged by the Turkish army, whose artillery reduced the inhabitants to such straits that 'Abdullah was compelled to capitulate on a Turkish guarantee that the lives and honour of his subjects would be respected. He himself and the more important members of the royal family were reserved to grace the triumph of his conqueror at Cairo; the rest of the royal family, the *Wahhabi* priesthood and other leaders of the people were disposed of by the simple expedient of a general massacre; and the walls and palaces, mosques and mansions of Dara'iyya were razed to the ground, where their ruins lie to this day, a monument of the great days of the *Wahhabi* Empire, of its rapid rise and headlong fall and of its victor, whose name and race are still execrated by the descendants of his victims after the lapse of a whole century.

For the next thirty years the Turks maintained a precarious foothold amid the wreckage of the Empire they had destroyed, and Arabia knew no peace. Ever and anon the Turkish Viceroys were challenged by some survivor of the *Wahhabi* dynasty, and the history of these years is little but a record of guerilla warfare between the Arabs and the Turks. Turki, the son of 'Abdullah, who had been absent from Dara'iyya at the time of the final tragedy, rallied the drooping spirits of his people about 1830 by the reoccupation of his father's throne and the creation of a new capital at Riyadh; and ten years later 'Abdullah ibn Thunaian, a scion of a collateral branch of the Sa'ud family, reigned for a brief space over the *Wahhabi* territories; but it was reserved for Faisal, the son of Turki, who had been carried off into exile with his grandfather, and who had escaped from his prison in Egypt, to reorganise the shattered fortunes of his country and to put an end to Turkish dominion therein.

After two failures he finally established himself on the throne of Riyadh about 1842, and by the time of his death, about a quarter of a century later, had restored something of the vigour which had characterised the *Wahhabi* state in its early days; but by this time the rival state of Jabal Shammar had risen into prominence under the skilful leadership of the founders of the Ibn Rashid dynasty, and Faisal was never strong enough to reassert the claim of his ancestors to suzerainty over Haïl. Be that as it may, we have the contemporary testimony of Palgrave and Pelly that, shrunk though it was from its original dimensions, the state that he bequeathed to his successors differed little, if at all, in essentials from that which his great-grandfather had inherited from the great Sa'ud and was well ordered in all respects but one.

Of the disastrous dispute over the succession which arose between his two eldest sons at his death, of the Rashidian occupation in which that dispute resulted during the eighties of last century and of the eventual recovery of the *Wahhabi* throne in 1901 by a cadet of the royal family, who still holds it to the great advantage of his subjects, I shall have occasion to give the details in the course of the ensuing narrative of my sojourn in the heart of Arabia during the last year of the Great War.

The dramatic revival of the *Wahhabi* power was, to say the least, somewhat disconcerting to Turkish policy, which had arrived at a satisfactory *modus vivendi* with Ibn Rashid; and Turkish troops were sent to help the Shammar to stem the northward advance of Ibn Sa'ud in 1904. But the Qasim was recovered by the latter in 1906, and an invasion of that province by the troops of the Sharif of Mecca in 1910 did not materially check the re-establishment of *Wahhabi* authority throughout the territories which had acknowledged the rule of Faisal. There remained, however, little doubt in the mind of Ibn Sa'ud that the Turks were only awaiting a favourable opportunity to crush him as they had crushed his great-great-grandfather a century before, and it was but natural in the circumstances that he should seek about him for the means of averting the danger which threatened him.

It was to Great Britain that he looked—though for a time in vain. Dark clouds were already rising over the political horizon, and Turkey was rapidly becoming the cat's-paw of German ambitions. The Baghdad railway was slowly bringing the forces of Germany within striking distance of the nerve-centre of the British Empire. Ibn Sa'ud, who had been brought up in exile at Kuwait, the ultimate destination of the German strategic railway, realised that his own security was involved in the coming struggle, and it was not without purpose that he encouraged the visits to his own territories and cultivated the friendship of the late Captain W. H. C. Shakespear, who was Political Agent at Kuwait during the fateful years which preceded the bursting of the storm.

None knew when that storm would burst upon the world ; but early in 1914 Ibn Sa'ud felt himself strong enough to strike a blow at Turkey on his own account. He descended suddenly upon the Hasa province, which the Turks had held since Midhat Pasha had annexed it in 1871 ; his victory was complete and the Turkish garrisons left his territories for good ; before they had time to organise an expedition to avenge their defeat they were swept by their own amazing folly into the vortex of the European War.

Sir Percy Cox, who accompanied the Mesopotamian Expeditionary Force as Chief Political Officer, immediately sent Captain Shakespear to spur Ibn Sa'ud into active operations against the Turks and their natural ally, Ibn Rashid. The campaign was launched in January 1915, and I have always thought that, had it not been for the unfortunate accident of Shakespear's death in the very first battle between the rival forces, Colonel Lawrence might never have had the opportunity of initiating and carrying through the brilliant campaigns with which his name is associated, and as the result of which he entered Damascus in triumph at the head of the army of the Hijaz.

For a time our faith in the ability of the Arabs to co-operate with our forces in modern warfare was shaken, and, though the continuance of cordial relations between ourselves and Ibn Sa'ud was ensured by the ratification of a formal treaty in 1916, it was not to him that we looked for assistance when circumstances necessitated an effort on our part to secure the active co-operation of the Arabs in our operations against the Turks.

The Sharif of Mecca stepped into the breach from which Ibn Sa'ud had withdrawn, and the subsequent course of events in the Arabian theatre of war is sufficiently well know to need no recapitulation. The initial successes of the Hija forces, however, encouraged the Mesopotamian authoriti to hope for a corresponding effort on the part of Ibn Sa'u whose co-operation, if it could be secured on reasonable term might be of value in connection with the blockade operatior then in progress on the Euphrates. It was hoped, moreove that, in view of the growing tension between Ibn Sa'ud an King Husain, the energies of the former might be usefull diverted to an attack on Haïl, where Ibn Rashid, with th fitful encouragement and assistance of the Turks, was alway a potential thorn in our sides.

And so in due course it was decided that a British Missio should be sent to Riyadh to study the possibilities of th situation on the spot, and to the charge of that Mission, whic left Baghdad in October 1917, I had the great good fortun to be appointed. With me, as military expert and represen tative of the Commander-in-Chief of the Mesopotamia Force, went Lieutenant-Colonel F. Cunliffe Owen, C.M.G. R.F.A., who was attended by his batman, Private H Schofield, a young Yorkshireman of great charm an promise, while Lieutenant-Colonel R. E. A. Hamilton, C.I.E., I.A., Political Agent at Kuwait, was to join us a Riyadh, whither he had already set out in connection wit an incident arising out of our blockade operations.

Time was precious, and we could not wait for the fruitio of plans then under consideration for the inclusion amon our number of representatives of the High Commissione for Egypt and the King of the Hijaz, as also of a medica officer and a wireless party. The first two were to join u at our destination by way of the Hijaz, but for reason which will appear in the course of my narrative failed t keep their tryst; no medical officer was available at th time, and the idea of keeping the Mission in wireless touc with the world was also abandoned. Within a month moreover, of our landing in Arabia the Mission, as such ceased to exist, and the departure first of Colonel Hamilton and afterwards of Colonel Cunliffe Owen and Schofield left me the sole survivor of a company that might have

[1] Now Lord Belhaven and Stenton.

been imposing, and for the best part of a year the sole representative of Great Britain in the heart of Arabia —the bearer to the Arabs of Wahhabiland of that great message of goodwill, which went forth in the dark days of the war to assure a proud race long ground down under the heel of the Ottoman Turk of the freedom which awaited it when the storm should be gone. In calling upon the Arabs to play their part in operations designed to achieve their liberation from Turkish tyranny we specifically disclaimed for ourselves and our Allies any ulterior motive of material profit or imperial ambition. Two years have rolled by, bringing forgetfulness of the heartfelt relief with which we acclaimed the news of our hard-won victory; and the Arabs, long patient but growing restive, still await the redemption of our pledges. As one of the least of the mouthpieces used by His Majesty's Government for the conveyance of an assurance of their goodwill to the Arab peoples, I may express the hope, nay, the firm conviction that, whatever temptings there may have been or may yet be to a contrary policy, the word of Britain will not be broken in the East.

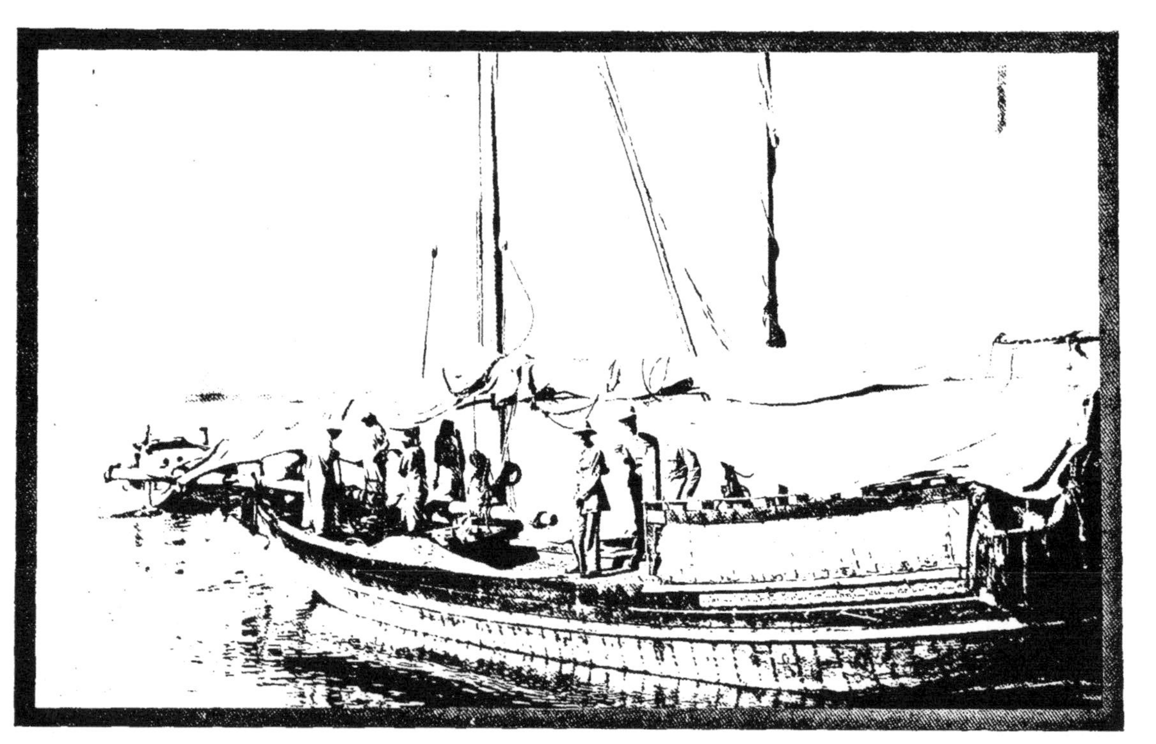

DHOW WITH BRITISH MISSION ON BOARD BEING TOWED BY STEAM CUTTER OF H.M.S. "LAWRENCE"; COLONEL F. CUNLIFFE OWEN IN CENTRE

THE THRESHOLD OF ARABIA

1. Al Bahrain to 'Uqair

No ripple stirred the oily surface of the Gulf of Bahrain at noon on the 14th November 1917, when the steam-cutter of H.M.S. *Lawrence*, leaving us to our fate at the entrance to the narrow channel which cleaves the submerged reefs, sped back to the good ship which had brought us thus far from Basra. Ruddy lay the sea on either side, warning the mariner of its hidden perils, green the channel, the narrow margin of safety, and the high seas behind. We lay becalmed. Idly flapped the sail full-spread to court the breeze; languidly drooped the ensign of Wahhabiland at our stern, pale green, white bordered, mirrored in the pale green sea. Behind us lay Bahrain, the last outpost of civilisation; before us lay Arabia. To right and left rose the rock masses of Jabal Dhahran [1] and Jabal Dukhan,[2] the one on the mainland north-westward, the other to the south-west on the island of Bahrain, hills of no great height but seeming high and fitting portals to the unknown beyond.

Our craft was a small *dhow* and we our three selves and a crew of seven, whose captain, 'Ali, had in similar but larger ships braved the perils of the ocean even to far Zanzibar. Many a *Baduwi* have I since met in the midst of Arabia, who has told me of the time when he tempted Providence on the sea in search of a livelihood, always hard to earn on the mainland. Many there are of 'Ataiba, Dawasir and others who come down to Bahrain for the pearling season; some of them thereafter take to a sea-

[1] 500 feet above sea-level. [2] 410 feet above sea-level.

faring life to earn the wherewithal to buy camels and a wife.

A transient breeze filled our sail for a brief space in the afternoon, but ere sunset it had failed us, and we drew in to anchor off a small promontory of the island abreast of Jabal Dukhan. At midnight we moved forward again before a gentle breeze, which held till midday, when again we lay becalmed within sight of the watch-tower of 'Uqair. Under normal conditions they reckon the run from Bahrain to 'Uqair at eight hours, while it was now some twenty-six hours since we had left the *Lawrence*, and it was not till 2 P.M. that we found the breeze again. Then, however, we made steady progress and rapidly approached the low-lying spit of Al Hadd, which separates the deep-water harbour of 'Uqair from the shallow reef-strewn gulf.

A crazy pole set in the sea off the southern extremity of the spit serves as a beacon to guide ships into the harbour, into which we turned before a sudden stiff blow from the southward,[1] every timber and rope straining and creaking as we raced towards the pier. And so, at length, after a run of thirty-two hours, as the sun was setting behind the sand-hills of the mainland, we reached our goal and stood on the threshold of Wahhabiland.

2. 'Uqair

We had scarcely made fast to one of the two old guns, set up on end, muzzle downwards, at the extremities of the jetty to serve as mooring-posts, than the local *Amir* or governor, 'Abdulrahman ibn Khairullah, appeared in person to welcome us in the name of Ibn Sa'ud and to invite us to his apartments in the fort. The local garrison, consisting of some forty armed men, was drawn up at the entrance to receive us and, passing into the courtyard, we ascended to the *Amir's* reception-room on the upper storey, a small and dingy apartment furnished with abundance of carpets and a few cushions, against which we reclined conversing with our host and two of his chief retainers, while tea and coffee passed round. A native of Qatif, 'Abdul-

[1] Known as *Kos*.

rahman had occupied the post of *Amir* for wellnigh four years since the early spring of 1914, when ʿUqair with the rest of the Hasa province was wrested from the Turks by Ibn Saʿud. In all that time he had visited his home but once for a month's leave during the previous *Ramdhan*; the fort had no accommodation for ladies, and he made no secret of his desire for transfer to a more congenial post, where he could enjoy the society of his wife and family. "Nevertheless," he declared, "it is the will of the *Imam*[1] and that for me is law." He spoke, too, with much enthusiasm of the great change which had come over the whole province with the change of rulers; the weak Turkish garrison had never been able to do more than hold the towns and various posts on the line of communications, with the result that the roads and the surrounding country were ever infested by *Badawin* marauders, whereas Ibn Saʿud, by punishing raids with counter-raids pressed home often into waterless deserts, whither the offenders would retire till their offences were forgotten, and by a judicious policy of tribal subsidies, had reduced the tribes to unprecedented order. At any rate they had ceased to trouble ʿUqair and the towns and villages of the Hasa and to molest the shipping on the coast.

As we rose to take our leave I hinted at our anxiety to begin our journey without delay, whereat, with the glib mendacity of all well-bred Arabs, the *Amir* replied that he had expected us two days before and had had camels ready for an immediate start, but that since then, having given up all hope of our early arrival, he had sent the animals away to graze. As Saʿdi has it: "*Durugh-i-maslihat amiz Bih az rasti-yi-fitna angiz.*"[2] The obvious but politic falsehood was, however, tempered by an assurance that the camels would be forthcoming the following day; so, arranging provisionally for a start to be made at dawn on the day after, we returned to our ship, postponing the worries of disembarkation and the pleasures of sight-seeing till the morrow.

[1] ʿAbdulʿaziz ibn Saʿud, ruler or *Hakim* of Najd, is also the titular *Imam* of the Wahhabis, though he himself always refers to his father, ʿAbdulrahman, by that title.

[2] "A politic lie is better than an annoying truth."

Unlike Qatif and Jubail,[1] where agriculture has played a more important part than commerce in fostering the growth of considerable settlements, dating back for many centuries, ʻUqair, situated on a narrow and barren strip of foreshore between the sand-hills and the sea, has in all probability never been more than it is to-day, a *caravansarai* of growing commercial and decreasing strategic importance, whose floating population of troops and merchants eke out a weary existence at the call of business or duty until relieved. Its name and excellent harbour tempt one sorely to speculate whether this may be the site of Ptolemy's Gerra, an identity for which, I am aware, there are other candidates, but speculation is idle in the absence of material remains, and it is unlikely that any permanent settlement could have existed in a locality where to-day there is but a single well.[2] The old seaport of Gerra, whence before the beginning of the Christian era and for a few centuries of it flourishing caravan routes radiated to the uttermost ends of Arabia—to ʻUman, to the Hadhramaut, to the Yaman and to Petra—is doubtless to be identified with an extensive ruin-field said to have been discovered long since at the southern angle of the Gulf of Bahrain. It lost its importance probably when the southern caravan routes ceased to be practicable and was supplanted by Qatif at the northern extremity of the Gulf opposite Bahrain, while ʻUqair cannot be of any great antiquity, though its name—pronounced ʻUqair, ʻUgair or ʻUjair—seems almost certainly to preserve the name of the original settlement and port.

Be that as it may, the only buildings of ʻUqair are a square turreted fort and a large warehouse,[3] forming together a continuous oblong block of clay, some 150 yards in length and 70 in breadth, facing the jetty, which projects southwards into the harbour from a blunt promontory of low-lying land jutting out from the mainland to within

[1] More commonly called by the Arabs ʻAinain = the two springs.

[2] Other wells have been dug from time to time but have been found to contain brackish water.

[3] This is an oblong building with a central courtyard round which on the ground floor are store-rooms for merchandise, while the upper storey consists of the living-rooms and offices of the Customs staff and local agents of Hasa merchants.

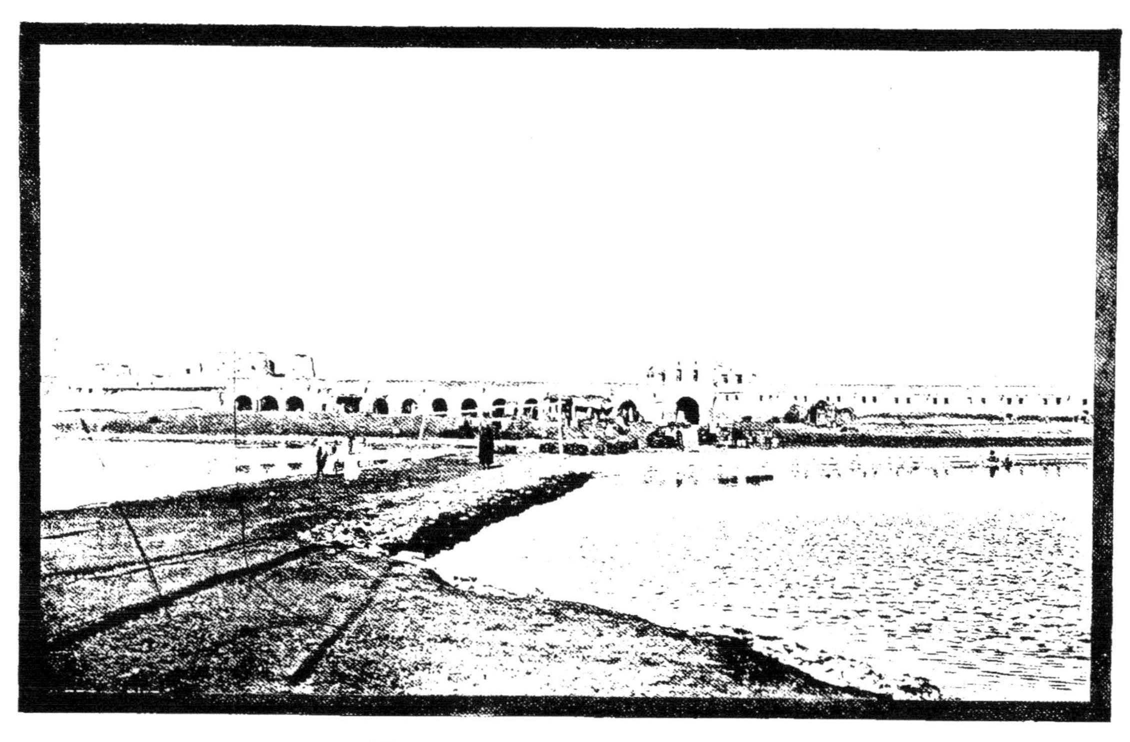

'UQAIR—JETTY, WAREHOUSES AND FORT.

100 yards of the long thin spit of Al Hadd. The harbour is enclosed by the mainland, the 'Uqair promontory and Al Hadd, between whose southern extremity and the coast opposite lies the entrance, itself protected on the south by the island of Zakhnuniyya several miles distant. A narrow channel, lying between the 'Uqair promontory and Al Hadd, connects the harbour with a lagoon extending about a mile northwards to the point at which the spit of Al Hadd projects from the mainland. Eastward of the warehouse lies a flat stretch of saline land, which serves as a camping-ground, while westward, between the fort and the sand-hills, runs a broad line of reeds and bushes, on the farther edge of which is the well already mentioned, guarded by the circular watch-tower of Abu Zahmul.[1] A small and dilapidated cemetery completes the scene, commemorating the forgotten sojourn of a Turkish garrison.

The following morning we landed and, after some time spent in sorting out our baggage and pitching our tents, repaired to the fort, whither the *Amir* had bidden us to breakfast—a simple meal of rice, mutton, vegetables and dates served on a circular mat in the reception-room. Coffee and conversation succeeded to breakfast, and the *muadhdhin's* voice, summoning the faithful to the Friday service in the fort mosque, warned us that it was time to depart.

As far as I was able to ascertain, the *Amirate* of 'Uqair is little more than an ornamental, though necessary, sinecure, involving no burden of work or responsibility more serious than the command of the local troops and a vague supervision of the customs department presided over by a special director or *Mudir*. The latter, also a native of Qatif, was

[1] A second watch-tower a few miles south of 'Uqair faces the island of Zakhnuniyya; such towers are known as *Maftul* (pl. *mafatil*); in shape they are circular, tapering slightly towards the top, where a parapet surrounds the watch-platform. Below the latter is the murky living-room of the guard, and below that again, on the ground level, a store-room for ammunition, etc. A small doorway on the ground floor is the sole means of entrance and exit, and is kept jealously bolted; I was only admitted as a great favour after a long argument. The guard at that time consisted of ten men, all, like the rest of the 'Uqair garrison, armed with modern rifles.

assisted in an undefined capacity by his brother and a number of subordinate myrmidons, and his duties consisted in examining every incoming ship and assessing the duty payable on its cargo and on stuff brought down for export from the interior. At the time of our visit there were seven *dhows* in port discharging a mixed cargo of rice, sugar, coffee and empty kerosene-oil tins, which with piece-goods, tea and spices make up the sum of Central Arabia's requirements from the outer world, the empty tins being required for packing dates and *saman*.[1] The last two with skins and reed-mats are the staple articles of export, dates and mats coming almost exclusively from the Hasa, while skins and *saman* represent the *Badawin's* contribution to the markets of the world.

The customs tariff of Wahhabiland is that enjoined in the *Quran*, fixed for all time by the Prophet himself, eight per cent *ad valorem* on all goods imported or exported, with a fixed rate of one dollar per maund or tin—calculated, of course, on the same basis—in the case of dates and *saman*. The only variation of this all-round rate—and this I had from the lips of the Director of Customs himself, though subsequent experience makes me hesitate to accept the evidence of my senses or suspect the Director of dishonesty—is in the case of tobacco, which pays duty at twenty per cent, though its import into the territories of Ibn Sa'ud is prohibited under the direst penalties. Nevertheless it is well known that tobacco finds its way regularly into all parts of the Hasa province, and no objection is raised to its consumption in decent privacy, a practice in which the Director and his brother themselves indulge when assured of their company. Of the manner and extent of its use in the heart of Arabia I shall have other occasions to speak.

The standard coin of Arabia is the *Riyal*[2] or Maria Theresa dollar, but rupees are freely current everywhere in the Hasa, and to a lesser extent elsewhere, at the prevailing rate of exchange, which, during my sojourn of twelve months in the country, fluctuated between Rs.230 and Rs.260 per 100 dollars. Small change is represented by the

[1] *I.e. ghi* or clarified butter.

[2] Plural *Aril*.

Masqat *baiza*, the equivalent of the Indian *paisa*, which is current everywhere in Ibn Saʿud's territories, while Indian and Turkish nickel and silver coins of the lower denominations enjoy a restricted popularity in commercial centres. In addition to the above, the Hasa, and the Hasa alone, has a special copper token known as the *Tawila*[1] and shaped thus— ; three *Tawilas* are equivalent to two *baizas*.[2] Paper money is, of course, used nowhere in the interior, though, doubtless, it would be accepted at a reasonable discount and as somewhat of a favour to the tenderer by any substantial merchant. Gold, both British and Turkish, is readily accepted at the prevalent rate of exchange,[3] but can scarcely be said to have been current for ordinary purposes before the Sharif's revolt,[4] since when it has swept across the peninsula in an ever-broadening stream ; it is, indeed, so plentiful in the west that, in less-favoured Najd, many relate and some believe the story of the *Baduwi*, who paid a sovereign for a box of matches and walked away without the change.

Customs duty is for the most part paid in rupees, the total revenue accruing to the Riyadh treasury from this source at the three Hasa ports during the year 1917 being some Rs.4 *lacs*. That year was, it must be remembered, one of war and restricted shipping, and it would, perhaps, be reasonable to assume that under normal conditions customs duty would contribute between Rs.8 and Rs.10 *lacs* to Ibn Saʿud's coffers, representing import and export trade of the gross value of between Rs.100 and Rs.130 *lacs*, of which not less than two-thirds would represent the value of imports, excluding of course all goods imported on Ibn Saʿud's own account. The merchants of the Hasa draw their requirements for the most part from Indian markets, which receive payment in kind to the extent of the surplus

[1] *I.e.* the long thing.

[2] For all ordinary purposes the *Riyal* is reckoned as 140 *Baizas*, 2 *baizas* as 10 *paras* (Turkish) or 3 *Tawilas* ; rupees tendered in payment of goods are converted in terms of dollars at the prevailing rate, and change given in *Baizas* and *Tawilas* on that basis. The merchant never loses on the deal.

[3] Varying between 6 and 7 dollars per £1 sterling.

[4] June 1916.

produce of the country, and in cash for the balance, and dispose of their wares in the interior in exchange for the produce of oasis and desert—dates, garden produce, skins, *saman*, mats and, last but not least, camels, the sole stock-in-trade of the true *Badawin*, whose lot, though still one of hardship and anxiety, has improved in the last decade and particularly during the four years of the war out of all proportion to the general rise in the standard of living, largely on account of the increased value of the camel. Forty years ago Doughty reflected that the few *Riyals* still left to him in the world would suffice to carry him from the Qasim to Kuwait; to-day the normal hire of a camel from the interior to the coast is 30 dollars, and but a few months ago[1] I sought in vain to hire five camels at that price from Zilfi to Kuwait. Men far from old tell of the days when a baggage animal could be purchased outright for 20 dollars, while now prices range from 80 to 150 dollars. Never, indeed, was *Badawin* Arabia more prosperous than it is to-day, but the golden stream has stopped, and soon there will be as little trace of it in the black-boothed settlements as there is of the winter torrents in their barren water-courses when summer has gone.

In the absence of exact statistics it is impossible to dogmatise on the relative importance of the three Hasa ports under present conditions: Qatif, while competing for the inland trade, is by no means solely dependent on it, and enjoys an unchallenged monopoly of supply to the populous and prosperous agricultural district of which it is the capital; Jubail is yet in the embryo stage of commercial development, but likely to make rapid progress if the necessary financial support is forthcoming for the construction of wharves and warehouses; while 'Uqair, which at present handles probably not less than half of the total inland trade of the Hasa coast, and enjoys the advantage of close proximity to the oasis of the Hasa, seems doomed to surrender its inland connections to Jubail as soon as that port is ready to play its part, unless in the meantime its splendid harbour, one of the best on the Arabian coast, can be freed, by dredging or otherwise, of the incubus of a

[1] October 1918.

bad approach, which at present militates against the passage of any but light-draught[1] vessels.

Meanwhile the Hasa ports are at the mercy of Bahrain, where Shaikh 'Isa, to the profit of his own treasury, levies duty on consignments booked for Najd at the time of their transhipment in his waters, with the result that the great bulk of Central Arabian trade is deflected to Kuwait, where goods intended for sale in the territories of Ibn Sa'ud and Ibn Rashid pay duty to Shaikh Salim and pay but once. Thus, while the Hasa pays double duty on all goods imported for her consumption, her merchants find themselves cut out, in respect of the more valuable commodities, in the markets of Riyadh and Southern Najd by the traders of Shaqra, who import their wares from Kuwait and carry them thence to the *Wahhabi* capital.[2]

The principles of economic science have obviously not penetrated to the courts of the princes of Arabia and, so far as I know, it has never occurred to Ibn Sa'ud, who is a substantial loser by the present state of affairs, either to question the right of his neighbours to profit by the advantages of their geographical position at his own expense or to combat their control of the situation with weapons more effective than vague dreams of creating a practicable rival port on his own coast. We must however make allowance for the fact that the existing position is an heritage from the days of Ottoman rule and that four years of war with their train of political difficulties have militated against the solution or even the discussion of the economic problems of Wahhabiland. The development of 'Uqair or Jubail will be a long and costly process, involving the sacrifice of much revenue meanwhile, whereas the simple expedients of a

[1] The present channel is just possible for ships drawing 12 feet.

[2] The distance from Kuwait *via* Shaqra to Riyadh is approximately double that from 'Uqair to Riyadh direct. Suppose, for instance, that a camel-load of costly silk valued at Rs.500 be imported *via* Bahrain (customs duty, 11 per cent) and 'Uqair (customs duty 8 per cent) to Riyadh (camel hire, 20 dollars), the cost to the importer of the consignment on arrival at Riyadh would be Rs.500 + 55 + 40 + 20 = Rs.615. The same consignment imported from Kuwait (customs duty, 11 per cent) to Riyadh *via* Shaqra (camel hire, 40 dollars) would cost Rs.595. Food-stuffs, being of less value, are imported to Riyadh direct from 'Uqair in spite of the double duty.

tariff agreement with Bahrain or the establishment of a land cordon [1] round Kuwait would fill the coffers of Riyadh with funds, which would be useful for the creation of a port.

From time to time during the day groups of camels appeared and disappeared over the sky-line of the sand-hills, and the foreshore presented an animated appearance as boat-crews and cameleers struggled with bundles of merchandise ; the groans of couching camels mingled with the cries of their masters, uncouth *Badawin,* who stared wonderingly at our outlandish English dress, as we wandered in their midst ; and with the camels came great white asses of the Hasa attended by their owners, all villagers, plying for hire like the cameleers ; and so to and fro all day long flowed the motley stream, but our camels came not and, as the sun went down, we wondered whether they would come on the morrow.

3. 'Uqair to Al Hasa

The following morning we were up betimes ready for an early start, but we were yet new to the ways of Arabia and consequently doomed to disappointment. Not a sign anywhere of the camels of yesterday, much less of new arrivals ; the *dhows* rode lazily at anchor in the harbour ; the shore lay, as it had been left at sunset, littered with bales and bags ; not a living soul was about. It seemed very doubtful if a start would be made that day. I accordingly went over to remonstrate with the *Amir* for his breach of promise ; he admitted that the camels had not arrived, and protested that they would soon be in, but at the same time suggested that we should find donkeys more comfortable to ride. This was an ominous suggestion ; it was clear that no arrangements whatever had been made for us, and that, even if the camels arrived, we should have to ride on baggage animals—and so it turned out to be. Even as I was talking with the *Amir* on the parapet of the fort, five camels lumbered over the sky-line and down

[1] A customs cordon on land is, I think, foreign to Arab ideas, but would present no great difficulty, as the posts for the collection of duty would obviously be established at the series of wells known collectively as Tawal al Mutair, *i.e.* Safa, Qara'a, Haba, etc.

the slope of the sand-hills: "Here they come," he exclaimed with evident relief, and as there seemed but little prospect of hastening the advent of the rest of the caravan by detaining the *Amir* in conversation, I returned to our camp to report on our prospects of departure.

Scarcely, however, had we settled down, resigned to indefinite delay, than an imposing procession, headed by the *Amir*, the Director of Customs and others, arrived to announce that the camels had come. With them came a pleasant but garrulous individual, Sultan ibn Suwailim, who told me that he was the brother of ʿAbdulrahman, the *Amir* of Qatif, and was telling me of a confidential mission, on which he was about to set out to Masqat on behalf of Ibn Saʿud, when the camping-ground was invaded by scores of camels and asses with their attendant men and women, and there ensued a scene of indescribable confusion, as camels were couched and our baggage hauled about in every direction. Conspicuous for the energy they displayed in sorting out the baggage into loads suitable to the known capacity of their various beasts were a number of women, whose decisions, shrilly announced from behind their hideous face-clouts of thick black muslin, seemed to command general respect and acceptance.

Meanwhile the asses had been loaded with the lighter articles of our baggage; the heavier loads lay sorted on the ground on either side of the camels destined to bear them; and peace reigned once more, as the unnecessary beasts and men removed themselves from the scene. Down came our tents, up went the loads and all was ready for a start. Three of the more promising camels had been couched apart for our riding, and the rest, snarling and groaning, as they rose, at the intolerable tyranny of man, lurched off towards the sand-hills in the tracks of the asses, which had preceded them.

Pointing towards the departing cavalcade, and doubtless congratulating himself on his good luck, the *Amir* chid me sadly for my impatience of the morning; "all's well that ends well" after all, and small is the difference between dawn and noon. I soothed his ruffled feelings with fair words and the gift of a watch, and just before noon on the

17th November we mounted and set forth on our journey into the interior.

Our party consisted of our three selves on camels, a cook and handyman called Ahmad, whom we had picked up on the *dhow* and who deserted us without pay or permission on our arrival at Jisha, an armed escort of four men provided by the *Amir*, fifteen baggage asses with half-a-dozen attendants and finally twenty-two baggage camels in charge of one ʿAli of the Ibn Shuraib[1] section of the Murra tribe, with whom were three men, one old man in his dotage, who rode along placidly mumbling to himself the whole time, and two women, all of the same section. We and our escort rode the whole way, while the rest, except the old man, took it in turns to walk and ride, the women particularly earning our admiration by the monkey-like agility with which they climbed from camel to camel adjusting loads and tightening ropes, when they were not walking, which was more often than not.

The white ass of the Hasa, big as a mule and creamy-white of hue, appears to belong to a class of its own. They are not unlike, though by an expert eye easily distinguishable from the asses of the Suluba,[2] which I saw on subsequent occasions; the latter, used by their gypsy-like owners in their hunting expeditions in the vast *Nafud* tracts of the north, are famous for their speed and endurance of thirst, while the Hasa product, used exclusively on the draw-wells of the oasis and for the carrying-trade between Hufuf and the coast, are heavier and slower, but very efficient substitutes for camels even over sand, provided that water is obtainable at reasonable intervals. So far as I know they are never used on the desert route between Hufuf and Riyadh.[3] Bred in large numbers by the villagers of the Hasa, they are said to be in great demand at Mecca and Madina, possibly for riding purposes, and I have seen them extensively used at Riyadh, Shaqra and in the Qasim in connection with well irrigation. A good ass of this type sells for about a hundred dollars, and inferior animals at anything between fifty and sixty.

[1] For the Murra tribe see Vol. II. p. 217.

[2] *Vide* p. 268 *infra*.

[3] But *vide* p. 44 *infra*.

In a quarter of an hour, leaving the watch-tower on our right, we reached the foot of the sand-hills, from the top of the first ridge of which we looked back on the port of 'Uqair with the azure expanse of the Gulf of Bahrain behind it, while before us lay a rolling sea of sand, into which we plunged towards the small dark patch of Suwad, a clump of dwarf-palm [1] bushes interspersed with *Markh*,[2] lying in a shallow trough about two miles from 'Uqair. The dwarf-palm bears a diminutive tasteless date eaten only by the hungry *Badawin*. Far away to the south showed a little hillock called Al Qara.

For nearly fifty [3] miles the dreary wilderness interposes its barrier of sand between the sea and the Hasa oasis; southward it skirts the Qatar promontory on the land side and presumably merges beyond it in the sand waste of the Rub' al Khali; northward, I believe, it follows the coast-line to Kuwait. Up and down, over trough and ridge, the weary camels padded, while the asses striking out on a line of their own were soon lost to sight, and did not rejoin us until we had camped for the night. The sand of this wilderness, which is called Barr al Hasa, is of white particles; its foundation, if one may judge by occasional outcrops of rock seen from time to time, is limestone; vegetation is plentiful both on the sand slopes, where grasses of various kinds predominate, and in the troughs, which support their lines of more succulent plants. The track is trodden down by the ceaseless passage and repassage of caravans.

Some 3½ miles beyond Suwad we passed the depression of Lasaf, where a few shrubs sustain existence on brackish subsoil water. Abu Khayala and its holes of sweet water lay 1½ miles beyond it, and shortly afterwards we crossed the trough of Umm al Dharr, which like other depressions of its kind seemed to trend towards the sea in a north-easterly direction. Southward of our course at this point lay the water-hole of Naba', with the well of Al Ghina three miles to the westward. We now reached a low ridge of limestone, called Al Jasra, lying north and south for a

[1] Called *Khis*.

[2] A sort of broom.

[3] The distances given in the text throughout are approximate; the maps give a more accurate idea of them.

distance of half-a-mile across the desolate sand; the track divided, one road leading to the north of the ridge towards the well of Qahdiyya, while we followed the other and, passing between two buttresses of rock, whence for the last time we looked back upon the distant sea beyond the sand-hills, descended to the shallow depression of Buraiman, where we pitched camp for the night.

We were now about 15 miles from 'Uqair and some 250 feet above sea-level; around us lay scattered patches of dwarf-palms struggling for existence with the drift-sand, which had entirely obliterated the ruins of a Turkish block-house, once garrisoned by Turkish troops for the protection of the caravan-route. In the old days, we were told as they kindled our camp-fire, the traveller tarried not in this place for fear of the *Badawin*, but hastened on after drawing water at the shallow water-holes, scooped by each newcomer in the sand, for the Turkish garrison, safe enough within its walls of clay, was no protection to those who lay without. We shared the camping-ground with 'Abdullah ibn Sharida, scion of a Buraida family, who was returning from a visit to the interior to his adopted home at Bahrain; with him were his womenfolk, who lay behind the shelter of a palm-clump, while I joined the men for coffee round their cheerful fire. Our men had brought no provision for the way, but accepted without question a tin of "bully-beef" from our store; the women slept fasting.

The night passed without other incident than the visit of a wolf, and our sleep was not disturbed by the rifle shot, which rang out just too late to save the sheep intended for Ibn Sharida's dinner at 'Uqair; the still warm carcase was pointed out to us in the morning and left to rot in the desert sun, the hungry *Badawin*, who had not rejected our "bully-beef" overnight, spurning the unhallowed meat. In matters of religious prejudice public opinion is all-powerful, yet the meat of the chase may be hallowed with the knife after death, if the trigger is pressed "in the name of God, the merciful, the compassionate."

Pursuing our south-westerly course, we continued over the sand-hills of a tract known as Nuqai'at al Aish, whence we passed on to an upland of higher sand billows called Al A'la, getting from time to time, as we rose to their crests, fleeting glimpses of the hills of the Hasa—Al Buraiqa westward, a long rough ridge; Al Qara[1] to the south-west ahead of us, a flat-topped hillock; and the four hummocks of Al Arba' to the S.S.W., said to lie athwart the road from Qatar to Al Hasa. The country over which we marched was strewn with desert scrub, and everywhere we saw the tracks of grazing sheep, belonging, they said, to the Bani Hajir. Southward lie the pastures of Al Murra and Manasir; northward those of the 'Ajman and Awazim.

At a distance of some 14 miles from Buraiman the sand-waste is traversed by a broad strip of salt-impregnated soil, the dry bed presumably of a watercourse, which, lying due south and north across our course, appeared to trend from south-east to north-west. Where it begins and where it ends I was unable to ascertain, nor was any other information about it forthcoming, except that, whereas the water is briny in the wells of Shatar on our course, that of Muraizib and Makku, situated respectively south and north of Shatar and, like it, on the edge of the salt strip, is sweet. Reaching Shatar, we followed the bed of the watercourse, which for want of a name is generally called Al Sabkha,[2] in a southerly direction to the point where it bends round from the south-east. Here, between a patch of bushes on our left, known as Sah al Barrani, and an old fort called Khuwainij, invisible to us and at some distance to our right, we passed again into the sandy wilderness at a clump of dwarf-palms, called Al Khisa, which appears to be the point of junction of the three alternative routes between 'Uqair and Al Hasa. The best of these tracks is the one we had ourselves followed; the others lie on either side of it at no great distance, the more northerly route branching off from our road in front of the Jasra ridge and following a line through the wells of Qahdiyya, Zuqain, Abul Maris, Makku and Khuwainij, while the southern route, not often favoured by travellers, branches off in the neighbourhood of Abu Khayala and,

[1] Not the same as the one mentioned above; the word signifies "flat-topped hill," and is of common occurrence.

[2] *I.e.* salty tract.

touching at the wells of Naba', Ghina and Muraizib, rejoins the main route at Al Khisa by way of Sah al Barrani.

The track now traverses a series of parallel ridges, on which the sand lay comparatively thin over a limestone foundation—a regular switchback called Al Nuqairat—ending in a barrier of deep drift-sand, between whose tumbled masses we meandered wearily, now in a deep hollow and now along a sliding flank, until, shortly before 4 P.M., having marched without respite since 8 A.M., we topped the last sand-wave of the wilderness and looked down upon a scene of wondrous loveliness—a broad black band of palms backed by the setting sun.

4. Al Hasa

"*La ilaha illa 'llah! La ilaha illa 'llah!*" Each weary man, as he topped the rise, paid his tribute of witness to God, the author of all contrasts, the maker of day and night, the creator of the sea and the dry land, the designer of the desert and the sown. Before us lay the oasis of the Hasa in its sordid setting of boundless desert, and the ascending smoke of its scattered hamlets warned us to hasten if we would be in by nightfall.

Near as it seemed, the edge of the palm-belt was yet three miles distant, a full hour's journey for the slow-padding camels, and it was 5 P.M. before we crossed the intervening plain and couched our beasts on the open space between the village of Jisha and the palms. Sore and weary with a long day's travel, we left our men to pitch the tents and chaffer with the villagers, who soon appeared with wares for sale—lucerne for the camels, dates for the men—and wandered in the date groves. Pleasant were the babbling streams, coursing through the groves, pleasant the fields of lucerne and new-sprouted corn and the fruit trees, lemon and pomegranate, fig and vine.

As the shades of night descended upon the scene we returned to camp to find that the men, who had been sent to the village to procure food for a feast, had returned with nothing but a small goat, for which the owner demanded no less than five dollars. Other emissaries were sent at once to the local *Amir*, who not only provided all that was required, but visited us in person with his son and, after partaking of coffee round our camp-fire, insisted on my going with him to drink coffee at his house while dinner was being prepared.

Ahmad ibn Saïl, *Amir* of Jisha, was an old man, sorely stricken with some infirmity of the eyes ; yet, blind as he was, he was but newly returned from Mecca, whither he had gone to perform the rites of pilgrimage for the first time in the great cavalcade which had set out from Najd in the summer ; four months had he been absent from home, and in his absence the duties of his post had devolved on his son, Nasir, a pleasing, intelligent lad of some sixteen summers. The narrow parlour of the *Amir's* residence soon filled as pestle and mortar rang out their summons, and I was pressed to the place of honour in uncomfortable proximity to the glowing hearth, behind which, our host being too feeble to do the honours himself, some elder member of his family sat preparing tea and coffee. Of the company was one Hamud, apparently a resident of the village and possibly related to the *Amir*, who led the conversation and showed by his own observations that he was interested in and not ignorant of the affairs of the world. "Where," he asked, "is 'Ajaimi al Sa'dun ? What has become of 'Abdullah, son of Falih, and his brothers ? Is it true that the British Government have confiscated their properties ?" and much more in the same strain. He had been to Basra on business and was deeply interested in its future ; possibly he contemplated migration thither, if ever the rigours of the *Wahhabi* creed should take root in his native Hasa. Tea was at length served round, milk is not used, but sugar is placed in the pot with the tea-leaves, and the pot is left near the fire to simmer ; the resulting liquid, unpleasantly acrid in spite of the sugar, is served round in cups of glass, a second and a third cup being pressed upon honoured guests. Then comes the coffee ; here in the east of Arabia it is the coffee of India except in the richer households, which reserve their precious stock of berries from the Yaman for special occasions, when the aromatic beverage is handed to the guest with all the ostentation that a notable vintage commands in England ; in the South, as I shall relate in due course, the poorest of the poor may be content to go coffeeless, but would be insulted by the offer of other than Yaman coffee. Little as he understands or appreciates tea, the Arab is a born coffee-expert ; coffee is his only stimulant, for wine and tobacco are forbidden ; it is served out in the smallest quantities in small earthenware cups, of which Japanese enterprise appears to be making a speciality, and the cup is filled only to honoured guests, not, as I have seen it stated, to hated foes—that, at least, is my experience in Najd, where I have heard the timid outpourings of the Hijaz coffee-man severely criticised and ridiculed. To fill to your foe as a hint to hasten his departure may well be in keeping with the civil manners of the great cities—Mecca, Damascus, and the rest of them—but is totally foreign to *Badawin* society and its unwritten "three-day" law of hospitality, binding alike on host and guest, and seldom abused by either.

As I rose to take my leave they detained me in their courtly fashion. "*Tutaiyyib, ya sahib ; hat al tib, ya walad*,"[1] said my host, and for the first time I saw the simple mystery of the preparation of incense ; a censer of coarse *Ithil*-wood,[2] roughly ornamented with strips of tin, was produced from the cupboard by the hearth ; in it were placed a few live embers from the fire, on the top of which was thrown a twig of fragrant aloes. A blow or two into the embers and a slender spiral of smoke ascended from the censer, which was then passed round from hand to hand, each recipient holding it for a moment under either flap of his head-kerchief and under his beard, and finally, before passing it to his neighbour, placing it under his nose to inhale its fragrance with an apparently natural but quite inimitable snort. Three times the incense goes round, being blown into fresh flame each time it returns to the coffee-host and, when the rounds are complete, one may rise to go.

Late as it was when I returned to camp, the evening meal was not ready and I joined the circle round the fire ; to my knowledge none of them had had anything to eat since they left 'Uqair except the tin of "bully-beef" of the

[1] "Take incense, friend ; boy, bring the incense." The word *Sahib* is rapidly acquiring the special meaning it has in India.

[2] Tamarisk.

previous night and the remnants of the cheese and biscuits we had carried with us for lunch. The latter I had taken care to distribute individually, not forgetting the two women, whose evident appreciation of the food was sufficient token of the gratitude they left unexpressed.

At length the food was cooked; a large tray had been borrowed for the occasion from the village, and on it the limbs of the sheep were piled high on a mound of steaming rice. A murmur of expectant thanksgiving burst from every lip: "*Lillahi al hamd wa 'lshukr, bismillahi 'lrahmani 'lrahim*";[1] and a dozen right hands reached towards the dish, a dozen mouths received a handful of rice, for it is Arab etiquette so to open a meal, and then ensued a struggle as of ravening wolves. Never before or since have I witnessed the like of that strange scene of hungry men sitting to meat by the garish light of the camp-fire; my fingers, tender from long desuetude, shrank from the boiling rice and felt cautiously round the edge of the dish for cooler spots; the steaming joints defied my timid attempts, while morsels placed within my reach by my thoughtful guests sorely tried my tongue and palate. The while the struggle proceeded, the rending and swallowing, and I wondered, as I watched the rapidly disappearing pile of meat and rice, whether any portion had been set apart for the two women, who at least had every reason to be no less hungry than the men.

Jisha, the farthest outpost of the Hasa towards the sea, is a dingy little village standing out from the palm-belt on the limestone plain at an elevation of 370 feet above sea-level; round it the surface of the plain is pitted with the quarries, whence they extract stone for building; all houses are of limestone blocks rough-hewn and roughly mortared with a mixture of earth and coarse cement of *juss*; the better houses are plastered over with *juss* of finer limestone[2] found in patches round Taraf, a village within the palm-belt to the southward; the village is walled around

[1] "Praise be and thanks to God; in the name of God the merciful, the compassionate."

[2] This cement is doubtless made of gypsum, which occurs in great quantities everywhere in the limestone desert.

and, as near as may be, four-square, 300 yards upon a side with a gate in each. The streets are narrow but clean and without any pretentious building, while a weekly market is held on Mondays in a *Suq* of modest dimensions for the sale of the garden produce of the neighbourhood. Such is Jisha with its population of some 3000 souls, peaceful and prosperous, fearing no drought in their land of plenty and, since the departure of the Turkish garrisons, fearing no foe; such doubtless is many another village of the Hasa oasis which we saw not—'Amran to the north, Taraf to the south and others.

The following morning we resumed our march; the narrow track ran westward through the heart of the palm-belt, crossing and recrossing the maze of murmuring streams on rough bridges of palm-logs or, more frequently, on culverts of solid cement; hedges of palm-fronds lined the groves on either side; here and there lay open patches of emerald green, lucerne or young corn; now and then a strip of rice struggling for existence in a reedy marsh; everywhere the stately rows of palm-stems, and beneath the grateful shade of their spreading tops a profusion of fruit-trees, weeds and vegetables.

At a distance of two miles from Jisha lies the oval village of Jafar in a broad clearing surrounded by palms. Outside its walls stood numerous booths of matting, erected after the Hasa fashion on market-days; around them a gay and merry crowd bought and sold, while towards them from every direction hied people from the neighbouring villages bringing their wares, for Monday is market-day both at Jafar and Jisha, and those who find no customers at the one have but little way to go to the other. Walking they came or riding on ass or camel, their wares on their heads or their beasts; everything seemed to be marketable—dates of good quality, inferior dates for cattle, oranges, lemons, pumpkins, egg-fruit, lady's fingers, lucerne, reed-mats, palm-fronds, palm-fibre—in fact everything or anything emanating from their prosperous gardens; the buyers are for the most part the petty merchants who collect supplies to sell at the bigger centres, for here in the villages, where each man is a husbandman of his own or others'

Group at Hufuf; (from left to right, seated,) Muhammad Effendi, 'Abdullah ibn Jiluwi and his son Sa'ud; attendants standing behind.

groves or fields, it is inconceivable that garden produce should find customers among the villagers themselves.

The population of Jafar may be 1500 souls; Subat, nestling in the palms half-a-mile to the north, has some 400 inhabitants, while Al Markaz, often called Markaz al Qara on account of its position close under the Qara hill, may have as many as a thousand. Other villages there, doubtless, are among the groves on either side of the road, but I did not get their names.

Beyond Jafar lie the finest gardens of all the Hasa, magnificent, well-kept groves with orange and lemon trees of sombrest green set out in regular rows amid the colonnades of great palm-stems; Mardhiyya, once crown-property of the Ottoman *Sultan* and now registered as *Bait al Mal*, the personal property of the *Wahhabi* monarch; Abu Laila, commemorating by its name a romance of years long past, when its former owner, infatuated by the beauty of a certain lady of Hufuf, who still survives to enjoy the fruits of her easy bargain, bartered the birthright of his children for one night of bliss; and another, of which I did not note the name, belonging to a Hufuf merchant of the Ja'fari[1] sect. Through these groves flows the main stream of Barabar, which with two others, the Sulaisil and the Wajjaj, are the parent stems of the irrigation system of this part of the oasis.

From east to west the palm-belt extends to a depth of about four miles; from north to south it is probably not less than twice that length; around it lies the desert, which on the west rises abruptly some forty or fifty feet to a low bare plateau, beyond which again lies another palm-belt—the main oasis of the Hasa—on a yet higher level. So far as I could ascertain the Hasa district consists[2] of these two oases, the eastern and the western, between which there is a difference in level of more than a hundred feet and a distance from edge to edge across the intervening plateau of about two miles. The road leaves the eastern oasis and ascends to the plateau at the walled village of Fudhul, more or less circular in shape and situated on the

[1] *I.e. Shia'.*

[2] There appear to be also a few outlying villages with palms besides the two main oases.

edge of a much-worked limestone quarry; a mile away to the north-west and on the fringe of the palms lies the smaller village of Munaizila; the ragged crags of Buraiqa show up prominently to the northward, while Qara lies nearer, half hidden by the palm-belt to the north-east. Fudhul may have a population of 1000 souls, and Munaizila, so far as I could judge from a distant view, but half that number. Taraf, which I never saw, is said to be no smaller than Jisha, and is, as already noted, famous for the quality of its limestone. With Fudhul it shares the waters of the streams Wajjaj and Sulaisil, while the settlements of the northern portion of the oasis depend on the Barabar. In all, making allowance for the existence of other villages than those I have mentioned and for the dwellers in isolated garden residences, I would estimate the whole population of the eastern oasis at about 15,000 souls, but it must be remembered that a considerable proportion of its gardens belong to merchants and others resident at Hufuf.

Hufuf itself, the capital of the Hasa, lies at an elevation of 475 feet above sea-level at the southern extremity of the western oasis, our route running slightly south of west from Fudhul diagonally across the plateau; the road, after crossing a well-built masonry culvert over the rapidly flowing Wajjaj, whose source is a spring in the western oasis, is dotted at intervals by a series of guard-towers, most of which, abandoned since the departure of the Turks, bear witness by their ruinous state to the peace and security which now prevail, in striking contrast to the anarchy which reigned supreme in the days of Turkish rule. From post to post the Turkish *pashas* rode under military escort; the villagers avoided the main roads, where the guardians of the peace were not less rapacious than its disturbers and more inevitable.

Striking across the plateau we reached the fringe of the western oasis at the guard-tower of 'Uwaimil after a march of some four miles, and another mile through the walled palm-groves brought us to the edge of a vast open space, at the other side of which the great white dome of the Ibrahim Pasha mosque towered above the flat roofs of Hufuf, not far beyond the gateway, by which in a few

Hufuf, capital of the Hasa.—General view with Ibrahim Pasha Mosque in background.

moments we entered the Rifa' or north-eastern quarter of the city, to traverse it and the broad market-place of Suq al Khamis dividing it from the Kut or citadel—our destination and the headquarters of the provincial government.

We sojourned at Hufuf two days till the afternoon of the 21st November, when we moved out to the camping-ground by the neighbouring fort of Khizam preparatory to an early start on the following morning on the long desert journey before us. During this time we were accommodated in apartments, spacious enough but scantily furnished, set apart for our use on the upper storey of one of the several courts constituting the *Sarai*, as the government offices are still called after the Turkish style. On our arrival at the gate of the *Sarai* we were received as we alighted from our camels by Muhammad Effendi ibn 'Ali, Director of the Revenue Department, and formally welcomed a few minutes later at the head of the stairs leading up to our apartments by 'Abdullah ibn Jiluwi himself, *Amir* of all Hasa, including Qatif, Jubail and 'Uqair, over whose *Amirs* he exercises a general supervision ; he is a first cousin once removed of Ibn Sa'ud himself, being the son of Jiluwi, brother of the great Faisal ; conducting us to our sitting-room, where he remained for a few minutes of formal conversation, 'Abdullah took his leave and disappeared through a little door connecting our court with the court of audience, leaving his secretary, Khalil Effendi, a Turk of Salahiyya in the Mausal *Wilayat* and, like Muhammad Effendi, a relic of the former Turkish administration, to minister to our wants.

Later in the afternoon we were summoned to the *Amir's* presence for an audience, and passing, ushered by Khalil Effendi, through a narrow hall lined on either side by slaves, gaily uniformed in long *Zabuns* of flame-coloured plush and armed with swords, entered a long narrow chamber, set about with rows of chairs and long benches, at the farther end of which 'Abdullah rose to receive us. Coffee was served round on a tray by a slave, who at a sign from his master approached me first ; I deprecated the honour and nodded in the direction of the *Amir*, who cut short the contest in courtesy by a laconic "*Ma ashrab*,"[1] accompanied by a characteristic, almost imperious upturning of the corners of his mouth ; I yielded and helped myself, whereupon he followed suit and such, at his insistence, was the order of our drinking whenever we sat together.

Middle-aged and of the middle-height, neither stout nor lean, with a short but full black beard, somewhat weak-featured and morose of countenance, dull of wit, cautious and formal in his talk, 'Abdullah ibn Jiluwi is numbered in popular estimation among the great men of modern Arabia, second indeed in Wahhabiland to his master alone. Ever since that fateful day in 1900,[2] when he stood by his young cousin in the desperate venture, which restored the Sa'ud dynasty to the throne of Riyadh, he has enjoyed and merited the implicit confidence of Ibn Sa'ud ; serving throughout the period of constant conflict, which followed the recapture of the capital, as the right-hand man and ever trusty counsellor of his sovereign, he was appointed *Amir* of the Qasim on the reconquest of that province from Ibn Rashid and remained at that difficult and delicate post, of whose duties he acquitted himself with conspicuous success, until 1914, when Ibn Sa'ud summoned him to the Hasa to create order out of the confusion left by Turkish misrule. Some men have greatness thrust upon them, and of them is 'Abdullah ; modest and utterly unambitious, he yearns for nothing but the peace and quiet of home-life in his native land ; his merits have condemned him to almost perpetual exile on the far frontiers ; in the Hasa he has made himself indispensable, and never for a moment is he allowed to leave his post. Thus, resigned to the dispositions of an all-wise Providence, loyally and conscientiously but without enthusiasm he devotes himself, year in, year out, to his appointed task ; dividing his time between the solace of his *harem* and the cares of state, he seldom, if ever, passes beyond the four walls of the Kut, where, in open court, to which all are admitted who would enter, he hears and disposes of the suits of his people and receives reports of their doings and misdoings. From the marches of Kuwait to far Jabrin and Jafura in the southern sands

[1] "I am not drinking."

[2] *Vide* p. 101 *infra*.

his name inspires wholesome terror, his writ runs unquestioned and the unerring justice of his summary judgments no less than the swift execution of his deterrent sentences have won him undying fame. Without fear or favour he conducts his administration on the principle of *Parcere subiectis et debellare superbos* and, if what they say of the turbulence of the tribes of the Hasa in the past be true, no further testimony to the success of his methods is required than the peace, order and security of the present day. *Si monumentum quaeris, circumspice.*

One day, as ʽAbdullah sat in public audience, there entered a poor old man of the people of Hufuf; "*Tawwal allah ʽamrak, ya 'l Amir!*"[1] he wailed the customary address before opening his case, "I was walking along in the public street when there came a man riding on a horse from behind and I saw him not nor moved from the path, when lo! he struck me with his stick and cursed me. Justice, O *Amir*!" "And who was the rider?" "*Ya tawil al ʽamr! ibnak, Fahad.*"[2] "Send for my son, Fahad," ordered ʽAbdullah, and, as he appeared: "Is this the man who struck you? that the stick?" "*Ai billah!*"[3] said the old man. "Did you strike him?" asked ʽAbdullah of his eldest son, a short sturdy lad of about eighteen. "*Ai billah!*" he replied. "Then take you that stick," said ʽAbdullah, turning to the old man, "and lay it across the lad with all your might, or else, by God! these slaves shall lay it across you till you cry again." The old man fell at the *Amir's* feet and begged forgiveness for his impertinence, implored to be spared the disgrace of raising his hand against one of the house of Saʽud. "Come here then," said ʽAbdullah to his son, "*Dhibb bishtak.*"[4] And with his own hands he clad the plaintiff in his son's mantle and dismissed him with a present of money.

On another occasion a villager came to him complaining that a certain *Baduwi*, passing with his camel by his unfenced patch of lucerne, had turned the animal in to

[1] "God lengthen your life, O *Amir*."
[2] "O thou of long life, thy son, Fahad."
[3] "Yes indeed" (*lit.* "by God").
[4] "Doff your mantle."

graze in spite of his protests ; the offender was summoned and denied the charge. "Very well," said 'Abdullah, "the matter is simple enough ; the camel shall be butchered and, if lucerne be found in its belly, the complainant shall have the meat as compensation for the damage to his crop, while, if none be found, the accused shall receive the value of the camel from the complainant."

Of such simplicity and deep knowledge of human nature is the wisdom of the ages ; yet the judgment of Solomon evokes more applause than imitation, and, in Arabia, the *Taghut* or unwritten code of *Badawin* customary law is condemned by the jurists of Islam not on its merits but as a product of "The Ignorance,"[1] prejudicial to the preaching and practice of the true faith.

The term Al Hasa signifies "limestone," and is strictly applicable only to the limestone plain between the Summan steppe-desert and the eastern sandbelt, and more especially to the actual neighbourhood of the twin oases ; for administrative purposes, the term is used more loosely to include the whole area of the jurisdiction of the *Amir*. The western oasis alone bears the distinctive name of Al Ahsa, a word which signifies "whispering" or "murmuring," *i.e.* of the streams which nature has provided for the irrigation of the fertile lands of the oasis. In Najd generally *hasa* is the generic term for all rock or stone, the word *hajar* is seldom or never used and varieties of rock are distinguished by colour rather than material formation ; thus red granite is *hasa ahmar*, basalt, grey granite and volcanic rock are all *hasa aswad*, greenstone is *hasa akhdhar*, and so forth; as far as I remember, I never heard any specific name for any variety of rock ; at the same time the average *Baduwi* is never at a loss for the name of a plant ; as he rides, his eyes are ever on the ground, seeking fodder for his mount and signs of possible foes, and at sight of a clump or tuft of any favourite herb off he goes—his whole wealth and his only care is the camel he rides, and he is happy if it has food, though he be without himself.

[1] *Al Jahiliyya* or The Ignorance in orthodox *Islam* means the period prior to the appearance of the Prophet, but in *Wahhabi* jargon it is more often used to denote the period preceding the appearance of Muhammad ibn 'Abdulwahhab.

Hufuf, Suq al Khamis on market day with Qaisariyya colonnade on left and walls of Kut to right.

Hufuf, with its reputed 6000 houses and probably not far short of 30,000 inhabitants, is by far the biggest town in the dominions of Ibn Saʿud; roughly oblong in shape and completely enclosed by a wall of unequal height, built of locally quarried limestone blocks, mud-plastered in parts, the town lies roughly N.W. by S.E. and falls into three well-marked divisions: the Kut, the Rifaʿ and the Naʿathil quarters, to which may be added the extra-mural suburb of Salihiyya; the western wall, closely fenced about with palm-groves, has no regular gate and was in parts in a dilapidated condition and perforated by unauthorised short cuts into the gardens; the southern wall has a single gate, the Bab Najd, the channel of all traffic to and from the interior; the eastern wall is pierced by two gates, the Bab Salihiyya, on the road leading from Taraf in the eastern oasis and passing through the suburb whose name it takes, and the Bab Jisha, by which we, like all travellers from the Hasa ports, had entered; finally the north wall also has two gates, one of which, the Bab Ibrahim Pasha, gives admission direct into the Kut in the neighbourhood of the great mosque and fort which recall the name of a former Egyptian viceroy,[1] while the Bab al Khamis leads, as its name suggests, into the broad *piazza* of the Thursday market, the Suq al Khamis, which bisects the town longitudinally to its central point, the Hamidiyya, the Town Hall of Turkish times but now converted into a warehouse for the produce of the *Bait al Mal* properties; in it at the time of our visit was a great store of dates, about which, coming in through the gaping windows, buzzed myriads of hornets.

The Suq al Khamis is a broad dusty street about fifty yards across and perhaps two hundred yards in length; on the west it is bordered from end to end by the moat and high bastioned wall of the Kut, to which admittance is obtained from this side through a strongly fortified gate provided with a portcullis. At the corner of the Kut nearest

[1] Not the destroyer of the *Wahhabi* power, but apparently a viceroy of the province when it formed part of the Ottoman dominions before the rise of the *Wahhabi* dynasty, but I was unable to obtain any very precise information about the mosque.

the Hamidiyya stands a lofty bastion, from which a high wall runs westward to join the outer wall of the city, the Kut quarter thus forming a regular square fortress within a fortified town ; in it, besides the *Sarai*, the *Amir's* private residence, the houses of other officials and the fort and mosque of Ibrahim Pasha, are a jail and several rows of ordinary houses and shops of all kinds ; the Kut is thus complete in itself and fully provided against the emergency of a siege, as it needed to be in the days of Turkish rule, both from within and without—a bulwark to the town against foreign invasion and a refuge for the garrison in the event of a popular rising. But the Turks, with all their capacity for excellent theory, failed to provide safeguards against their own negligence, and, on a certain night in the spring of 1914, their drowsy sentries were woken from their sleep in circumstances which made resistance hopeless, and a hundred *Wahhabi* desperadoes, whose presence in the neighbourhood had not even been suspected, drove the terrified officers and men of the garrison before them and by dawn were in possession of the whole quarter except the mosque of Ibrahim Pasha, in which the commandant and his officers with their wives and families, together with such of the garrison as had escaped in the confusion of the night, were gathered together to resist the invaders. The people of Hufuf, who had no reason to desire the continuance of Turkish rule and perhaps as little to hanker after *Wahhabi* overlordship, maintained a neutral attitude, but the gates of the town and the Kut were opened to Ibn Sa'ud the following morning by his own men and his handling of the situation was characteristic. A mine was rapidly driven under the floor of the mosque, all available powder was collected and placed in position, and the commandant received a politely worded ultimatum. He did not hesitate long in making his choice between the alternatives of unconditional surrender and sudden death.

Thus, almost without the shedding of a drop of blood, Ibn Sa'ud became master of the Hasa, and the Turkish garrison marched out unmolested but under escort to the coast, where they took ship for Bahrain ; the garrisons of Qatif and 'Uqair surrendered without resistance and were similarly treated; and the last vestige of Turkish rule in the Arab districts of the Gulf coast disappeared for ever.

The Suq al Khamis has a deserted appearance on all days except Thursdays, when the little booths of reed matting are set up in rows and buyers and sellers come in in their thousands for the weekly market. Then brisk business is done in dates and garden produce of all kinds and meat, great blood-red haunches of camel and droves of goats and sheep; for meat is eaten in all households but the poorest on Friday, the day of public prayer, and each householder does his own marketing; here are no fixed rates and all is done by bargaining; no sheep or goat is bought but is first kneaded by expert hands.

East of the Suq lies the Qaisariyya, a great maze of arcades, roofed or open, in which are the permanent shops—grocers, milliners, haberdashers, cloth-merchants, carpet-sellers, metal-workers, harness-makers, money-changers and so forth; all day long, except at the hours of prayer, the arcades are paraded by townsmen and *Badawin* looking for bargains, longing to buy, restless so long as they have money to spend. In it for the most part are wares from India, supplemented by local work in metals, wood or leather—coffee-pots, saddle-bags, saddle-frames, censers, sandals and, last but by no means least, black mantles with collars of simple silver- or gold-thread filigree work for which the Hasa is justly famous. With this one exception, however, there seemed to be little in the place of any real merit, and prices ranged high.

The Rifaʿ quarter includes the Qaisariyya and occupies the whole length of the eastern side of the town; in it are the dwellings of the merchants and other people of substance, buildings of modest enough appearance from the outside, being of the common limestone plastered over with *juss* or mud, but doubtless more or less luxurious within according to the means of their various owners. Unfortunately owing to the shortness of our stay I had no opportunity of seeing the interior of any house but the *Sarai*.

The Kut and Rifaʿ quarters occupy perhaps three-fifths of the whole town, and the remainder or south-western section constitutes the Naʿathil or slum quarter; here the streets are narrower and less regular than elsewhere and the houses are less elegant for want of plaster, while here and there they seemed to be in a ruinous condition. A narrow street separates this quarter from the Rifa', running from the Hamidiyya to an open space, called Al Qirn, in front of the Najd gate.

The Salihiyya suburb, lying outside the wall of the south-eastern portion of the town, is of comparatively recent growth, and takes its name from a fort erected by the Turks for the protection of the city on that side; formerly its residents were for the most part Turkish officers and officials with their families, for whom sufficient or suitable accommodation was not available in the congested Kut. Muhammad Effendi, the secretary Khalil and a few others are survivors of the old *régime*, deep-rooted in the soil of their adoption, providing for themselves with the same zeal as of yore and serving a new master not less faithfully than the old; the rest are gone and the wise laxity of the Islamic code has made provision for the wives and families, who brightened the dreary days of their long sojourn in a far-off land.

Simple is the administration of an Arab town—no education, no sanitation, no illumination, and therefore no expense and no taxation except on what we should call "imperial" account; and in this respect the Hasa is the milch-camel of the *Wahhabi* empire, the only province, except possibly and to a lesser extent the Qasim, which, after defraying the expenses of local administration, renders a substantial surplus to the central Treasury. Customs[1] dues and *Zakat* or land-tax are the main sources of revenue; the latter is the *'ushr* or tithe levied on the gross produce of all primary crops such as dates, wheat and rice, and brings in an annual revenue of about Rs.6 *lacs*; subsidiary cultivation, such as fruit, vegetables, fodder-crops and the like, is exempt from the payment of tax, and on Crown lands and other large holdings is also rent free. Such a system, far as it falls short of the principles of scientific assessment, has at least the merit of giving tenants every encouragement to improve their holdings and to cater for the requirements of

[1] *Vide* pp. 6 and 7 *supra*.

Hufuf, Mosque of Ibrahim Pasha; Khalil Effendi on left with Sulaiman Hariqi next to him, and two attendants on right.

the market, while it is a great improvement on the ingenious but obviously unjust device favoured by the Turks in some parts of Mesopotamia, for instance on the lower Euphrates, whereby palm-lands classed as *kharab*,[1] owing to the absence of subsidiary crops, are assessed at higher rates than *ʿamar*[2] groves, where vegetables and fruit-trees are cultivated in addition to palms, the resulting loss to the Treasury being made good by the levy of a vegetable tax, not on all vegetables cultivated, but on those brought to market in the towns. The intention—to encourage the cultivation of vegetables—is excellent, but the best of intentions cannot make amends for bad policy and the last state of *kharab* gardens is generally worse than the first. In addition to these sources of revenue, a tax of one dollar is levied at Hufuf on every camel entering the town, and all booths set up in the *Suq* on market and other days are liable to the payment of ground-rent at the rate of one dollar per mensem on each booth.

The collection of taxes devolves on Muhammad Effendi, a native of Mausal, who, after a service of nearly thirty years under the Turkish administration, elected to remain at his post after the fall of the Hasa, and receives a salary of 200 dollars per mensem in addition to such perquisites as he cares to credit to his own account. No questions are asked so long as a plausible balance-sheet and a substantial balance are remitted at irregular intervals to Riyadh ; the prevailing system of annual assessment by appraisement of crops allows considerable latitude to the man on the spot, whose accounts, it was whispered to me at Riyadh by the envious, would not stand the strain of a professional audit. Ibn Saʿud is his own finance minister and personally supervises the disbursements of his Treasury in every detail ; yet it never seems to occur to him that his coffers might be fuller if the revenue administration of his dominions were under closer expert supervision. The mysteries of Hasa finance are jealously guarded by Muhammad Effendi and his lieutenant Khalil, whose removal from office would be followed by a period of financial chaos. Taxes are assessed in kind and paid either in kind or cash, the *Amir* of each

[1] Waste, uncultivated. [2] Sown, cultivated.

village unit being responsible for the collection and payment of his people's dues—the villager is thus spared the incubus of an official collecting agency, and even the work of crop-appraisement devolves on the village authorities, subject to official check at the discretion of the Director.

Some three or four miles to the north-west of Hufuf lies the sister town of Mubarraz with a population of perhaps 20,000 souls ; it has none of the elegance of the capital, its streets are narrow and crooked, its houses of the inevitable limestone are low and unplastered, the wall which surrounds the town is without bastions, and the gates are featureless gaps, one in each of the four sides of the square. Within the eastern gate is an exiguous open space along one side of which stands the house of the *Amir*, Muhammad ibn Thunaian, on whom I called on one of my excursions from Hufuf. Warned of my arrival, he emerged from the house bearing his sword of state and attended by a few followers, and conducted me to the mat-spread clay bench built out from the wall which serves as his judgment-seat at the daily outdoor *majlis*. Tea and coffee passed round the little gathering of townsfolk which had assembled to see the stranger. The *Amir* is a native of the town, whose administration he conducts under the general supervision of 'Abdullah.

The villages of the western oasis I had no time to visit ; among others are Ruqaiqa, about two miles southwest of Hufuf, Shahrin to the northward on the eastern fringe of the oasis, both of which I saw from no great distance, Mutaifi and Julaijila ; of the rest I learned only a few names,[1] but it is safe to surmise that the total population of all the outlying villages of this section does not exceed 10,000, a figure which would bring the population of the western oasis up to 60,000, and that of the whole of the Hasa proper up to 75,000. I had no opportunity either of visiting or of estimating the population of Qatif and Jubail, which, however, cannot fall far short of 25,000. If these estimates, all of them necessarily rough, are approximately correct, the conquest of the Hasa

[1] Among them are 'Uyun, Kilabiyya and others.

has added some 100,000 souls to the settled population of Wahhabiland, a barrier, as it were, of orthodoxy and even heresy—for a considerable proportion in the Hasa and a substantial majority at Qatif subscribe to the doctrines of the Shiaʿ faction—between the puritan masses of Central Arabia and the heterodox multitudes of the great world beyond its ken.

The wealth of the Hasa lies in its mineral springs and running streams and abundant water; few are the houses in Hufuf without the luxury of a private well with water at a depth of from twelve to twenty feet but of varying quality, the wells of the Kut and Naʿathil quarters being sweet, while those of most of the Rifaʿ and the whole of Salihiyya are marred by a brackish taste; the streams, on which all the gardens of both oases depend, have their rise in a number of springs dotted about the western oasis, and flow in open channels following the natural slope of the land from west to east; the flow is perennial and the supply ample, but wasteful methods of irrigation, facilitated by the absence of any system of control and heavy intensive cultivation, have sorely tried the soil, and here and there a patch of marsh or grove of decadent palms tells its tale of woe. The sources from which the streams of the Hasa derive their being are, so far as my knowledge goes, ten in number; others there are, but mostly of little practical importance or utility, mere jets of water welling up in rock-clefts, attributed by popular belief or fancy to the falling of stars, the most notable of these being the sulphur spring of ʿAin Najm, situated in a small hill-mound of that name, north of Mubarraz.

The great springs are these: (1) The "Hot Spring" or ʿAin al Harra, bubbling up distinctly hot into a large tepid lake formed of its waters, from which channels lead in various directions towards the palm-groves around Mubarraz.[1] The lake lies about one mile north of the town and extends about 400 yards in length and 100 yards across; on its edges are patches of palms, a well or two, and the remains of some abandoned dwellings. It is one of the beauty

[1] And also, I believe, in the opposite direction to an oasis called ʿUyun, but I did not myself see either the stream or the oasis.

spots of the province, and much resorted to by both sexes for bathing, the ladies being relegated by custom to the farther extremity of the lake, where high reeds and the shade of a palm-grove provide some approach to privacy; the water, though hot in the immediate neighbourhood of the spring itself and tepid in the rest of the lake, is tasteless and, so far as I could ascertain, entirely neutral in its effect on the human system. (2) and (3) The Khudud and Haqal springs situated within a quarter-mile of each other in a palm-belt about one and a half miles to the east of Hufuf; both springs rise from the sandy bottoms of deep ponds of no great size, from each of which a channel leads southwards to a point at which they unite to form the Nahr Sulaisil, already mentioned as one of the streams which water the eastern oasis; in the ponds, which are surrounded with rank vegetation and about which are extensive patches of rice cultivation, the water is tepid and of a beautiful transparent green and the sides are deeply scooped out by the perpetual motion of the rising water. (4) Close by the Khudud lies the small spring-pool of Umm al Jamal, which irrigates a few fields of rice in its immediate vicinity. (5) Somewhere in the neighbourhood of Mubarraz rises the stream of Umm al Khuraisan, which flows along the road to Hufuf; its waters are believed to possess peculiar chemical properties harmless to natural dyes but unerringly destructive of synthetic imitations; the black mantles of Hasa manufacture are tested by dipping in this stream and, to judge by the black colour of its water, it must have saved many a would-be purchaser from a bad bargain. (6), (7) and (8) The Mutaifi, the Julaijila and the Jauhariyya, of which the first two irrigate the villages of the same names, while the third waters the palm-groves known as Battaliyya near Hufuf; I was unable to visit any of these. And finally (9) and (10) the Wajjaj and Barabar, whose sources I did not visit, and are, I believe, situated somewhere in the northern end of the western oasis.

The Kut or citadel of Hufuf constitutes, as I have already noted, a self-contained unit complete in all essentials, with access to the outside by the northern gate and to the rest of the city by a gate of massive dimensions in the wall

'Ain al Harra, the hot spring, near Mubarraz.

aligning the Suq al Khamis. Within the former gate is a spacious *Baraha* or camping-ground, on one side of which and adjacent to the gate stands a fort-like building, now used, I was told, exclusively as a jail. On the other side lies the inner keep, as it were, of the citadel, a spacious thick-walled fortress, in the midst of which rises the splendid mosque of Ibrahim Pasha, whose great dome and graceful minaret, blending the salient features of Byzantine and Saracen architecture, contribute to make it without exception the most beautiful building in all Central and Eastern Arabia. We were naturally very anxious to examine this thing of beauty at closer quarters than was possible from the roof of our apartments and other distant vantage points, and not only were we anxious to visit the mosque, but it seemed to us also very desirable that we should acquire at first hand some idea of the military assets, which, in an incautious moment, Khalil Effendi assured me were stored therein, including, it seemed, some machine-guns which the British authorities in Mesopotamia had presented to Ibn Sa'ud on the occasion of his visit to Basra the year before, in the hope that he would use them against Ibn Rashid. It soon became apparent, however, that our host was not over-anxious to display the whole of his military resources before us, and although he answered my first tentative suggestion with a nonchalant "*Ma yakhalif*" ("Oh, by all means"), I gathered, when I came to suggest to Khalil Effendi that a visit should be arranged, that his master had instructed him to discourage me if possible. I was determined, however, to see both the armament and the inside of the mosque, and my importunity eventually won the day and a visit was duly arranged. On the way to the fort we paused a moment in the *Baraha*, a portion of which is divided off from the rest to serve as an open-air stable, to inspect some twenty or more—some of them first-rate—Arab horses, the property of our host; and then we moved across the camping-ground to the fort gate, where we were received in state by Sulaiman al Hariqi, the commandant, and a part of the local garrison, some fifty men arrayed in garments of spotless white and armed with good modern rifles. The whole military force, permanently at the disposal of 'Abdullah ibn Jiluwi for the garrisoning of such posts as ʻUqair, Qatif, Jubail and the Hasa itself, is probably not more than some 500 or 600 men, of whom perhaps one-half are stationed at the capital. The commandant now conducted us round the fort; along the parapet lay at intervals in front of as many embrasures some seventeen great guns of antediluvian type, carriageless and entirely useless; in chambers beneath were gathered the store of modern ammunition and serviceable guns, the four machine-guns so recently received from the British Government, and a number of Turkish seven-pounders captured from the last Turkish garrison; three of the former were still in the packing-cases in which they had arrived, and only one had been taken out for inspection and perhaps for occasional practice; but the real trouble and disappointment lay in the fact that of the four men who had been specially instructed in the management of machine-guns by the British military authorities at Basra only a year previously, three were already dead, and the survivor, Husain by name,[1] had apparently forgotten most of what he had learned. We were not, therefore, greatly impressed by the military display at Hufuf, and I must confess that, though at one time I thought that Ibn Saʻud's Arabs might be able to make good use of guns if available, my subsequent experiences with his army and the lamentable results achieved by the Sharif's artillery during the various phases of the skirmishing round Khurma have led me to believe that an Arab army is more effective without artillery than with. Having inspected the armament of the fort, we repaired to the great dome, whose interior has apparently been converted for use as a barrack, its floor being entirely bare except for a few bedding-rolls of the garrison, while from the summit of the dome hung chains apparently used in former times to bear the weight of suspended lamps or candelabra. Our visit was of too official a character to permit of my taking any measurements of the dimensions of the dome, and I had to be content with photographing the commandant and his chief myrmidons against its great spread of dazzling white.

[1] *Vide* p. 384 *infra.*

CHAPTER II

THE EASTERN DESERT

1. Al Khizam

Pleasant and all too few were the days of our sojourn at Hufuf, where, under escort of Khalil Effendi and a few sword-girt myrmidons of the *Amir's* guard, we were free to wander where we would, now on foot within the precincts of the town, and now on horseback, when we would fare farther afield, for 'Abdullah had placed the whole of his stable at our disposal. Nevertheless our foreign garb was ever a serious impediment to free movement and an obvious source of much embarrassment to our companions; crowds collected wherever we paused in our progress through the bazars, and bands of thoughtless children dogged our steps and ran round by byways to peep at us, not always in silence, from the street-corners; the exasperated swordmen of 'Abdullah showered oaths and imprecations on the ill-mannered youths and exhibited a persistent tendency to steer homeward through unfrequented lanes, while our one desire was to prolong our wanderings through the busy thoroughfares; but worst of all was the sacrilege of booted feet and bare heads in the presence of the *Amir* himself. We were yet but on the threshold of Wahhabiland, and among people not ignorant and therefore tolerant of the vagaries of the ungodly, but the stir we had created here promised ill for the future, and the advice of Muhammad and Khalil confirmed me in the conviction that we should profit little by emphasising the barrier of nationality and religion which separated us from the people of the country. We decided, therefore, and certainly we decided rightly, to adopt the dress of the country from the moment of our departure from

Hufuf, and Khalil busied himself on the morning of our last day under the roof of ʿAbdullah in procuring the requisite garments.

Meanwhile all necessary preparations had been made for the journey before us, and on the afternoon of the 21st November a long string of camels wended its way down the Suq al Khamis and the lane, which separates the Rifaʿ and Naʿathil quarters, to the Najd gate, issuing from which we turned slightly south of west towards the square fort of Khizam. Here we were to stop for the night to allow of a final watering of the camels at dawn of the next morning and to make sure that all was in order before launching out into the desert. All was not in order as indeed everybody knew but ourselves, but this was our first experience of the *tabriz* [1] or "breather," the false start without which no Arab would ever go upon a journey or successfully accomplish one, for in the bustle and turmoil of a town the Arab loses all capacity for serious thought, and spends in coffee-drinking or, if a resident of the place, amid the blandishments of his *harem* the time which he should be devoting to preparation for the venture of the morrow; and so the morrow finds him unprepared, with empty saddle-bags and leaking water-skins, and he counts on the morrow's night to redeem the forfeits of his thoughtlessness.

We had marched but two miles from the Kut, and Khalil Effendi, who had accompanied us thus far, lingered while the tents were pitched and our baggage sorted for a final inspection, which disclosed a serious shortage of water-skins and other deficiencies, whereupon he took his leave promising to return at dawn with the missing articles. Others of the party drifted away on one excuse or another, most of them to return to their homes in the town for a last night with their families, and we were left with the camels and the baggage.

We took advantage of the short interval before sunset to visit the fort, which we found tenanted by a garrison of some twenty men, all armed with good rifles of modern

[1] The name Mubarraz is from the same root, betraying the fact that the present town was probably in origin no more than a watering-place for caravans leaving Hufuf.

The Author

type, under a commandant, in whose company we made a tour of the interior. On the parapet at irregular intervals with their muzzles pointing outwards through slits in the thick walls lay about ten antediluvian guns without carriages or fixings of any kind; they must date back at least to the Egyptian invasion of 1818 and have apparently never been used since. From one of the turrets we obtained a commanding view of the surrounding country, the palm-groves of the Hasa behind us, and the desert around dotted with mounds and ridges to the western horizon.

Returning to camp we busied ourselves to make all ready for the morrow, and, with the assistance of the few men who had stayed behind and exhibited much interest and delight in the operation, proceeded to transform ourselves into the semblance of Arabs. The garments of Arabia, designed at once for comfort and dignity, differ but little from those of Mesopotamia; the *Fez* and other outlandish articles of dress affected by the townspeople of 'Iraq are of course not tolerated, though they occasionally appear in the privacy of houses with pretensions to elegance both in the Hasȧ and the Qasim; the heavy head-dress of Mesopotamia is seldom seen elsewhere than in the Qasim; and for the rest there is little variety; the *dishdasha* or long linen shift is worn next to the skin down to the waist whereafter it covers the baggy linen pantaloons called *sirwal*; the latter is gathered round the waist by a tape or string drawn through the hem and is generally made with outlets so small as to defy the passage of a normal European instep; over these garments is worn the *thaub*, an overshirt of ample proportions with long and very full sleeves; over the *thaub* comes the *Zabun* or coat, usually of some bright-coloured material, reaching to or below the knee; and over all is worn the mantle (the *aba* of Mesopotamia, but generally called *bisht* in Arabia), usually of black or brown colour with a collar of gold- or silver-thread work. On the head is worn a kerchief or *Kafiya* (more commonly called *qatra*) of white or red and white, pressed down upon the head by a simple headband of black or white wool, about half an inch in diameter and slightly compressed, but not twisted, and worn in a double circle. Sandals on the feet complete the outfit.

The poorer classes, which include most *Badawin*, frequently wear no more than a *dishdasha* or a *thaub* with a *bisht*, if they can afford it, for protection against the cold or, on special occasions, when, for instance, they are in a town ; the head-dress, which is often no more than a piece of dirty rag, is never dispensed with.

Over the *Zabun* is girt the leather cartridge-belt, strapped at the waist and supported by crossed shoulder-straps ; into it is tucked the *janbiyya* or short curved dagger by those who possess one, while the rifle is slung from the hinder upright of the camel saddle ; the mantle is generally thrown back while riding, but is always kept handy in case of need, for etiquette demands that it be worn when entering a town or village, while in the open the waving of a mantle on approaching a *Badawin* camp or a caravan betokens the absence of hostile intentions, for a *ghazu* or raiding party leaves all superfluous and precious articles at home before taking the field.

The two women, who had accompanied us from 'Uqair and with their menfolk were still with us, wore one a red and the other a black smock over drawers of black, a face-clout and a black muslin veil enshrouding their heads and descending in front over their shoulders and bosoms. Their feet needed no protection. Such seemed generally to be the garb of women of the lower classes.

Our transformation complete and a dinner of cold mutton, unleavened bread and dates, kindly provided by the *Amir*, disposed of, we composed ourselves for sleep, hoping that the morrow would see us launched on our way.

2. The Summan

The camp was in a state of animation when we woke the following morning ; the truants had returned, and Khalil Effendi had sent one of his henchmen, 'Abdullah, with the missing articles ; the loads were all ready, each assorted to its animal, and it took but a few moments to strike and pack the tents ; the sun rose as we breakfasted hurriedly, congratulating ourselves on the prospect of making good progress in the cool of the morning ; all was ready. So, at least, we thought; but before us lay 150 miles or nearly five days' journey over a waterless desert, and in such circumstances the Arab, ever mindful of his beasts, leaves it to the very last moment to water them; the wells of Ruqaiqa were half-a-mile away to the southward, and we possessed our souls in such patience as we could muster, while the camels lurched off to the watering.

At length, somewhat before 8 A.M., the last camel, snarling and ruckling in a passion of indignation at the tyranny of man, had received its load and the caravan filed slowly past the fort into the wilderness. Half-a-dozen men still sat by the smouldering embers of the camp-fire draining the last drops in the coffee-pot; their mounts and ours lay ready; "*Ya 'llah!*"[1] exclaimed the leader, rising from the circle with a weary yawn, "*tawakkalu 'ala 'llah!*"[2] and we climbed without much skill into our saddles, while our companions kept down our *dhaluls* by standing on their knee-joints. Then with groans and a grating of tough-skinned limbs on the flint-strewn ground the ponderous beasts rose to their task and followed in the wake of the baggage-train.

Before us lay the great steppe-desert of the Summan, which extends without interruption from the Batin in the north to the southern sand-sea, and from the sand-hills of the east to the central sand-barrier of the Dahana. Sections of this vast tract bear specific names, but all are one in essentials, the whole a dreary waste of barren limestone, here smooth as any sea, there a gentle rolling down, and ever and anon worn by wind and weather into low sharp ridges and hillocks like breakers on a reef-bound shore.

Our course lay to the south-west towards the flat-topped ridges of Malda; to northward were the squat peak of Abu Ghanima and the double cone of Jabal Farr backed by the downs of Ma'ma with the ridge of Ghawar westward; southward of Malda lay a double flat-topped hill called Tamatain, and far distant in the same direction rose the ridges of 'Uwaisa and Kharma; the track, deeply scored in the hard soil by generations of soft-padding camels, ran up a mile-wide valley towards a prominent humped

[1] "O God!" [2] "Put your trust in God."

peak called 'Uthmaniyya at the edge of the Ghawar ridge, whence from our higher ground we looked back for the last time on the dark palm-groves of the Hasa eighteen miles away.

We now held on over featureless lumpy country across an occasional grassy depression towards the low dark line of a ridge ahead, reaching which, after a march of some twenty-five miles from our starting-point, we camped at the foot of a sharp escarpment known as Ghar al Shuyukh, the "royal cavern," so called because once, or more than once, visited by Ibn Sa'ud or one of his ancestors. The "cavern" is no more than an overhanging ledge of rock, some forty or fifty feet high,[1] affording pleasant shade for a midday siesta to any one reaching it after a long desert march. Having marched throughout the heat of the day under a sun, which was sufficiently trying as it beat upon the stony soil, we were not sorry to be at the end of our journey and to rest in the shade of a friendly sand-hill watching the weary camels driven forth to pasture, the pitching of tents, the lighting of fires and all the other accompaniments of a *marah*.[2]

As before, we had our own commissariat arrangements, and six water-skins [3] had been filled for our exclusive use; the rest had each his own skin, but our experience of the improvidence of the *Badawin* on the march to the Hasa had warned us to add a sack of flour and another of rice to our stores for the common weal, and well it was that we did so, for, with the exception of the myrmidons of 'Abdullah, who accompanied us as a personal escort, none of the party had brought anything but dates.

Our caravan comprised rather more than thirty camels and, including ourselves, about twenty-five persons; in charge

[1] Palgrave, who grossly overestimates the height of the rock at 1400 feet, adds a touch of local colour to his narrative by hiding a village among the neighbouring sand-hills. The nearest water is about twenty miles away.

[2] *Lit.* "resting-place," but technically restricted only to the place where one halts for the night.

[3] The *qirba* (pl. *qarab*) consisting of a whole goat- or sheep-skin; whole camel-skins (*mizada*) are also used when special camels are detailed to carry water for an entire party.

of all arrangements and especially appointed to the charge by Muhammad Effendi was 'Amir, a *Dausari* by origin, but a townsman (*hadhari*) by generations of residence at Hufuf, between which place and the interior he practises the lucrative profession of conductor to trading caravans, while he is also joint owner with his patron, Muhammad Effendi, of not a few camels plying for hire on his beat; somewhat obsequious and greatly addicted to singing his own praises alternately with those of his hearers, he exercised but little authority in the caravan, and was eternally sparring with the members of our escort, who never lost an opportunity of pointing out that they derived their authority not from his patron but from his patron's patron, 'Abdullah ibn Jiluwi himself, the vicegerent of Ibn Sa'ud, and that they cared as little for Muhammad Effendi as for his creature; nevertheless I must admit with gratitude that 'Amir, alone of the whole party, had an intimate knowledge of the country we traversed and was always ready to impart it. His chief rival was 'Aïdh, like himself a townsman of Hufuf, but of *Qahtani* origin, a regular swashbuckler, crafty of mien and small-featured, always clad in a *Zabun* of brilliant hue, overbearing, insolent and useless, always hurrying on ahead to make coffee for himself and one or other of his boon companions of our so-called escort; Sa'ud the slave, haughty, reserved, sulky and, like his kind, delighting in gaudy raiment, was much of the same kidney; the onus of escorting us, if indeed escort we needed, fell on Salih and Gharib, men of a different type, merry uncouth rascals, always jesting and singing, but not disdaining to lend a hand occasionally with the tent-pitching and loading.

These, like ourselves, rode *Dhaluls* or female riding camels unencumbered with baggage except that each man carried his own water-skin. The baggage was distributed among the camels of the *Badawin*, hired or requisitioned for the purpose, drawn from four different tribes and thus serving as *rafiqs* as well as carriers. They were of Dawasir, Murra (those of our journey to Hufuf including the women), Qahtan and Bani Hajir, among these last being Dhib, joint *shaikh* with Muhammad ibn Taiza of the Muhammad section, and his son, who were on their way to Riyadh in obedience to a summons from Ibn Sa'ud, and if they spoke true, to receive monetary recognition of special services rendered in addition to their regular annual subsidy of 400 dollars.

Our party was completed by two men of Hufuf, who had tacked themselves on to us uninvited at the Khizam fort and who were going to Riyadh on business, riding on diminutive asses, which, by dint of early starts, kept pace with us surprisingly well and showed themselves no whit the inferior of the camels in endurance of thirst, for not a drop did they have for four days and a half; and a half-witted *darwish* on his way to the house of God, who, having no vehicle but his feet to carry him over 800 miles of desert, thought to procure an occasional lift and provision of food and water by accompanying our caravan as far as Riyadh; he was not disappointed, and rendered profuse thanks to his god and his benefactors in broken accents of some hybrid tongue; for some reason he early acquired the sobriquet of Al Sindi, to which he answered readily; he came, he said, from the Garmsir, but his Persian was as weak as his Arabic, while he exhibited gleams of intelligence when I tried him with such Pashtu as I could muster; he had certainly travelled, and travelled mostly on foot, from a far country, whither he will doubtless return as he came, if strength be vouchsafed him, from the Holy City.

As the sun sank below the horizon, each man, obeying the call to prayer, left his task and took his place in the line of worshippers drawn up behind a semicircular mark in the sand representing the Qibla or Mecca-ward niche; one of the number stood forward of the line to lead the prayer, and as he intoned the formal sentences, he bent and knelt and bowed down and rose, and so they did after him the appointed number of times, until the final formula, "Peace be upon you and the mercy of God," spoken by the *Imam*, turning his head to right and left, released the congregation to their mundane tasks.

The following morning (November 23) we were up betimes, and for the next twelve miles marched in a south-westerly direction over a dreary expanse of bare gravelly downs, distinguished by the name of Na'la and

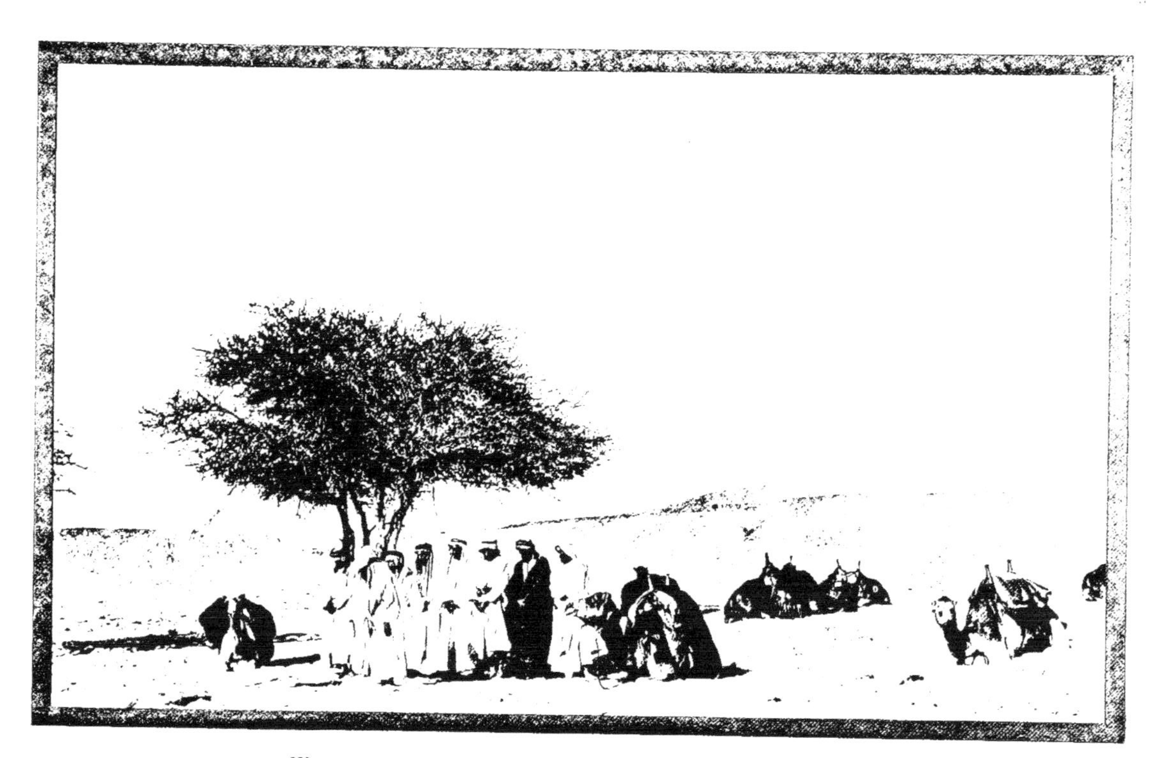

Wadi al Shajara—A halt for the afternoon prayer.

extending from the low ridge of which the rock of Ghar al Shuyukh forms part to the edge of Wadi Faruq. Here and there the folds of the downs were carpeted with coarse *Thamam* and other grasses, and during the morning we passed through the grazing herds of the Ibn Da'ath section of Qahtan, droves of camels moving leisurely to the northward in search of new pastures, for the rain had not yet fallen, and at the latter end of the dry season the *Badu* are condemned to perpetual movement if they would not lose their stock. At intervals of four or five days the camels go down to water about Hufuf, but when the rains set in the desert provides man and beast with water enough.

Wadi Faruq, near which we passed a caravan from Najd bound for the Hasa, is a broad valley or depression of sandy soil lying south by north in the midst of the desert, in all probability with an escape into the Sahaba channel at the southern end for the drainage it receives from the downs to east and west, but on this point I was unable to procure exact information and therefore cannot speak with certainty. Some six or seven miles in breadth, it lies twenty or thirty feet below the level of the desert and is bordered on the west by the rough plateau of Rubaida, which we entered along the course of a little ravine, Wadi Shajara, so called on account of a group of three acacia trees standing a little way above its junction with Wadi Faruq. These were the first trees we had seen since leaving Hufuf, and are the only ones visible from the road in all the desert between the Hasa and the Turabi plain beyond Abu Jifan. We had outdistanced our baggage train and the afternoon sun beat fiercely upon the barren wilderness; it was time for the afternoon prayer and 'Aïdh had coffee utensils at hand; so we spent a pleasant hour in the grateful shade of those wretched trees, near which a century ago the troops of Ibrahim Pasha had camped and laboured in vain to dig a well.

A further march of three miles brought us to the Sha'ba, a grassy dip in the Rubaida plateau; we had marched over twenty-five miles and were utterly weary; so we pitched our tents and rested in the midst of the infinite waste.

Next morning we resumed our march over the lumpy

plateau, utterly bare but for a patchy covering of a prickly scrub called *Shibram*, with here and there cairns of stones loosely set up on knolls to serve as beacons to the wandering *Badu* or travellers gone astray ; imperceptibly the unsteady wriggling lines of the well-worn highway passed into a vast bare plain, extending with scarce a ripple to the far horizon on every side ; this they call the Summan, and beyond the ridge, which determines it on the west, is the Sulb tract or Huzum al Sulb, a gently swelling plain broken at intervals by low ridges. The soil is sometimes sandy, sometimes gravel or shingle, and again, in patches, a sandy loam or "*pat*" ; here and there lies a small depression with a clump of stunted acacia bushes or *Aushaz*, where, after rain, water lies ponded long enough to give life to the desert herbs. One such depression, dignified by the name of Raudhat al Hanaï, lay across our path, while another, the Raudhat al Baidha, marks the transition of the Sulb into the whitish gravel tract of Baidha, in which we camped on the third night out from Hufuf within sight of the Dahana sands. We were now nearly done with the steppe desert of the Summan, with which I was destined to renew acquaintance on two further occasions during the time of my being in Arabia, and which for unrelieved monotony and weariness may indeed have its fellow, but is assuredly surpassed by nothing in all the wide world.

In camp each company or *Khubra* lies apart, each tribe by itself, and the townsfolk a separate division, each circle round its own camp-fire with their camels couched about them as a screen against the cold blasts of the winter wind. That evening I was made welcome at the fire of the Hawajir,[1] and seated on a sheepskin between Dhib and his son, shared their simple meal of boiled rice and *saman*, the latter the sole luxury of nomad Arabia, and of their bounty they poured it with no sparing hand over my part of the platter, assuming, as they do in all things, that that which gives them most pleasure is also exceeding pleasant to all men. The meal over we sat round for coffee, pounded in a brass mortar with a marble hand,[2] as they picturesquely term

[1] Pl. of Hajir, *i.e.* Bani Hajir.
[2] *Yad* = pestle, *niqra* = mortar.

the pestle ; the marble or some sort of greenstone, as I think, is quarried at Mudhnib, south of the Qasim, and made into pestles of varying lengths, some two feet and more, by the stoneworkers of ʿAnaiza and Buraida for export to all the settlements of Arabia ; sometimes they use brass pestles, but stone is preferred. Talking of stone, they told me of Jafura, where they find a marvellous moving stone, which travels, so they say, of its own volition over the sands, leaving a trail to betray its course ; some time before ʿAbdullah ibn Jiluwi, hearing of this portent in the southern sands, sent messengers to secure specimens, and in due course the messengers returned with two, found in the act of walking ; that evening ʿAbdullah summoned guests to his roof, and there before them the stones were loosed to show their powers, but disappointed the expectations of the wondering onlookers by exhibiting not the slightest sign of life. The test had failed, but the *Badawin* retain their conviction, for they have seen them walk ; I hoped to secure specimens for myself, but left Arabia disappointed. What may be the true facts of the phenomenon I cannot say, but perhaps the apparent motion of the stones over the sands is in reality due to the motion of the sands themselves. Of Jafura itself more hereafter.[1]

Of wonder-talk they never tire ; in the northern part of the Summan there is, they say, a water-hole of some depth, at whose bottom water may be found by scraping away the earth, but one should not descend into it without a rope to secure one's return, for at Haïl there is a man, white-haired and white-skinned, who lost his natural colour some ten years ago as the result of his experiences in the underworld, whither the waters, suddenly rising about him, carried him by a subterranean channel and whence, after subsisting some months on naught but grass, he reappeared to tell the tale far from the original water-hole. There is in fact in the tract known as the Duhul,[2] or "the water-holes," whither I came later, a maze of subterranean galleries, apparently natural, into which men descend in search of water, and in which one might well lose oneself by adventuring too far.

[1] *Vide* Vol. II. p. 221.

[2] *Vide* p. 270 *infra*.

As *shaikh* of one of the tribes which in Turkish times lived by blackmail and robbery on the highways between the Hasa and the coast, Dhib had from time to time come in contact with the Turkish authorities and visits to Bahrain had made him familiar with the sight and reputation of the British. A Bahrain astrologer had recently predicted the victory of the *Bani Asfar* or white folk over the *Muslimin* in seven months or seven years or seventy years; and a Turkish officer had said to him: "Give us but 'Abdul Hamid and the Ottoman Empire will remain strong, but with Muhammad Rashad calamities will multiply." England, the Arabs firmly hold, lies to the east of their country, for do not the ships of the *Inqlis* come from the eastward?

Though *shaikhs* of a great tribe, Dhib and his son wore but a cotton smock and went unshod, though at night they drew their mantles of coarse homespun wool about them like the rest. Perhaps at Riyadh God would vouchsafe them a better cloak, for on the return journey it would be cold at night; the best of them scorn not to beg.

The Bani Hajir roam from the Kuwait border to the Qatar coast and their westward limit is Wadi Faruq; the leading sections are Al Muhammad with two coequal *Shaikhly* houses and Al Mukhadhdhaba, whose two sub-sections, the Mudhafira and the Yazid, yield allegiance to Shafi ibn Salim as paramount *Shaikh*. To the south, but overlapping the marches of the Hawajir, are the Manasir or Ahl Mansur and the Murra, while northward are Bani Khalid, based on Qatif, of whose palm-groves they are part-owners, and the two home tribes of the Kuwait principality, Awazim and Rishaïda, to say nothing of the 'Ajman, once rulers and owners of all the Hasa, but now banished and living in exile in the territories of the *Shaikh* of Kuwait. The Qahtan and Dawasir tribes from the far south-west roam as far afield as the Hasa border, between which and Wadi Faruq they overlap the marches of the eastern group; westward of the *Wadi* are Dawasir, Qahtan, Subai' and Suhul, with the Murra in the south and the Mutair to the north.

3. The Dahana

We now passed across a narrow strip of desert herbage into low, gently undulating down-country of gravel and sand bestrewn with boulders of limestone rock. This is Malsuniyya, the connecting-link between steppe and sand, which extends to a depth of four miles and ends abruptly some way short of the Dahana itself in the arid stone-strewn flat of Salabikh, covered as far as eye could see to north and south with curious weather-worn cylindrical stones [1] and rock fragments. From this, some five miles on, we passed imperceptibly into a broad causeway of similar formation, called Jasra, which runs like a wedge for another four miles into the Dahana, whose outer sand-barrier gradually converges on the track.

The Jasra, now no broader than the road, turns sharply to the left and is engulfed in the sea of sand. At last we had set foot upon the Dahana and passed over the first ridge close by a nameless dilapidated cairn. The track, heretofore scored deep in the firm soil of the desert, is now at the mercy of wind and rain; a few steps on we came to a prominent sand-knoll crowned by a cairn, known as Rijm al Shuwair; thereafter he who would make the road to the next watering must have an experienced guide or a compass to direct his march, unless he be fortunate enough to find the spoor of a passing caravan yet uncovered by the wind-swept sand; even so he may be misled, for the Dahana, far richer in vegetation than the desert on either side, is a favourite grazing-ground of the *Badu*, and woe betide the traveller who follows the tracks of grazing camels.

Nevertheless the terrors of this barrier of sand have been grossly exaggerated; we were to cross it now where Palgrave had crossed it five-and-fifty years before, and unless Dame Nature has repented of her frowardness and levelled the fearsome obstacles with which she guarded the mysteries of Central Arabia from the prying eyes of the West in times

[1] Unfortunately I omitted to bring away any specimens of these stones for examination, but, if I may trust my memory, they were not unlike some specimens which I brought home from a locality near Sadus in Jabal Tuwaiq, and which have been classified as corals and sponges of the Jurassic (Corallian).

long past, I make free to say that he drew more on the imaginings of his own brain than on actual fact for the lurid picture he painted. Apart from the risk, now happily a thing of the past, of meeting with human hostility, no one, who has taken the ordinary precautions of ascertaining the general direction to be followed and of providing himself with water sufficient for the journey, has anything to fear from the passage of the Dahana, while Arabs have been known to set out on foot on the journey from Abu Jifan to Hufuf without encumbrance of food or water, trusting to their own powers of endurance and chance meetings with caravans or wandering *Badu*, and to reach their destination without mishap.

Before us lay a seemingly endless down of sand-ridges and scattered hummocks covered with grasses and low scrub withered by the long drought; the going was easy enough and the difference in level between trough and ridge seldom more than thirty or forty feet with a gentle gradient, but we had covered nearly seventeen miles [1] before entering the real sands, and our camels, now four days athirst, began to show signs of weariness; so we decided to halt for the night on reaching the low twin ridges of Bani Badali eight miles from the eastern edge of the sands, our elevation above sea-level being now about 1550 feet.

Attempts were now made to induce us to resume our march during the night; the Arab normally travels by night over waterless distances, in fact travels day and night with the occasional halt for coffee so dear to him, but we had made it clear at Hufuf that we had come not only to traverse but to see the country and that, therefore, we would travel as long as they desired by day, but only by day. Our intention, they pretended, had been misunderstood, and they had made certain we would consent to a night march over the last part of the journey; they had therefore made free with their water and now many were waterless; besides last night one of the skins had been ripped open by a wolf. Incidentally one of our own skins had been found in the morning less full than it had been left overnight; possibly, I suggested, some thirsty *Jinni*

[1] *I.e.* since starting from our last camp.

had helped himself unseen. We remained unshaken in our determination not to move till morning, and that night there was neither coffee nor dinner round the camp-fires, for water, the foundation of both, was wanting, and what there was was carefully husbanded for the morrow's march.

Next morning all was bustle and stir betimes and anxious voices urged us to make haste if we would reach the watering before night. We had husbanded our resources so well that, in spite of occasional tampering, we still had two skins out of the original six intact, but the rest of the party were in a sorry plight, and before we had marched long it was clear that their straits were serious. Here the superiority of *Badu* over townsmen became apparent at once, the former enduring thirst with all the fortitude of long custom, while 'Aïdh and his fellows broke away into the wilds on the pretext of searching for game, for the tracks of herds of gazelles were crossed at frequent intervals, but in reality in search of wandering graziers, from whom to beg or rob their scanty supply of water.

They did not rejoin us till we were well beyond the Dahana; fortune had not favoured them in the chase, but, in spite of their asseverations to the contrary, it was clear that they had been more successful in the main object of their excursion. That, however, did not prevent them waylaying and taking a tribute of water from a small caravan which passed by on the long journey to Hufuf shortly before we reached our own camp. To my protests against such behaviour 'Aïdh, with all the insolence of the townee and, it must be admitted, not without some show of reason, retorted that it was not for nothing that he and the like of him had entered the service of Ibn Sa'ud to protect the highways against the depredations of just such people as those whom he had relieved of their water; "*Alladhi ma yadhlim yudhlam*" ("He who oppresses not will be oppressed"), and the *Badu* respect not but those who enforce respect by tyranny. There was certainly something unanswerable in the rascal's simple logic, but it would have appealed to me more strongly had he shared the proceeds of his robbery with his thirsting companions.

From the Bani Badali ridges we passed after a march

of ten miles into the Miz'alat, a tract of deeper sand and higher hummocks, about which we meandered apparently aimlessly for some six miles, now over the crests of wind-swept waves of sand, now skirting their flanks, and now along the troughs of firmer sand between them. Well is this place named the " abodes of anger," where the camels labour and the way is not certain. Suddenly we found ourselves clear of the Dahana on a narrow strip of low dune country known as the Marbakh and ending three or four miles farther on at the edge of the 'Arma steppe. The sand-ridges behind us, more sharply defined on this side than on the east, extended north and south to the far horizon, receding as we moved on and ever becoming a deeper orange colour as the sun approached his setting. In all our passage we had seen no lofty pinnacle of sand, the alternating ridges and well-marked valleys of the north had disappeared, and the Dahana in this sector had seemed to us nothing but a low-lying belt of sand with little but its reddish tinge to distinguish it from the sand-tracts of India and elsewhere. By my reckoning its breadth from the first to the last ridge, that is to say, from the western extremity of Jasra to the eastern edge of Marbakh, was rather less than twenty-five miles or nearly an average day's march.

4. The Inner Steppe

Fearsome is the grim barrier which protects the core of Arabia from the consuming canker of foreign penetration and foreign influence ; tier upon tier it rises glacis-wise from the eastern ocean to the central plateau ; first the coastal sand-strip rising in 50 miles from sea-level to an elevation of 350 feet ; next the Summan rising slowly but steadily another 900 feet in 90 miles ; thereafter the Dahana ascending in 25 miles from 1200 to 1500 feet above sea-level ; still far off lay the citadel itself behind its last defence of graded steppe.

The stony causeway of Jasra on the east has its counter-part on the west in the Jari, which we now entered, a strip of clay richly covered with coarse *Thamam* and succulent *Harmal* and protruding wedgelike into the dunes of Marbakh.

As we advanced the sands on either side yielded abruptly to a gentle stone-strewn upward slope, up which ran the Jari, now a shallow mile-wide depression rising to low ridges on either side. To north and south stretched the infinite expanse of the 'Arma steppe, ending to the far westward in a low rim outlined by the light of the sinking sun.

We were yet far from the watering and slender was our chance of reaching it before nightfall ; on, however, we marched with what speed the jaded beasts could make ; a solitary gazelle, the only one we had seen in all the desert though we had seen countless tracks of them in the Dahana, crossed our path, to be pursued in vain by some of our thirsting but stout-hearted *Badu* ; anon we passed a *Dausari* driving a small flock of sheep Hasa-ward to sell at next Thursday's market in the great *Suq* ; wearily we called a halt to buy of him meat for the night, and with one accord we agreed to march no farther ; meat we had, two fine sheep purchased after much bargaining at ten dollars apiece, but water wherewith to cook it we had none ; a couple of the stoutest camels were despatched forthwith to fetch a skin or two of water from Abu Jifan and we pitched our tents and waited for their return ; at length we ourselves, despairing of their coming, supped on bully beef, and it was nearly midnight before our sleep was disturbed by the happy cries which heralded the arrival of the camels ; now all was good cheer and merriment ; the long thirst was slaked and the dead embers of the camp-fires were rekindled to cook the meat ; we slept.

Next day we resumed our march up the Jari depression through the same desolate steppe country relieved only by a prominent hillock called Farha and the short low ridge of Thaniyyat al Bilal on our left hand somewhat west of south. On our right at some distance we saw a clump of bushes, which is known as Raudhat al Hilal, and is an alternate watering to Abu Jifan, lying on a more northerly branch road, which eventually joins the path we had trod in the Dahana. Its water is less plentiful than that of Abu Jifan and it is frequented mostly by those travelling in haste from Riyadh, the direct road from the 'Aqla wells to the *Raudha* avoiding the long detour to Abu Jifan.

The Jari came to an end, after about four miles' march from camp, on a low watershed, beyond which the road descends a gentle downward slope to the westward; the surface of the steppe now became more undulating with here and there about the road a low bare hummock. We passed a large caravan from the Qasim wending its way wearily eastward with Bahrain as the goal of a wealthy 'Anaiza merchant, who with his womenfolk and children rode in the train. They had left Abu Jifan the previous afternoon and had spent the night in a considerable bush-clad bottom called Raudhat al Dhulla, which we soon reached. This is a favourite *mubarraz* or breathing-place for caravans outward bound from Abu Jifan, whither water-skins emptied during the night's halt are sent back to be filled before next dawn, when the caravan finally launches forth into the desert. As we entered the bushes a great wolf went away on the left unharmed by the fusillade which greeted its appearance.

The surface of the steppe now broke up into rough boulder-strewn hummocks; the headland of Khashm Ausa'[1] showed up prominently ahead and suddenly we came upon the brink of a deep gorge running south-west; here at last was Abu Jifan; at our feet in the rocky bed of the ravine lay the wells of which we had talked and dreamed so much in the last five days. It was now 124 hours since we marched out from the fort of Khizam and the camels had last tasted water at the wells of Ruqaiqa.

From ledge to ledge the weary animals laboured with a heavy jerking motion down the steep boulder-strewn incline to the wells, where busy hands of those who had preceded us were already at work drawing water and filling the stone-bordered earthen troughs about the wells for their own beasts and those yet to come. Another party bound for the Hasa were still in the place, but had finished their watering, and only delayed their start to give and receive such news as there was to exchange. The camels were couched and driven, after unloading, to the troughs,

[1] Pronounced by the people of the south Asa'; *Khashm* means a nose, *Khushaiyim* a little nose, *Khushum* (pl.) noses, the whole series of headlands being referred to collectively as Khushum 'Arma.

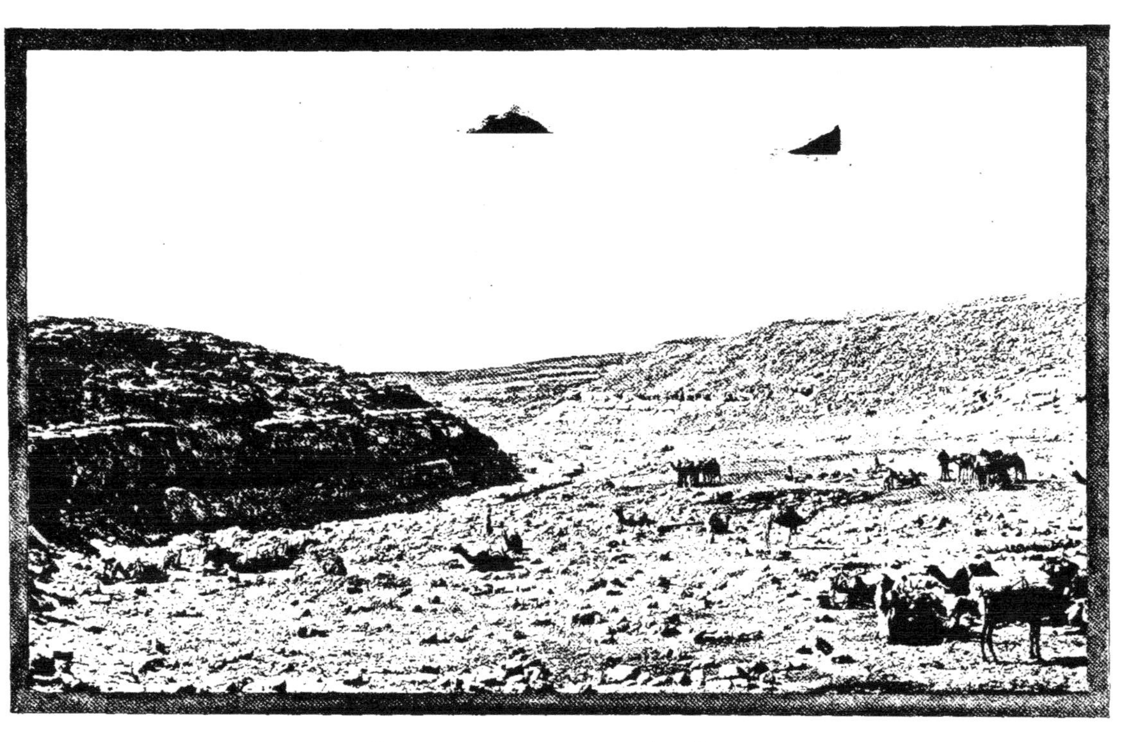

The ravine and wells of Abu Jifan.

where the thirsty brutes pushed and struggled for a place, and, extending their long necks to the water, drew in long draughts, pausing awhile to shake their dripping blubber lips, and again descending to the troughs, which the men, drawing and pouring amain, had much ado to fill as fast as the outstretched necks absorbed their contents.

For us, our carpets and bedding were spread under the shade of a great ledge of overhanging rock, where we took our ease. The ravine of Abu Jifan is a deep cleft in the steppe, a boulder-strewn torrent-bed about sixty yards across between high crags of rock from fifty to a hundred feet in height; in the midst of it lie the wells, some twenty-five in all, as they say, but of these only three are in regular use, the rest being partly buried with *débris* and partly exhausted. The Qammus, as the best of the wells is called, is like the rest about twelve feet deep to water and roughly lined with limestone blocks, worn at the top into deep ruts by the well-ropes of centuries. The water in the three wells now used is sweet and plentiful; the soil of the ravine between the interstices of rock is sandy and covered everywhere with the *jalla* or pellet-excrement of camels. In the middle of the gorge they have cleared a narrow space of sand and in it outlined a praying-place, neatly marked out with stones, complete with *Mahrab* and all. Here doubtless generations of passing caravans have raised their voices in prayer and thanksgiving to the true God while their camels slaked their thirst; in such places, where stone is ready to the hand, the pious *Muslim* spends the hour or two of his idleness in laying out a permanent though simple memorial to the Almighty, as the pagan *Baduwi* of old whiled away the hours of his shepherding by erecting some cairn to mark a grazing-ground, as indeed he does to this day. In the desert stones are fascinating playthings, and often have I, when sitting on some barren prominence to survey a barren landscape, turned round to find my companions engrossed in their building. "Look," they would say, broadly grinning, "have you put down the name of this?" "What is its name that I may write it?" "*Tara, ya Sahib, iktib ismuh Zubb al Mutawwa'*";[1] and they would go off into

[1] "Look 'ee, sir, write its name, '*The Zelator's member.*'"

peals of joyous laughter as I recorded their little jest, at once coarse and impious. I often wondered why the desert was dotted about with cairns in bewildering profusion ; the explanation is simple enough and a warning to the unwary.

" Drink and make room for others " is the Arab rule in the desert ; seldom do they camp at a well except in the neighbourhood of a village or nomad *manzil*, and the rule is a sound one, for where water is scarce wells are the lodestar alike of honest and dishonest men, of friend and foe, and a sleeping caravan is at the mercy of a passing enemy. The period of our siesta under the shady overhanging cliffs drew all too soon to a close, and the afternoon sun beat fiercely down on the narrow gorge as we loaded up and set forth. The ravine runs between high cliffs to the south-west, draining this part of the ʿArma steppe through its outer fringe into the Turabi plain, which in turn drains southward to the great Sahaba channel ; but to follow the ravine would have taken us too far to the south, and the Riyadh track leads through a gap in the right bank on to a rough plateau, terminating in the steep western escarpment of ʿArma. Following this track, we passed the prominent pyramid-hill of Sanam al Hawar on to the plateau, making, it seemed, for the brink of the precipice. From here a splendid view opened up before us ; to right and left the headlands of Khashm Ausaʿ and Khushaiyim Ridhi stood sentinel over the approach to the broad plain of Turabi, extending green and bushy to a distant line of hills, the low coast of Shadida to the southward shutting off the fertile district of Kharj, the ridges of Jabha and Jubail to the north.

Our guides now led us aside to the brink of an immense fissure ; some 150 or 200 feet below us lay a pleasant copse of acacias and desert plum-trees,[1] surrounded on three sides by the frowning crags of the escarpment supported by avalanches of precipitated *débris* and opening on the fourth or western side into the plain beyond. A steep and narrow zigzag path led over the edge of the cliff and down the sliding avalanche to the copse below. Dismounting, we beat the unwilling camels over the brink ; thereafter they

[1] The *Sidr*.

looked after themselves and reached the bottom without mishap. The copse is named appropriately enough Abu Khishba, or "the father of timber."

Descending ourselves on foot, we remounted and shortly entered the Turabi plain; from Hufuf our course had lain generally somewhat south of west to this point, but from now onwards we steered north of west across the plain. On our right hand to north and south as far as we could see lay the steep precipice of the ʿArma escarpment, rising abruptly out of the plain to a height of from 200 to 400 feet, the haunt of eagles and ibex,[1] but from this side unscalable by man except at certain points where practicable tracks have been found or made; on our left across the plain ran the ridges already mentioned. The whole plain is scored by the channels of freshets running down southward to the Sahaba.

For the time being we kept close in under the escarpment and, after passing a mighty buttress, standing out from it like some great fortress, we approached and camped for the night within half-a-mile of the headland of Khashm Ausaʿ, which towered majestically above us in the clear light of the full moon.

Since leaving Hufuf, we had been consistently favoured by gentle northerly breezes, which tempered the fierce heat of the sun by day and made the nights delicious; the climate had cooled perceptibly as our altitude increased, and that morning at the Jari camp my thermometer recorded 48·2° Fahrenheit at 6 A.M. During the day, however, the wind had changed suddenly to the south, and for a space a warm and steady *Kos*, as the south wind is called, raised the temperature, which from 55·4° at 11.30 P.M. on the previous night (26th November) jumped up to 73·4° at the same time on the night of our camping in Turabi. The change was, however, a transient one and, soon after midnight, the wind veered round to the north again and, becoming a gale, levelled our tents over our heads ere we could scramble out into the open; as suddenly the wind abated and we slept peacefully in the open by the *débris* of our camp. Next morning the thermometer recorded 62·6° at 6.30 A.M., but

[1] *Waʿl* (pl. *Wuʿul*).

there was a wintry chill about the air, and a start was delayed by some trumped-up story of a camel gone astray.

It was nearly nine o'clock before the camels were loaded and the march resumed. The Turabi plain was a welcome change from the dreary wilderness we had left behind us, and it was well on in the day before the sun gained strength enough to neutralise the chilly blasts which swept down upon us from the north. Here was grass, green grass, in plenty and scattered bushes of stunted acacia; ever and anon the green was broken by a band of black, some torrent channel sweeping down from the 'Arma precipice across the plain, as it were the path of a lava stream. Scattered hummocks dotted the plain, and to the north lay tumbled ridges; the hillocks of Al Abraq and Rahaiya stood out prominently in front of the escarpment, the former marking the track of the Darb al Hajj, one of the caravan highways between Riyadh and the Hasa, joining our route at the 'Aqla wells. The northward horizon was closed in by the indeterminate ridges of Huzum Sailan and Dughm, and behind the latter lay the watering of Miyahiyya, marking yet another track between Riyadh and the Hasa. The direct route from the Hasa to the Kharj district avoids Abu Jifan and strikes water at the wells of Wasi'a, near the junction of the Turabi plain and the Sahaba channel, passing thence to the southward of the Shadida ridge.

Animal life was more in evidence here than it had been hitherto; gazelles were seen and chased without success, and one *Hubara* or lesser bustard flopped across our path, its sluggish flight belying its speed; as in India this bird is most easily secured by circumvention, if hawks be not to hand, and he who would hunt it more directly is doomed to disappointment; here the black pebble strands are pitted with holes of the tough-skinned *Dhabb*, a lizard eaten with relish by the *Badu*, but endowed with incredible speed; here also the *Jarbua* rat has its abode, and can be dug out of its hole if no time be lost in starting operations when he is seen to disappear; this, too, is considered a delicacy. Eagles or vultures we saw from time to time soaring high above the cliffs of 'Arma.

Here, too, were shepherds of Dawasir and Subai' grazing

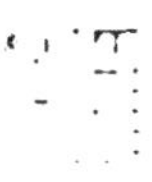

Khashm Ausa'—Camp levelled by storm in the Turabi plain.

their flocks, and one large caravan bound for the Hasa passed us during the day. The *Shuwwan* or shepherd elements of the great tribes stand lower in the social scale than the *Badu*, rearers of camels, raiders and naught else.

On we padded the livelong day over the never-ending plain; at length the low mound of Jabal 'Aqla appeared ahead and we pressed on, but the camels had drunk their fill and we had water enough, so we camped for the night some miles short of the wells, being now at the eastern edge of the long slope of Jubail.

Continuing our march next morning, when the thermometer registered 48·2° at 6.45 A.M. and a keen northerly breeze blew freshly over the bare steppe, we reached the 'Aqla wells in rather more than half an hour. They lay, some nine or ten, of which only three appeared to be in use, in a shallow sandy depression amid low bare hummocks and ridges; round the edges of the saucer the ground was black with the excrement of sheep, of which a flock still lay where it had lain all night, waiting to be watered before moving out to pasture. We borrowed troughs, consisting of a leather basin stretched on a wicker frame, from the shepherds, and water was drawn and poured into them, but the camels merely snuffed at the surface and refused to drink.

On we marched up the long drag of the bare stone-strewn steppe of Jubail, rising gently from ridge to ridge, now through a sandy depression, now across a broken torrent bed, and now over the dreary slope until, at a distance of about fifteen miles from our starting-point, we descended into the deep gorge of Sha'ib [1] Abbanas, which, coming from the north in two branches, here becomes a single channel flowing southward in its deep fissure and eventually issuing into Wadi Sulaiy. The gorge is not unlike that of Abu Jifan, but has no wells. Here we rested for a short while and, three miles farther on, suddenly found ourselves on the brink of the steep bluffs, which form the outer rim of Jubail; before us lay a confused landscape of low downs, and beyond them, far away to the westward, towered the bold outline of Tuwaiq.

[1] *Fiumara* or dry watercourse.

In configuration the steppes of 'Arma and Jubail are but the forerunners of Tuwaiq itself, small-scale miniatures, as it were, of the great steppe-plateau which forms the backbone of Arabia ; in each case there is a long gentle slope from the eastward to a frowning line of precipitous bluffs, opposing as it were a barrier of mighty bastions to the west. The descent here, however, presented no difficulty, and we soon found ourselves in a circular plain protruding bay-like into the ridge and surrounded on three sides by steep precipices, while the fourth was closed in by a line of rough bare downs, through which the track led at first on an easy level and later down a steep winding fissure to the broad sandy valley of Wadi Sulaiy.

We were now within easy reach of Riyadh, and pitched camp by a solitary acacia in the valley, with the majestic headlands of Jubail behind us, Khashm al An farthest north, Khashm al Sulaiy hard by our camp, and Khashm al Hith southward. The long flat summit of Tuwaiq stood out sharply against the evening sky, while a dusty haze hung over the serrated ridges of Duraibat al Khail. Beyond them lay Riyadh. "Make thy bourne by day and not by night"[1] is a favourite Arab proverb, for the Arab day closes with the evening prayer, and the hours of darkness are a man's own for his family and his friends, and it is unseemly for the stranger to claim his attention and hospitality at such a time. There is another reason, a relic of wilder times ; one should look before one leaps, and in the darkness one cannot distinguish between the *manzils* of friend and foe ; therefore approach strange tents by day and approach circumspectly, if haply there be blood between you or yours and any man.

The camels were loosed out to pasture in the valley, and we gathered about a single fire to discuss the long journey behind us, and for the last time to dip hands in a common dish ; the petty dissensions and hard words of the long-drawn desert march were forgotten in the common joy and the needy greedy companions of our travel without shame assessed the value of their services. Round and round passed the coffee-cups, and the hollow of an upturned mortar

[1] "*Sabbih al dar wa la tamasiha.*"

served as a censer, 'Aïdh producing some twigs of aloes, which he had carefully preserved in the recesses of his saddle-bags; and those who smoked, Dhib and 'Aïdh and one or two others, produced their pipes, talking the while with bated breath of the gloomy asceticism of the capital, its eternal round of prayer enforced by the rod of zealous monitors, and the unrelenting persecution of the smoker by the guardian sleuth-hounds of the *Wahhabi* creed. Poles apart in spirit as in space, Riyadh and Hufuf face each other over the boundless wilderness, the one a bulwark of puritan spiritualism, the other a champion of heterodox materialism, mutually disapproving and disapproved, and "never the twain shall meet," though they be for all time as now members of a single political unit.

I now wrote a letter to Ibn Sa'ud informing him of our arrival thus far, and we composed ourselves to rest while Dhib and 'Aïdh rode out into the moonlit night to precede us with the news of our coming. Next morning, the last of November, we were up and astir betimes and, leaving the baggage train to follow in our wake, set out with a small company on the last lap of our journey. Rising and falling, up slope and down valley, we proceeded until we came to the foot of the last long slope of the Duraibat al Khail. Up and up we went towards the line of pointed hillocks which line the summit of the slope. At length we reached the summit. "*La ilaha illa 'llah! La ilaha illa 'llah!*" Before us in the folds of the grey valley below lay a streak of emerald green; it was the gardens of Riyadh. The clay towers of the *Wahhabi* capital showed dimly through a screen of palms.

CHAPTER III

THE WAHHABI CAPITAL

1. Arrival at Riyadh

As we stood, dismounted, on the summit of the ridge, taking in the details of the scene before us, there came towards us three horsemen galloping up the slope. As they reached us, they leaped nimbly to the ground and, approaching, welcomed us to Riyadh. One of them was ʿAïdh, who had preceded us and who now introduced his companions, one of them a slave of the royal household named Saʿid, and the other, the spokesman of the party, one Ibrahim ibn Jumaiʿa, master of the ceremonies to Ibn Saʿud and a captain of the guard, to whom I took a strong instinctive dislike at sight, with whom I was destined during the following months to become intimately acquainted, and for whom my antipathy grew with every day of our acquaintance, until, more than six months later, I shook myself free of the incubus of his attentions by an open rupture. The reader of these pages will make his closer acquaintance and judge between us as my narrative proceeds; for the nonce he was the bearer of Ibn Saʿud's welcome.

After the customary interchange of formal greetings, we all remounted and moved slowly down the hill towards the palms, Ibrahim, a magnificent figure in his splendid raiment and sitting his breedy palfrey with the Arab's natural grace, riding level with me, exchanging news and compliments. Half-way down the slope a group of Arabs awaited our approach, their *Dhaluls* couched beside them; as we came up to them and their leader stood forward to greet us, we recognised in him Colonel Hamilton, the Political Agent at

Colonel R. E. A. Hamilton on left with Fahad of the Royal Bodyguard at Riyadh.

Kuwait, who had reached Riyadh by way of the Qasim some three weeks before us.

Joining forces, we all rode on together to the edge of the palm-belt, where a halt was called to await the opening of the city gates, for the day was Friday and the hour noon; the whole male population, high and low, was gathered in the Great Mosque for the weekly public prayer and all the gates were shut against ingress and egress. We dismounted on a dusty road leading between walled palm-groves and sat down to wait in the shade of a high garden-wall until the coast was clear. The while the long-drawn wail of a neighbouring well-wheel accentuated the deathly stillness of the scene, as it were the shrill cry of some ghostly *Muadhdhin* calling the world to endless prayer.

Suddenly there was a stir as of rustling leaves; somehow it was known that the gates had been flung open; life resumed its sway over the world that had seemed dead. We rose to our feet; saddles were adjusted and we mounted; once more we moved forward through the avenue of walled groves, from which we emerged into an open space to find ourselves looking upon the walls of Riyadh. Black booths of *Badawin* lay here and there before the city, and we wended our way through them to the northern gate. Through the gate and up a dusty street past the turreted fort, gazed at by the passing crowds just issued from the Mosque, we marched slowly forward to the palace square, now full of people, and, couching our beasts at the palace gate, entered. Ibrahim ushered us along a crowded passage, into an inner courtyard, up a flight of steps lined by armed slaves and men of the guard, along a corridor, similarly crowded, and through an open vestibule to the royal study.[1]

Shuffling off our sandals at the threshold, we entered a large square room, to be received with much cordiality by a little old man, somewhat inclined to stoutness, sharp-featured and bright-eyed, who led us towards the cushioned settees at a corner of the room by an open window; by a sort of instinct I became aware of another presence in the room, hidden at our entry by the central supporting column,

[1] They call this room *Daftar* or office, in which Ibn Sa'ud transacts such business as cannot be done in public audience.

a stately figure, tall and upright, clad in flowing robes of white overlain by a mantle of light brown, with a kindly, manly face, standing apart as if from shyness. This was Ibn Sa'ud himself, 'Abdul'aziz ibn 'Abdulrahman ibn Faisal al Sa'ud, *Imam* of the *Wahhabi* sect and ruler of Wahhabiland; the other was his father, 'Abdulrahman, styled by courtesy the *Imam*. Never again did I see father and son together, and I count ourselves fortunate in the accident of our arrival on a Friday, whereby we were privileged to witness two peculiarities of the *Wahhabi* system: the closing of the city gates at prayer time, and the strict observance of the canons of family etiquette in circumstances to which it would be hard to find a parallel. Every Friday, after the *Jum'a* or congregational prayer, for which alone in these, the days of his old age, the pious *Imam* issues forth from the seclusion of his house, he pays a formal visit to his son in the palace; on this particular Friday we happened to arrive at the very moment of his visit, and so it was that, coming as envoys of the British Government to the ruler of the country, we were received and entertained on our first arrival in the hall of audience by his father, while Ibn Sa'ud himself, sitting apart in a far corner, humbled and effaced himself in obedience to the laws of God. In India I have seen a father and his son in the same room, the one sitting on the floor cross-legged, the other, a barrister educated at an English University, lolling comfortably in a deep arm-chair and leading the conversation, the one fondly proud of his fine child, the other just a little ashamed of his parent; in Wahhabiland they are yet far from that stage of civilisation, and the laws of the old world still hold good, binding alike on sovereign and subject. A son will not wittingly enter an upper room if his father be in the room below; in public he sits in the lowest place if his father be present.

The *Imam* 'Abdulrahman now took his seat by the window, motioning us to seats by his side; a slave appeared first with tea and then with coffee, each time serving the *Imam* first, then ourselves, and then going over to pour to Ibn Sa'ud. Conversation in such circumstances could only be formal and complimentary, and after a few minutes

'ABDUL 'AZIZ IBN 'ABDUL RAHMAN IBN FAISAL IBN SA'UD, THE RULER OF WAHHABILAND, ON RIGHT, WITH HIS COUSIN SALMAN AL 'ARAFA.

ʿAbdulrahman rose from his seat, remarking that we must be tired after our long journey, and walked out of the room without further ado. Ibn Saʿud now came over to take the vacant place and the round of tea and coffee began afresh, the first cup now being handed to him as a matter of course; a further interchange of compliments ensued; I thanked him for the arrangements he had made to facilitate our journey and congratulated him on the peace and quiet which now prevail in his dominions as the result of his administration; he expressed the great pleasure he felt in receiving the emissaries of the British Government and enquired after the health of the many friends he had made on his visit to Basra twelve months before; and so on until he suggested that we might like to rest after the fatigues of the march.

Taking our leave of him, we were conducted by Ibrahim to our apartments, in which Colonel Hamilton was already installed, a suite of three rooms and a bathroom on the upper storey of a large courtyard, forming part of the east wing of the palace and separated from the court of audience by a small open quadrangle, whence a special flight of steps led up to our private door. The rest of the courtyard appeared to be occupied by slaves of the household and their families, and the doors giving access therefrom to our apartments had been barred up to effect a complete separation. As I afterwards learned, the suite we now occupied was usually reserved by Ibn Saʿud for the occupation of any *Baduwiyya* he might take to himself as wife from time to time in the course of his provincial tours and desire to retain on the "active list" on his return to town. Of this more hereafter; the purpose for which the apartments were reserved suggests that they are probably a good specimen of the domestic arrangements obtaining among the well-to-do at Riyadh. The outer staircase would serve as the private entrance of Ibn Saʿud himself; the inner doors for the admission of female servants from within; the apartments themselves comprise a large central room supported on three pillars, with a partition running across it for two-thirds of its breadth close to the inner door and serving to shut off the interior from the vulgar view when the door is opened to admit the servants ; this room is, as it were, the drawing-room, from which a door gives access to a smaller and square sleeping apartment ; the third room is a small oblong and apparently superfluous, leading, like the bathroom, out of a small hall at the head of the outer stairs ; the bathroom consists of a small vestibule, giving access to the bathing apartment, beyond which is the privy, the latter a small room without other furniture than a pile of stones for an obvious purpose and a slightly raised platform of clay with a runnel sloping down to a hole in the centre ; the bathroom furniture consists of water vessels of brass or pewter ; the other rooms are furnished with mats, carpets and cushions, with a few dilapidated plush-covered chairs, the last possibly introduced for our benefit. Such is what I take to be a typical *andarun* suite of Riyadh ; it was destined to be my home for seventy days in all at various times during the following months.

Our arrival was soon followed by the appearance of a princely repast, to which, seated on the floor round a large mat spread with manifold plates and dishes of vegetables and other delicacies grouped round a central pile of rice and mutton, we did ample justice in company with Ibrahim and Mulla ʿAbdullah ibn ʿAbdulillah, the Kuwait Agency *Munshi*, who had accompanied Colonel Hamilton on his journey. After the meal we received a visit by an attractive-looking young man, ʿAbdullah Saʿid Effendi, an Arab of Mausal, and incidentally the son-in-law of Muhammad Effendi of the Hasa, who had studied medicine for several years at Constantinople, held a Turkish medical diploma, and had spent several months in Paris ; he was, I think, at Basra just before the outbreak of war between Great Britain and Turkey, had thence gone to Hufuf either to marry or because he had married the daughter of his fellow-townsman, Muhammad, and, being cut off from access to his home by the opening of hostilities in Mesopotamia, had resigned himself to remaining in Arabia for the period of the war and offered his services to Ibn Saʿud, who used him freely in the double capacity of medical and political adviser. He spoke excellent French, and being specially deputed by Ibn Saʿud to attend to our wants, became our constant companion and much-valued friend.

The rest of the afternoon was spent in unpacking and making ourselves at home in our new quarters; letters and presents brought by us for Ibn Saʿud were despatched to him by the hand of ʿAbdullah Effendi; largesse in the shape of money and mantles was distributed to our companions of the journey from the Hasa; dinner was served at 5.30 P.M. and followed by a peaceful interval, of which I took advantage to have a much-needed bath; and at 7.30 P.M. we were summoned to our first formal conference with Ibn Saʿud.

2. Riyadh—The City and its Surroundings

During the ten days of my sojourn in the *Wahhabi* capital on this occasion my time was so fully occupied with the official business of my Mission and in protracted discussions with Ibn Saʿud on the problems which had brought me to his court that I had but little leisure to study the life and topography of Riyadh in the detail necessary for a description that would do them justice. Moreover, I was the more content to leave so vast a field for future exploration in the months that lay before me for the reason that I could scarcely hope to amplify, correct or, at any rate, improve upon the vivid picture of the city and its citizens painted some five-and-fifty years before by the *Jesuit* traveller of Jewish antecedents, William Gifford Palgrave, who abode here for forty-two days in all disguised as a Syrian leech during the austere reign of Faisal, the grandfather of my host.

Nevertheless no account of Wahhabiland in modern times would be complete without a sketch of its chief city and the life that pulses therein; and the stage I have now reached in the narrative of my wanderings in Arabia seems to be an appropriate moment for collecting and piecing together the information and impressions gathered haphazard at various times during a sojourn of seventy days comprising three different periods separated by intervals of several months; and I am emboldened to attempt the task in the presence of a greater artist by a variety of considerations : in the first place, the vicissitudes of fortune and the political and social upheavals by which they have been accompanied cannot but have left their mark, not only moral but physical, on the capital of the *Wahhabi* state in the long interval of years which has elapsed since Palgrave's visit; secondly, the conditions under which we sojourned at Riyadh were such that I was able to carry and freely use compass and other scientific instruments which Palgrave dared not include in the *paraphernalia* of his travelling pharmacy; and last but not least—I say it in all modesty and without any personal claim to infallibility—there are occasions when he stumbles, be it through forgetfulness or excess of imagination or for other reasons—*quondam dormitat Homerus.*

But of Palgrave more anon in due course.[1] As I rode up from the eastward to the low ridge of Duraibat al Khail and looked down from its brow for the first time on "Riad,[2] the main object of our long journey, the capital of Nejed and half Arabia, its very heart of hearts," I wondered whether the scene before me was indeed that, at first sight of which from the opposite hill-brow my predecessor had thrown open the flood-gates of a poet's imagination. I sought in vain "the blue hills, the ragged sierra of Yemamah" in the southern background, and "the fertile plains" of the same province, "thickly dotted with groves and villages"; I sought in vain the landscape "wider and more varied" than that of the approach to Damascus, where "the circle of vision embraces vaster plains and bolder mountains; while the mixture of tropical aridity and luxuriant verdure, of crowded population and desert tracts, is one that Arabia alone can present and in comparison with which Syria seems tame and Italy monotonous." [3]

Of tropical aridity and desert tracts there was indeed enough and to spare ; before me lay a shallow pear-shaped basin in the dip of an upland wilderness, whose far-flung desolation of wasted naked rock threw out in strong relief the narrow streaks of green or black, which constitute the oases of Riyadh and Manfuha, in the hollow. A narrow

[1] *Vide* Vol. II. p. 117. [2] W. G. P. vol. i. p. 388.
[3] W. G. P. vol. i. pp. 390, 391.

The Royal Palace at Riyadh.

tongue of the arid slope on which we stood separates the two oases, projecting south-westward between them towards a cleft in the slope beyond, wherein a scattered patch or two of palms mark the position of the Batin oasis and the course of Wadi Hanifa, where it carves out a passage for itself through the heart of Tuwaiq. The great clay towers of the capital stood out serenely above the palm tops near the northern end of the oasis ; elsewhere a tower or house showed through the screen of trees ; and the ruined watch-towers on the Manfuha road still told their tale of ancient strife.

Since that day of my first arrival I have looked down upon the same scene from the high ground on every side of the Riyadh basin ; from every point of view it is the same—a long dark screen of palms against a desert background—except only from the south, whence, owing to the slope of the basin in that direction, the whole extent of the double oasis may be seen at once and appears as a vast lozenge of vegetation based on the course of Wadi Hanifa.

Of Manfuha and the Batin I shall speak in a later chapter [1] in connection with visits I had occasion to make to those localities ; the oasis of Riyadh, parted from the former by the desert strip already mentioned and from the latter by the upward slope of Tuwaiq, extends from the left bank of Wadi Hanifa at a point midway between the two northwards up a shallow bay or trough which forms part of the Shamsiyya basin ; roughly diamond-shaped with its angles oriented towards the four points of the compass, its length from its southerly extremity to the Shamsiyya garden on the north is about three miles and its breadth considerably less than one mile across the widest section, in which stands the city itself, closely invested by dense palm-groves on all sides except the north-east, where only a few scattered groves break the view towards the Abu Makhruq uplands, whence the Shamsiyya watercourse, the main artery of the oasis, runs down to the garden which bears its name and thence past the east wall of the city towards Manfuha.

The city of Riyadh is built on a low platform of

[1] *Vide* p. 366 *infra*.

limestone rock shelving down on all sides from a central eminence, on which towering above the surrounding houses stands the noble pile of the royal palace. Palgrave's plan of the *Wahhabi* capital—a plan which apparently does not pretend to be anything but a rough sketch from memory—gives it a roughly symmetrical rectangular periphery with a pronounced inward indentation of the north-eastern angle and a spread from east to west about half as great again as that from north to south ; changes may well have taken place in the outline of the city in the course of half-a-century of strife and turmoil, but the plan is too vague and lacking in definition to be convincing in spite of some excellent internal detail, though in most respects it is more suggestive of modern Riyadh than the description of a recent traveller, who makes the town L-shaped and places the palace at the angle of the L.

Many a pleasant hour did I spend with compass and notebook pacing the walls of the city in the endeavour to arrive at something like a correct idea of its shape, orientation and dimensions ; the result of my labours, often interrupted by the suspicious inquisitiveness of the inhabitants but steadily persisted in until my object had been obtained, may be seen in the accompanying plan, which shows the *Wahhabi* capital as an irregular many-sided figure, which with the help of a little imagination may be regarded as an equilateral spherical triangle with a base-line of rather more than 600 yards on the north and its apex to the south, with a superficial area of about 100 acres and with streets radiating in every direction towards the circumference from a central and roughly circular enclave dominated by the palace.

The city is completely encircled by a thick wall of coarse sun-baked mud-bricks, about twenty-five feet in height and surmounted by a fringe of plain shark's-tooth design ; at frequent intervals [1] its continuity is interrupted by imposing bastions and less pretentious guard-turrets, circular for the most part and slightly tapering towards the top but some few square or rectangular, varying from thirty to forty feet in height and generally projecting slightly outwards from

[1] Twenty-two in all, I think.

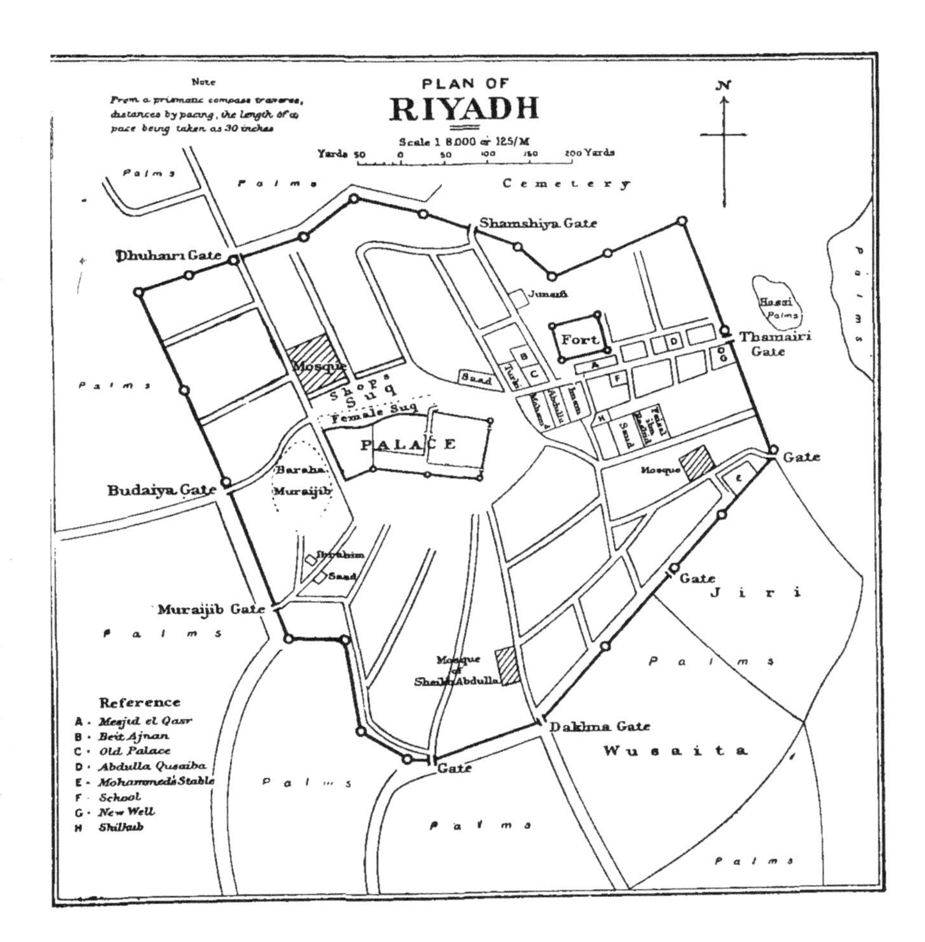

Note
From a prismatic compass traverse, distances by pacing, the length of a pace being taken as 30 inches
PLAN OF
RIYADH
Scale 1 8,000 or 125/M
Yards 50 0 50 100 150 200 Yards
N
Palms
Palms
Cemetery
Shamshiya Gate
Dhuhari Gate
Junaifi
Fort
Thamairi Gate
Hassi Palms
Palms
Mosque
Shops
Suq
Female Suq
Saad
Turki
Imam
PALACE
Palms
Baraha Muraijib
Budaiya Gate
Gate
Mosque
Ibrahim
Saad
Muraijib Gate
Gate
Jiri
Palms
Palms
Mosque of Shaikh Abdulla
Dakhna Gate
Wusaita
Gate
Palms
Palms
Palms
Reference
A - Masjid el Qasr
B - Beit Ajnan
C - Old Palace
D - Abdulla Qusaiba
E - Mohammed's Stable
F - School
G - New Well
H - Shilhub

the wall-line for greater facility of defence. Much of the wall and its fortifications as they are to-day, more particularly on the north and east sides, are of comparatively recent structure, for the *Rashidian* occupation of the *Wahhabi* capital had been marked by the demolition of its defences—a factor which eventually proved the undoing of its perpetrators inasmuch as Ibn Sa'ud was able to enter the city over the ruins of its walls unobserved; but both the walls and the bastions on the west and south sides seemed from their comparatively greater massiveness and solidity, as also from the presence of a moat-like trough, to be part of the original fortifications possibly dating from the time when Manfuha and Riyadh were rivals well matched in strength; this impression was further strengthened by the presence on the outskirts of the oasis to south and west of groups of ruins, apparently of fortified hamlets or outposts, in the construction of which much use had been made of the plentiful limestone rock of the neighbouring slopes with or without a binding of mud-mortar, as also by the fact that the finest and most mature palm-groves of the settlement, reaching as they do right up to the walls on these sides, seem to indicate that the walls, as they now are, mark the original limits of the city in this direction.

Tradition points to an insignificant group of ruins, known as Hajar al Yamama, about a quarter-mile to the north-east of the modern city towards the Shamsiyya garden, as the original site of Riyadh, but the inconsiderable extent of the remains would seem to justify the conclusion that the traditional site was no more than that of a petty hamlet dating back to the days before the rise of Riyadh, when Manfuha was the undisputed mistress of the whole basin.

The perimeter of the wall is pierced in nine places by gateways, some of which have ceased to be in regular use except as means of access to the walled palm-groves in their vicinity; of the others the most important are the Thumairi and Dhuhairi gates, the first situate on the east side of the city and serving as the regular outlet to the main tracks to the north and east and also to the southern road towards Manfuha, while the other at the north-west corner gives access to the north-western route to Washm and the Qasim and to the western pilgrim road to Mecca; next in importance are the Dakhna and Muraiqib gates on the south-west and a nameless outlet between them, all of which give access to the southern and south-western routes; the Budai'a gate, which leads out towards the Batin; and finally the Shamsiyya gate, by which one may pass out on to the northern route.

The internal arrangement of the streets is without symmetry except for the natural convergence already mentioned of all main traffic lines on the central enclave; the chief street is that which leads in a straight line from the Thumairi gate to the palace and thence through the market-place to the Budai'a outlet, with a branch going off from it at right angles from the western end of the *Suq* to the Dhuhairi gate.

The market-place, which occupies the whole of the open space to the north of the palace, slopes westward down a sharp incline and is divided into two sections by a partition wall, the section between this wall and the wall of the palace being reserved exclusively for the use of women—vegetable-sellers, purveyors of domestic necessaries and the like—while the other and larger section comprises about 120 unpretentious shops ranged partly along either side of a broad thoroughfare and partly back to back on a narrow island of no great length in the midst thereof; the shops along the north side of the *Suq* are backed in part by the outer walls of ordinary dwelling-houses and partly by the south wall of the Great Mosque itself. On market-days and during the busy hours of ordinary days the *Suq* presents a lively scene indeed; the shops display a miscellaneous assortment of wares ranging from imported piece-goods and indigenous leather-work and saddlery through the whole gamut of tea, coffee, sugar, spices, meat, rice and other necessaries of life to such articles of luxury or desire as rifles, ammunition, watches, field-glasses and what-not; the thoroughfare is blocked by droves of sheep, the object of much chaffering between their owners and would-be buyers, who pass from one animal to another with the

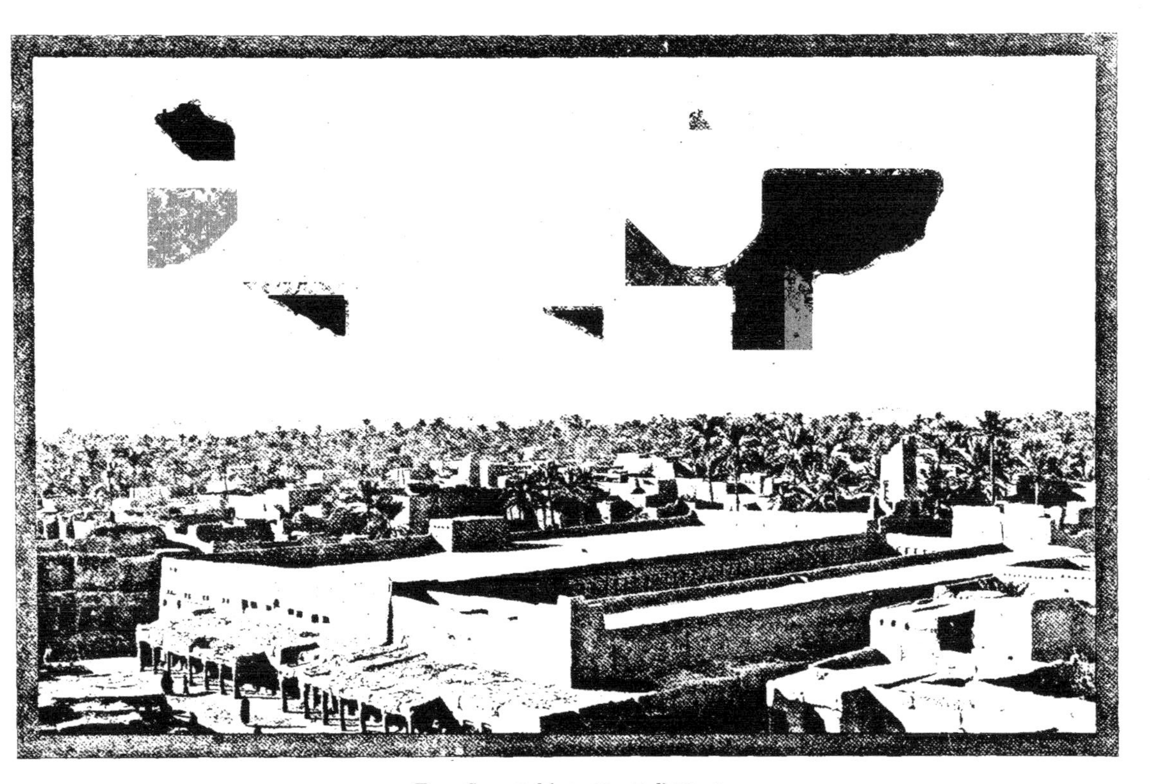

The Great Mosque at Riyadh.

patience of men determined to make a good bargain or none, kneading the fleshy parts of the unfortunate beasts with expert fingers; here and there a shopman or paid hawker passes in and out among the clamouring crowd with a rifle or pair of field-glasses, or a mantle of Hasa workmanship crying the last price bid and endeavouring to get a better offer; and now and then a camel or two loaded with fodder or fuel wends its indifferent way through the press of man and beast, picking its path through the crowd with the clumsy intelligence peculiar to its kind and brushing the bystanders aside with its trailing load. At the hours of prayer the scene changes with dramatic suddenness; at the first sound of the *Muadhdhin's* cry the shops are closed down, the crowd vanishes to perform its ablutions and the proctors prowl through the empty streets; in a moment the streets are filled again with people decorously stalking with downcast eyes towards the mosques, and thereafter the silence is broken only by the deep responses of a dozen congregations; the shops reopen at the close of prayers, and once more the market-place is filled with the clamour of men. And so they alternate between noise and silence the livelong day.

The Great Mosque or *Jami'a* of Riyadh is a spacious rectangular enclosure about sixty yards by fifty in area, whose main entrance faces the *Suq* through a gap in the row of shops lining its southern wall, while the Qibla or prayer-direction, by which the whole building is oriented, is marked by a very slight south-westerly bulge in the longer western face, near which as also on the east side is a subsidiary entrance. The internal space is divided into three sections, of which the central one forms an open court occupying about a quarter of the whole building, while the other two are covered over by low flat roofs supported on several rows of massive stone pillars to form *Liwans* or cloisters for the convenience of worshippers during the hot hours of the day; the inward faces of these cloisters towards the central open court form colonnades of pointed arches of typical *Wahhabi* architecture and of considerable merit, though the workmanship is rough and simple; the *Liwan* on the *Qibla* side occupies about half of the whole enclosure, leaving the remaining quarter to the other; the roofs are without ornamentation, being encircled by a low parapet with a low stepped structure of very ungainly appearance near the centre of the north side to serve as a minaret, for minarets of the types known to other *Muslim* countries are anathema to the puritan *Wahhabis,* who regard any embellishment of their praying-places as the work of the Devil. A similar but much smaller projection adorns the south-eastern corner of the building, while the *Qibla* niche also projects slightly above the level of the roof.

Besides the Great Mosque and the palace itself the only building of any architectural distinction in the city is the fort, a great square building with massive walls and ponderous bastions at the four corners situated slightly to the north of the main street about midway between the palace and the Thumairi gate; in its present form it apparently dates back about half-a-century to the latter part of the reign of Faisal or to the beginning of that of his son and successor, ʻAbdullah, to whom it owes its existence. It is now used only as an arsenal, jail and storehouse by Ibn Saʻud who, in the spacious times of peace which he himself inaugurated by his return from exile, has found the generous dimensions of his grandfather's palace more in keeping with the *rôle* of a great monarch than the thick-walled dungeon in which his uncle sought to parry the treachery of an ambitious brother.

Be that as it may, there is, with the possible exception of the fort at Buraida, no building in all his territories so splendid in its proportions, so beautiful and so representative of all that is best in modern Arabian architecture as the royal palace of Ibn Saʻud. Its merit lies in its superb simplicity of design and in an almost complete absence of ornament so appropriate to an edifice intended to provide not only comfort but security for those dwelling within its walls. Much of the western wing of the building was, during the time of my visit, in a somewhat dilapidated state, and masons were busy creating order out of chaos and incidentally increasing the available internal accommodation for the growing family and household staff of Ibn Saʻud, whose own private apartments occupy a central position adjoining

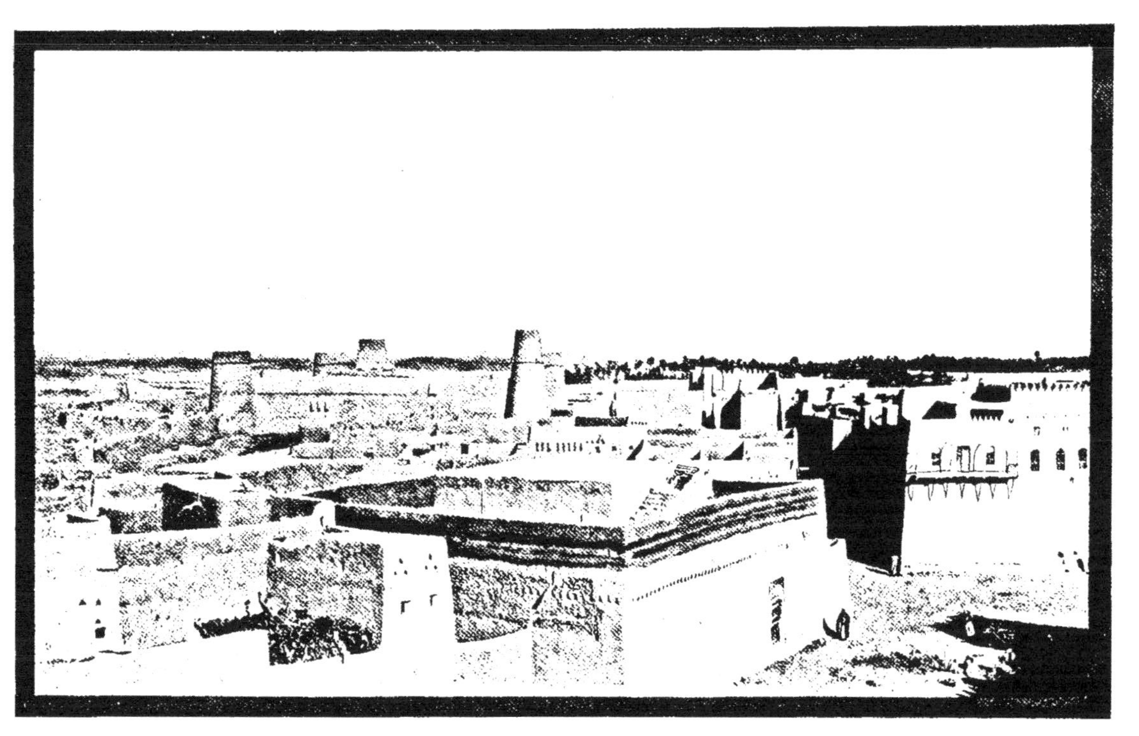

THE FORT AT RIYADH AND GENERAL VIEW NORTH-EASTWARD FROM PALACE; THE HOUSE OF MUHAMMED IBN SA'UD ON RIGHT AND THAT OF THE LATE SA'UD IBN SA'UD IN CENTRE FOREGROUND AND MAIN STREET TO NORTH-EAST GATE BETWEEN THEM.

the southern wall and are connected by passages with a corresponding edifice in the middle of the northern wall, in which are the audience-chambers and offices of the central administration. To these the main doorway facing eastward from a projecting machicolated structure gives direct access to the throngs which at all times besiege the entrance and which can be conveniently overlooked from a number of latticed windows in Ibn Sa'ud's private sanctum on the first floor of the projecting portion immediately above the door. The eastern section of the building is for the most part relegated to the domestic staff, the slaves and servants of both sexes, who occupy a courtyard in the north-east corner, and to the kitchens and stables which spread over the south-eastern portion; to these two separate doors give access on the east side. Bastions afford protection to the palace at intervals in its periphery, but the most elegant portion of the whole building is certainly that which first meets the view of one advancing towards it along the main street leading from the eastern gate of the city. The spacious turret at the corner, the great expanse of clay wall, with its minute triangular perforations and surmounting fringe of stepped pinnacles, broken at the farther end by the angle formed by the projecting tower and the raised central portion extending inwards from the latter and at the same level as its summit —all these together form an exceedingly picturesque front, facing the open square and the *Suq*. In the hot weather the roof of the raised central portion was allotted to my use at night, and from that commanding position, the highest point in the whole city, I could scan not only the surrounding roofs, but the country around far and wide. On it stands a tall rickety pole, which looks like a flagstaff, but is in fact a lamp-post, a great arc-lamp procured from Bombay being hoisted to its top every night to give light to the many roofs of the palace, on which its inmates spread themselves out to enjoy the cool air of the evening; ordinarily the lamp was lowered and extinguished somewhat before midnight or when Ibn Sa'ud retired to his bed, but during the month of *Ramdhan* the great light was left there all night to illuminate the praying congregation, and its removal just before dawn gave the signal to the whole city that the next day's fast would soon begin.

The palace, whose irregular mass covers the greater part of the central enclave, and the residences of the various members of the royal family occupy, as I roughly estimated, about a quarter of the whole area of the city. Mosques, to the number of between fifteen and twenty,[1] but including none of any architectural pretensions besides the Great Mosque, and the fort probably occupy nearly as much space again, while the remaining half of the area enclosed by the circuit wall is thickly dotted with ordinary dwelling-houses, of which no special mention is necessary.

All round the city, except towards the north-east, lie the dense palm-groves of the oasis, in many of which there are buildings which serve as country residences when their owners want a respite from the routine of city life. In them are the deep, and in many cases very capacious, draw-wells or *Jalibs*, which night and day seem from the unceasing long-drawn-out drone of their pulleys to be perpetually at work. One of these is very much like another, and that which stands in the midst of and irrigates the garden called Wusaita, a splendid grove on the south-east side of the city belonging to the *Imam* 'Abdulrahman, must serve as a type of the rest. The pit of this great well is about ten feet square at the top and tapers very slightly downwards to the water level, which lies between forty and fifty feet below the surface; hewn out of the solid limestone rock, its upper portion for about one-third of its depth has an additional strengthening of stone-slabs roughly cemented together. The mouth of the pit is surmounted by a ponderous triangular superstructure called *'Idda* and constructed of palm-logs with *Ithil*-wood for the stays and subsidiary parts; the top cross-beam of the *'Idda* is furnished with

[1] The next in importance to the Great Mosque is the *Masjid al Shaikh* eastward of the palace and so called because the chief priest, Shaikh 'Abdullah ibn 'Abdulwahhab, of the *Wahhabi* hierarchy officiates therein at all prayers except on Fridays, when he conducts the congregational midday service at the Great Mosque. The *Imam* 'Abdulrahman has a private chapel in his own house, and there is another in the palace which Ibn Sa'ud ordinarily attends when he does not go to the Great Mosque. Another mosque lies alongside the fort between it and the main street.

Gardens in Riyadh oasis 'Abdullah Effendi seated on wall.

six pulleys (*Mahala*) on either side or twelve in all, while the basal beam resting in masonry sockets over the actual mouth of the well is provided with a corresponding number of rollers (*Darraja*). Stout hempen ropes, to one end of which are attached the leathern buckets (*Qarab*, sing.: *Qirba*) generally consisting of whole goatskins, run over the pulleys to be harnessed in this case to great donkeys of the Hasa breed and in the case of some wells to mules and donkeys[1] combined, while thinner cords running over the rollers are attached at one end to the donkeys and at the other to the necks of the skin-buckets, which are weighted by stones tied to their thicker extremities. On either side of the well-mouth lies a sharp incline, whose length corresponds to the depth of the pit to water; the donkeys, each harnessed to its bucket by the thick and thin ropes, start in a line, six on each side, down the incline, and as they descend draw up the buckets full of water; when they reach the bottom, the thick ends or bodies of the buckets reach the level of the pulleys in the upper beam, while their thin ends or necks, being simultaneously drawn over the rollers, discharge their contents into a masonry reservoir immediately below them, whence the water flows out into the channels by which it is distributed over the garden. The animals, having reached the bottom of the incline, pause for a moment and turn round, each pivoting on his own centre; the line then ascends the incline as it descended, and by so doing lowers the weighted *Qarab* into the water, whereupon the process here described is repeated without end. Clumsy as it looks, this simple well-machinery seems to work very smoothly and efficiently; occasional repairs are required by the woodwork and the surface of the incline, but the worst that can happen in the ordinary course is the snapping of a cord by friction with the roller; on such occasions the weighted bucket of course remains at the bottom of the well, and one of the attendants, taking a spare end with him, slithers down the main rope to the scene of action

[1] Camels are not used on the wells at Riyadh, though they are more frequently used than donkeys elsewhere. In the poorer villages cattle and inferior donkeys also perform this service.

and, having effected the necessary repairs, is drawn up again on the bucket to the pulley level, whence by an exhibition of agile gymnastics be brings himself again to dry land. The mules used in some of the gardens of Riyadh are the exclusive property of Ibn Sa'ud, who acquired them by capture from the last Turkish garrison of the Hasa. Though the Wusaita well may be regarded as typical in its general structure of the wells of the oasis, and indeed of the whole of Central Arabia, it is by no means the largest ; one in the garden called Hauta for instance is worked by fourteen donkeys, seven a side, while the 'Ataiqiyya well has room for eight donkeys abreast on either side, and I have been told of, though I do not remember actually seeing, a *Jalib* worked by twenty animals—ten a side. Ibn Sa'ud, talking to me on one occasion of the art of swimming as known to the Arabs—it is extraordinary that a race which lives in a country where water is so scarce should be able to swim at all, and yet the Arabs are expert swimmers—assured me that he had known men to dive into these wells from the basal beam and to emerge unhurt, and promised me an exhibition of their prowess in this direction, but unfortunately I forgot to remind him of the matter and never saw the feat performed. The depth of water in these wells varies, of course, with the seasons, but is probably seldom greater than twenty or thirty feet, if as much.

In the open clearing between the Shamsiyya gate and the encircling palm-groves on that side, which include the Hauta garden and extend northwards to that of Shamsiyya, lies the greater of the two cemeteries which accommodate the people of the capital when their earthly course is run. A mere wilderness of low earthen mounds and tumbled *débris*, it serves to remind those who yet live of the vanity of human life, for here in these dusty mounds prince and peasant lie side by side without distinction, and though those who have buried their dear ones remember the position of and at intervals visit their graves to ask God's pity on the departed, their successors will forget, and none could—or perhaps would—point out to me the last resting-places of the great Faisal and his predecessors. I am not even sure whether these lie here or in the smaller or so-called royal cemetery farther east on the left bank of the Shamsiyya torrent-bed, where members of the royal family are nowadays interred.

About midway between the two cemeteries and in front of the main east gate lies the *'Id* praying enclosure, a large bare oblong space enclosed by a low mud-wall with a *Qibla* niche in the middle of the western side. This enclosure is used for congregational prayers only on the great feast days, and is reckoned to be large enough to contain the whole male population of praying age of the city, the women, who are permitted to join in the *'Id* prayers, being excluded from the enclosure itself and left to pray on the open ground behind it.

Such are the main features of Riyadh, the *Wahhabi* capital, the queen of Desert Arabia, set on a throne of rock and screened about with palms from the encircling waste of a wilderness, whose desolation is reflected in the barren hearts of its denizens.

3. First Days at Riyadh

It did not take me long to realise that Ibn Sa'ud was a man of inexhaustible energy, a man who put the affairs of his State above all other considerations and spared neither himself nor his subordinates in the ordering thereof; endowed with a splendid physique and with a stature rarely attained by Arabs—for he stands about six feet three inches and looks considerably taller by reason of the simple flowing robes which he affects—he restricts himself to but few hours of sleep, perhaps four hours at night and two during the day, and to such recreation only as the demands upon his time permit; for the rest he is punctual in the observance of the appointed hours of prayer and somewhat casual and irregular in the matter of meals; the remaining hours are fully taken up by the duties, which devolve upon him as the ruler of the land, and in the administration of his household, in which he always takes the keenest personal interest, mindful perhaps of the experience of his predecessors, which has taught him that a monarch, who is at the same time a *paterfamilias* on a large scale, cannot with impunity neglect the cultivation of close personal relations with the members of his own family. A marked tendency to uxoriousness is perhaps in his case but a natural development of a pronounced domestic trait in his character, which makes him no less efficient in his capacity of head of a family than in that of head of a State.

His capacity for work may be judged by my experience during this first period of my sojourn at Riyadh; I had come to him on a mission from my Government with instructions to discuss matters with him and report on the situation in Central Arabia in relation to the war, in which it was hoped that he might be induced to take a more prominent part than theretofore; the policy of His Majesty's Government, as represented by the Civil Commissioner of Mesopotamia, aimed at a threefold object: firstly, the cultivation of friendly relations between the various Arab states, which had adhered to the Allied cause; secondly, the efficient prosecution of the blockade of enemy territory on the Arab side; and lastly, the utilisation of the military resources of the friendly Arab states in the direction most convenient in each case. Ibn Saʻud, conscious of his ability to assist us and willing to do so, was at the same time quick to perceive the advantages which might accrue to himself from a policy of co-operation with us in these aims—those advantages being, firstly, the stabilisation of his own position in relation to his neighbours, and secondly, the financial backing of the British Government so necessary to him for the proper development of a country which still bore the marks of a long period of anarchy and discord.

Nothing was to be gained by delay, and the rapid rise of the Sharif of Mecca to a commanding position in Arabian politics warned him that his own future depended on the adoption of a vigorous policy for which the time was fully ripe. The arrival of a British Mission at his capital provided him with the requisite opportunity of setting his house in order, and he seized the opportunity with characteristic energy. Audience followed audience with bewildering rapidity, and at the end of the fifth day of my stay I calculated that of the 132 hours which had elapsed from the time of my arrival to midnight of the 5th December, I had spent no fewer than 34, or more than one quarter of the whole period, in formal interviews with Ibn Sa'ud, to say nothing of the time spent in informal discussions with his secretaries, who visited us in season and out of season during the intervals between audiences, to clear up points which had been raised or to prepare the ground for matters yet to be mooted.

At this stage, having covered and re-covered the whole range of the Mission's mandate, I felt, and I think Ibn Sa'ud shared the feeling, that we had reached bed-rock in all the matters under discussion; I was able to draw up a report of our proceedings with recommendations for the consideration of the British authorities, which being despatched the remaining portion of my sojourn was of a less strenuous character, and I was able to walk abroad occasionally to see something of the city and its surroundings.

Up to the afternoon of the 4th December, when I said good-bye to Colonel Hamilton on his departure on the return journey to Kuwait, he accompanied me to most of the royal audiences, which were also attended, though less regularly, by Colonel Cunliffe Owen, who appeared only when military matters were likely to come under discussion, while Ibn Sa'ud on his side was generally supported by his cousin and political *aide-de-camp*, Ahmad ibn Thunaian, and by 'Abdullah Effendi. When our negotiations had reached an advanced stage, however, and showed signs of becoming unduly protracted owing to the variety of views voiced in our meetings, I made bold to ask Ibn Sa'ud for a private interview, and the finishing touches were put on the first stage of our negotiations in a *tête-à-tête* conference lasting five hours in the privacy of a cosy little boudoir adjoining the royal apartments.

On one occasion Ibn Sa'ud did us the honour of visiting us in our own apartments, following so rapidly on the heels of the messenger, who came to announce his coming, that Colonel Cunliffe Owen and I had barely time to stuff pipes, tobacco-tins and other evidences of our bad habits behind and under the cushions of our divan, when our visitor stalked into an atmosphere heavy with pungent smoke, and, after an exchange of greetings, took his place between us, conversing as if he had noticed nothing; but we were not to be let off so lightly, for a slave, who had accompanied his master to our threshold, shortly afterwards reappeared with a censer, and having passed it round to each of us in turn, left it on the floor before us to purge the noisome air. It was the first but by no means the last time that I was surprised almost *in flagrante delicto* by Ibn Sa'ud, who, however, never even remotely betrayed a knowledge that I was addicted to smoking, or a suspicion that my company was a refuge for those of his own people who were in the same plight, though, whenever the subject of tobacco cropped up in conversation, he made no secret of his loathing for the forbidden weed.

Ibn Sa'ud's only recreation during the periods of his residence at his capital takes the form of occasional excursions on foot or on horseback to convenient spots within or on the fringes of the oasis. One such outing, which I attended during these days, was arranged, by way of formal farewell to Colonel Hamilton, to take place on the afternoon before his departure; in order to facilitate an early start on the next day he had had his tents and baggage moved out from the city to the camping-ground near the Shamsiyya garden, and it was thither that we repaired in company with Ibn Sa'ud, many members of his family and his court, all on horseback; a goodly cavalcade it was as we streamed out of the city and up the sandy watercourse, Ibn Sa'ud leading the way with our three selves in close attendance, together with the children of the royal family, each on a pony suited to his size and attended by slaves; as we got clear of the walls Ibn Sa'ud, raising himself to his full height on his stirrups and turning in the saddle towards his following, intoned the opening verses of some stirring war-chant, which being taken up by those in the rear, the cavalcade broke into a canter, and spreading out as they went over the open plain, the horsemen ranged themselves into two groups for a military display; at a given signal the tournament began; at and through each other, and back and through again and round about they rode at a hand-gallop with loud challenging cries, with swords or rifles poised aloft as in an Arab combat, but there was no firing, for in Arabia, or at any rate in Central Arabia, ammunition has its price and is not squandered in sham fights ; in the midst of them rode Ibn Sa'ud, a splendid figure on a splendid mount, and his elder sons, enjoying the fun as well as any of the rest, and posing consciously as they galloped past the knoll on which I had taken up my position with my camera to view the scene.

When they had had enough of the game we repaired in company to the shade of the Shamsiyya garden wall, where, reclining on a spacious mound of earth, we talked for a while until it was time to go on to Colonel Hamilton's tents, where coffee was being made ready. It was now near the hour for the sunset prayer, and in due course the whole gathering lined up on the open plain behind Ibn Sa'ud, and from a respectful distance we watched the ordered harmony of the inclinations, prostrations and uprisings of *Muslim* worship —an impressive ceremony, very simple and austere. The conclusion of prayers brought the outing to an end, and leaving Ibn Sa'ud and his people to return to the city, we stayed behind for tea in Colonel Hamilton's camp, where we were joined by 'Abdullah Effendi, who brought with him by his master's command a pair of oryxes,[1] those splendid animals of the great sand-deserts, full-grown specimens with white pelts and long straight horns, for eventual presentation to the King of England. Before dark we returned to the city, leaving Colonel Hamilton in his camp, which was to be struck before dawn.

It was at this outing that I saw for the first time and was introduced to Turki, the eldest son and heir of Ibn Sa'ud ; after many months spent in the Qasim in command of the troops in that province he had only just returned to Riyadh to recuperate after a bad bout of fever ; a handsome boy he was, with pleasant easy manners and a complexion somewhat sallow as the result of his recent indisposition ; but there was nothing in his slender frame and delicate features to indicate either the possession of the heroic

[1] One of these animals arrived in England in May, 1920, as a present to H.M. the King, and was by his command deposited in the London Zoological Gardens on the 14th May. It is a hind of the species *Oryx Leucoryx*. I do not know what happened to her mate.

qualities, with which unanimous public opinion credited him, or long experience of campaigning; he had, nevertheless, begun his military career at the age of eight, and was now second only to his father in command of the army at the age of eighteen.

Among the children present on this occasion were Muhammad and Khalid, younger sons of Ibn Sa'ud, aged nine and six respectively, and Faisal, Fahad and Sa'ud, ranging from eight downwards, the orphans of his favourite brother, Sa'd, whose death in 1915[1] at the hands of the 'Ajman tribe he has never forgotten, forgiven, or ceased lamenting, though, truth to say, Sa'd had richly deserved the fate he brought upon himself by an act of shameless treachery. Hatred of the 'Ajman and a determination to avenge his brother were at this time one of the key-notes of Ibn Sa'ud's policy and provided him with a dramatic *leit-motif*, as it were, with which to work on the feelings of his audience when necessary; to this end he had taken his brother's widow to wife—she was with child by him at this time, and was delivered of a daughter in the following April; to the same end he paraded the little orphans, as it were his own children, before the public gaze on every suitable occasion; and often, pointing to them, he would launch forth into a homily on the treachery of the 'Ajman and the necessity of settling accounts with them. The tragedy of Sa'd is a blot on the annals of Ibn Sa'ud's reign, though but an incident—perhaps by no means the final incident—in a long record of strife between the 'Ajman tribesmen and the ruling branch of the Sa'ud dynasty.

Another day we were honoured with a summons to an audience with the *Imam*, 'Abdulrahman, whom we had not seen since our first meeting with him in Ibn Sa'ud's office, and Colonel Cunliffe Owen and I accompanied the bearer of the invitation to the old man's house, a large but unpretentious building in the main street opposite the fort. Passing through the outer door into a courtyard surrounded with coarsely-frescoed earthen walls, we ascended a narrow winding flight of steps to the first floor and entered the audience-chamber, a long bare hall, forty feet in length,

[1] *Vide* p. 103 *infra*.

Group at Riyadh; royal children in front, and standing behind from left to right: Faisal ibn Hashr, Faisal ibn Rashid, Ibn Sa'ud himself, Sa'ul ibn 'Abdul, 'Aziz al 'Arafa, Turki ibn Sa'ud, Sa'ud ibn 'Abdul Rahman ibn Sa'ud, and two other members of the royal family.

half as much in width, and about eighteen feet in height, with a central row of plastered pillars supporting the roof; the floor was covered over with carpets, and one corner of the room was furnished with two cushioned elbow-rests on either side of the *Imam's* own sitting-place, and a few other cushions for visitors to recline against; the *Imam* appeared soon after our arrival, and coffee was served while we conversed with our host. He had visited Baghdad as a young man forty years before, and since then, during the period of his exile, he had once visited Basra about twenty years before; otherwise he had not been farther afield than Bahrain and Kuwait, where he and his family had spent the years of their voluntary exile from Najd; during the preceding summer he had set out with his second son, Muhammad, and the *Wahhabi* pilgrim-train in the hopes of achieving the common ambition of all good *Muslims*, but the fatigues of the long journey had proved too much for his old bones and he had been compelled to return home from the fifth stage towards his goal, leaving Muhammad and the others to see the pilgrimage through. It had been a notable ceremony, the first of its kind under the auspices of the new-made King of the Hijaz, and it was said that the *Najdis*, who rode in the pilgrimage, were not less than 7000 souls,[1] men, women and children. ʿAbdulrahman spoke with much enthusiasm of the bond of amity which the war had forged between his country and ours; in his early youth he had seen the beginnings of the present alliance in the visit of Colonel Lewis Pelly [2] to the court of his father, Faisal; he spoke too with conscious pride of the great position his son had won for himself, and of the bonds of loyalty which in these days unite the royal family in the service of God and their country; Ibn Saʿud visits his old father once at least every day when he is in residence at his capital, and never undertakes any important measure

[1] The number was inclined to vary considerably; *e.g.* Muhammad himself told me his following comprised 17,000 persons (*vide* p. 378 *infra*), but 7000 was probably something like the correct figure.

[2] This was in 1865 when Pelly, then H.M.'s Political Resident in the Persian Gulf, visited Riyadh with a small British Mission: *vide* "Report on a Journey to the Wahabee Capital of Riyadh in Central Arabia," by Lt.-Col. Lewis Pelly. Bombay, 1866.

without consulting him; when he is absent the current duties of administration devolve on the old man, who also takes an active personal interest in the development of his own estates and those of the crown. Of late years he has exhibited an increasing tendency towards sedentary habits; seldom or never does he leave his own house except to attend the public prayer in the Great Mosque on Fridays and to visit his son at the palace on his return; much of his time he spends in prayer, in a mosque in his house, and in reading or meditation; for he is, he feels, near the end of the human span, and there remains but little between him and the blissful state on which he has set his best hopes and endeavours without stint since the days of his early youth.

Our presence in the *Wahhabi* capital as the guests of Ibn Sa'ud naturally enough did not pass without remark, for, though there was no outward exhibition of disapproval or hostility towards any of us, I gathered from my host's remarks that there was much covert criticism of his policy in the air; at one of our interviews he produced and read out to me a long anonymous letter, in which he was warned that the English had come to Najd for a selfish purpose, that, though they might give him what he wanted in exchange for his assistance in the furtherance of their designs, it was not out of any love for him, and that they would eat him up when it suited their purpose to do so. It was the letter of an ignorant fanatic, but served to illustrate a tendency of public opinion and as a warning that the greatest circumspection was necessary in our deportment in public. Like Colonel Hamilton, who had preceded us to Riyadh, we too had adopted Arab dress before our arrival, but Colonel Cunliffe Owen had done so only partially under persuasion from me in spite of a strong conviction of the impropriety of such a course, while Schofield, for all his willing efforts, never came within measurable distance of looking like an Arab. Similar differences divided us in the manner of our eating; Hamilton and I had acquired sufficient facility with our fingers to sit at meat with such visitors as joined us at our meals without any serious breach of table etiquette; Schofield battled manfully, but with little success, with meat and rice and soup; while Cunliffe Owen, secure in the privacy of our apartments, generally preferred to feed himself with knife, fork and spoon. That Hamilton and I were right in the view that those who would travel in Arabia should learn to do as Arabs do in every respect, I personally harbour no shadow of doubt, and I have no sympathy whatever with the prejudice which condemns the dissimulation by a Britisher of his identity as a "British officer and gentleman,"—a prejudice which perhaps cost Shakespear[1] his life in 1915, and cannot but add to the difficulties of travel in fanatical countries; but the idiosyncrasies of travellers are queer phenomena, dependent on the temperament of the individual and the circumstances of each case, and not to be lightly discussed—*quot homines tot sententiae*; each individual must decide for himself, using the experience of his predecessors so far as it may be applicable to his own case, but to any one who would ask my advice in such a matter, I would have no hesitation in recommending the principles and methods of Carlo Guarmani, the Levantine Italian, who penetrated into the Shammar country and has left his views on record:[2] "At the gate [of Haïl] the corpse of a Persian Jew lay rotting, he having been massacred by the populace for pretending to be a Mussulman and then refusing to repeat the formula. . . . If his fate was a sad one, it must be owned he had deserved it. When a man decides to risk himself in a great adventure, he must use every means in his power and be prepared to suffer all the consequences of his enterprise. His death was believed to be my own . . . my poor family were informed through the tactlessness of a friend and mourned me in earnest, whilst all the time I was in excellent health, eating *pilaff* or *temmen* and making my *rikat* to God in my heart but to Mahomet with my lips in all due reverence; and, remembering Christ's Sermon on the Mount, not to mention the stench of that Jew's rotting corpse, I was determined not to be amongst the poor in spirit and enter Paradise with the fools."

The circumstances of our Mission rendered conformity

[1] *Vide* p. 384 *infra*.

[2] Page 54, *Northern Nejd*, by Carlo Guarmani. Translated by Mr. D. Carruthers. Cairo Government Press, 1917.

in the matter of religious observances unnecessary and even undesirable, but 'Abdullah ibn Jiluwi had been very insistent on our assuming Arab dress against chance encounters in the desert, and Ibn Sa'ud was no less pointed in his references to the necessity in our own interests and his of our making ourselves as little conspicuous as possible during our sojourn in his territories.

Our meals came from the royal kitchens, where a staff of professional cooks was employed in the preparation of vast quantities of rice and meat for the household and its guests, while the more delicate items of the daily menu devolved for the most part on the female slaves, experts in the baking of bread and the preparation of cakes, sweets, sauces, spices, egg-dishes and the like, and were served only to Ibn Sa'ud, his immediate entourage and family, and, of course, to ourselves. In the morning, before we rose from our couches, they brought us tea and *chupattis* with honey from Taïf when available ; an hour or two later a train of slaves would file in with our breakfast ; a large circular reed-mat being spread upon the floor, a metal platter piled high with steaming rice and crowned by joints of excellent mutton would be placed in the centre ; around this they would array the subsidiary dishes—bowls of tasty soup or gravy with tit-bits of meat and bone floating therein, all piping hot, to be ladled according to taste on to the rice ; bowls of fresh camel's milk or curdled sheep's milk ; dishes of dates ; bowls of fresh water ; and rounds of girdle-bread, some leavened, some not ; plates of sweet *Muhallibi* of milk and sugar with spices ; and dishes of button-like roasted cakes which they call *Qaimat.* " *Sam*—set to," says Ibn Musallim, the chief steward, who seldom failed to superintend the laying of our table, and we would rise ; a slave comes forward with ewer and basin, towel and soap, and each of us in turn goes through the formality of washing, which done we take our places on the floor round the mat with such guests as are present, and set to work on the viands before us ; each one as he finishes rises, washes his hands with soap and water over the basin held ready by a slave, and takes his seat on the carpet against the wall, waiting till all are finished and coffee is served. Tea was always ready for us, did we need it, during the afternoon; coffee was ready at all times; and dinner—generally an exact replica of the breakfast above described—was served to us about two hours after sunset, though the royal household ordinarily dined soon after the afternoon prayer.

Whether at meals or on excursions abroad or at the royal audiences 'Abdullah Sa'id Effendi was our ever-present companion and *aide-de-camp*; outwardly conforming to the narrow tenets of the *Wahhabi* creed, which forbids smoking but sanctions polygamy, he betrayed the influence of an European upbringing by being in practice a monogamist—though still young enough to have plenty of time to revise his views on that subject—and a devotee of tobacco, in which, of course, he indulged only in the privacy of his own apartments or ours; regarding the deserts of Arabia as nothing more than a temporary refuge for the troublous period of the war, he often hinted at a desire to find suitable employment later on in Mesopotamia, which he already regarded as an appanage of the British Empire, though he never dreamed that his own native land, the town and *Wilayat* of Mausal, would then be under British control; at the same time he always evinced the greatest admiration for Ibn Sa'ud, whom he held out as a striking example of the possibilities of indigenous Arab rule under favourable conditions no longer to be found—thanks to the Turks—either in Mesopotamia or in any other part of the far-flung Turkish Empire; he had steeped himself during the period of his voluntary exile in the politics of Arabia—a study for which his medical sinecure at the *Wahhabi* court left him ample leisure—and his intelligent application of the lessons of a wider experience to the special problems of his adopted country as well as his acquired practice of seeing things from different points of view made him an invaluable counsellor to Ibn Sa'ud, and an efficient medium of communication between him and ourselves on points of difficulty, which demanded careful consideration on both sides before they could be discussed in formal audiences. His knowledge of French, his keen interest in the affairs of the world beyond the limits of Arabia, and, above all, his hedonistic temperament made his society a source of unfailing pleasure to us during these first days of our residence in a strange inhospitable land; when I left Riyadh on my journey to the Red Sea, it was he who remained in attendance on the companions I left behind and piloted them back safely to the Persian Gulf; it was some months before I saw him again—for his home and the wife of his heart were at Hufuf and nothing could draw him thence—but I have no doubt that Colonel Cunliffe Owen would bear witness to the invaluable character of his services to himself and Schofield during the six weeks or so they remained in Arabia after my departure from Riyadh.

Of very different temperament and character though of like education and attainments was another of our constant companions during this period; Ahmad ibn Thunaian, a young man of about twenty-eight, extraordinarily fair for a native of Arabia, old in appearance far beyond his years, almost toothless, of exceedingly frail physique, and already betraying the ravages of a disease which was diagnosed two years later during his visit to England with the Central Arabian Mission as diabetes, was a member of the royal family, a third or fourth cousin of Ibn Sa'ud, and the grandson of 'Abdullah ibn Thunaian, who had occupied the throne of Najd from A.D. 1840 to 1842 as a vassal of the Turkish Sultan under the control of Khurshid Pasha, the last Turkish Viceroy of Central Arabia, and had lost it together with his head on the resumption by Faisal of a reign twice interrupted by Turkish interference; Ahmad's father, 'Abdullah, had then retired either voluntarily or otherwise into exile and had eventually taken up his residence at Constantinople, where his four sons were born and brought up, and where three of them remained behind when Ahmad himself, having conceived a desire to see something of the world, set out on a journey which landed him at Bahrain after periods of sojourn at Tunis and Cairo. He came in due course to the land of his fathers, where he settled down, rejoicing at the chance which had relieved him of all obligation to serve the rulers of Turkey in the rash adventure on which they had already embarked. His delicate constitution had turned his thoughts in the direction of letters and learning rather than towards a more active career ; Turkish was of course a second mother-tongue to him, and I have known him break off from Arabic into that language without realising that he had become unintelligible ; he had attained also to a considerable degree of proficiency in French, which he still spoke fluently, but not so well as 'Abdullah ; in addition to his linguistic attainments he was fairly well read in Arabic literature and in European and Oriental history. Ibn Sa'ud had recognised his merits by taking him into his innermost counsels, and though he never seemed to me to have derived as much benefit from his early training or to be as much a man of the world as 'Abdullah, he enjoyed the advantage over him of being not only a member of the royal family but a strict *Wahhabi* both in profession and in practice. Proud as he was of his direct descent from an actual ruler of the country, he was always careful to keep his pride in the background in the presence of Ibn Sa'ud, and it is improbable that even in his wildest dreams he ever visualised himself or his progeny as the occupants of the throne of Riyadh; at any rate Ibn Sa'ud never entertained the slightest doubt of his loyalty, and he always appeared as a matter of course at all interviews during this period, when State secrets were freely discussed. He had an excellent knowledge of the history of Najd and of the Sa'ud dynasty and was always interesting on that topic, but his opinions on world politics were somewhat jejune, the more so, it seemed to me, for being oriented in accordance with inapplicable *Wahhabi* standards of judgment.

One afternoon of our sojourn was spent in a visit to the fort, for which we obtained permission on the pretext that Colonel Cunliffe Owen, as an artillery officer, would be glad of an opportunity of inspecting Ibn Sa'ud's artillery, and might be in a position to advise him regarding its maintenance. On the side of the open square in front of the fort, opposite its only gate, they pointed out to us a plain square building known as *Bait 'Ajnan,* the official residence of the *Rashidian* governor of Riyadh in the days of the foreign occupation ; high up in its front wall was the narrow wooden lattice, at which Ibn Sa'ud and his handful of bold companions had sat through a whole night, reading passages from the *Quran* and sipping coffee, and always watching the wicket of the fort beyond the square until the dawn which witnessed the final conflict with the *Rashidian* forces and the restoration of the Sa'ud dynasty to the throne of Riyadh.[1]

Within the gateway of the fort we found ourselves in a courtyard of narrow dimensions surrounded by high walls, the rest of the internal area of the building being taken up with storehouses, guard-rooms, etc., which we were not invited to inspect, though through one of the doors opening on to the court we saw two men apparently undergoing a period of imprisonment, while from another came a ceaseless patter of unintelligible nonsense emanating from a woman incarcerated in a prison cell for lunacy; another such door gave admission to the arsenal itself, the inside of which we did not see, as the whole of the local artillery, consisting of only two somewhat ancient field-pieces, had been drawn up for our inspection in the courtyard; both guns were seven-pounders, the one a serviceable but old Turkish piece, while the other was of German make and bore the mark "*Von Broadwell—Karlsruhe*—1872"; the ammunition in stock appeared to belong to the latter piece and consisted of some old pattern shells and case-shot—all the worse for rust.

Official preoccupations prevented me during this period from availing myself of my host's invitation to attend one of his public audiences—a pleasure which I deferred till a later visit—and the only social function at which I assisted, apart from the Shamsiyya outing, was a wedding feast given by Ibn Sa'ud in honour of the marriage of a member of the royal family—I forget who; both bridegroom and bride having been married before, the pomp and ceremony, customary even among the *Wahhabis* on the occasion of the marriage of a virgin and an unmarried youth, were dispensed with, and we were spectators of nothing more than a muster in force of the male members of the royal family and a few honoured guests[2] to partake of dinner. The conversation naturally enough turned on the subject of

[1] *Vide* p. 101 *infra*.

[2] It was on this occasion that I first made the acquaintance of Faisal al Duwish, a leading light among the *Ikhwan*, and until recently chief of the Mutair tribe.

marriage and divorce. "Why is it," asked Ibn Sa'ud, "that you English allow divorce to be so difficult? among us when a wife no longer pleases we get rid of her by thrice repeating a simple word: *Talliq, talliq, talliq*; that is enough. *Wallah*, in my lifetime I have married five-and-seventy [1] wives and, *Inshallah*, I have not done with wiving yet; I am yet young and strong. And now with the great losses caused by the war assuredly the time will come when the people of Europe shall take more wives than one." Those of his wives who establish a claim to special consideration by bearing him children, whether subsequently divorced or not, are provided by Ibn Sa'ud with houses and establishments of their own, in which to bring up their royal children, and are not as a general rule passed on to other husbands, as is the case with the divorced wives who have borne no children. The mother of Turki, the heir to the throne, lived at this time in single state with her son, having long been divorced by Ibn Sa'ud, who generally has three wives at a time and keeps the fourth vacancy open to be filled temporarily by any girl to whom he may take a fancy during his expeditions abroad; on such occasions, having pitched his tents, he sends out trusty deputies to search out some suitable candidate, whom he marries for the nonce with a simple ceremony, demanding no more than the presence of priest and four witnesses, and returns to her parents when he has no longer need of her.

Ibn Sa'ud's chief wife or queen, who occupied the royal apartments in the palace and was the mother of his favourite sons, Muhammad and Khalid, was his cousin, Jauhara bint Musa'id, a woman from all accounts of great charm and beauty; her death during the influenza epidemic of the winter of 1918 was a cruel blow to him, a cause of greater sorrow than that of his eldest son and the two other sons he lost on the same occasion, and when his representatives visited England a year later, they told me that her place as queen had not been filled up, and that the apartments which had been hers had been left as they used to be in her lifetime—a striking tribute to her memory and to the place she had occupied in the affections of the *Wahhabi* monarch.

[1] The number is now, I believe, above a hundred.

Another of his wives at this time was the widow of his brother, Sa'd, whose death in battle with the rebellious 'Ajman had, as I have already mentioned, prostrated him with grief; and yet another wife, Bint Dukhaiyil, was at this time in the Qasim, where she apparently resided permanently, seldom seeing her royal spouse except when State business carried him to her neighbourhood; she had, however, not been divorced, as Ibn Sa'ud joined her in the autumn of 1918 on the occasion of his visit to the Qasim in connection with his preparations for the campaign against Haïl. His fourth wife was Bint al Sudairi, a daughter of the leading family of the province of Sudair, but she must have been divorced in my absence from Riyadh during the winter, as I found Ibn Sa'ud on my return free to celebrate another marriage;[1] the divorce doubtless took place when he moved out into the desert for his annual camp of exercise in the early spring of that year, his custom being, as I have already remarked, to keep or create a vacancy in his conjugal establishment, which of course is strictly limited to four wives at a time by the injunctions of the *Quran*, especially when he is likely to be absent from headquarters for any length of time; on occasion too he takes advantage of the privilege allowed by *Muslim* law to the possessors of unmarried female slaves to use them as concubines, though it was not till many months later, when I accompanied him to Buraida, that I became aware through the indiscretion of a slave of his indulgence in this practice, which till then I had supposed to be contrary to *Wahhabi* doctrine.

If, as occasionally happens, the tale of four wives is complete and Ibn Sa'ud in his wanderings is attracted by the rumour of some local lady's beauty, the lax law of *Islam* as interpreted by the *Wahhabi* creed does not stand in his way, for all that is needed is that he should despatch a letter to one of the four wives awaiting his return at Riyadh to the effect that he will return to her no more, and from that moment he is free to go through the marriage ceremony with the new bride of his choice. The divorce of Turki's mother seems from all accounts of it to have been a some-

[1] *Vide* p. 326 *infra*.

what pathetic affair, and to have been forced on Ibn Sa'ud by one of the few complications which cumber the *Muslim* code, for by that code it is forbidden that one should take to wife the sister of a woman to whom one is already married, and it so chanced that Ibn Sa'ud, being in the Hasa, filled an existing vacancy in his complement of wives with a girl who turned out, to the horror of her royal spouse not only after the wedding ceremony but after the consummation of the marriage, to be the sister of Turki's mother; the matter could only be rectified by the latter's divorce, which was accordingly announced to her by letter.

Cavalierly as he has treated the marriage bond to the point of exposing himself to the imputation of uxoriousness, it must always be remembered that Ibn Sa'ud has largely used his freedom to contract alliances of this kind for political ends, with a view to cementing together in loyalty to his person the scattered and naturally centrifugal elements that make up the population of his territories, for there can now be but few of the great families of Central Arabia which he has not conciliated at one time or another by marriage ties with himself or other members of the royal family; such alliances are not affected by divorce, to which no stigma attaches, while those which result in the birth of children, especially sons, to the royal house cannot but have a permanent beneficial effect on all concerned. On the other hand, his long and sincere attachment to his cousin, the Queen Jauhara, and his unblemished record as son, brother and father are in themselves sufficient testimony to his possession of domestic qualities of a very high order; of that aspect of his character I naturally saw a great deal less than I should have wished to, but such glimpses as I obtained from time to time of my host in the bosom of his family, for instance in the presence of his father or in the company of his younger sons and nephews, especially in the free-and-easy atmosphere of picnics in the palm-groves about Riyadh, or again in the company of his brothers and cousins, more than bore out the burden of the many delightful tales I had from the household officials and slaves of the domestic life within those great clay walls of the palace.

Few days pass but Ibn Sa'ud makes the round of the family circle, visiting his old father in his retirement, his sons and brothers, and particularly his sisters, with whom from all accounts he indulges freely in schoolroom romps, the sounds of whose mirth often came to me in my room through the doors which shut off my apartments from the great courtyard ordinarily reserved for the women of the household. His eldest sister, Nura, in honour of whom he is often addressed as Akhu Nura [1] in accordance with a common and picturesque custom of Central Arabia, is entrusted with the superintendence of all the domestic side of the household, the kitchen, the management of the slaves, the store-cupboards and so forth, and appears, on the testimony of those who knew her well, to be as delightful and charming as she is capable and energetic ; the remaining sisters, some fifteen in number, range down from the thirties to mere children, for the *Imam* 'Abdulrahman continues to beget children in his old age, but play a subordinate part in the household to their eldest sister, just as his brothers do to Ibn Sa'ud himself in the scheme of the State. The royal children at this time numbered seven sons and perhaps a dozen daughters, the former, alas, now reduced to four, for Turki, Fahad and Sa'd, the eldest, third and youngest sons of the monarch, died in the winter of 1918–19, leaving Sa'ud the heir-apparent, and his half-brothers Faisal, Muhammad and Khalid to carry on the line and traditions of their father. So far as I know, Turki left no offspring, for though his several marriages resulted in the birth of, I think, two daughters, they both died in early infancy.

Infant mortality is a terrible scourge in Arabia, thanks mainly to smallpox, and, though circumstances obviously did not favour my taking a census of such losses, I made a rough calculation, on the basis of enquiries from those with

[1] The ruling Ibn Rashid of Haïl is also addressed by the same appellation, which in the case of that dynasty has become a hereditary title ; that is not so at Riyadh, and Ibn Sa'ud is so addressed because Nura happens to be the name of his eldest sister. He is as commonly styled Abu Turki after the name of his eldest son, but is rarely addressed as 'Abdul'aziz or Ibn Sa'ud. Strangers address him as *Imam* or more rarely as *Hakim* ; while speaking of him to others they say *Al Shuyukh* or *Al Imam*.

whom I came into contact, to the effect that between seventy-five and eighty per cent of the children born in Wahhabiland fail to survive the first few years of life. That is indeed a terrible state of things, and is made worse by the ravages of warfare among those who survive to adolescence. Old men are rare in Arabia, but, now that modern weapons are much commoner among the Arabs than they used to be, it is difficult to envisage anything but the rapid decimation of a population which infant deaths already keep at a dangerously low level, unless the time-honoured pastime of war is seriously discouraged. This is exactly what Ibn Sa'ud has been attempting to accomplish ever since he succeeded, by dint of a series of vigorous campaigns, in stamping out the dangers to which his own throne was exposed; moreover, he has shown himself alive to the necessity of introducing the benefit of modern medical methods into his country, and not only is 'Abdullah Effendi a great improvement on the local quacks by reason of his European medical training, but twice during the last few years Riyadh has received the benefit of visits by Dr. Harrison of the American Mission at Bahrain. Rumour had it when I was at Riyadh in the winter of 1917 that his departure on the occasion of his first visit[1] had been precipitated by the discovery by some of his patients that the drugs he dispensed were wrapped in Christian Arabic tracts, but the fact that he was invited to visit the capital again during the influenza epidemic of 1918–19 shows that his use of tracts for such a purpose—if he did so use them—had not seriously militated against his popularity. Arabia is, however, not a promising field for missionary zeal, though it has good reason to be grateful for the excellent medical work done for many years past by the various branches of the American Mission scattered along the coast of the Persian Gulf.

Happy as Ibn Sa'ud is in his domestic affairs, he cannot forget the warning, writ large in the annals of his dynasty, that a polygamous system is inevitably subject to periodic ebullitions of domestic strife. The presence at his court of his cousin Sa'ud ibn 'Abdul'aziz ibn Sa'ud ibn Faisal;

[1] During the summer of 1917.

his difficulties with the 'Ajman tribe, which had so recently resulted in the death of his favourite brother Sa'd; and the unsatisfactory relations between himself and the *Shaikh* of Kuwait; all these things served to remind him that he occupied his throne in virtue not of hereditary right but of his own merit, and that he was surrounded by enemies who would gladly see him overthrown; all these things, moreover, came very much into the purview of Colonel Hamilton and myself during the first few days of my sojourn at Riyadh, when we took advantage of our opportunity to discuss the whole matter with our host, between whom and Shaikh Salim of Kuwait the British Government, being on the most cordial terms with both, were anxious to see the rapid re-establishment of friendly relations.

The Sa'ud family, and particularly the present *Wahhabi* ruler himself, had during the time of their exile at Kuwait during the last decade of last century owed much to the hospitality and assistance of Muhammad ibn Subah and his brother, assassin and successor, Mubarak, that doughty champion, whose guiding principle throughout his reign was to rely on friendship with Great Britain as the sole means of saving his little state from being swallowed up by the Ottoman Empire, and who, having lived to see a British army put an end to Turkish hopes of achieving that object, died full of years and honour in December 1915. During all this period, in spite of occasional storms, the relations between Najd and Kuwait had remained on a very amicable footing,[1] and Mubarak's son and successor, Jabir, continued the same policy until his lamented death eighteen months later. Jabir was succeeded not by his son Ahmad,[2] but by his ambitious brother Salim, who has reigned ever since, and whose accession was immediately followed by the decline of the friendly relations with Ibn Sa'ud which had

[1] This was certainly largely due to the splendid work of the late Captain W. H. C. Shakespear, who, being Political Agent of Kuwait during the years preceding the outbreak of the Great War, travelled extensively in Ibn Sa'ud's territories and cultivated the most friendly relations with that ruler.

[2] It was he who headed the Kuwait Mission to this country in the autumn of 1919 on behalf of his uncle. He succeeded Salim on the latter's death in February, 1921.

characterised the policy of his predecessors. It was held that Salim, as a fanatical *Muslim* of the *Maliki* persuasion, was at heart in sympathy with the Turks, but, however that may be, there is no doubt that his attitude towards Ibn Sa'ud was consistently hostile, and that his hostility took the form of harbouring the 'Ajman tribe in Kuwait territory in defiance of Jabir's undertaking not to give the tribe asylum.

The 'Ajman problem was therefore at this time at the root of the difficulties between Najd and Kuwait, which it was the British Government's desire to smooth over in the interests of all concerned. The 'Ajman had deserted Ibn Sa'ud with studied treachery at the battle of Jarrab in January 1915, and in the following summer had killed his brother Sa'd in a battle in the Hasa, in consequence of which actions the whole of Ibn Sa'ud's ire was roused against them and he was determined to avenge the outrages by the extermination of the tribe; but his unrelenting hostility towards them was due also to deeper causes, which take us back to the end of Faisal's reign in the late sixties of last century, and which have a bearing on the presence at Riyadh to-day of the cousin Sa'ud ibn 'Abdul'aziz, above mentioned.

Faisal at his death left his throne to his eldest son, 'Abdullah, well knowing that his own burial would be followed by a furious struggle between him and his second son, Sa'ud, the son of an 'Ajman wife, who during his father's lifetime had made no secret of his hatred for 'Abdullah, and who had taken advantage of the important military commands entrusted to him with the object of keeping him away from the capital, as also of his more pleasing personality, to seduce the troops and tribes under his command from the allegiance which they would one day owe to his brother; he had further fortified himself in the graces of his mother's tribe, one of the most powerful and warlike tribes of Arabia, by marrying into one of its *Shaikhly* families.

The train was thus laid for future troubles, and Faisal's gloomiest forebodings were more than realised; the ordered state he had built up with so much patience and trouble was soon wrecked by the dissensions of the two sons he had left to wrangle for his throne, and 'Abdullah, despairing of holding his own single-handed, invoked the assistance of Muhammad ibn Rashid, the ruler of Haïl and at that period the most powerful man in Arabia. Sa'ud had in the meantime occupied Riyadh and the throne left vacant by his brother's flight to Haïl, but before many years were out he was called upon to meet the whole force of Jabal Shammar, and a decisive battle took place at Judi in the Hasa desert, apparently about the year 1885. Sa'ud was defeated and killed; the pretender's cause collapsed; but 'Abdullah in the hour of his victory soon realised that he had sold his country to his saviour. Muhammad ibn Rashid decided to annex the *Wahhabi* country to his own empire, and 'Abdullah spent the rest of his days a prisoner-guest at Haïl, where he died, leaving no children.

In the meantime the remnants of the Sa'ud family had gone into exile in various parts of Arabia rather than live in a homeland subjected to the yoke of a foreign usurper, the sons of Sa'ud betaking themselves to the Hijaz, while 'Abdulrahman, the fourth son of Faisal,[1] withdrew with his growing family of young children to the shores of the Persian Gulf. For more than a decade Wahhabiland lay prostrate under the heel of Haïl while those children grew to manhood, Muhammad ibn Rashid being succeeded in the fulness of time by his nephew 'Abdul'aziz.

During this period the sons and grandsons of the unsuccessful pretender apparently remained resigned to their lot, and it was not they but 'Abdulrahman who, with the steady encouragement and assistance of Mubarak of Kuwait, assumed the obligation to free the land of his ancestors from the foreigner. In 1899 or 1900 the first serious move was made, 'Abdulrahman and Mubarak moving out with their main body towards the Qasim, while 'Abdul'aziz, the eldest son of the former and now a young man of eighteen summers, set out with a small following to create a diversion in the direction of Riyadh itself. The main forces of the opposing sides met in the saltpan of Tarafiyya during a shower of rain, and the victory went to Ibn Rashid after a great slaughter on both sides, so great, I was assured by

[1] The third son, Muhammad, died childless; whether before or after the fall of Riyadh to Ibn Rashid I do not know.

several who had taken part in the battle, that the rain mingling with the blood of the fallen flowed in a broad red stream into the snow-white basin of salt. The news of ʿAbdulrahman's defeat caused ʿAbdulʿaziz to retire from his adventure with nothing achieved, and the father thereupon formally abdicated his right to the throne of Riyadh in favour of his eldest son.

The latter lost no time in embarking on the task thus set him, and in the winter of 1900–1901 marched out of Kuwait with a small but select following of two hundred men, including his staunch friend and cousin ʿAbdullah ibn Jiluwi. Arrived within a short distance of the capital, he halted his little band and, selecting therefrom only fifteen men, went forth into the dusk, leaving the remainder with instructions to return whence they had come if they had no news of him next morning. "Look ye," he said, "there is no power or might save in God ; but, if no message reaches you to-morrow, haste ye away ; you will know that we are dead."

In the dusk they entered the capital over its dilapidated walls and made their way to the *Rashidian* governor's house over against the fort ; the door was opened to their knocking by a woman ; the governor was gone to the fort, where he was wont to spend the night for greater security, and would not return to the house till the morrow's dawn ; ʿAbdulʿaziz and his followers entered nevertheless, and, placing all the women together under guard in one room, with a warning against making any sound, took up their positions by a lattice overlooking the square before the fort ; and there they watched the livelong night, fortifying their bodies with dates and coffee taken from the governor's store, and their souls with readings from the *Quran*, till dawn, when the massive gates of the fort were thrown open and the governor stalked out with his bodyguard towards his house. The bold sixteen were waiting at the door, and, flinging it open, darted, swords and revolvers in their hands, upon the foe. A moment of furious struggle decided the issue, and ʿAbdulʿaziz ibn ʿAbdulrahman ibn Faisal ibn Saʿud was acclaimed by the astonished populace lord of the land of his fathers.

The following years were spent in reclaiming province after province of his country from the domination of the foreigner, but the success of a cadet branch of the family in recovering the land of their ancestors roused the jealousy of the elder branch, the surviving sons of Sa'ud the pretender. 'Abdul'aziz ibn Rashid welcomed their accession to his side in the ensuing conflict, in which he posed as being desirous of restoring the rightful heirs to the throne, but success favoured the cadet, and the final battle took place in the cornfields of Raudhat al Muhanna, not far from the scene of the battle of Tarafiyya. Ibn Rashid was vanquished and slain, and the conquerors, proceeding to the plundering of his camp, found cowering among the baggage those of Sa'ud's descendants who had taken part in the fight and whom they acclaimed by a term applied by the *Badawin* to raided camels recovered in battle, a term which has clung to that branch of the family ever since as a nickname—Al 'Araïf.[1]

That was the first step in a policy of conciliation, from which Ibn Sa'ud has never departed, and the success of which is strikingly demonstrated by the presence of Sa'ud ibn 'Abdul'aziz or Sa'ud al 'Arafa, as he is commonly called, and others of that branch of the family at the *Wahhabi* court of to-day. But that result was yet to cost Ibn Sa'ud some trouble, and the 'Ajman, true to their family ties with the 'Araïf, were yet to play a part. In 1910, Sa'ud al 'Arafa, who had apparently not been at the battle of Raudhat al Muhanna, raised the standard of revolt at Hariq, and for a moment had the south country at his back, but Ibn Sa'ud crushed him in characteristic style, as I shall relate hereafter,[2] and his flight to Mecca and eventual submission seemed for a time to have finally settled the question of the succession, and with it the 'Ajman problem. At any rate we find that tribe contributing a contingent to the *Wahhabi* forces at the beginning of 1915 in the campaign against Ibn Rashid, but the treacherous tribesmen could not resist the temptation put in their way by a doubtful situa-

[1] Plural of *'Arifa* or *'Arafa*—a thing recognised or lost property recovered.

[2] *Vide* Vol. II. pp. 78 and 275.

tion, and their desertion at a critical moment in the battle of Jarrab turned a victory into a virtual defeat.

Ibn Sa'ud neither forgot nor forgave their treachery, but the proclaimed outlawry of the 'Ajman brought about a recrudescence of the dispute regarding the succession, and two members of the 'Araïf, Salman ibn Muhammad ibn Sa'ud and Husain ibn Sa'd ibn Sa'ud, enlisted the assistance of the tribe in another—and the last—bid for the throne. Ibn Sa'ud, accompanied by his brother Sa'd, moved down to meet the danger, and the rival armies began to manœuvre for position ; the 'Ajman, seeing themselves outmanœuvred, asked for a truce with a view to an amicable discussion of the issues involved, and Ibn Sa'ud granted their request in the absence of his brother, who was away making preparations for a surprise attack on the enemy camp. Sa'd, having made his dispositions, returned to find that his labour had been wasted ; furious with Ibn Sa'ud for his misplaced clemency, he pleaded for the carrying out of his plans in spite of the armistice, and in a weak moment Ibn Sa'ud yielded to his counsels of treachery. The surprise attack was made and the 'Ajman, finding themselves duped and trapped, fought heroically; they lost the day, but Sa'd lost his life, and Ibn Sa'ud counted his brother's blood to the long list of 'Ajman crimes demanding expiation. The tribe fled the country to the borders of Kuwait, where they have remained from that day to this, a thorn in the side of Ibn Sa'ud—for they nullified his plan of campaign against Ibn Rashid in 1916 by occupying a threatening position on his flank—but nevertheless in imminent danger of merciless extermination should he ever, as he hopes, find himself in a position to attack them with advantage.

Intriguing now with Ibn Rashid and now with Salim, they maintain a precarious existence in the desert borderlands, but at the period of which I write, the winter of 1917, Salim had afforded them asylum in spite of Jabir's undertaking to the contrary, and the British Government were naturally desirous of removing a potential source of trouble between Najd and Kuwait. It was therefore a source of considerable satisfaction to Colonel Hamilton and myself to be able to agree, after full discussion of the matter with

Ibn Sa'ud, to an arrangement whereby, in return for the exclusion of the 'Ajman tribe from Kuwait territory, Ibn Sa'ud undertook to receive them back into his fold in the event of their being prepared to make submission to him under proper guarantees; to concede to Shaikh Salim the disputed right of taxing the Awazim, a nomad tribe residing alternately in Kuwait or Najd territory according to the seasons; and finally to co-operate whole-heartedly with Shaikh Salim in the blockade of enemy territory by ensuring that none but properly authorised persons went down from Najd to purchase provisions at Kuwait. The 'Ajman did not, as a matter of fact, accept the alternative offered them of making their submission to their lawful ruler, nor did the friction between Najd and Kuwait wholly disappear, but something was achieved by the formal outlawry of the rebellious tribe, and I shall have occasion later to show how a solution of the blockade problem was arrived at.[1]

For the time being the arrangement arrived at with Ibn Sa'ud cleared the ground for the main object of my mission, namely to induce Ibn Sa'ud to undertake and prosecute with vigour a campaign against Haïl. This involved prolonged discussions of ways and means for the accomplishment of the object in view and resulted in the despatch of proposals for the consideration of the British Government before I left Riyadh on my journey to the Hijaz; but these are matters which can be more appropriately dealt with when the time comes to record the course of the Haïl campaign of the autumn of 1918.

I had left Baghdad in the belief that an officer representing the High Commissioner for Egypt would join me at Riyadh with a view to joint consideration of the political situation in Central Arabia in its bearings on the Arab problem as a whole, and particularly on the position in the Hijaz. It was well known that the relations between Ibn Sa'ud and the Sharif were none too cordial in spite of their common alliance with ourselves, but it was not known how utterly incompatible the ambitions of the latter were with Ibn Sa'ud's conception of the *rôle* he himself was destined to play on the Arabian stage. The Sharif, it is

[1] *Vide* p. 359 *infra*.

true, had already begun to pose as the natural leader of the Arab cause, and had, without authority or other justification, arrogated to himself the title of "King of the Arab Countries," but the steps by which he hoped to achieve the recognition of his claims by those whose independence was affected thereby were still known to none but himself. For the time being he was the recipient of a substantial subsidy from the British Government, and Faisal's projected campaign on the borders of Palestine together with the preliminary fighting it involved on the Hijaz railway provided him and his advisers with enough to think about. The door was still open to him for the adoption of a conciliatory policy towards his Arab neighbours, and competent judges thought, though I confess I never shared their view, that such potentates as Ibn Sa'ud and the Idrisi would in the fulness of time consent to surrender their independence in return for the honour of being included among the King's vassals. In a word, there seemed at any rate to be no reason to despair of bringing about an amicable understanding among the various units of our Arab alliance, and the proposed visit of an officer from Egypt to Riyadh was a step in that direction.

It very soon, however, became clear that the Sharif had no desire to assist that project, and it was while I was at Riyadh that I heard of the King's refusal to allow any British officer to come to Najd from the west, on the ground that the routes over which he would have to travel were unsafe. Ibn Sa'ud, who was exceedingly anxious in his own interests to have an opportunity of explaining matters personally to Mr. Ronald Storrs,[1] the officer designated to represent the High Commissioner, immediately begged me to suggest that he should come by sea to Bahrain, but, on my pointing out that not only would such a proposal involve too long a journey, but the journey itself would be meaningless unless Mr. Storrs came after consultation with the King, he was sufficiently convinced by my reasoning to throw himself whole-heartedly into a subtle scheme which I proceeded to propound to him.

I should confess, perhaps, that my motives in making

[1] About this time he became Military Governor of Jerusalem.

that proposal were of a mixed character, and not wholly based on the actual requirements of the situation, but that is a trifle and I have never regretted my action. The Sharif, I pointed out, had refused to further the project of Mr. Storrs' visit solely, so far as we knew, on the ground of the danger involved ; "There is only one way of ensuring that Mr. Storrs shall come," I continued, "let me go with an escort from you to Taïf to bring him back with me."

Ibn Sa'ud was as much alive to the possibilities of such a plan as myself ; his attitude towards the Sharif was one of consuming jealousy, rapidly developing into thinly disguised hatred. "Was he not," he would burst forth in his more unguarded moments when carried away by the impetus of his own eloquence, "was he not till recently but *Qaïm-Maqam* of the Hijaz under the Turks ? Who is he then to call himself King, King of the Arabs, forsooth ?" But what rankled most with Ibn Sa'ud was the princely stipend lavished on his rival by the British Government, who were content to palm off a modest pittance on himself, and it was of no avail to explain that the Sharif's subsidy was paid him in recognition of substantial services rendered or yet to be rendered in connection with the war against the armed forces of the Turks. In his candid moments he would confess that he expected to be treated on an equality with his rival politically and financially, while he also demanded that the latter should in no way infringe his sovereign rights, as he had evinced a desire to do in claiming suzerainty over the 'Ataiba and Harb tribes within the confines of Najd.

For the moment, however, he was concerned to turn the Sharif's refusal to countenance the mission of Mr. Storrs to his own advantage and my proposal provided him with the opportunity of so doing. "*Wallah, ya Sahib!*" he said. "*La haula wa la quwwata illa billah!* on a journey as at all times we are in the hands of God ; but I will send you with a party of my men to Taïf as you propose, and, *Inshallah*, you will reach it without misadventure, for the Sharif lies when he says that the road is beset with dangers." And so it was arranged ; immediate action was essential if the main object of my journey was to be achieved, and on the evening of the 5th December I despatched a courier informing the authorities at Baghdad of my decision. The next three days passed in an agony of suspense lest I should receive orders or information incompatible with the execution of my plans, but fortune favoured me and I was safely in Jidda at the other side of Arabia when I received the next communication from Baghdad.

CHAPTER IV

THE PILGRIM ROAD

1. DARA'IYYA

ON the morning of the 9th December there was stir and bustle in the palace; the camels, promised for the previous morning, had not arrived till the evening; now gnarling and complaining they lay in the palace square amid a vast concourse of people, gathered to see the departure of the caravan, for the departure or arrival of a caravan is a great event in a *Badawin* town; news may be had from newcomers, friends and long-absent relatives welcomed among them, while the departing has friends to bid him farewell and to remind him of the letter or commission entrusted to him for delivery or performance at his journey's end. In the inner court lay four *Dhaluls* gaily caparisoned with superior saddle-bags and long tassels; one was for me, the rest for the leaders of the party which was to accompany me. In our apartments there was all the wild confusion of packing and the distribution of doles to a host of underlings, none of whom could be forgotten, though it was hard to remember what they or most of them had done in the past ten days to deserve what they got. At 10 A.M., all being now ready so far as I was concerned, breakfast appeared, and after the meal I was conducted to the study to take my leave of Ibn Sa'ud.

"All is now ready for you," he said; "I have allotted you a goodly host of the best of my camelry and all should be well; you have a far way and a hard way before you, but be of good cheer; *La haula wa la quwwata illa billah*, there is naught to fear; you have men of every tribe with you, men staunch and loyal; have a care for the animals

Part of Author's escort on journey across Arabia; standing from left to right: Mutailij, Tami, Ibrahim, the Author, Sa'd, Izmai, Hailan and Badr; seated: Shaya, Sa'id, ?, Ibn Nassar, Abu Nura and Jarman.

and press them not too hard, but travel steadily and return without delay, for I shall await your coming eagerly; see, I will in your presence give my final instructions to the men, whom I have placed in charge of your party." In answer to his summons there appeared before us two men, Ibrahim ibn Jumai'a and Sa'd al Yumaini, the latter a tall slim man with long braided locks hanging down to his shoulders about a countenance strikingly handsome and refined. "Sit ye down," said Ibn Sa'ud, and they dropped to the ground reclining against a column, as he proceeded to give them detailed instructions for the ordering of the march: "And when ye get to Taïf," he continued, "look ye, *al dibra bid Allah, thumma bid hal rajul hadha*, the ordering is in the hands of God and thereafter in the hands of this fellow here (pointing to me); obey him without question in all things and contrary him nowise; rise, put your trust in God." And they rose and went forth, each stepping forward and kissing their master on the side of the nose by way of leave-taking. I rose to follow them; "Put your trust in God," said he, "in the keeping of God, farewell."

Descending, I found my *Dhalul* already led forth to the palace square, and there amid the mighty concourse, making my final adieus, I mounted; with a shuffling and gurgling the host was up; we lurched slowly through the crowded *Suq* to the Dhuhairi gate at the north-west corner of the city and passed forth on the road to Taïf; henceforth in all my wanderings in Arabia I was alone; Colonel Hamilton had already returned to Kuwait; Colonel Cunliffe Owen and Schofield lingered at Riyadh, paying a short visit to the Kharj [1] district in the interval, till the end of January, when they returned to the coast and sailed from Qatif.

Our course now lay north-westward, the palm belt soon yielding to a bare slope of calcareous limestone, up which we wended our way along a well-scored track, having the rough hillocks of the Mugharrizat and Abu Makhruq on our right hand and the gorge of Wadi Hanifa with the dark palm

[1] They were almost certainly the first Europeans to visit this district, *pace* Palgrave, but see Vol. II. p. 117.

patches of the Batin in its midst on our left ; before us the dreary steppe rolled up in gentle undulations intersected at intervals by freshet-channels trending towards the *Wadi*. The greatest of these was Sha'ib Maidhar, three and a half miles out from Riyadh, a stony, sandy torrent-bed which runs down from the upland on our right into the *Wadi* at the Batin ; somewhat in front of it lies a grange or *Qasr* amid a small plantation of new-planted palms and a patch of corn. A newly excavated well stood on the roadside three miles farther on near the village and oasis of 'Arqa,[1] whose palm tops appeared over the bank of the Hanifa gorge to our left.

Beyond lay a bare undulating down, vaguely known as Hishat al Dara'iyya ; we directed our march on a prominent hillock surmounted by a cairn called Rijm Sa'ud, a landmark in the troubled history of Najd, for it was on this prominence that Ibrahim Pasha in A.D. 1818 planted his guns for the fierce bombardment, which, reinforced by treachery from within, resulted in the capitulation of the *Wahhabi* forces, the destruction of the proud city of Dara'iyya and the temporary eclipse of a dynasty, whose empire had extended to the farthest limits of Arabia, the crushing weight of whose hand had been felt by the holy cities of Mecca, Madina and Karbala.

We soon reached the brink of Wadi Hanifa and stood before the noblest monument in all Wahhabiland, a city of the dead ; in the midst of a great oval bulge in the valley stands a mighty rock, its base swathed around with a shroud of terraced corn plots, palm gardens and orchards, its summit crowned by the fallen towers and palaces of Dara'iyya, once the proud capital of the great Sa'ud, emperor of all Arabia. The lower ground of the valley to north and east is covered by a forest of palms, amid which lie the hamlets of peasant folk, to whom has descended the empty heritage of an honoured name with the fertile gardens of their fathers. Through the palms and dividing to east and west round the central rock winds the white line of Hanifa's pebbly torrent-bed coursing to southward. Round about the valley is girt in by frowning cliffs rising sheer to

[1] Pronounced 'Arja.

the ponderous ruins of the stone wall of the outer circuit, marked here and there by a gaping turret or dismembered portal. Over the scene of desolation broods the cairn of Sa'ud.

The road descends into the valley by a dip in the eastern cliff and thence runs up the torrent-bed. We had marched ten miles from Riyadh, sufficient for the first day of a long journey, and camped for the night under the central rock opposite the little hamlet of Malwi. I wandered among the ruins of the old city and the outer battlements accompanied by Sa'd al Yumaini until sunset, when I returned to camp, to dinner and to bed.

The ruins on the rock are distinguished from the rest of Dara'iyya by the name of Turaifa, and are entirely deserted; the old buildings, battered as they are, still stand, a pillar here, a wall there, a tumbled arch, a houseless doorway, the whole forming a picture of magnificent desolation; all are of massive clay except the pillars, which are of rounded limestone blocks mortared together with mud and outwardly plastered over with the same material; the arches are pointed and supported on pillars with undecorated capitals. The east side of the city was occupied by the palaces of the Sa'ud family, the chief mosques and other public buildings, the guest-houses and the dwellings of the great, while the poorer classes, labourers and artisans and others, appear to have congregated on the west side of the rock, which is covered by the remains of inferior buildings. A great open square at the north-east corner of the city was doubtless the public market-place, and the streets leading off it the commercial quarter. Life in those days of the birth of *Wahhabism* must have been very like what it is at Riyadh in these days of a militant revival; in 'Abdul-'aziz ibn Sa'ud and Shaikh 'Abdullah, the ruler and high-priest of an established spiritual state, we can recognise their own ancestors and prototypes, Sa'ud ibn Sa'ud and Muhammad ibn 'Abdulwahhab, the patron and the preacher of an infant creed; in the uncouth *Badawin* passing their days in prayer, striving in adolescence or old age to master the mysteries of the alphabet, to con by rote the very words of God, we can see those sturdy warriors of old, who poured in to the court of one of the many *Amirs* of those days, drawn by the rumour of a revelation ; in one of those splendid halls sat Muhammad, the prelate, culling from the *Quran* and the *Traditions* choice passages for a simple treatise for the use of simple souls ; the *Badawin*, distracted by wordy argument and complicated ceremonial, had left God and his meddlesome ministers to fend for themselves, and had relapsed into the joyous path of paganism ; they could be brought back by sweeping away the ecclesiastical cobwebs which had gathered about the creed of the shepherd Prophet ; in those old halls in the public *majlis* one day the idle coffee-bibbers were startled ; Muhammad ibn 'Abdulwahhab was speaking :—

> "Hear what said the Prophet of God—
> 'Behold Jewry, it is divided into seventy and one divisions ;
> And lo ! the Nazarenes, into two and seventy divisions be they divided ;
> Verily, I say unto you, this people of mine shall be divided into seventy and three divisions ;
> They be, all of them, for the flames of Hell—except one.' "[1]

That appealed to them ; their curiosity was aroused ; the result we know. In those days even as in these the courts of the prince and the houses of God seethed with an ever-growing multitude of frightened men, seeking desperately the path to Paradise ; they found it then on the far-flung battlefields of Arabia. Round a court famed for its lavish hospitality to the stranger within its gate and its generous patronage of priests, a moribund *Suq* eked out a precarious existence by catering for a small and poor population of resident citizens. In all things the Dara'iyya of old was but the prototype of modern Riyadh, built to replace it, as it were by the irony of fate, on the ruins of its own former rival and first victim.[2]

Modern Dara'iyya consists of five scattered hamlets, of which two, Al 'Auda and Al 'Ilb, lie on the right bank of the storm channel higher up the valley, while the rest

[1] "*Qad iftaraq al Yahud ila wahid wa saba'in firqa wa qad iftaraq al Nasara ila ithnain wa saba'in firqa wa sitaftariq hadhihi 'l umma ila thalatha wa saba'in firqa—kulluhum l'il nar illa wahida.*"

[2] Manfuha, *vide* p. 366 *infra*.

Oasis of Dara'iyya with storm channel in centre, the ruins of the old city on left and the hamlets of Malwi, Dhahara and Ghusiba to right.

Malwi, Al Dhahara and Al Ghasiba, lie in an almost continuous line embedded in the palm forest on the left bank of the channel, on which Malwi stands. All these hamlets are insignificant unwalled groups of mud huts without any conspicuous feature; collectively they may contain a population of 7000 souls, the bulk of whom are of the ancient stock of Bani Tamim, being of the Abu Hanifa section, which, as they believe, settled in and gave its name to the *Wadi* in the days of the *Ignorance*;[1] their original seat was Jubaila farther up the valley, which I visited on a later occasion, and whence they migrated on its destruction by the prince of 'Ayaina.[2] Other elements in the population are immigrants of Qahtan and Dawasir origin, and the inevitable Bani Khadhir of ultimate servile extraction, the droppings as it were of the migrating hordes, which have swept across the Arabian peninsula from time immemorial, from south-west to north-east, from Yaman to 'Iraq, driven from the prosperous spice country of Arabia Felix to the fertile plains of Mesopotamia perhaps by the bursting of the great reservoir of Marib.[3] As the Arabs say, "Yaman is the cradle of the Arabs, 'Iraq their grave."

Four or five or more times a year, when the storms of winter and spring break upon the cliffs of Tuwaiq, a raging torrent swirls down the bed of the *Wadi*, the roaring foaming flood reels from side to side on its unsteady course, racing to the southern sands, beating vainly against the unbending cliffs, spreading havoc in unguarded fields and gardens; in a few hours the storm is spent, the flood is past and a hundred tiny rills ripple over the pebbly strand to little pools and ponds; the thirsty soil revives to bear the burden of another crop. Here and there along the storm-channel the banks are strengthened to resist the flood by stout retaining-walls of solid stone, quarried in oblong blocks two feet long from the limestone steppe and laid symmetrically one upon another without mortar to a height of ten feet or more.

[1] *I.e.* before Muhammad, the word *Al Jahiliyya*, the Ignorance, being used here in its classical sense and not in the sense in which it is commonly used by the *Wahhabis*—the period before the advent of Muhammad ibn 'Abdulwahhab; *vide* footnote, p. 26 *supra*.

[2] Ibn Mu'ammar.

[3] This took place in the first century of our era.

The level of the valley is about 2250 feet above the sea, or nearly 400 feet above Riyadh, and the summit of the central rock must be higher by 100 feet.

During the night clouds began to gather from the south, precursors of the first storms of the season, and the thermometer recorded 54·5° at 10.30 P.M. I had a 40-lb. tent and the rest of the party a couple of large canvas shelters. The next morning it was yet dark at 5.30 A.M. when I was woken, a quarter-moon lit up the gaunt skeleton of the dead city above and the cliffs around echoed the solemn responses of the morning prayer. Early as it was a crowd of village folk had gathered about the camp, mostly women and children, collecting the dung-pellets piled up behind each camel after the night's couching, and some, bolder than the rest, thrusting forward to my tent to beg until driven off by Sa'd with a shower of stones and imprecations.

By 6.30 we were a-saddle and moved off up the torrent bed ; in a few minutes we passed the northern extremity of the central rock, and palm-groves lined the channel on either side ; on the right hand stood a low rock covered with ruins of a former village ; for a space the palms stopped and soon resumed on either side as we reached the hamlet of Al 'Auda, a small dishevelled group of huts on the right bank. The palms rapidly thinned out and soon gave way to a thick copse of dwarf poplars [1] spreading across the whole width of the valley, here narrowed to 300 yards ; again the valley spread out at the last palm-groves of Dara'iyya, among which stood the hamlet of Al 'Ilb, surrounded by a low irregular wall ; these palms are the private property of 'Abdullah ibn Jiluwi, *Amir* of the Hasa.

The *Wadi* now bends round sharply to somewhat west of north and runs straight on, a bare sandy valley about 400 yards across between cliffs from fifty to seventy feet high. The sand was spotted here and there with drops of rain which had fallen during the night. Thus we marched for rather more than two miles to a wide circle formed by the confluence of three *Wadis* : from the north Wadi Hanifa ; from the east the insignificant freshet of Sha'ib Malqa, with the palms and small hamlet of Malqa, the personal property

[1] *Ghāf*

of Ibn Sa'ud, at its junction with the Hanifa; from the west Wadi 'Ammariyya. In the middle of the circle lay the ruins of a small village of the past.

2. Wadi 'Ammariyya and Jabal Tuwaiq

Up the Wadi Hanifa lay the high road to Washm and the Qasim, the main track of pilgrim caravans, for which the easy pass of Haisiyya provides the easiest passage through the barrier of Tuwaiq; on that route lay the remains of ancient cities, Jubaila, 'Ayaina and Sadus;[1] up the 'Ammariyya lay a shorter but more difficult track. A hurried consultation was held at the confluence; some were for the easier road, others for the shorter; my preference would decide the dispute; the ancient cities tempted me, but I hoped to see them when, on my return, we should move up towards the north; the other route was, so far as I knew, unexplored. I decided for Wadi 'Ammariyya, and we turned to the west.

Our course lay up a rough valley of alternating sand, gravel and loam, 400 yards wide between bleak cliffs seventy to a hundred feet in height, with great buttresses of rock standing out from them at intervals on either side. Two miles up a wall of rock stood across the valley, deflecting it to the north-west through the ruins of a large deserted village, known as Shajara Abu Qubas on account of a group of tamarisks, which with a solitary watch-tower are the sole remnants of a once prosperous settlement. A few dead or dying palms are all that is left of the extensive palm-groves which surrounded the village in its halcyon days; around the whole runs the trace of a circuit wall, 700 yards in length and half as much along the sides; in the midst are the levelled remains of houses. The desertion of the village is said to have been due to a prolonged drought.

Soon after passing the ruins we turned again to the westward towards the prominent cone of Jabal 'Ammariyya; before it lay a dark mass of palms, behind it the dark line of the Tuwaiq plateau. Three miles farther on we crossed a low ridge projecting across the valley from the left and

[1] Sadus lies in a separate valley slightly off the main line of the track.

arrived at the village of 'Ammariyya, where we halted for a short rest and much-needed meal, for which there had been clamouring soon after we turned aside from Malqa.

The settlement of 'Ammariyya consists of two groups of palms with a hamlet attached to each, that to the south being wholly in ruins except for the *Jalibs* or draw-wells, which irrigate an extensive patch of palms and corn-land; the northern hamlet consists of a compact square block, 100 yards on a side, with a small palm patch to one side; its houses are so arranged that the outer walls form a continuous protective barrier; the corners are fortified with low towers and there are no public gates, each house having its own separate access to the exterior. The population of 500 souls are partly Dawasir and partly 'Anaza of the Suqur section, to which belongs the *Amir*, Muhammad ibn Burqa, who, being incidentally a relative-in-law of Sa'd al Yumaini, joined us at coffee after our repast. The cone hill lies near by the village on the west side, between them being a cemetery of typical *Wahhabi* fashion, in which the graves, all level with the ground, are marked only by head and foot stones not more than a foot high.

The chaotic jumble of ridges and hummocks round Riyadh makes it difficult to say exactly where the eastern edge of the Tuwaiq steppe begins; from the Batin downwards the Wadi Hanifa itself is undoubtedly the boundary, though even here the steppe projects in part beyond its left bank; north of the Batin the western boundary of the Riyadh oasis, prolonged through the Mugharrizat and Abu Makhruq hills to Banban, thence along the western edge of the sand strip called 'Arq Banban, and on up the valley which separates the steppe and valleys of northern Tuwaiq or Sudair from the 'Arma steppe, is, I think, the most suitable line for the eastern limits of the Tuwaiq barrier. It follows from this that from the moment of leaving Riyadh our march had lain over the outer flank of the range; from Dara'iyya onwards we had been ploughing through the very core of the steppe, gradually rising, and now, beyond 'Ammariyya, we found ourselves in the midst of the main plateau, though still not on its highest level. Before us opened out a wide valley sweeping round in a semicircle southward

THE SAQTA PASS IN JABAL TUWAIQ.

and westward between serrated ridges rising to a height of 400 or 500 feet; from the ridge on our right hand, behind which lay a yet higher ridge, marking the inner edge of the higher tableland, low projecting ridges ran down at intervals into the valley. The track switchbacked over these, negotiating here and there a steep rough descent, to avoid the longer detour of the storm channel.

Traversing a broad affluent of the *Wadi* from the right, called Sha'ib Muzaira, we reached in one and a half hours from 'Ammariyya a confluence of freshets which form the nucleus of the *Wadi* itself. From the north-west Sha'ib Dhubai'a ran down from the high plateau, and from the south-west came Sha'ib Saqta, up which we struck. Into the *Sha'ib* came affluents from either side, Abu Taiy, Abu Sus, Haddawi and others; ever narrowing between its high buttress cliffs it wound upwards into the heart of Tuwaiq, a narrow pebbly storm channel running from side to side of a valley often not more than 30 yards wide. Ever and anon we came upon signs of life; four *Hubara* flopped away at our approach up a bushy side-valley; on the ridge above the Abu Sus grazed a flock of sheep, whose shepherdess, a maiden of the Dawasir, stood on the summit watching our movements, her smock of brilliant vermilion giving a touch of colour to the drab hill-sides; up the valley on our road were some small children tending a flock of new-born lambs; beyond a bend of the ravine lay three black booths of the Quraidan, an offshoot of Shammar.

It was but 2 P.M., but loud cries arose for a halt; there had been clamouring in the morning for a halt for breakfast but two hours after our start; Tami the Aslami, nicknamed "the camel" or "the *Pasha*," led the clamour, protesting that he would die if food were not forthcoming at once; there was murmuring at my refusal to yield, which I allayed by a distribution of bread to be eaten on the move; food is a sovereign restorative of spirits among the Arabs. Now Sa'id the Qahtani, a pleasant youth with a pinched look and our guide for the early part of our journey, was brought up; "*Wallah, ya Sahib*," he said, "we should camp here for the night; see there is grass here and fuel and, *wallah*, there is neither grass nor fuel hereafter for a full day's journey" ; the clamour rose high, but it was clear that to yield would create a very bad precedent, and it was equally clear that Sa'id was lying, with the full approval of Ibrahim and the rest ; again I refused to yield and there was more murmuring ; what sort of a man was this who objected to taking things easy ? surely some madman. "*Inshallah*," said I, "God will show us a camping place full of grass and fuel." An hour later it was sulkily announced that they would stop for the afternoon prayer ; "Very well," I replied, "you stop and pray and I will go on slowly." But an inexperienced rider should never attempt to ride except in company, as I then found to my cost. My *Dhalul* looked anxiously round as I urged her on while the rest dismounted to pray ; we were now passing through the roughest and narrowest part of the gorge, the path running along a narrow boulder-strewn ledge with a sharp six-foot precipice to the torrent bed ; on I urged the unwilling beast with heel and rod ; snarling and casting longing glances at the couched animals behind she lurched along ; at last she struck, and, taking charge, turned and raced madly back along that narrow ledge, galloping ; I clung wildly to the saddle, pulled desperately at the rein, but we did not stop till we reached the line drawn up for prayer ; then we sat down and waited till the prayer was over "Don't you think," I said to my companions, upbraiding them, as we resumed our march, "that, knowing my inexperience and the temper of the beast, one or two of you might have kept me company, while the rest prayed ? Did not Ibn Sa'ud charge you to look after me ?" "You should have halted while we prayed," replied Sa'd al Yumaini. "If 'Abbas Pasha himself should come and bid me withhold from prayer, I should pray nevertheless at the appointed hour." "And who is 'Abbas Pasha ?" I asked ; Sa'd did not know, and a roar of laughter restored good humour all round.

We now reached a very narrow and steep rocky defile, up which the camels laboured heavily ; at the top we emerged on to a broad plateau bordered on the left by the ridge of Al Hamra running east and west parallel with our course ; on the right the plateau sloped down to a maze of deep rifts and gorges; far away stretched the uplands of Tuwaiq, fold upon fold, ridge upon ridge. We soon came to a little shallow freshet bed running down from the Hamra ridge to a sharp fall over great slabs of limestone rock, into the deep ravine of Sha'ib Mukhlab; here the sandy bed was dotted with bushes of acacia and carpeted with desert grasses; it was nearly four o'clock. "What is all that I see?" said I, "methinks there is fuel and fodder here." "Yes, yes," they replied in eager chorus unashamed, and we halted.

While the tents were being pitched I walked with Sa'd to the summit of a bluff of the Hamra; he brought his rifle on the chance of seeing an ibex but we saw nothing; I took out my pipe and sat down to survey the scene in comfort. "Why don't you smoke?" I asked. "Ibrahim has the pipe," he replied, "but I will have a puff of yours when you are done." I passed him my pipe. Far away to the west was a golden glimmer of the sands beyond Tuwaiq, whose outer rim was dimly silhouetted against them; to the north Sa'd pointed out the whereabouts of Haisiyya and Sadus. The storm-clouds lay thick and dark over the distant ridges, and flashes of lightning told of the raging storm; the sun sank in a blaze of glory and we descended to camp. The plateau, which is known as Al Dhahara, lies some 3000 feet above sea-level, and the highest points of the Hamra ridge must be 200 feet higher.

A few drops of rain fell early in the evening; the wind rose steadily as the night advanced; at 11.30 P.M. the thermometer recorded 60·8° Fahrenheit, the sky was heavily overcast, the wind howled over the bleak plateau, and occasionally a few drops of rain pattered down upon the tent. We had had a long day, marching nearly thirty miles over rough and difficult country. Ibrahim, Sa'd and Tami forgathered in my tent; we were beginning to know each other; we had differed during the day, but the Arab has a short memory for unpleasant incidents, and they readily understood or professed to understand my anxiety to lose as little time as possible in arriving at our destination. Tami beguiled us with lewd tales of his amorous adventures, his conquests, real or fictitious, past or future;

in early life he was a *Baduwi*, living like the *Badu* on his wits, raiding and robbing to provide himself and his family with food ; in course of time he had taken to himself some seven wives or eight ; he had begotten many children and almost as many victims to the smallpox, that pest of infant life throughout Arabia ; of all his children but two survive, both daughters, one married and the mother of his only grandchild, the other a child of five ; latterly he had settled down at Buraida with a wife, whose beauty and virtue he never tired of praising. Tami is a man of ripe middle age, with but few grey hairs amid his braided locks and well-trimmed beard, a dandy and withal a poet of no mean order, a singer, too, of high repute among the song-loving but untuneful Arabians. In the old days he was numbered among the subjects of Ibn Rashid, but for many years now has been in the service of Ibn Sa'ud,[1] who, appreciating his ready wit, knowledge of the world and freedom from prejudice, has of recent years used him freely to carry letters to the British authorities at Kuwait and in 'Iraq, and to accompany such British officers as have visited Najd. Before the war he accompanied the late Captain W. H. C. Shakespear[2] during part of his journey across Arabia in 1914; latterly he was among those who were deputed to accompany Mr. R. Storrs on his projected journey in 1917, and finally he was with Colonel Hamilton from the Qasim to Riyadh.

The next morning broke cold and dull with overcast skies and the thermometer at 6 A.M. recorded 51·8°. We continued our march across the plateau with occasional glimpses of the sands ahead and prominent headlands of the Tuwaiq escarpment, especially in the direction of the Jabal 'Alaiya ridge to the south, which looked considerably higher than any other part of the range. We came after about two miles' march to the head of the Saqta gorge and the brink of the escarpment ; north and south ran a long unsteady line of cliffs, facing west and rising by a sheer

[1] After my departure from Arabia he incurred the displeasure of Ibn Sa'ud and sought refuge with the King of the Hijaz, in whose service he died in 1919.

[2] From Riyadh to Buraida.

precipice from the plain below to the edge of the plateau, on which we stood 600 to 800 feet above it; majestic headlands jutted out from this line at intervals into the plain, which merged to the westward in a vast sea of sand. Immediately before us lay the Saqta gorge, between whose beetling crags and tumbled boulders a rough and narrow path descended precipitously to the plain below, zigzagging from ledge to ledge. We dismounted and, leading or driving the camels, began the descent; the gorge, narrow at first, opened out gradually as we advanced; the precipice towered higher and higher above us as we descended; here and there a suspended avalanche of boulders and shale hung on the brink of the abyss; about half-way down we saw a slender obelisk of rock standing out from the cliff on the left.

At length we reached the bottom; looking back we saw, as it were, a bastioned fortress, a semicircle of sheer rock with thirteen rounded bastions protruding from its face; from either end of the semicircle extended the frowning escarpment of Tuwaiq; of the path by which we had come we could see no trace; the barrier seemed unscalable, impregnable. To our left now as we faced the plain stood a nameless headland; southward lay the ridge and headland of Suquriyya; beyond rose the coast of ʻAlaiya; on the right the escarpment bent round to the north and was lost to sight. In front of Suquriyya lay two low ridges enveloping the unseen villages of Maghrafiyya and Muzahimiyya on the road from Riyadh to Ghatghat, which crosses the Tuwaiq range by the Abaljidd pass; the settlement of Ghatghat, a new town of the *Ikhwan* brotherhood built on the site of an ancient capital of the kingdom of Yamama, lies some miles to the west of Muzahimiyya on the edge of Nafud Jau; between us and the two low ridges lay the remnants of the old village of Bulaida.

3. Trans-Tuwaiq

Jabal Tuwaiq was behind us; the villages mentioned at the end of the last section were too far afield to admit of a visit, and in any case the hornets'-nest of Ghatghat was better unvisited; Muzahimiyya, the home of Sa'id the Qahtani, is little better than its greater neighbour, and though an old village, is largely peopled by devotees of the new sect, of whom Sa'id is one; in years past, however, he sought a livelihood on the pearl banks of the coast, thence he tried his fortune at the same trade in Ceylon and chance took him to Zanzibar; he has therefore learned to be tolerant and brought his toleration with him to his new creed. The population of these villages, which are included in the province of 'Aridh, is for the most part Qahtan and 'Ataiba with an admixture of Subai', Suhul and Dawasir, Ghatghat is always spoken of as having a population as big as that of Riyadh, but 8000 would probably not be short of the actual number; the other two may have 500 souls apiece.

The plain shelves from the foot of Tuwaiq to the valley of Dhruma, often called the Butin; the first section is a level scrub-strewn coombe, the Raudha as they call it; on the right runs the Tuwaiq escarpment screened in parts by tumbled masses of rubble, one of which standing out prominently in a lofty pyramid is crowned by a curious obelisk of stone, called Al Khunsar or "the finger," though it was held by some, who professed to know the country and who were strongly supported by the expert anatomical opinion of Tami, that its real name is Zubb al Hamudh.[1] That the latter is the name of some prominence in this neighbourhood admits of no doubt, but whether it is this particular one or not I cannot say. I prefer the politer name.

We now passed on to a gentle upward slope, strewn with rough flints of sandstone and called Hazm al Sufaira; the cliffs of Tuwaiq could be seen in all their grandeur extending as far as eye could see to north and south. At the end of the slope a short steep drop brought us down to the Butin, a sandy valley about two miles wide and bordered on the west by three ridges lying north and south in an almost continuous line, Abu Talh farthest south, Al Mushamra in the middle and Al Barqa to the north; to the east of the last-named lay the dark patch of the palms of Dhruma in the distance;

[1] "The spicy penis."

behind the ridges lay the sand barrier of Nafud Jau, beyond which stood out a prominent basalt rock called Al Ma'anij. In the valley to our left lay scattered granges, small groups of fortified houses standing amid plots of corn-land, for the irrigation of which water is drawn from wells within the granges. In all there were eleven groups scattered over a considerable area, the more important of them being Riqaï, Safaï, Jufran, Umm al Khushaïf and Zunaiqa, the last-named lying close under the Mushamra ridge in front of the *Ri'* or low pass, over which lies the direct road to the Ma'anij. We were anxious, however, to visit Dhruma, where, as I heard months later, Sa'd was paying court to a girl, who afterwards became his wife; the baggage animals were accordingly despatched by the direct route with instructions to await us at the Ma'anij, while we turned up the valley, making for Dhruma, behind which rose the imposing jagged mass of the Quraidan hill on the boundary between 'Aridh and Mahmal. The sand soon gave way to a firm loamy soil, which continued uninterrupted till we reached the palm belt of Dhruma, shortly after passing the solitary grange of Qasr Sha'lan close by the Barqa ridge.

Dhruma consists of two thick belts of palms about a quarter-mile apart, lying roughly east and west across the valley and each about half a mile long and half as broad. Dotted about among the palms stand fort-like garden-residences, while the village itself, square and surrounded by a wall with turrets at the corners and at intervals along each wall, lies in a bay of the northern belt; each wall is perhaps 300 yards in length, and so far as I could see there is only one gate at the north-western corner. The space between the palm-belts and a considerable area around them is corn-land, the whole irrigated from wells within the gardens, which are all walled. As we approached the outer palm-belt a man of the inhabitants of the village, which we had not intended to enter, came forward with a pressing invitation to us to partake of refreshments at his house. We had as a matter of fact halted a short while before reaching the place to break our fast, but I yielded readily enough to the man's insistence, as, our baggage having gone ahead to camp at the Ma'anij, there could be no fear of our being pressed to stay the night.

'Abdullah al Nafisi, our host, preceded us on foot along the path leading through the first palm-belt and across the open space beyond and conducted us through the gate of the village to his house, where in a very dingy little oblong room we arranged ourselves on the bare matting round the coffee-hearth. Our host went through the tedious process of roasting and pounding the coffee beans, pouring the resulting powder into a large beaked coffee-pot, pouring it from that into a smaller one and so forth until the refreshing beverage was ready; it was then served round and soon followed by the appearance of a large dish of excellent dates, in the middle of which was ensconced a bowl of *'Iqt* or compressed shards of butter-milk pounded up and mixed in liquid *saman*; we fell to, each man taking the dates, dipping them into the *'Iqt* and conveying them to his mouth, the stones being thrown back on to the mat; I preferred the dates without the *'Iqt* after making trial of the combination. Our hunger appeased, 'Abdullah removed the tray and sat down to prepare a substitute for tea, a concoction called *Zinjabil*, and consisting of hot water flavoured with ginger—a mild aperient. The entertainment closed with the passing round of incense. My companions realised as we sat there that the prayer-hour had come upon them and, rising without ceremony, spread their mantles on the floor and went through their devotions, while 'Abdullah and one or two villagers (who had dropped in to see the visitors) and I kept up the conversation. In such circumstances among the Arabs there is no ceremony whatever, and it is not considered irreverent to talk and laugh while others pray. They themselves had already prayed in the mosque at the *dhuhr*, nominally midday, but actually an hour or so later, and it was not yet time for their *'asr* prayer. Travellers enjoy the privilege of syncopating [1] the five appointed prayers of the day into three, the dawn prayer by itself, the prayer of *bain al 'asrain* [2] combining the *dhuhr* and *'asr* prayers and performed at any time

[1] This is called *takhfif*, lightening.

[2] Between the two afternoon (prayers).

after the appointed hour of the former and before that of the latter, and the *salat al maghrib* performed at sunset and combining the sunset and evening (*'asha*) prayers. Each prayer is gone through in full to the smallest detail, and in the case of the double prayers, the prescribed service for *dhuhr* and *maghrib* is completed and rounded off by the terminal blessing, "Peace be upon you and the mercy of God," before the *'asr* and *'asha* services are begun, these being invariably preceded by the "secondary" call to prayer, the *Adhan* not of the *Muadhdhin* but of the *Imam*. When the time of the afternoon prayer approaches and the travellers are actually on the march one of their number intones the call to prayer, which differs from the orthodox call only in the addition of a twice-repeated "*La ilaha illa 'llah*" at the end; the call sounded, a suitable spot is selected for the prayer, the camels are couched, the *Imam*, after making sure of his direction, marks out a line on the ground with a kink towards the *Ka'ba*; he takes up his position behind this recess and the rest line up as he intones the "secondary" *Adhan*, which differs from the first only in the addition of the formula, "*Qad qamat al salat, qad qamat al salat*,"[1] to signify that the service is actually in train.

'Abdullah, a citizen of a village renowned for the martial spirit of its people, is numbered among the envied few, who have had their "faces whitened" for valour in the field, being the first man up on the battlements of the Kut at the assault on Hufuf; military prowess is rewarded in Najd only by public acclamation of the hero; on that occasion it was proclaimed in the camp of Ibn Sa'ud: "The Kut is captured, 'Abdullah al Nafisi was the first man over the parapet; *Baiyidh allah wajhhu*,[2] may God whiten his face (in Paradise)." The rescue of a wounded man under fire is, as amongst ourselves, reckoned an heroic act worthy of the "whitening." In all Wahhabiland the yeomen of the 'Aridh villages are reckoned second to none in the field.

The population of Dhruma, including the outlying granges, which are only inhabited during the winter and

[1] "Verily the prayer is in train." [2] *Vide* Vol. II. p. 173.

spring for the sowing and harvesting of wheat and barley, is probably not more than 6000 inhabitants, if as many, though local pride claims an available military contingent of 2000 men. The predominant element is ʿAnaza, to which ʿAbdullah himself belongs; the rest are Bani Tamim, Dawasir, Subaiʿ, Qahtan and perhaps others. The village lies at an elevation of nearly 2200 feet above sea-level or about 300 feet higher than Riyadh.

The Butin drains southward to Shaʿib Ausat[1] and Shaʿib al Ha, both of which penetrate the Tuwaiq range from west to east and flow into Wadi Hanifa at Haïr, which marks the southern extremity of the ʿAridh province; the head of the Butin lies in the Mahmal district, where a number of freshets from Tuwaiq pour down their waters into the common drainage.

After an hour's halt in the village we took our leave of our host, who did not disdain a present of fifteen dollars, and set our faces south-westward towards the sands. After one and a half miles we reached the Riʿ al Barqa, a dip in the Barqa ridge, beyond which we entered the depression of Jau al Saibani, whose surface at first sandy thereafter became a friable salt-encrusted loam. We were once more on the main pilgrim track between Central Najd and Mecca, which comes southward to Dhruma after passing the Tuwaiq barrier at the Haisiyya pass. At a distance of four miles from Dhruma we passed the four wells of Jau al Saibani and entered the sands of Nafud Jau. Negotiating a gentle sand slope we soon reached the first wave, thereafter toiling laboriously over wave after wave of sand up to the summit of the *Nafud*, whence we had a fine view over the valley behind us and the long cliff barrier of Tuwaiq; far away on the left we saw the palms of Muzahimiyya and directly behind us those of Dhruma; before us was seemingly endless sand broken only by the dark mass of Maʿanij rising from a narrow depression almost at our feet. The descent to the valley, though shorter than the ascent, was infinitely steeper, and it was a matter of wonder to me how the camels managed it; I was, however, gradually acquiring

[1] Its lower reaches appear to be known as Shaʿib Baʿaija; *vide* Vol. II. p. 300.

experience of camel riding and, acting on the advice of my companions, let my *Dhalul* have her head down the precipitous slopes, pulling her up only at the bottom of each to prepare for the next slide ; thus sidling and sliding, now straight forward, now slanting across an avalanche of sand, now thrusting forth her long neck to pluck some luscious herb always in the most precipitous parts, the beast reached the bottom and I dismounted with a sigh of relief. The ascent from the eastern edge of the sands to the summit had taken fifty minutes, the descent to the Ma'anij only fifteen ; the base of the latter lies some 2250 feet above sea-level, its summit 100 feet and the summit of the *Nafud* 200 feet higher. The width of the *Nafud* is not more than three miles, but for difficulty and gradient it surpasses anything I experienced subsequently ; its length from north to south may be fifteen miles or more.

The clouds, which had cleared during the day but began to gather again soon after we resumed our march from Dhruma, discharged a few drops of rain after our arrival in camp and the night was bleak and chill, the temperature at 11.30 P.M. being 52·7°. Next morning the world wore a dreary aspect ; the thermometer recorded 49·1° at 6 A.M. ; the sky was overcast with a pall of dull grey clouds and a drizzling mist chilled us to the bone as we moved off at 7 A.M.

Crossing the Ma'anij depression we entered the sands of Nafud Qunaifida, a southern prolongation of the arm of the great encircling sand waste which runs down along the western boundary of Washm ; at this point its breadth from east to west is ten miles ; in character it is a gentle undulating down of sand without high ridges or waves and offering no serious obstacle to the voyager. It extends southward to the granite or basalt masses of Al Bukhara and Khashm al Dhibi, which we saw during the day's march perhaps ten miles away, and in which lie the sources of Sha'ib Nisah, one of the great level-crossing drainages, which pierce the barrier of Tuwaiq in their course to the Sahaba. After marching about four miles we crossed a broad depression in which on our right hand lay the basalt hummock of Dhuwaiban. Thereafter, re-entering the undulating sand down, we continued over a featureless course, while the rain came down at first in a gentle drizzle and then in a steady stream ; on we padded, becoming more and more miserable with every step we took, until, soaked through and through, we reached the western edge of the *Nafud* soon after 11 A.M. and decided to camp. We chose a shallow depression in the sands ; the camels were let out to graze ; firewood was collected and the tents pitched ; we proceeded to dry ourselves as best we could, and for the rest of the day I sought comfort in the snug shelter of my tent, while outside the rain pattered on gently with but few breaks.

Soon after noon the temperature was down to 45·5° ; just before 3 P.M. it had fallen to 42·8°, after which it rose to 46·4° at 5 P.M., only to sink to 42·8° again by 6.45 P.M. It was the coldest day I experienced in all my sojourn in Arabia, and whether it was owing to the cold or to the rough food I felt far from well, and turned in early to sleep after the sorriest pretence at dining and a strong dose of brandy. I had decided before leaving Riyadh to share the lot of my companions in every respect, and had, in consequence, left behind everything but a bottle of brandy, a bottle of lime-juice and a bottle of quinine tabloids in addition, of course, to tobacco, all except the last to be used only in the last resort as medicine ; when I reached the coast the bottle of lime-juice was unopened, the bottle of brandy short of only one dose, the quinine practically untouched, and only the tobacco seriously depleted, and that not wholly by myself.

It was raining fairly hard when I fell asleep and the rain continued without a break through the night ; it was still raining at 6 A.M., when I was woken after the dawn prayer, and the temperature was down to 41·9°, the lowest temperature but one recorded by me in Arabia. I resisted a strong temptation to lie abed and was rewarded by the clearing of the weather by 7.30 A.M., when, steeling myself against piteous pleas for a further delay, I insisted upon a start. Well it was that I did so for in a quarter-hour the rain came on again, and if it had found us still in camp it is most unlikely that we should have moved that day.

In ten minutes from our start we passed out of Nafud Qunaifida into the immense plain of Maruta, sometimes called Al Jilla, over which we marched, ascending steadily but gently for over twenty miles ; the soil was for the most part sandy with occasional streaks of black pebbles and every now and then a low ridge of blackened rock ; thus it rose westward tier by tier by the easiest of gradients to the final and highest ridge of Sudaira, beyond which there was a slight descent to the edge of the Dalqan *Nafud*. The rain had left its mark upon the plain, whose every dimple or depression was a pool of water ; from these pools we filled our water-skins, for rain-water is accounted far superior to that of wells, partly because it falls from heaven and partly because the well-water of these parts, though reckoned sweet, is inclined to have a brackish or mineral flavour.

The pilgrim route across the plain touches water at the Tubraq wells three miles from the eastern extremity, three wells being in regular use with good water at not more than twenty feet, while many are fallen in and abandoned ; again at the Sudaira wells six miles farther on, which we left somewhat to our right ; and finally at the Dalqan watering, some miles north of which lie the wells of Al Anjal.

Rather before 11 o'clock the rain, which had poured down upon us without cessation for three hours, stopped, and we halted in a large patch of *Hamdh* bushes, which provided excellent fuel for a fire. Here we broke our fast and dried our clothes, the Arabs complaining bitterly of the cold and declaring that it was entirely contrary to Arab custom to march under such appalling conditions. I felt no less miserable than they, but cheered them up by telling them that in my country half the days of the year are just such days as that.

Animal life was more in evidence than hitherto ; gazelles bounded away at our approach ; pigeons clattered up from the depths of the Tubraq wells in which they had been sheltering from the storm ; flights of sand-grouse wheeled round the rain pools, and crows hopped about the plain. Every now and then we passed small groups of black booths of Qahtan graziers, here a flock of sheep and goats, there a herd of pregnant camels; we were at the beginning of the dropping season; young lambs we saw in plenty, and occasional young camel calves but a few days old. The camel's period of gestation is thirteen months, and an interval of ten or eleven months is allowed before the next covering; without it the stock deteriorates.

From our midday halting-place we had a wide view of the country round; to the south stood the prominent landmarks of Khashm al Dhibi and Al Bukhara, while another mountain mass could now be seen farther south and somewhat east of them, the Mirka, so called from its resemblance to the camel's shoulder-pad, and apparently no more than a headland of the Tuwaiq cliff in the neighbourhood of the valley which runs down to Hariq and Hauta; ahead of us appeared the distant coast of the Ardh range, far beyond the Dalqan *Nafud*; northward the scene was one of unrelieved monotony.

From the Sudaira ridge we had a clear view of the Ardh uplands and the prominent double-peaked mountain of Idhnain Shamal, the "Ears of the North," which towers above it. The Sudaira ridge itself is of blackened rock. Beyond it and across a narrow depression lay the line of the Dalqan *Nafud*, which we entered immediately after passing the wells, from which it takes its name. These are three in number, excluding several abandoned shafts with somewhat inferior water at a depth of thirty feet, each well lined with masonry and the large sand circle, in which they stood, black with the droppings of sheep. Far and wide about the circle lay the traces of the great *Najdi Hajj* of the previous summer, which had spent a night here. "There," said Izmai' the *Buqumi*, who had guided the *Hajj* as he now guided us, "was the tent of Muhammad ibn Sa'ud, and there is his *masjid*, and over there, O Sa'd, was the camp of your mother and sisters, who rode with him." The round circles, where the tents had stood, the long prayer-lines, the charred embers of a hundred hearths and the piles of unused brushwood, all remained unobliterated to mark the spot; they say that the number of people who rode with the *Hajj* was seven thousand.[1]

[1] *Vide* p. 85 *supra*.

'Abdulrahman, father of Ibn Sa'ud, had started out from Riyadh but broke down under the fatigues of the journey, and returned home either from this camp or the one before it near the Tubraq wells. 'Abdullah Effendi had also been of the party. The *Hajj* of 1917 is a notable landmark in Arabian history.

The Dalqan *Nafud*, a southward prolongation of the broad Nafud al Sirr, another arm of the encircling sands, is at this point barely one mile across and without difficulty; a distinct track leads over its gentle undulations. On reaching the western edge we turned aside into a deep hollow and camped for the night. We were now on the fringe of the 'Ataiba marches; hitherto from the coast westwards it had never been necessary to take precautions either to conceal our presence or to guard our camps; now it was different; we had turned aside from the road to be out of the way of chance passengers; we had camped in a hollow to conceal our camp-fire; among us were four men of the 'Ataiba tribe, who now assumed responsibility for our safety; at intervals they went forth to the surrounding sand-hummocks and proclaimed to the world: "Look you, O men of the 'Ataiba, here am I, Jarman, a man of the Barqa, and I say to you, we are men of Ibn Sa'ud journeying to the Sharif; so let none molest us; and whoso hear my words, let him come to us and share our dinner or drink coffee and welcome; but molest us not or, if you do, say not you knew not who and what we are." The invitation fell on the deaf ears of the night and our peace was not disturbed.

4. The Highlands of Najd

Before us lay the vast flat plain of Hadba Qidhla, extending to north and south as far as eye could see between the parallel lines of Nafud Dalqan behind us and the long low ridge of Al Ardh ahead; out of the latter, towering above it, rose the twin peaks of Idhnain Shamal somewhat south of west; north of them ran a jagged range of hills losing itself in the distant haze; southward a bare monotony of sandstone steppe, interrupted only by a slight serration marking the point, a few miles south of the great peaks, at which we were to enter the Highlands of Najd by way of Sha'ib Quai'iyya. The breadth of the plain was between fifteen and twenty miles; its slope southward and slightly eastward.

Ibrahim, who had contracted a sore throat and stiff neck as the result of our recent drenchings, had not risen for the dawn-prayer and I was not woken till it was over, in spite of my injunctions that I should be roused before the Call. My companions warmed themselves by the camp-fire, imbibing coffee, while I made ready for the march, and at 7 A.M. we were in the saddle. The sky was clear, the rain had passed away, and the air was crisp though not cold, as we set forth in a south-westerly direction over the sandy plain, the camels browsing as they went on the plentiful desert herbs, withered by the long autumn drought and drenched by the recent rain, which would be green ere ever we should return. The misery of the last two days was forgotten in the cheerful thought of spring; they talked joyously of the *Rabi'*, how the camels would fatten on the grasses grown girth-high, how the hump of every animal would swell and rise. The Arab is a true optimist, forgetful of past pain, depressed by present troubles while they last, and for the future imagining naught but undreamed-of good; *hal tul* [1] they would say of the desert herbs of spring, eking out the imperfect instrument of their desert speech with gestures conjuring up in my mind visions of impenetrable forests of pampas grasses far exceeding the utmost possibilities of a perfect *Rabi'*; doomed to disappointment in either case they magnify the camel's springtide hump as they do man's body come to Paradise; years of bitter experience dull not their visions of an ever-imminent camels' paradise; can we then wonder if nothing on earth will shake their tenacious faith in the Paradise of Man?

A march of eight miles brought us to a narrow strip of drift-sand, a miniature *Nafud* called Dughaibis, running diagonally across the plain from the neighbourhood of the Idhnain Shamal peaks south-eastward to join the

[1] Pronounced *ha'tul* for *hadha 'ltul* = thus long, thus high.

Oasis of Quai'iyya in the Ardh highlands with Wahhabi cemetery in foreground.

Dalqan *Nafud* near its southern extremity. The sight of dry bushes of *Arta*, the best of the desert fuel plants, produced an outcry for a halt, but the morning was yet young and I insisted on the continuance of the march; it took us but five minutes to cross the sand strip, and again we plodded on over the plain towards our still distant goal. At noon we halted in mid-plain to break our fast; at 2 P.M., having covered some twenty miles, we passed out of the Hadba Qidhla plain into the low tumbled foothills of the Ardh ridge at the confluence of two torrent-beds, Sha'ib Harmaliyya, rising in the bosom of the Idhnain Shamal and issuing into the plain some miles to the north of this point, and Sha'ib Quai'iyya traversing the Ardh barrier from west to east. The combined *sha'ibs* run down under the single name of Harmaliyya southward to the trunk channel of Wadi Sirra.

We now followed the scrub-covered bed of Sha'ib Quai'iyya, varying from one mile to half a mile in breadth, between bleak buttressed cliffs of sandstone rising to a height of thirty to fifty feet above the level of the valley, and, circumventing a projecting arm of the bluff on our left, came into view of the scattered palm-groves of the village of Quai'iyya itself, a charming vision of green fertility in the midst of desolation. Here and there a basaltic hummock or stream of black pebbles broke the brown monotony of the surrounding sandstone, while the yellow buds and dark green stems of a broom-like bush called *Qirdhi*, the first of all the herbs of the desert to don its garb of spring in response to the winter rains, stood out in strong relief against the dreary greys and browns of acacia bushes and withered grasses. Down the middle of the valley ran the winding course of the pebbly storm channel.

The village, an oblong block of dingy mud-built houses, surrounded by an outer wall with turrets at each corner and a turret in the centre of each of the longer sides, lies close under the left bank of the *Sha'ib* and may be some 200 by 100 yards in area. Over it towers a prominent cairn-crowned pyramid of rock, supported by huge fallen slabs of smooth-worn stone, down which, so it was related to me, the lads and lasses of the village use to slide on high days and holidays, making merry as it were after the fashion of our tobogganing, greasing them beforehand for greater smoothness with some concoction of *saman*; wherefore the name of the rock is Zill Laila or "*Laila's slide.*" It is difficult to believe that the practice of such levity is permitted by the strict puritanism of the present generation, and the name is in all probability the last and only relic of an old-world frolic. At the foot of the slide lies the best well of the village, named appropriately enough Riq al Banat or *Maidens' spittle.*

Towards the farther side of the valley lies the local cemetery, one of the best specimens of a *Wahhabi* graveyard [1] I have seen, a forest of low flint head- and foot-stones marking out graves otherwise scarcely distinguishable from the level ground around. This I visited with Sa'd, with whom again I shared my pipe, turn and turn about, as, leaning upon his saddle-bow, he mumbled the formal salutation to the departed souls: "*Salam 'alaikum*, peace be upon you and the mercy of God, ye who are gone before us to the joys of Paradise," and so forth. The worship of the dead, be they saint or sinner, and supplication for their intercession with the Almighty are anathema to the followers of the *Wahhabi* creed, but there is no harm in breathing a prayer for the mercy of God on those already gone to appear before his judgment-seat, and the humiliation of a living soul by the contemplation of their last resting-place on earth is an act of merit. Death is ever before the eyes of the pious *Muslim*, and he never mentions a dead man by name, but he adds: "*Allah yarhamhu*—God have mercy upon him."

Between the cemetery and the village lay a considerable tract of open corn-land divided into little squares, about which were disposed small piles of prepared manure [2] ready for application; up and down the valley, over a distance of about one and a half miles and for the most part downstream of the village, extended a chain of some fifteen palm-groves varying from one to four acres in extent, and each self-

[1] *Vide* Vol. II. p. 47.

[2] *Samad*, consisting of mixed refuse and dung finely powdered, while dung or sheep-droppings undiluted are called *dimal*.

contained within a low mud wall and provided with a *Qasr* or fortified grange, within which stands the *Jalib* or draw-well of the type common to all Najd. The settlement lies within the danger zone of *Badawin* depredations, and the *Qasrs* provide a ready refuge for the tillers of the groves in the event of an alarm ; the *Badawin* will not attack manned walls, and the wells being within the granges, they cannot stay for a siege. These, however, were until recently not the only source of danger to the inhabitants of Quai'iyya, mainly Bani Tamim of the Bani Zaid section, between whom and their Bani Khalid neighbours of the rival village of Miz'al farther up the valley there was incessant war, until Ibn Sa'ud himself intervened to impose upon both sides peace and a compromise, whereby Miz'al was excluded from the general jurisdiction of the *Amir* of Quai'iyya and granted autonomy under its own chief, while Quai'iyya was left to queen it over most of the scattered settlements of the Ardh range.

Ibrahim had gone on with the rest of the party to the village, while Sa'd and I wandered, and on our arrival we found the camels couched outside the south gate awaiting the provender already being brought out in headloads, while Ibrahim under instructions from me was unwillingly protesting with the *Amir*, Sulaiman ibn Jabrin of the Bani Zaid, that we would not halt as we were anxious to push on without delay. Such a course, protested the latter, was utterly unthinkable ; how could he endure that we should pass by his open door and go to sup with his rival ? I was appealed to and yielded to his importunity, to the great satisfaction of my companions, and we passed on foot through the gate and along a narrow dusty street to the *Amir's* house. His coffee-parlour was a small dark room with a floor of sand without mats or carpets, and we ranged ourselves along the walls on either side of the hearth at which our host sat to prepare coffee and tea for his guests. Meanwhile other preparations, of which I knew nothing, were on foot for our entertainment, and after tea and coffee had been disposed of, the *Amir*, disappearing for a moment, returned to announce that dinner was ready for us. "*Sammu*,"[1]

[1] "Say *bismillah*."

he said, as he led the way up a narrow dingy flight of steps to an open upper-storey veranda facing the inner court. Here coffee and tea were served again as we took our places along the walls, and in a few minutes a number of servants appeared, some bearing large round mats which they placed in the centre of the veranda, and others raised platters of metal piled high with a wheaten mess called *Qaimi*[1] and mutton. The former is identical with the *Jirish* of other parts of Najd and, I think, with the *Burghal* of Syria, a whole-meal porridge mixed with sodden girdle-bread and liberally besprinkled with *saman*. We had but recently broken our fast sufficiently well and it was only 3 P.M.; nevertheless my companions did ample justice to the generous meal, and I did not fail in my duty, regretting only that my host was so busy feeding me that he had but little time to talk.

The population of the village may be some 3000 souls. Until the settlement already mentioned Sulaiman was the sole administrative authority of the Ardh district answerable to Ibn Sa'ud alone, and so far from him that he was for all practical purposes an autocrat in his limited sphere. He is yet far from reconciled to the diminution of his dignity imposed on him by his master and makes little secret of his hatred and jealousy of the *Amir* of Miz'al. Lying as it does on the main route of the Mecca pilgrimage, the settlement serves as a commercial centre for the surrounding villages, whose inhabitants come down annually in normal times to exchange the produce of their groves and fields with the merchandise of the outer world brought in the train of the *Hajj*. At other times there is little communion with the world, though from time to time a caravan from the Hijaz passes by this route to Shaqra, and there is little prosperity in the place.

The sandstone rapidly gave way to basalt as we resumed our way up the *Sha'ib*, now narrowed to half a mile or somewhat less between cliffs or detached hummocks from seventy to a hundred feet in height. Topping a slight rise of the

[1] I think the word is strictly applicable to the grain (wheat) itself rather than to the mess, while *Jirish* and *Burghal* are applied only to the latter.

valley we came into view of the oasis of Miz'al, the place of wrath, so called[1] owing to the warlike character of its turbulent people, a colony of the 'Arafa section of Bani Khalid, transplanted from the deserts of the Hasa less than twenty years ago apparently by Ibn Sa'ud himself to strengthen the older settlers of Tamim, Qahtan and other elements against the marauding 'Ataiba. The new blood, under the leadership of one 'Abdullah ibn Muhammad al 'Arifi, lost little time in making things uncomfortable for the proud people of Quai'iyya, and a few years later Ibn Sa'ud intervened as already recorded. It is not indeed improbable that Ibn Sa'ud foresaw and desired the consequences of his action, his main object being the establishment of a strong party unquestionably partial to himself in country scarcely worth the trouble of subduing, but, nevertheless, desirable as a rampart against foreign aggression and the natural turbulence of the 'Ataiba already on more than one occasion exploited against him by his enemies.[2]

The village itself and the greater part of the plantations stand in a circular bulge of the valley, into which four *Sha'ibs* run down from the surrounding basalt screes, two from each side. The greatest of these is the Nakhur, at whose confluence with the valley stands the village; it comes in from the north, while the Makharr runs in from the south at the entrance to the bulge, and the other two, whose names I was unable to discover, come into the circle from north and south respectively.

Two ruined *Qasrs* stand sentinel over the eastern approach to the oasis; behind them are three small patches of *Ithil* trees, between which and the village stand a dozen walled palm-groves similar to those of Quai'iyya except that the palms are more thickly interspersed with *Ithil*, the *Qasrs* are more ruinous, and a few of the gardens, particularly those under the left bank of the valley, are either dead or moribund. A few more gardens masked the mouth of the

[1] So it was related to me, but I am inclined to think that the explanation is an instance of popular aetiology; the name of the place is probably older than the Bani Khalid colony.

[2] Once by the Sharif of Mecca and on another occasion by the 'Araïf pretenders, both about 1909–10.

Nakhur *shai'b* and dotted the valley farther up-stream. The ring of black hummocks around it and the black skeletons or stumps of dead palms convey the impression that the settlement has been the victim of a devastating conflagration, but the failure of water is given locally as the reason for its desolate aspect.

The village, at which we camped for the night, lies at an altitude of 2850 feet above sea-level and is built in a rough square, perhaps 130 yards on a side, with an unpretentious mud wall about it, studded with occasional towers. The streets and houses are mean and dingy, but the *Amir's* parlour, to which we were invited for coffee though not for dinner, was furnished with mats and a few rugs thrown over the sandy floor. The reception was attended by several of the villagers including Sulaiman al 'Arifi, uncle of the *Amir*, clothed in rich raiment with an embroidered *Zabun* and girt with a fine sword, contrasting strongly with his nephew, who concealed his dirty and well-worn shift under a mantle of the commonest make. The uncle took the place of honour, with myself on his left and his nephew officiating at the coffee-hearth on his right; conversation was dull and intermittent, and I was ignored until the *Amir* abruptly introduced the subject of the war, on which he certainly had little and imperfect information; "How long has Egypt been in the hands of the English?" he asked, "and when were the Turks driven out? The English are the friends of Ibn Sa'ud; *ai billah* and the friends and enemies of Ibn Sa'ud are my friends and enemies; but *inshallah* it will not be long before all Englishmen have subscribed to the true faith." I endeavoured to enlighten their ignorance, while Ibrahim added a touch of romance. "Hundreds of Arabs who have joined the Sharif have received instruction in the art of flying; *ai billah* and I have myself met many returned to Najd who were pilots." I ventured to question the accuracy of this statement, but he assured the company that he spoke the truth. "Have you a writer?" he asked, turning to the *Amir*, and the only "writer" of the village was produced, a blear-eyed boy of twelve or fourteen, who, taking pen and paper, knelt down in front of Ibrahim and wrote at his dictation in a round childish hand by the dim light of a spluttering oil-lamp. It was a letter to Ibn Sa'ud announcing our safe arrival so far on our journey. We sought in vain to purchase a sheep for our next evening meal, but succeeded better in hiring four or five camels to share the burden of our baggage with the animals brought from Riyadh, which were already showing signs of fatigue after some 150 miles of steady travel under somewhat unfavourable weather conditions. The population of Miz'al may be about 2000 souls, and 'Abdullah, the *Amir*, struck me as an utterly unintelligent and uncouth man with no enthusiasm for anything but the true faith and Ibn Sa'ud.

It was still dark when I was woken next morning before the dawn-prayer. The sky was now clouded over and soon after we had started the scene was blotted out by a thick chilly mist through which we marched up the valley to the small settlement of Ibn Sa'dan, comprising two little hamlets or unwalled groups of houses with a population of not more than 300 souls, and about one mile distant from Miz'al. Passing some eight or nine small palm-groves we watered our beasts at a stone trough outside the largest grove, round which lay a considerable area of corn-land ready for sowing; the valley now broadened out into a bare fan-shaped plain, on either side of which scattered hummocks of basalt loomed through the fog; a grey fox scuttled away to the refuge of the rocky wilderness pursued by a couple of long dogs, which gave up the chase at the foot of the hills and returned to the village. As the mist lifted before the rising sun we perceived a small party somewhat ahead of us travelling in the same direction as ourselves; Tami went off to make enquiries, and returned with the information that it was a bridegroom returning with his bride from Quai'iyya, where the wedding ceremony had taken place the previous day, to his home at Ruwaidha; the bride was a widow and was carrying with her the infant offspring of her former marriage; with them was a servant. Marriage [1] in Central Arabia is a simple unceremonious affair; the bridegroom repairs to the village of his future wife, and in the afternoon, after the *'Asr* prayer, all legal requirements are satisfied

[1] *Vide* p. 93 *supra*.

in the presence of witnesses representing both contracting parties; the marriage of a youth with a virgin is often accompanied by a simple feast, the sole form of entertainment known to dour and hungry Wahhabiland; on other occasions even that is dispensed with, and after the *'Asha* prayer the bridegroom goes in to his bride.

The valley was now about four miles wide and dotted with outcrops of sandstone rock; here and there we passed over or between great slabs and boulders of porous rock, scored by wind and weather into fantastic shapes; the soil was generally of loam with a thin covering of gravel-strewn sand, thickly dotted with *Hamdh* bushes, while in the mile-wide bed of the *Sha'ib* itself was a plentiful sprinkling of acacias and scattered patches of corn-land cleared for cultivation round a series of seven walled granges constituting the settlement of Quai'. Before us lay the long granite range of Al Jidd, the backbone, as it were, and watershed of the Ardh system, extending north and south from the high peaks of Idhnain Shamal through the mountain masses of Muhairqa, 'Amar, and Jafar to the distant peak of Fura'.[1] The storm-clouds were gathering thick and dark over this range as we advanced, and our camels started nervously at each low rumble of distant thunder; the lightning flashed about the peaks, and it looked as if we were in for a heavy deluge. Nevertheless we pressed on across the *Sha'ib*, which here bent round to the north-west, and whose bed was thickly covered with undergrowth of coarse grasses and thorny acacia bushes.

At length, at a distance of about twelve miles from Miz'al, we reached the fringe of Al Jidd and the pilgrim road, scored deep in the hard rock, led at a gentle gradient up a narrow glade to a low saddle of rock connecting the peak of 'Amar on our left with a nameless hill on our right. At this point we must have been, so far as I could judge, some 3000 feet or more above sea-level; the granite masses on either side of us and Muhairqa close by on the north towered above us at least 700 feet, while

[1] Beyond this peak the twin ridges of Hasat Qahtan rise out of the sands of Nafud Dahi to a height of nearly 5000 feet, but were nowhere visible from our line of march. They are presumably of granite.

the more distant and far more imposing peaks of Idhnain Shamal, Jafar, and Fura' cannot well be less than between 4500 and 5000 feet above sea-level; it may be safely assumed that the general level of the summit of the Jidd range runs at an elevation of 3500 feet above sea-level, and that its highest points rise to another 1000 or 1500 feet. The section between Idhnain Shamal and some point to the southward of 'Amar drains eastward by the Harmaliyya and Quai'iyya *Sha'ibs,* rising respectively in the Idhnain Shamal and Muhairqa masses, to their junction already described, and thence southward to Wadi Sirra, and it may be safe to assume that the southern section of the range drains direct into the Wadi Sirra itself; westward the whole range drains down to the Sardah valley, to which we now descended by a narrow bush-covered glade; its bed trends southward parallel to the range, and is white with quartz [1] pebbles of every size and occasional outcrops of solid quartz rock; here we camped for our breakfast, having a magnificent view of the Idhnain Shamal on the north, and the whole range southward to the dim outline of Fura'. In a small freshet descending into the valley from the 'Amar hill lies a well of brackish water known by the same name; this name in the form 'Amariyya is locally used as an alternative appellation both of the Jidd range, of which it forms part, and indeed of the whole Ardh range, but the terms Ardh and Jidd are in more general use.

The storm-clouds grew thicker and blacker as we breakfasted and the thunder rumbled and cracked about the "Ears of the North," whose gaunt masses stood out purple and deepest blue against the gathering gloom. We hastened on our way, and reaching the farther side of the valley, entered a belt of tumbled ridges and hummocks called Suraidih, and forming as it were a screen for the Ardh range on the west. Passing a long low ridge of slaty rocks, known as Umm al Jilat from the water-pools which collect in its recesses after rain, we rode rapidly through a bewildering maze of quartz and schist and green granite rocks; the rain overtook us and we hastened on with mantles drawn over our heads and seeing not where we went;

[1] Called *Maru.*

the rain came down in torrents and drenched us through, while all around us the rocks poured down their babbling runnels. This lasted for about an hour when, wet to the bone, we found ourselves beyond the maze of foothills, beyond the rain, and looking out over as fair a prospect as one could wish; before us a broad bushy valley glittering with little running streams and standing pools; beyond it the red granite hills of the "Red Range" rain-washed and sparkling in the bright sunlight.

The whole of the Ardh range was now behind us, some thirty miles across on the line of our south-westerly course and rather more than twenty miles in a direct line from east to west; its salient feature is the high central range of Al Jidd of massive granite; to the east thereof lies a low sandstone plateau thickly interspersed with basaltic rocks, while westward lie the Sardah valley and the Suraidih foothills, a rubbish-heap as it were of granites, schists and quartzes. The whole chain trends southward to Wadi Sirra, where it loses itself in the sands of Nafud Dahi, from a line somewhat south of Duadami, whose extremities lie at the waterings of Mausal and Mughaira; northward of that line lie, so far as I could ascertain, the sand-waves of the Shuqaiyija *Nafud* stretching up to the borders of the Qasim. From north to south the length of the Ardh range may extend to 100 miles; we had crossed it in the neighbourhood of its centre along a line dotted with fertile oases, Quaiʿiyya, Mizʿal, Ibn Saʿdan, and Quaiʿ; to south and north of the pilgrim road are said to be many islets of cultivation; those to the south are Rain, a newly planted settlement of ʿAtaiba *Ikhwan*, and Hilwa, lying about one mile apart at a distance of from fifteen to twenty miles south of Mizʿal, while ten miles farther south is Qasr al Saih, the "grange of the stream," lying, if one may so conjecture from its name, on the course of some spring-fed perennial brook probably issuing from the bowels of Furaʿ. The other two villages lie perhaps in a watercourse having its source on the flank of Jafar; these three settlements are of small extent with scanty palms. Northward of the pilgrim road a group of little villages clusters round the foot of the Idhnain Shamal: Khanuqa in the Harmaliyya *Sha'ib* to the eastward and ten miles north of Quai'iyya; Sudairi and Juzaila to the south-east; Muhairqa to the south-west under the northern face of the hill of the same name; Nukhailan to the north-west some twelve miles from Miz'al, and finally Dahis four or five miles to the north-west of Nukhailan. In all these villages there are palms and corn patches tended by a wild, shy population of highland folk, seldom in contact with the outer world, having no camels but small sturdy hill ponies and plough cattle of similar dimensions. The total population of all the Ardh villages off the beaten track is probably not more than 3000 souls, and if this estimate is approximately correct, the whole settled population of the Ardh district may be reckoned at 8400 or 8500 souls. I saw flocks of black sheep grazing in the coombe of Quai' as we passed, but that was the only sign we met of *Badawin* life. Hares were plentiful in the same valley and also in that of Sardah.

Before the storm our party had been cheerful enough, running foot-races over extremely short distances for small wagers of three or four dollars made among themselves, with myself to witness the pact, and as it turned out, to provide the stakes; thinking to encourage them in their amusements I offered to pay the stakes for the loser in a race between Tami and Izmai; it was at once assumed that I would accept liability for all previous bets, an assumption I could not with honour repudiate, but I had to be firm when our progress threatened to develop into a series of foot-races; nevertheless I noted the cupidity of my companions, and on subsequent occasions made good use of it in the later stages of a day's march by fixing a distant goal and announcing a prize for the first man to reach it, with a subsidiary prize for the first man of the baggage train to do likewise. As a short-distance runner the Arab leaves much to be desired, but up a flint-strewn hill-side he has few equals, and I marvelled to see them scramble up a pathless crag regardless of ugly gashes and blood streaming from their wounded feet; I never could induce them to submit to a test of endurance over long distances. Of all our party Izmai, though but little short of fifty years of age, was the fleetest and soundest of wind and limb;

he was our chief guide, with Sa'id as his second, over the whole track from the beginning of the 'Ataiba marches to the borders of the Hijaz ; born in Buqum territory he had migrated at the age of twelve or fourteen to Najd and had never revisited his own country until the summer of 1917, when he was selected by Ibn Sa'ud to guide the *Hajj* to Mecca ; yet, as he himself declared, the scenes of his boyhood had stamped themselves so sharply on his retentive brain that he knew his landmarks as if he had left them but yesterday, and in all the time of my being in Arabia I was never privileged to meet his equal in geographical temperament and knowledge of local detail ; every knoll and ridge and valley he recognised by name with unerring precision. He was a member of the inner circle of the *Wahhabi* brotherhood of the *Ikhwan*, and had incurred the severe displeasure of Ibn Sa'ud by stoutly protesting against his inclusion in my party on this occasion ; forced against his will to accompany me he had held aloof from me up to the day of our arrival at Miz'al, and, though one of the leading members of our party, had preferred to sit at the servants' platter rather than break bread with an infidel. As my intimacy with the members of our party increased and I discovered his special qualifications as a guide, I was compelled to protest to Ibrahim at his conduct with the result that from this day onwards he was forced to ride at my side ; the ten dollars which he pocketed as a prize for his prowess in the race was the first step in an acquaintance which ripened rapidly into intimacy and friendship only to wither as suddenly under the influence of separation and his return to the numbing atmosphere of Wahhabiland ; it was yet to be some days before he risked his prospects of salvation by sitting at meat with me, when I discovered that he extended his left hand to the platter, his right hand being deformed and fingerless from birth. Meanwhile I profited by his extraordinary knowledge of the highlands through which we were passing and found him to be an excellent exponent of *Badawin* ideas. Thunder, he told me in all simplicity and seriousness, is caused by the angels shouting and beating on iron gongs among the clouds to precipitate the rain on places selected by God.

A gentle slope led down to the bushy depression of Wadi Jarbu' before us; beyond the latter a few conical peaks of granite rose at intervals out of the tumbled hills and ridges of the Hamra range; Za'aba due west marking the position of Ruwaidha our goal, Umm al Madaq, Al Mughara and Al Khurs in that order to the southward, each separated from the one before it by low and indeterminate ridges. We were soaked to the skin and some voices were raised in favour of camp and a fire to dry ourselves by, but the bright sunshine, which had displaced the storm, and the prospect of meat for dinner at Ruwaidha decided us to advance.

The Jarbu' depression, somewhat less than two miles across and trending southward, was of a sandy loam with a thick sprinkling of acacias grown almost to the dignity of trees; from its farther side a broad bushy passage led up a gentle slope between ridges and hillocks of greyish schist to a low granitic ridge with two *Sha'ibs*, called Khanuqa and Jarbu', flowing down across it at some distance on our right from the heart of the Hamra range into the Jarbu' *Wadi*. We afterwards learned that a small party of Qahtan raiders was actually lying up in Sha'ib Jarbu' at the time of our passing, and it was doubtless due to the recent storm that they had been too busy drying themselves to watch for unexpected and unsuspecting victims; had we halted and lit fires on the other side of the depression we should certainly have attracted their attention during the night, though from what we heard they were too few to dare a direct attack on our superior numbers.

We halted at the ridge for afternoon prayers, after which a poisonous snake was slain as it tried to wriggle away to the shelter of a bush; *Dab* (plural *Diban*) is the generic term for all snakes, which local science further subdivides into *Haya* and *Hanish*, the former term being, I think, applied to all vipers and the latter to all other poisonous snakes, though on this point I cannot speak with authority, as the Arab in general has but the vaguest knowledge of the reptiles which are found sparsely scattered over his limitless deserts.

The peaks of the Jidd range showed up grimly behind us as we continued our march over a series of low ridges, beyond which the main ridge or backbone of the Hamra system ran from the prominent hill of 'Arwa to the north along the series of granitic knolls known collectively as 'Araiwiyat, and across our front to the fantastic jagged hill of Tuhaiy and thence southwards in a winding line. Immediately in front of us stood the cone of Za'aba, passing which we debouched into a considerable loamy plain, in the midst of which stood the scattered palm groves and walled village of Ruwaidha, the capital of the Hamra district. The groves, ten in number, were in great part in a moribund condition scattered about at wide intervals round the village, which is a small irregular oblong about 100 yards long and 50 yards broad, containing a population of not more than 1000 souls. These are mainly of the Suhul tribe, the sole remnants in western Najd of a flourishing nomad and settled community driven forth long since by the Qahtan to wander in the steppes east of Riyadh. The village is walled about and its streets and houses are of the dingiest, though of the interior of the latter I had no opportunity to judge as the *Amir* was away on a visit to Riyadh, and we were invited to no hospitality. The *Amir's* function of providing for the wants of travellers was performed by an inferior official, styled *Naib*, who produced a sheep for ourselves and fodder for our animals in spite of the rain, which set in heavily with thunder and lightning soon after our arrival and continued for some time.

The Hamra range is dotted at frequent intervals by small villages or rather groups of granges surrounded by cornfields; of these two, called Jarbu' and Khunaifisa, lie in the bed of Sha'ib Jarbu'; Khurs and Mughara lie below the hills bearing those names; Khuraisa and Mishash al 'Arqan are situated to the north of Mughara; Qasr al Tuhaiy nestles against the crags of Tuhaiy, while to the north-west of Ruwaidha are the cornlands and granges of Qasr al Sahib. Westward of Ruwaidha and on or about the pilgrim road lie Qusuriyya, Hufaira, Sa'diyya and Riqaï al Sa'dan. Such, so far as I was able to ascertain, is a complete catalogue of the settlements of Al Hamra, whose total settled population, including that of Ruwaidha, is probably not more than 2000 souls.

The range starts southward of the line Sha'ra-Duadami, these two places lying about thirty miles north-west and north-east respectively of Ruwaidha, and extends southward to the high mountain of Sabha at the southern extremity of the 'Arwa - 'Araiwiyat - Tuhaiy ridge. The village of Ruwaidha stands at an elevation of 3200 feet above sea-level ; the summits of the main ridge stand not more than 500 feet higher, but the isolated mass of Sabha cannot very well be less than 5000 feet above sea-level and may be still higher ; in popular estimation it is the highest mountain in the Najd highlands. From east to west the Hamra range extends about twenty miles along our route from the Jarbu' depression to Qusuriyya and slightly less than that in a direct line. In ancient times the whole of this *Dira* belonged to the great tribe of Mutair, with elements of Suhul and Subai' living in peace among them, but the pressure of the Qahtan from the south-west and the 'Ataiba from the west drove out this group, and at the present time the southern extremities of the Hamra and Ardh ranges, including the Sabha and Hasat mountains, fall to the Qahtan, who also strive eternally with the 'Ataiba for the marches immediately south of the pilgrim road, while the latter tribe are in unchallenged occupation of the Hamra range north of that line and of all Ardh almost down to Al Fura'.

The rain stopped at 9.30 P.M. but began again about 2 A.M., with the result that I was not woken as early as usual and my companions had had plenty of time to dry themselves by the morning fire before we were ready for a start at about 7 A.M. The rich loam of the plain had become a veritable quagmire, and for the first hour of our march the camels laboured heavily and had considerable difficulty in keeping their feet. We then rose to firmer ground and reached the watershed of the range, beyond which the slope was westward towards the Haliban plain. The road now led between low ridges a mile apart into a bay of the main ridge, which here bulges westward into a wide circle, wherein lie the granges of Qusuriyya ; gaps in the ridge disclosed a distant view of the third rib of the highland system, the Damkh range beyond the plain, and it was from here that we obtained our first view of the great Sabha mountain.

In the way we passed a small cemetery, doubtless marking the scene of a tribal encounter of the past and shortly afterwards espied in the distance two men riding a single *Dhalul* towards us, who, catching sight of our imposing cavalcade, turned and fled at full speed towards Qusuriyya until, reassured by our shouts, they stopped and awaited our coming. It was from them that we learned of the Qahtan *Ghazu*, for which, being themselves 'Ataban, they naturally mistook us; they were able to give us the satisfactory information that our onward path was, or had till recently, been clear of disturbing elements.

We now reached Qusuriyya, a group of six fortified granges scattered about a large patch of arable land, part of which was prepared for the winter sowing while the rest had but recently been shorn of a millet crop. A track leads hence southward to the *Qasrs* of Hufaira nestling against the western face of the Hamra ridge three miles away, while the main road led south-west up a slope, at the summit of which we found ourselves clear of the Hamra system and facing the broad plain of Haliban backed by the long range of Damkh. Westward of Qusuriyya there are no habitations of settled folk until Khurma is reached —a distance of about 200 miles which it took us six and a half days to cover.

The Haliban plain extends to a breadth of some fifteen miles between the Hamra and Damkh ranges, trending southward to Wadi Sirra, and is traversed diagonally from north-east to south-west by the narrow torrent-bed of Sha'ib Haliban, which rises in or near the 'Araiwiyat ridge and flows to the Haliban wells at the southern extremity of a long basalt ridge called Samra Haliban, whence it runs south to Wadi Sirra. The plain on both sides of the *Sha'ib* bed and of lesser tributary *Sha'ibs* running into it from east and west is thickly covered with undergrowth of *Sharr* and various kinds of acacia, of which the *Wahat* with its bare stiff branches and large claw-like thorns was much in evidence. The pilgrim track strikes due south-west from Qusuriyya to the wells some twenty miles distant, but

The mountain of Farida in the Damkh range.

the rains had made us sufficiently independent of water to strike off on a more direct track W.S.W. through the heart of the Damkh range ; the camels required no watering and our skins were filled as necessary from the rain-pools left by the storm in every depression and rock crevice.

We entered the Damkh range at the northern extremity of the Samra Haliban ridge and camped for the night in a sandy hollow surrounded by basalt hummocks, from the summit of one of which I was able to obtain a fine view of the granite masses of the main ridge darkly silhouetted against a glorious sunset. We were now at an elevation of 3250 feet above sea-level; the summit of the Samra ridge ran at a mean level of about 3700 feet, while the ponderous granite masses of Ghurur, Nasifa, Kahila and Farida, forming the backbone of the range and lying in that order from north to south, with Kahila somewhat to the east of Nasifa, over a length of perhaps twenty miles, rose, it seemed to me, to a height of from 4500 to 5000 feet above sea-level ; the greatest of these is Ghurur. Far away to the south I could see the extremity of a great range or mountain mass called Idhqan lying to the south-west of Sabha presumably in the midst of the Dahi sands and reputed to be not less lofty than the greatest mountains of the Najd highlands ; but in considering native estimates of mountain heights we have to remember that the Arab is entirely ignorant of the sea-level criterion and that the slope of the continental mass is southerly ; thus Sabha, vaunted the highest of the Najd mountains, lies so far to the south that, though its summit may be reared higher above the plain than for instance that of Ghurur, the latter has the advantage of standing on a considerably higher base and it is probable that in elevation above sea-level there is little to choose between the two. In any case any attempt to estimate the height of these great peaks must necessarily be largely a matter of conjecture and my endeavour has been to avoid exaggeration in all cases.

According to Izmai, whose information on this point I had no subsequent opportunity of testing, the great mountain of Jabal Nir towering over Sha'ra to the north forms as it were the base of both the Hamra and Damkh ranges, the 'Araiwiyat ridge of the former being continued in a north-westerly direction by the Mujaira and Dha'lan ridges to the base of Nir, while a south-westerly projection of the range, of which the latter is the highest peak, runs down to within a few miles of the northern extremity of Ghurur.

Next morning, the 17th December, we made an early start and after threading a narrow tortuous passage among the basalt hummocks which spread out northward from the end of the Samra entered the broad bushy depression which separates that ridge from the main range. Over this we marched in a south-westerly direction towards a low saddle connecting the Nasifa and Farida crags. Here and at intervals during the day we saw animal life in abundance, hares scurrying away among the bushes, small herds of gazelles bounding away at our approach, standing a moment to protest at our intrusion on their peace and then trotting off in disgust; crows played about the pools of water, and a large flight of twelve *Hubara* flapped away up a side valley. The bushes were for the most part acacias, the *Wahat*, the *Samar*, the *Salam* and the gum-bearing *Talh*, on which for the first time I saw in plenty the great pendant combs of transparent amber gum; here and there stood great bushes of the desert broom, one spreading its flowered stalks so wide around that sixteen camels gathered comfortably round it browsing on the juicy stalks till little was left; the sandy floor of the depression was covered with *Thamam* grass and tufts of *Arfaj* not yet recovered from the autumn drought.

Reaching the saddle we descended along a broad strip of bare black gravel between the great buttresses of Nasifa and Farida; a *Jarbu'* rat went to ground before us and half a dozen of the Arabs leaping to the earth set to work briskly with hands and camel-sticks to dig out their quarry, which they brought along in triumph, but even as we were discussing the propriety of slaughtering it at once for a future meal, passing it round the while from hand to hand, the little beast slipped to the ground and, tail in air, bounced away with incredible speed followed by half-a-dozen of our fleetest runners; with all the disadvantage of strange surroundings against him and headed from point to point by pursuers his superior in cunning, he managed by sheer speed and rapidity of manœuvre to make good his escape, and the men returned crestfallen at the loss of a dainty though minute morsel. The *Jarbu'* is eaten by all *Badawin* except the Harb, and those of the party who belonged to this tribe made merry at the expense of the rest, twitting them with the eating of a beast unclean by *Islamic* law.

We now passed over a low belt of outer foothills and stood at the threshold of the Sirra plain ; behind us ran the dark ridge of the Damkh chain, whose depth from east to west in a straight line is about ten miles ; beyond the plain lay the *Nafud* belt of Sirra, dotted with outcrops of basalt, Makhyat with its five pointed cones, Junaih resembling, as its name suggests, the outspread wings of a raven fallen upon the sandy wilderness, and others ; the background was occupied by three long basalt ridges, 'Alam to the north reaching down to a point due west of us, Zaidi of great length continuing it after an interval of sand to the far southward, and the *sierra* of Jirdhawi to the south-west screening the distant Idhqan just visible over its summit.

Traversing the intervening strip of plain strewn far and wide with black gravel we entered the bushy and grassy freshet-bed of Sha'ib Qahqa, down which the drainage of the western slopes of Damkh pours south-westward to its junction with Wadi Sirra, whose sandy bed, streaked here and there with long streams of black gravel, we reached after another five miles of marching. This great *Wadi* rises on the flank of the 'Alam ridge and runs southward along the eastern fringe of the *Nafud*, which bears its name and separates it from the Zaidi range, to the Jirdhawi, against whose solid barrier it is bent back eastward and flows along the northern flank of Sabha and the Hasat, collecting the drainage of the Haliban, Jarbu', Sardah and Harmaliyya valleys on the way, and thence between the Dahi *Nafud* on the south and the Dalqan and Qunaifida sands on the north to the barrier of Tuwaiq, which it pierces on its way to the Sahaba outlet by the great level-crossing channel of Sha'ib Birk.[1] Ignorance of the existence of Wadi

[1] *Vide* Vol. II. p. 282.

Sirra and of its connection with the Sahaba drainage through the Birk and ʻAjaimi channels had led geographers to postulate a uniform north-easterly slope of the Arabian peninsula on the assumption, justified by knowledge of the actual facts in one case, that its two main drainage arteries of Wadi Rima and Wadi Dawasir trended in that direction; but the data now available necessitate a modification of that hypothesis. In the first place, as I shall show hereafter, Wadi Dawasir trends not in a north-easterly direction but somewhat south of east; in the second place the great river system of Sirra-Birk-ʻAjaimi-Sahaba, flowing in the main eastward from the heart of the Najd highlands through the barrier of Tuwaiq to the sea in the neighbourhood of the Qatar promontory, postulates a divide between it and the Dawasir and Rima drainages on either side; and lastly a study of the levels of the three valleys shows that the Sirra system lies at a higher level than the other two, 800 feet higher than the Rima and about 400 feet higher than Wadi Dawasir. We must therefore conclude that, while the main slope of the peninsula is from west to east, that is to say from the Hijaz mountains towards the Persian Gulf, a central ridge, running, so far as we can judge, in a north-easterly direction across the peninsula along a line marked by the mountain chains of Hadhb Dawasir, Mankhara, Zaidi and ʻAlam, creates a diversion of the general slope in a northward and southward direction on either side of it towards the Rima and the Dawasir respectively. The peninsular slope assumes, therefore, something of the character of a pent-house with a broad flattened summit and gentle northerly and southerly inclines from either side of it—the whole being tilted downwards from west to east; or, in other words, the surface of the peninsula is traversed roughly in the direction of its dominant slope by three broad but shallow valleys, of which that of the Sirra is the most elevated and occupies a central position in relation to the other two.

From this point onwards the highlands present a scene of wild confusion, the details of whose features are extremely difficult to unravel; unlike the first three units of the highland system, which we had just traversed, well-marked

The Sirra plain looking eastwards towards the Damkh range—Farida on right and Nasifa on left.

mountain-ranges lying north by south and separated from each other by well-marked valleys, the fourth or Zaidi unit, as we may call it for convenience, may best be described as a vast sea of storm-tossed sand, dotted at frequent and irregular intervals by long islands or isolated rocks of basalt; the confusion is worse confounded by Arab perversity, which not content with inventing a name for every rock and ridge must needs mark out the sands themselves into spheres, to each of which a name is allotted. This *Nafud* is doubtless a northward projection of the vast sand tract of Dahi to the south and, so far as I was able to ascertain, it comes to an end somewhat to the southward of the latitude of Sija'. From east to west between the eastern extremity of the Sirra *Nafud* to the eastern edge of Wadi Na'im its average breadth may be some forty miles, our course which of necessity followed the line of least resistance along such depressions as could be found being somewhat longer.

The outer edge of this tract comprises the 'Alam range and the sands out of which it rises to the north, Nafud Sirra three miles deep in the centre and the Jirdhawi ridge to the south; this belt we crossed by the *Nafud*, whose four ridges of sand presented no serious difficulty, to camp at the foot of the Zaidi ridge, where our camels refreshed themselves on the abundant *Nussi*, the most nourishing and most eagerly sought after of all the desert grasses, which grows in such profusion in the whole of this sand tract that the latter is reckoned one of the best grazing grounds in western Arabia. Nevertheless, we traversed the whole area without falling in with any signs of human life though I was assured that it would not be long before the place was alive with the flocks and herds of the 'Ataiba.

On the following day we set ourselves to negotiate the central strip consisting of the Zaidi range to the south and the Sakha *Nafud* northward of it. Coasting along the outer edge of the former we came to its most northerly point, a sharp hog-backed lump of granite called Khanzir, between which and the Junaih hummock we entered a broad strip of gravelly plain surrounded by the sands of the Sirra, and Sakha *Nafuds* here mingled in inextricable confusion.

On our left lay the highest peak of another basalt ridge, called Karsh,[1] standing back at some distance and properly belonging to the third or western section of this system. We passed out of the Darat al Junaih, as the plain is called, up a sandy pass dotted here and there with outcrops of greenstone, which added a pleasant touch of colour to the monotonous yellow and black of sand and basalt. From here we descended to a saline depression, called Jau Dahu, which runs down southward along the western flank of the Zaidi range, at whose foot in the bed of the *Jau* some ten miles lower down are the brackish wells of Muraifiq; in parts the depression glittered in the sun snow-white with a salty efflorescence.

Beyond it lay some scattered low black rocks marking the position of the Sakha wells, which we reached in a few minutes; they lie in two groups in the midst of an extensive bottom surrounded on all sides by high-piled sand and shaped like a horseshoe,[2] the only really good specimen of such a phenomenon I saw in all my wandering. The surface of the bottom is flat and smooth with occasional excrescences of greenstone at the northern end; in the centre lies a chain of six or seven wells lined with greenstone blocks and containing plentiful though brackish water at a depth of only five feet, in which during our halt the men bathed after watering the camels; the water in these wells is not fit for human consumption, for which provision is made by nature at the north-western corner of the bottom, where in a patch of sand sweet water may be had for the trouble of scraping out the sand to a depth of two or three feet; a number of unlined shafts have been scooped out here in the course of time, in which there is always a little muddy water yielding an inexhaustible supply under the influence of patient scraping.

The bottom, perhaps one mile across at its longest, lies roughly north by south, the sand-slope being steeper and higher at the curve of the shoe on the south than at the

[1] Farther to the south of this ridge another ridge and peak, called Idhn, rose out of the sand.

[2] These horseshoe hollows, called *Falj*, are apparently more frequent in and, indeed, a characteristic feature of the *Nafud* north of Jabal Shammar.

northern end where low black rocks mingle with the sand; the soil is of clay without vegetation except a few stray bushes of *Sharr*, though it appears, superficially at any rate, to be a suitable site for a permanent settlement, if Arabs can be found to settle permanently in a place so remote from all civilisation. The idea has already suggested itself to Ibn Sa'ud in connection with his scheme of *Ikhwan* settlements, but so far it has met with little acceptance on the part of the *Badu*, among whom none but the 'Ataiba would be in a position to colonise such a spot. It was about the year 1912 that Ibn Sa'ud, who had at this time [1] never penetrated farther west than Sakha, made these wells his base for a notable attack on the 'Ataiba, from which he returned crowned with success and loaded with booty. Nevertheless, his hold on this tribe, disputed as it is by the Sharif, has always been somewhat precarious, and, though recently the *Ikhwan* movement has received considerable attention from its leaders, the advantages of having in a spot so well adapted for the control of the tribe a colony, whose loyalty and fanaticism would be above suspicion, cannot be gainsaid.

Ascending the sand-slope from the southern end of the Sakha bottom we soon reached the low ridge of Mandasa, by the side of which we marched south-west until we emerged on a wide sandy plain called Sha'ib Raddadi, where we camped for the night under the lee of some greenstone outcrops and loosed out the weary camels to browse on the bounteous *Nussi*.

The following morning we were all ready to start before the call to the dawn prayer, and as my companions prayed I noticed for the first time low down on the southern horizon the Southern Cross, which they call *Nu'aim*. According to Izmai, Sha'ib Raddadi, which we now traversed, is a blind depression rather than a watercourse, in which the rain-water drained down from the neighbouring ridge is absorbed by the sand, *yahir* as they say. We now passed across

[1] In May, 1919, however, he passed this spot again on his way to Khurma and Turaba far beyond it, to superintend the military operations which resulted in his decisive victory over the *Sharifian* forces commanded by 'Abdullah, the King's son.

the northern extremity of the Karsh ridge, which extends southward for several miles to the main peak, under which lie the brackish[1] wells of Kuwaikib; the waters of these wells like those of Mahdath some twenty miles to the north under a prominent solitary rock and of Budai'a farther on in our course are said to have a deleterious effect on human beings though good enough for cattle. To the north-west lay the ridge of 'Aqqar running north and south. Next on our path came the sand-sprinkled basalt ridges of Buwaibiyat which we left to southward of us; southward again of these lay the rocks or ridges of Wa'la and Arwisa with Sha'than westward of them, these three forming as it were a broken extension of the 'Aqqar-Buwaibiyat line.

We next passed over the double ridge of Abu Nubta into the vast Nafud Bishara extending northwards as far as we could see, over which we steered towards the Budai'a ridge with the hummocks of Hamma and Umm al Jawaïr to our left. A shallow clay depression on the hither side of the ridge contained the Budai'a wells; we passed round the northern extremity of the Budai'a ridge and a gentle sandy slope led us down to Wadi Na'im. The fourth and last section of the Najd highlands lay behind us and we had traversed the 'Ataiba *dira* from side to side without mishap, and, with the exception of the two men who fled before us to Qusuriyya, without meeting a single individual of the tribe.

We had crossed the Harmaliyya *Sha'ib* into the Najd highland tract at 2 P.M. on the 14th December, and now passed out of the latter into Wadi Na'im at 9 A.M. on the 19th December, having covered in the five days about 150 miles in rather over forty hours of actual travel. Of the general features of these gaunt and sparsely populated highlands, whose area cannot well be less than some 10,000 square miles,[2] I have in these pages given a descrip-

[1] *Hamaj.*

[2] This highland tract is, I would suggest, but the northern extremity of a continuous chain of mountains—Hadhb Dawasir, Mankhara, etc.—which would seem to project from the mountainous country of Asir in a wide sweep to eastward with a gradual tendency to assume a northward direction. If this is so the Najd highland tract forms a southern counterpart to the mountains of Jabal Shammar, which are similarly an arm projecting eastwards from the mountains of northern Hijaz.

tion sufficiently if not indeed excessively detailed; I now passed from them probably to see them no more, regretting that the speed of travel imposed on me by the purpose of my journey had permitted of no deviation from the track trodden by the pilgrims of centuries hastening even as we hastened on the road to the holy city, and conscious that in the Najd properly so called, the true highlands of Central Arabia, whose limits I have attempted to define, I had left for the wanderers of the future many a knotty problem unattempted, many a hidden mystery unsolved. Of the three great mountain chains and the tumbled confusion of sand billows and basalt rocks, which complete the quadruple barrier; of the tempest playing over the massive granite of the "Ears of the North"; of the rain-washed red rocks of the Hamra glistening in the sunlight; of the mighty mountains dimly seen in the far south; of the charming groves and dingy villages and solitary turreted granges; of all these I carried away with me memories which words cannot describe nor time efface.

5. The Subai' Country

Wadi Na'im is a shallow depression, about one mile in breadth, dividing the highland tract from the immense steppe of Shifa, whose dull rim bounded the horizon to south, west and north; with the exception of a few low hummocks scattered over the gravel plain not a landmark was to be seen in all its expanse until we came into view of the sand-barrier of 'Arq al Subai' and simultaneously of the peaks and ridges of the Hadhb Dawasir, a considerable range, presumably of granite, lying west by east across the Dahi *Nafud* and separated from the Suwada range between it and the Hasat by the gravel plain of Jamra, in whose exiguous watercourses lie the small Qahtan settlements of Qara'a and 'Aifara at a distance of some fifty or sixty miles southward of our track.

The Shifa, whose northern boundary is practically the line of Wadi Rima between the Harra Kishab, or Harrat al Harb as it is commonly called, and the village of Sija' some forty miles north-west of our position in Wadi Na'im, rises steppe-wise westward by the gentlest of gradients. The storms of winter and summer pass over it unarrested from the Hijaz mountains to the Najd highlands, and rain falls upon it but at rare intervals; the showers which had drenched us so recently had left it dry, and it was said that this vast arid plain had had no fall of rain for several years; everywhere was the same unvaried desolation of gravel, black and brown and grey, with never a bush and scarce a blade of withered grass; yet they tell of years when the flocks and herds of the *Badawin* swarm over the steppe to graze on the luxuriant herbs which a slight shower draws from its virgin soil.

To right and left of us, as we entered the plain, lay the low short ridges of Barqa Na'im and Suwwan, and at midday we halted at the knolls of Aushijiyat; as we proceeded, the Humiyya ridge, with brackish wells at its foot, the small mound of Abul Hirran and the scattered cones of Hutaimiyat[1] appeared in the north-western distance, and we camped for the night close by the mound of Musaijira in the low loose ridge of the Hasiyat within view of the long coast of the Subai' *Nafud*.

We were now clear of the dangers lurking in the folds of the highlands; in the daytime no foe could approach without timely warning of his presence, but at night no friendly shelter concealed the camp-fire from prowling brigands, should any be about. For four days since leaving Qusuriyya behind us we had seen no living soul, but in the morning of the day just ended droppings of sheep gone by some day or two before had been observed, arguing the not distant presence of shepherd folk. A thin flight of hungered autumn locusts greeted our arrival in camp, but all hopes of a providential feast were dashed to the ground on examination of the wretched insects, and we settled down to our dinner of plain rice and the results of the day's chase, a single hare, shot as it slept under a tuft of herbage, among thirty men. Very pleasant it was to sit, as we sat that night, round the camp-fire, drinking round the coffee and I alone smoking, for in me they pardoned the offence, discussing the long weary days behind us and reckoning up those yet

[1] The largest of these, Barqa 'Arrada, lay at the north end of the chain.

to come; they chid me for my exacting demands on man and camel; the Arabs, they said, are inured to endure fatigue when exertion is necessary, but never in all their born days had they met with one who seemed to enjoy it; and Tami related his reminiscences of English travellers he had known, who had been more reasonable, while I countered his points by quoting the reports of the same travellers on the incurable sloth of their Arab companions. The idle banter froze upon our lips as a long low wail pierced the darkness around us. "Hark! a wolf," said one, "there, he howls again"; "or perhaps," said another, "a *Slugi* hound of some shepherd camp, but it is very near and we saw no sign of human life at sundown." "Nay," said a third, "'tis the signal of a *Baduwi* scout calling to his gang."

The fire was extinguished and the party scattered to their arms, while the *Rafiqs* strode forth to the four corners of the camp and one after another proclaimed our whence and whither to the silent night. Watches were set for the night, and next morning searchers found the tracks of the wolf which had alarmed us in the near vicinity of the camp.

A few miles farther on the summit of the Shifa was reached, whence there is a gentle slope down to the sands, on whose edge respectively due south and due west of us rose the rocks of Kabd and Ashhaila. Occasional bushes and tufts of grass now dotted the barren plain and a large herd of gazelles streamed away to our flank making for the *Nafud*, while almost at the same instant it was reported from the rear that riders had been observed far away to the northward, three of them, of whom one had galloped off immediately for what other purpose than to report our presence to the main body? I scanned the horizon with my field-glasses in vain, for a fold of the ground had swallowed up the remaining two, and after a brief consultation it was decided to continue our march. We were now entering the sand-barrier of ʿArq al Subaiʿ along the line of a well-marked clay-bottomed channel about two miles wide between high sandbanks at its mouth and rapidly narrowing to about a quarter of a mile farther on; the channel takes its name of Khudud from an irregular line of low basalt mounds almost obliterated by sand near by, and, running about S.S.W. for a distance of about thirteen miles, saves the traveller all the wearisome labour of traversing the sand-billows of the *Nafud* for nearly three-quarters of its whole width.

Our thoughts dwelt much on the three riders and the perils their presence might betoken; were they raiders out on business we were at their mercy, for they presumably knew our route as well as we did, and were in a position either to follow us up or ambush us at any point ahead, or descend upon us at night at their discretion; it was obviously our wisest course to push on with all possible speed and I strongly advocated that course, but Ibrahim, mindful that he had not broken his fast, was of a different opinion: "Let us leave our mark behind us and halt for breakfast at the next convenient spot," said he; "ho! Jarman, descend and mark our *Wasms* [1] on the track." The 'Ataibi did as he was bid, marking in the sand the brand-signs of Ibn Sa'ud, the Sharif, the Barqa section of the 'Ataiba and the Subai'; such is the simple desert method of communication, the *Badawin* substitute for writing, sufficient to proclaim the ownership of cattle and the identity of travelling parties, and sufficient to ensure at least circumspection in their approach on the part of marauding gangs. "But if that is sufficient," I asked, "what is there to prevent any party of travellers, whether accompanied by *Rafiqs* or not, from proclaiming a false identity to elude pursuit, or a gang of raiders doing the same to lure the unwary into an ambush?" The answer was simple and effective: "Such a thing is never done." The whole structure of *Badawin* society would totter to its fall, if the law of the desert were transgressed.

The graceful *Ghadha*, an *Euphorbia* allied to the common lowly *Hamdh* for all its resemblance to the tamarisk, I here saw for the first time dotting the sandy slopes; it is eaten sparingly by camels when other herbage is deficient, but is held in high repute as fuel wherever it is found, notably in the Qasim and in Southern Najd. We continued our march

[1] These are the tribal marks of the *Badawin*, primitive symbols enabling the unlettered to distinguish between the property of one tribe or section or family and another.

up the Khudud depression after a brief halt for breakfast, and at mid-afternoon passed up out of its southern extremity into the billowy sands, spurring our jaded beasts to a great effort in the hope of reaching the plain beyond the *Nafud* before sundown.

Tami, with Hailan of the 'Ataiba and Abu Nura of the Harb, was slightly in advance of Izmai and myself and a few others, while Ibrahim and the bulk of our party, including the baggage train, were some distance to the rear at the foot of a long sand-slope, up which we were painfully advancing; around us rolled the sea of sand utterly desolate in its emptiness. The leaders suddenly drew up: "*Sadiq, Sadiq, Sadiq!*" they shouted in different keys. We were with them before we realised what had happened, and found ourselves covered at a range of twenty yards by a dozen rifles; for all our precautions we had walked straight into an ambush, our rifles slung to our saddle-frames unloaded, and we were completely at the mercy of our surprisers, while the main body, still far behind, was hurrying up at its best speed. In the meantime there was nothing to be done but to hold up our hands under the menace of those ominous barrels and to parley with the foe; there then arose a hubbub such as I have seldom heard; three or four of our opponents, ill-clad and bare-headed, rose from their cover of bushes while the rest ceased not to cover us; of the negotiations which ensued, everybody shouting at the top of his voice and all together, to me not a single word was intelligible. The 'Ataiba *Rafiqs*, who had all been behind, now came up and advanced into the forefront of the wordy *mêlée*. "*Salam 'alaikum,*" "*W' 'alaikum al salam*"; the words of peace were spoken and the tension was over. "Come on with me," said Sa'd to me, and I followed him obediently aside, while friend and foe gathered on the summit of the ridge to fraternise. "Let us halt here for the night," said Ibrahim, and I yielded with but little murmuring as there was little hope of our now reaching the farther edge of the *Nafud*, and the north wind was blowing the whirling sands this way and that until we could hardly see about us.

We and our erstwhile enemy camped side by side in

adjoining hollows; I suggested that we might invite them to share our evening meal, but my proposal was negatived; in the first place it was still unknown to them that the party they had ambushed contained an Englishman, and the discovery of an infidel among us might cause them regrets at the moderation they had exercised in the moment of their undisputed ascendancy, and would certainly be blazoned abroad by them on their onward journey, perhaps to our undoing; in the second place, we had naught but rice and dates in our larder, while they were known to have a sheep. These arguments were unanswerable, and I rested content with the reflection that my identity was not as obvious to strangers as I had assumed it must be.

They were a small party, a dozen all told, of Shaqra merchants with carriers and guides, returning home from Khurma with foreign merchandise imported through the Hijaz; more wary in their progress than ourselves, they had been warned by their scouts of the approach of what they took to be a raiding party, whose numbers left them little hope of successful resistance in the event of an attack; they had accordingly decided to secure the initiative for themselves and the advantage of position; for the rest they had put their trust in God and determined to sell their lives and their goods as dearly as might be, or, if circumstances so permitted, to buy their way through; our negligence enabled them to score a complete success, only to find, much to their relief, that our purpose was as harmless as their own. Such are the daily anxieties and dangers of the desert; for day after day we had marched warily enough, ever on the look-out; but an hour or two before we had been warned to be on the alert; yet at the critical moment we were off our guard and, in other circumstances, might have paid dearly for our fault.

The country before us, they said, was in a state of ferment, and the Mecca-ward road from Khurma was barred against the Subai' by the Buqum tribe, acting under the orders of the Sharif. The local *Amir* had passed into the fold of the *Ikhwan* and had placed himself at the head of the Bani Thaur tribesmen, a section of the Subai', to resist the encroachments of their would-be overlord, and fighting might be expected to take place at any moment. This was cheerful news for us, and we repaid them for their information by warning them of the 'Ataiba and Qahtan outridings, of which we had heard much but seen little in the country now to be traversed by them. We left them next morning warming themselves at their fire at the chill hour of dawn, and continued our interrupted march over the sands.

A series of clay and slightly saline bottoms lay in our path, which at a distance of three miles from our camp emerged from the last sand ridge of the *Nafud* on to an immense plain. The 'Arq al Subai' sand strip, probably not more than ten or twelve miles across in a direct line from east to west, though the route we had followed along the Khudud depression and the nameless dips beyond it had been several miles longer than that, is said to extend from the Buqara ridge some thirty miles to the north to the Hadhb Dawasir range somewhat more distant to the south —a total length of perhaps seventy miles—and there seems to me reason, as I shall relate in a subsequent chapter,[1] to hold that it extends in a solid barrier across the upper reaches of Wadi Dawasir to the north-western corner of the great sand-sea of Rub' al Khali. The sands of the 'Arq appeared to me to be of a dull grey colour with a considerable admixture of black, presumably basaltic, grains.

Our course now lay south-west over the Subai' plain towards a distant low ridge rising from both extremities to a high central mass and called Tin; the ridge of Hisan lay to the S.S.W. with a small hillock called Ghuraimid between its right extremity and Tin, while due south rose the prominent double-peaked hill of Gharamin. For the rest, the vast expanse was bare except for a series of low basalt hummocks called Rughailat.

The surface of the plain showed considerable variety of formation, the slightly sun-cracked loam or clay on which we first entered, giving way to a strip of low sand dunes, the sand in its turn yielding to a shingle beach dotted with excrescences of slaty rock, and that to a broad expanse of rough sun-cracked clay covered with the *débris* of a forest of *Tarfa* or dwarf tamarisk, uprooted by floods and

[1] *Vide* Vol. II. p. 197.

scorched by the sun; vegetation was everywhere plentiful —*Arfaj*, *Hamdh*, *Ghadha* and a broom-like bush called *Tandham*, akin to the *Qirdhi*, and the usual grasses; in one spot scattered blocks of masonry marked the site of a buried and forgotten group of nameless wells, three or four miles beyond which we halted at the most southerly of the Rughailat mounds in a patch of acacias. One mile west of this point lay a dark patch of vegetation marking the eastern extremity of the Wadi Subai' channel, the Dhalma, as it is called on account of the dense undergrowth which covers the bed from side to side; from here in the flood season the waters descending from the Asir mountains pour forth over the plain, whose blistered surface and uprooted shrubs bear witness to the passing of the flood, which in years of exceptional rainfall piles itself against the 'Arq barrier and even penetrates its outer rim into the depressions along which our route had lain.

A march of three miles brought us to a monument of the past, the decrepit and long-untenanted fort of Qunsuliyya, dating back to the days of the *Wahhabi* Empire, when it formed a blockhouse to guard the route between the capital of the great Sa'ud and his outlying subject provinces of Taïf and Mecca. Nothing remains of the fort but a skeleton of roofless walls between a small cemetery of orthodox type and probably of recent date, possibly marking the resting-place of pilgrims overtaken by the messenger of death on their way to Mecca, and a group of seven wells, excavated to a depth of twenty-five feet in the natural rock soil, unlined, and containing plentiful though slightly brackish water. Here another halt was called to water the camels and to fill our skins from the one well reputed to contain comparatively sweet water; flights of sand-grouse wheeled about overhead, and the crows, disturbed by our approach, patiently awaited our departure at a respectful distance; gazelles had been observed and hunted in vain several times during the march.

We resumed our march parallel to and at a short distance from the Wadi Subai' channel, beyond which the dark conical mound of Biram rose out of the desolate plain. As we proceeded the ground became rougher and more undulating, with a thicker covering of flood-felled *Tarfa*, this tract, which is said to extend unbroken westward to the hills, being differentiated from the rest of the plain by the name of Al Taraf. In the far distance the dark lava masses of Harrat al Nawasif began to appear against the sky-line, their profile as seen from our camping place extending over forty degrees of the compass from south to south-west.

The next day was one of strenuous exertion; for six days we had fared on nothing but rice and dates, varied by a hare on only two occasions, and all were agreed that we must make Khurma before nightfall; to make matters worse my *Dhalul* had picked up a flint the previous afternoon and gone badly lame, with the result that the awkward gait, coupled with a series of long fatiguing days, made me ache all over; in this condition I mounted a *Dhalul* which I had discarded for its rough paces in the early stages of the journey, to face a march of eleven and a half hours, broken only by a single halt of less than an hour, my discomfort and agony increasing with every step until, by the time we arrived at our destination, I was in the last stages of exhaustion.

The country over which we marched, still parallel with and very gradually converging on the line of Wadi Subai', was a rough, gently-undulating down of gravel, seamed at intervals by streams of black stones and rocks descending from the Nawasif *Harra* and traversed in a south-easterly direction towards the Hisan and Gharamin ridges by two broad offshoots from the *Wadi*, called respectively Sha'ib Maqsan and Sha'ib Hathaq, about two miles apart and covered with a dense growth of acacia bushes and occasional patches of *Tarfa*. The monotony of the scene was varied only by the distant view of the black mountain range of Nawasif, whose greater peaks showed up more and more grimly as we drew nearer to them; our best view of these was obtained during a mid-day halt in the Maqsan trough, the highest points in order from south to north being Qaus, Sufira and Khal, in which doubtless lie the sources of Wadi Subai'.

My discarded *Dhalul*, whose pad had been roughly patched up after the extrication of the flint, had been allotted to

Sa'd, who made little secret of the discomfort he was experiencing and lagged behind; my own mount was little better and I joined him in the rear, but Ibrahim, determined not to leave us alone in our agony, drew up at intervals to await our coming and, doubtless with the best intentions in the world, insisted on prodding my *Dhalul* to a trot or clacking encouragement to her with his tongue, regardless of my own comfort. I protested in vain, but my protests he persisted in misunderstanding, and I resigned myself to the endurance of his officiousness, striving in spite of my growing irritation to maintain a show of respect and friendliness towards the leader of our party, but to Sa'd, in the intervals of our being alone, knowing that he was a bosom friend and boon companion of my persecutor, I confided something of my feelings, begging him to intervene before I should be compelled to take matters into my own hands. Betraying by his dark complexion the negro strain by which his pedigree was tainted, but for all that remarkably handsome for an Arabian, and uncommonly proud of his much-anointed braided locks of raven black, Ibrahim was an epitome of empty-headed vanity and coarse sensuality; his conversation, no lewder than that of Tami and some of the others, was relieved by no spark of wit; his manners at meals were revoltingly disgusting and, try as I might to avoid sitting near him, I always found him sitting at my side; and every night, when I retired to my tent to read or write, he would intrude upon me and, drawing together the outer flaps, would settle down to a secret smoke, haunted ever by the fear of discovery by his fellows, and breathing out the fumes from the depths of his lungs in ostentatious enjoyment, accompanied by spitting; at meals he would insist on feeding me; when I mounted my camel he would insist on assisting me; in the one matter in which he might have helped me to advantage, namely in quieting the clamour of my companions for shorter and more restful marches, he invariably threw in his voice with the majority; whenever I made a remark he would applaud; when I extricated myself from his company and entered into conversation with the others, he would join the party in a trice and monopolise the conversation. In all these trials of the past

THE VILLAGE OF KHURMA.

fortnight I had schooled myself to silent endurance of his all-pervading presence, because he was the *Amir* of the party appointed by Ibn Sa'ud to that charge; even on this last day of our march to Khurma I held my peace, though the cup of anguish and irritation was nearly full.

About 3 P.M. we sighted the little hamlet of Sulaimiyya nestling among its palms and tamarisks in the *Wadi* bed on our right, while the palms of Khurma itself showed up darkly ahead, with the ruined fort of Qunzan between the two on an eminence on the left bank of the channel; this *Qasr* had in former times been held by the Bani 'Amir section of the Subai', long since driven out by the Bani Thaur and now settled in Kharj, whither I afterwards came to their newly founded *Ikhwan* settlement of Dhaba'a, and in Eastern Najd.

We now reached the broad channel of Wadi Subai', which we followed along its high right bank up-stream with the *Ithils* and palms marking the course of the storm channel on our right; after about half a mile we slanted across the *Wadi*, and crossing the torrent bed of deep white sand entered the main belt of palms. The thickly grown stems with their heavy green tops formed a shady avenue, whose winding course we followed for some distance till we emerged upon an open space with little square patches of brilliant green, young corn and lucerne, in the midst of which stood the formless straggling village ot Khurma itself; the village children, with an idle man or two, gathered about us, and women peeped timidly from side streets as we passed along an outer street to a clearing on the north side of the settlement, where we couched our camels and pitched our tents in the empty angle formed by two court-yard walls before an ever growing and wondering audience. The sun was very near its setting and, continually dogged and watched by curious persons, I had but just time to walk round and inspect the outer face and surroundings of the village, when the shades of night blotted them out for ever, for we were well on our onward way next morning before the metallic sheen of the false dawn had yielded to the softer light of daybreak. The events of the following year made me regret bitterly that circumstances had not permitted of a longer sojourn at and closer inspection of a locality destined, for all its seeming insignificance, to a fateful share in the making of history, perhaps indeed to be the earthly grave of the Utopian ideal of Arab unity, perhaps, who knows ? to be the anvil on which that ideal may yet be hammered into reality. The name of Khurma, a little desert oasis seen but once in all the ages by European eyes, was during the summer months of 1918 heard in the courts of far Whitehall, and the dawn of the new year was clouded by the gathering storm of a medieval Armageddon, as the warring factions, serving in modern as in ancient times the Mammon of political ambition with their hearts and the true God with their lips, arrayed their uncouth forces for battle along the valley of the Subai'.

The course of that struggle between the Sharif on the one side and Ibn Sa'ud's *Wahhabi* host on the other falls outside the scope of these volumes, for it was not until the following June that the first clash of arms took place, resulting in the defeat of a *Sharifian* force sent to restore the king's authority in the " rebellious " oasis ; and it will be sufficient here to relate that, that first skirmish having been followed during the last months of the great war by two others of similar character with the same result, the crisis became more and more acute in spite of the efforts of the British Government to incline the disputants to reason, until in May, 1919 it culminated in a great battle fought at dead of night, not at Khurma but at Turaba, and resulting in a sweeping victory for the *Wahhabis*, who, surprising the sleeping camp of the enemy, put all they found therein to the sword and possessed themselves of all their guns, ammunition and equipment. 'Abdullah, the king's son and commander of the expedition, escaped in his nightshirt with a small following, leaving between 4000 and 5000 of his troops dead on the field ; and the news of his defeat created consternation at Taïf, whose panic-stricken inhabitants fled before the approaching terror —all except, as the story goes, an old lady of the Sharif's family, who remained in her palace, declaring that she knew enough of Ibn Sa'ud's record to anticipate nothing but honourable treatment at his hands. As a matter of fact Ibn Sa'ud did not follow up his victory, and his retirement to Riyadh left the Khurma question still a potential source of future trouble in Arabia, though for the moment he had gained and still holds an advantage in the possession not only of Khurma itself but of the Buqum oasis of Turaba.

For geographical reasons I regret that I was unable to explore towards the upper reaches of the *Wadi*, but when I left Khurma I had planned to return from Taïf by way of Turaba and Ranya, and thus to clear up the mystery of the origin and course not only of Wadi Subai' but of the Turaba and Ranya channels. My plans were frustrated by circumstances beyond my control, and I can do no more than conjecture the realities of the geographical arrangement of this tract from what I saw. From Khurma the *Harra* masses of Nawasif exhibited the peaks of Abu Ashdad and Raiyan in addition to those already seen, while the dim distant line of the Hadhn range met them from the north, forming an angle in which, they say, lies the village and oasis of Turaba, some forty miles south-west of Khurma and, I think, situated like the latter in the bed of Wadi Subai'[1] at the point where it enters the plain from the *Harra* gorges in which it rises. If this be true, the *Wadi* thereafter must descend in a north-easterly direction twenty miles or more to the ruined village and deserted oasis of Gharith, situated at the point from which the important offshoot of Sha'ib Sha'ba parts company with the main channel. The latter continues straight on to Khurma, whose village and scattered *Qasrs* extend up and down its bed over a distance of perhaps four miles, and thence runs somewhat north of east past the fort of Qunzan and the hamlet of Sulaimiyya, already mentioned, to its outflow at the Dhalma coppice, passing on its way the well groups of Wutta', Hunnu, Shudhu, Hujaif, Barida and Hanfa over against the Biram knoll. Local nomenclature, with characteristic precision or, from our point of view, vagueness, breaks up the channel of the *Wadi* into three sections, known as Wadi Turaba, Wadi Khurma and Wadi Subai'; the last two, however, are certainly one, and though we must keep an open mind for the possibility that the Turaba channel is separate from the Subai', and perhaps constitutes the upper

[1] The upper reaches of the channel are known as Wadi Turaba.

course or a tributary of Wadi Ranya, it is on the whole, I think, more probable that it is nothing but the upper section of the Subai' *Wadi*. As for Ranya,[1] whose oases lie, if my information is correct, about sixty miles due south of Qunsuliyya, it is sufficient here to say that it almost certainly rises like Wadi Subai' in the folds of the Nawasif *Harra*, and eventually coalesces with the *Wadis* of Bisha and Tathlith to form the great Wadi Dawasir.

The village, situated wholly in the *Wadi* bed but on a strip of ground raised somewhat above the level of the storm channel, consists of several straggling and unwalled groups of mud tenements of the type common to all Najd, but here and there a two-storeyed house of more pretentious appearance relieves the general dinginess of the place, and suggests the residence of people not unaccustomed to something more luxurious than the accommodation provided by a desert village. This indeed proved to be the case, for the settlement numbers among its population a small percentage, fifty or sixty souls I was told, of merchant adventurers from Shaqra, 'Anaiza, and other places in Najd, who have made Khurma their business centre and a sort of clearing-house for trade between Najd and Mecca. The unsettled condition of the country between the Hijaz border and the settled districts of Najd precludes the idea that this trade is or ever has been voluminous, while the blockade imposed on the village by the Sharif must have made it even more precarious than formerly, but it may be assumed that in normal times these enterprising foreigners enjoy a monopoly of local business, buying up the *saman* and other products of the pastoral *Badawin* for the Mecca market and purveying to the nomads and villagers coffee, sugar, piece-goods, and other commodities brought up from the coast. Commercial intercourse with Najd, which draws its ordinary supplies mainly from the east coast, must be of a fitful nature, though the Khurma merchants doubtless traffic in the vials of Zamzam water, which, though not in great demand in Najd itself, is highly valued in the Hasa.

For the rest, the population of Khurma, some 4000 permanent residents all told, though this number is swelled

[1] *Vide* Vol. II. p. 223.

perhaps to 10,000 by the annual incursion of the *Badawin* for the date harvest, consists of *Ashraf* elements comprising not more than 200 souls, semi-settled Subai' tribesmen and negro freemen, no longer slaves though still known as *'Abid*. The last category probably comprises at least three-quarters of the entire resident population; on them falls the whole burden of the cultivation of the soil, of whose fruits they deliver one half to the *Ashraf* or Subai' landlords, to whom the groves and cornfields belong. The cultivator is styled *Kaddad*. The Subai' here are mainly of the Bani Thaur section, while the *Ashraf* long settled here as at Turaba enjoy a hereditary prescriptive right to the hegemony of the whole community. The *Badawin* wander the livelong year with their flocks over the Subai' plain, the sands of 'Arq al Subai' and the Shifa steppe beyond as far as Wadi Na'im, visiting their headquarters about the beginning of the month of *Ramdhan* [1] and remaining there till the end of the date harvest.

At present the local *Amir* is Khalid ibn Mansur ibn Luwai, a scion of the leading family of the *Ashraf*, who had succeeded his uncle or first cousin Ghalib on his death some four years before; during the summer of 1917 he had apparently incurred the displeasure of the Sharif, for what reason I am ignorant, and had been thrown into jail at Mecca, whence he had been released at the intercession of Sharif 'Abdullah, with whom since then he had, at any rate until recently, been serving in the field about besieged Madina. Whether at the time of my visit to Khurma he was still with 'Abdullah I am unable to say; [2] he was certainly not at Khurma, where his brother Saif was officiating as *Amir*, or rather had been doing so, until he took the field with the Bani Thaur against the Buqum forces led by the *Amir* of Turaba.

The information given us by the Shaqra merchants

[1] That is to say when the month of fasting falls in late summer; in winter and spring when water is abundant in the desert they, doubtless, remain in the pasture lands.

[2] He had paid a visit to Riyadh about this time, and it seems probable that, deserting 'Abdullah during the later months of the year, he had repaired to Ibn Sa'ud to beg his assistance in the conflict about to be forced upon him by the Sharif or, indeed, actually begun by the Buqum threat, against which he had left his brother to guard the village during his absence.

turned out to be correct; the village was practically deserted by its able-bodied men except a few merchants, and the crowd which collected to gaze on us consisted largely of children in the foreground and women lurking more timidly but with all the prying curiosity of their sex in the background; our requirements in the matter of fodder and food were attended to by the local *Naib*, and a few of the resident merchants accosted us in search of news of their distant native land. One of these, a travelled man, who had apparently served the Turkish Government in Syria or on the *Hajj* route, as a soldier according to his own account but more probably as a *Hajj* guard, and who had only recently returned from a visit to Riyadh, where he had heard of the expected arrival of English visitors, made little secret of his suspicions regarding my identity; this to my surprise had apparently baffled the curiosity of the other villagers in spite of lively speculation as to the nature and business of the *Wakil* or agent of Ibn Sa'ud—for such I was proclaimed to be—who rode a *Dhalul* so gorgeously caparisoned, and by arrangement with Ibrahim the man consented to keep his suspicions to himself until after our departure.

Our long penance of low diet was interrupted that evening by a sumptuous feast comprising a large haunch of camel beef with rice and vegetables from the gardens of the oasis. We were fortunate in arriving on a day when butcher's meat was available, for, the *Badawin* being away, sheep or goats were unobtainable, and the people left behind in the village contented themselves with the occasional slaughter of a camel; the meat, which I now tasted for the first time, was coarse and very tough, but satisfying and not unlike inferior beef.

We were now within a few miles of the western frontier of Wahhabiland at an elevation of 3650 feet above sea-level and about 400 miles from Riyadh; the following day we were to enter the limits of the sacred territory of the Hijaz. At Khurma water[1] is abundant at a depth of a few feet in

[1] It appears that shortly before the battle of Turaba in May, 1919 a great flood had visited the valley, in consequence of which considerable reaches of the channel retained a fair depth of water for some time, and I was told that fishes of some size had actually been found therein.

the higher cultivated lands, and can be obtained anywhere in the actual bed of the storm channel by digging down a few inches into the sand; in quality it is excellent and as sweet as any to be had on the route we had traversed from the east coast. The temperature, which for several days past had maintained itself at an average level of 55° Fahrenheit and even higher at the chill hour preceding dawn, had dropped suddenly on the bleak plain of Al Taraf to only 41° at 4 A.M., but the drop was only temporary and due to a sharp northerly wind; during the next two days the thermometer showed a return to normal conditions.

CHAPTER V

THE HOLY LAND

1. THE SHARQI STEPPE AND THE FOOTHILLS

THE space between the left bank of Wadi Subai' and Sha'ib Sha'ba is known as Al Tarif, a bare plain of loose shingle forming the counterpart of Al Taraf on the other side of the *Wadi* and extending to a depth of six miles on the westerly course of our passage. The black masses of Nawasif now gradually receded from view in our rear, while the range of Hadhn loomed ever larger on the forward horizon.

"*Idhkar allah*," ejaculated the pious Izmai as he led the way down the slope into Sha'ib Sha'ba, and each man as he crossed the border discarded his habitual levity for a serious mien, calling on the name of the Lord. The broad bed of the *Sha'ib*, three miles across between its low banks and densely covered with thick acacia bushes, forms the recognised boundary between the Subai' and Buqum tribes, and thus, though the matter is still under hot dispute, between the Hijaz and Najd. Hitherto we had been in the territory of tribes among whom Ibn Sa'ud's writ runs unquestioned; henceforth we were in foreign territory, and as strangers coming from a blockaded region liable to obstruction should we fall in with the wardens of the marches, whom, therefore, it was our utmost endeavour to avoid. We moved warily with rifles unslung ready for instant use, threading our way through the thickly wooded coombe.

The Sha'ba, issuing as already noted from the Wadi Subai at the abandoned settlement of Gharith, is a waterway of no little significance in the hydrographic scheme of the continent of Arabia; being, as it is, the most southerly tributary of the great north-easterly drainage system, whose trunk channel is Wadi Rima, its right bank constitutes the boundary between that system and a considerable neutral tract, if we may use the epithet to denote an area provided with no drainage outlet and thus compelled to dispose of its surface waters by absorption, intervening like an immense wedge between it and the no less important south-easterly system, which embraces the Asir mountains, the Najd highlands, the Dawasir province, the southern section of the Tuwaiq barrier and the provinces of Aflaj and Kharj. Reinforced by a number of watercourses which drain the eastern flank of the Hadhn range, the Sha'ba eventually passes into Sha'ib Jarin and so by Wadi al Miyah—both of these descending from the northern extremities of the Najd ranges and Jabal Nir—into Wadi Rima westward of the Qasim boundary. Whether in point of fact this channel ever adds to the volume of the Rima flood in any but years of phenomenally heavy rainfall is doubtful, and I am inclined to think, on comparison of its bed with that of Wadi Subai' at Khurma, that under present conditions the latter carries the great bulk of the torrents, which descend from the Harra, over the broad bosom of the Subai' plain to the 'Arq sands, leaving but an exiguous stream to trickle down the almost imperceptible runnels ot the Sha'ba to revive the coppices in its upper reaches.

We passed now into the gently undulating plain of Al Sharqi, which extends from the left bank of the Sha'ba to the foot of the Hadhn range, traversed at intervals in a north-easterly direction by the three great watercourses of Adh'an, 'Iqtan and Qurainat, all of which descending from the slopes of the range pour their drainage into the main channel. Ridges of rough basalt alternate with stretches of coal-black gravel and slag, relieved by the broad bands of acacia bushes which mark the courses of the channels.

"Back, back!" our leaders suddenly cried; "keep down along the hollow." Fantastic shapes were thrown up afar off by the shimmering mirage of the black wilderness. "See there," said one, "*Gom,* hundreds of them!" I handed my glasses to another; "*Ai billah! Gom!*" he confirmed the worst, "they have not seen us and are moving along." "Look," said another, "they have stopped, they have seen us; down and by the right along the hollows." We moved along, deviating from the straight track, while our scouts kept the suspects under observation, following the contour of the slope. We halted again to examine them; to me there appeared to be a long line of camels marching along a low ridge. "They are not *Gom*," said Izmai with cheering decision; "*'Arab, naïrin al ma*" ("Arabs making for the watering"). Some still persisted in their first opinion, but admitted that, whoever they might be, they were moving away from us; they had probably not seen us; if they had, they were trying to avoid us. All was well and we resumed our course. An hour later we crossed the recent tracks of grazing camels moving to new pastures; our fears had been unfounded. The distinction between *Gom* and *'Arab* roused my curiosity: the latter term is applied exclusively to peaceful graziers and *Badawin* at home or encumbered with their household *impedimenta*, or, in other words, to harmless gatherings in general; *Gom*, a corruption of *Qaum*, signifies the tribe in its martial aspect, and is used loosely of any *Ghazu* or raiding party out on business and riding light, as it were "cleared for action." The tracks of baby camels and of a few horses mingled with the heavier marks of the ponderous milch cattle; they had passed but an hour or so before; their story was written on the plain for all to read who passed that way.

About our midday halting-place in Sha'ib Adh'an lay a group of low rock ridges partly covered over with sand, the Adh'an ridge, from which the *Sha'ib* takes its name, close by on our right with those of Thuwairi and Hazm al Ahmar beyond it to the north. Farther on we passed a low hummock called Saq at some distance on our right before crossing the 'Iqtan; thence we fared on towards the ever nearing Hadhn, halting shortly before sundown some miles to eastward of it in the bed of Sha'ib Qurainat. While our tents were being pitched our scouts went out to scour the country from the rocks and ridges about us; I accompanied one party to a low hill, where lying prone upon our faces to obviate detection we followed through my glasses the movements of a small party of horsemen wandering about in a distant coombe; there were five men mounted on *dhaluls* with three led horses, in all probability the scouts of a raiding party following the tracks of the grazing camels we had passed earlier in the day; the latter were probably Subai' and the party we now watched Buqum. They certainly had no suspicion of the interest they were creating or of our presence, and they could not possibly cross our own tracks before nightfall, so we returned to camp hoping that they would not stumble upon us by accident. Izmai, now our *Rafiq* as well as guide, proclaimed at intervals the desert password and nothing disturbed our peace.

The day had witnessed a further shuffling of our *Dhaluls*; I began the march on the beast I had ridden the previous day, but my discomfort had become so apparent to all that a change was unanimously voted necessary, especially as no lagging could be tolerated in the altered circumstances. Tami surrendered his mount for my benefit, and for the first time I experienced the delight of riding a perfect *Dhalul*; in Himra, as she was called from her coat of sandy dun, there was no blemish; she alone, long trained almost from infancy by Tami, answered to her name, the mere whisper of which was enough to make her arch back her neck to receive food from one's hand; all things came alike to her, a wisp of hay, a lump of dates, a slice of girdle-bread, and even a hunk of cold camel meat; her paces were perfect and buoyant, walking or trotting, and for me the day was one of perfect enjoyment marred only by the thought that I had robbed Tami of the beast he loved with a passionate love. Henceforth, to the end of the journey I rode her and her alone, proudly conscious that I bestrode as good an animal as any in Arabia.

The Hadhn range extends about fifteen miles across from east to west, projecting from the Harra in the neighbourhood of Turaba northwards to the pilgrim road which passes between it and a northerly prolongation of somewhat different character, comprising a jumble of sand-covered rocky ridges intersected by bushy valleys. At first we marched over a rough flint-strewn down, in whose folds between two prominent knolls called Buraim and Bruma lay the wells of Buraim ; farther back on the northern flank of the Hadhn, whose height is probably nowhere more than 500 feet above the level of the plain, were said to be the waterings of Sulaba and Haradha in petty *Sha'ibs* of the same names, which join the Buraim drainage channel on its way to join the Sha'ba. As we crossed this *Sha'ib*, Himra, much to my consternation, began to limp, stamping her pad upon the ground to free herself of a painful thorn, which Jarman, who was riding with me, was able to extricate without difficulty with the rude tools carried for the purpose by every rider. While halted for this operation we heard from beyond the hills, which veiled the wells from our view, unmistakable sounds of the presence of Arabs watering at them ; I marvelled that they had not taken the precaution of setting a watch on the hill-top to guard against surprise, and when Himra was restored to her former state, Jarman and I raced to rejoin our companions, who had left us far behind.

The Barqa tract into which we now passed consists of a low sand-covered ridge running parallel with the northern flank of the Hadhn and a series of sandy coombes running northward between finger-like projections of the ridge, the first of which extending across our path, which crossed it between two great mounds of rock and sand, runs north-westward and forms a protecting barrier for the whole tract ; to northward of this barrier lay the tumbled sand-hills and rocks of the Saisad and Bitila groups, the latter a prominent landmark in the scene.

As we rose over the rim of the second finger-ridge a wonderful scene burst upon our view, and for a moment there was consternation in our ranks ; a broad green valley extended before us as far as we could see, dotted with bushes and broken at regular intervals by the echeloned projections of the main ridge ; on the slopes and in the hollows grazed countless flocks of black sheep attended by their shepherds, and droves of ponderous camels nursing their new-born young ; here and there stood a group of black booths of the *Badawin*. We had broken in upon the peaceful home life of the Buqum, gathered here in their thousands to enjoy the desert herbs, quickened into new life by the winter rains. As a herd of gazelles will stand and gaze at sight of an intruder, then break and run, so for a moment after our sudden appearance there was a stillness followed by a great stir in the valley ; the shepherds seconded by their dogs drove their flocks to this side and that up the slopes, the sleepers in the tents emerged, and a group of horsemen rode towards us. It was as if the arena had been cleared for combat. Izmai with two others rode forward to meet the horsemen, who had challenged us, and the rest of us moved quietly on to one side of the valley awaiting the outcome of their encounter ; anon we saw them meet and mingle in friendly intercourse giving and exchanging the news of east and west. *Salam 'alaikum, ya Muslimin! W''alaikum alsalam! Halo marhaba, ya Izmai! Chaif ant? Chaif ant? Chaif ant? Halak taiyyib? Lillah alhamd ala 'l'adl. Chaif halak? Chaif ant? Wush al 'ilm? Chaif al Amir?*[1] *Jakum al matar? Ai billah dharabna fi Najd. Wa shlun al khad? Wallah jaiyyid; Rabi'!*[2] Such is the greeting of man to man meeting in the desert, hearty between friends mutually recognised, and more formal between strangers mindful ever of the pursuing vengeance of distant feuds, and, as it were, sparring for position. Every detail is taken in by their keen observant eyes, and as they part each party falls to discussing the other ; "Did you see that pony ? *wallah*, a perfect beast ! and that fellow's *Dhalul*, a regular *Dhabi*,[3] a gazelle," and so on.

All eyes were on the parleying delegates, at whose parting the valley resumed its normal life and the flocks and herds

[1] Non-*Wahhabi Badawin* use this title for Ibn Sa'ud and are often rudely corrected by the pedantic *Ikhwan*. "What *Amir*?" they would say. "Why, Ibn Sa'ud." "Oh, you mean the *Imam*—very well," and so forth.

[2] "Peace be upon you, O Muslims ! And upon you the peace ! Greeting, welcome, O Izmai ! How are you ? How are you ? How are you ? Are you well ? Praise be to God, (I am) in good health. How's your health ? How are you ? What's the news ? How's the *Amir* ? Did you get the rain ? Yes, by God, it came upon us in the highlands. And what's the country like ? Splendid by God ! The spring !"

[3] *Dhaluls* of the best strain, light and swift, are frequently compared to gazelles, the Arab's ideal of lightness and speed. *Dhabi* and *Dhabiya* (doe gazelle) are common camel names.

scattered once more to the pasture. As we passed on, men ran up to us to get the news ; from afar off without greeting they demanded our news and running to our side broke into greetings, walking by us until satisfied, when they would break off abruptly and return to their tasks. With one man, ill-clad and perched insecurely on the crupper of the heavy beast he rode, with his bare shanks tucked firmly under the barrel, we opened negotiations for the purchase of his mount. " By God," he said, " it is worth 120 dollars, but I will take a hundred for it and you are welcome." " Oh," we replied, " we wanted something for fifty or sixty dollars, and that camel of yours is not worth more ; come, we will give you sixty." The negotiations were continued during the short halt we made for breakfast, but resulted in no satisfactory arrangement and we passed on, Tami and Sa'd being deputed on the way to visit the tents of the *Amir* of Turaba, 'Abdullah, who had joined the Buqum to organise them on behalf of the Sharif for excursions against the Subai', and who sent by our messengers an expression of lively regret that we had passed his camp without giving him an opportunity to entertain us to a feast.

At length we reached the last ridge of the Barqa downs and looked out over the bare expanse of the Rakba plain, dotted far and wide with the black encampments of the 'Ataiba, to the distant mountains of the Hijaz, towards which we now marched, directing our course by a great saddle-back peak said to mark the position of Taïf. In two days' march we had traversed the Buqum territory from east to west ; southward their boundary is the foot of the Nawasif about Turaba, and northward a line drawn east and west from Sha'ib Sha'ba to the northern extremity of the ridges subsidiary to the Hadhn. The whole tract comprising the Sharqi plain and the Hadhn range may comprise some 2500 or 3000 square miles, with a population of 3000 nomads and perhaps as many settled people at Turaba. The Buqum tribe, including the negro element and *Ashraf* of Turaba, is thus somewhat smaller than the Subai', whose northern boundary may be taken to be a straight line drawn east to the Wadi Na'im from the north-eastern corner of the Buqum marches ; southward their range is bounded by a line joining Gharith through the oases of Ranya to the southern extremity of the 'Arq ; round these two tribes circles the vast region of the 'Ataiba, who march with the Qahtan in the south, the Harb in the north and the tribes of the Hijaz mountains on the west. One section, the Thibata, penetrates the mountains and occupies the foot-hills between Taïf and Wadi Shamiyya.

The Rakba plain, on which we now entered steering south-west, is a vast sandy wilderness with plenty of desert grass and patches of acacia bushes extending from a line connecting 'Ashaira and Marran on the north southward between the Hijaz range and the Hadhn to the Asir high-lands, whose clouded summits could be seen in the far distance. The southern part of the plain is called Al Jarad, and is said to be of fine white sand with a thin covering of grass but no bushes.

It was Christmas Eve and we camped far out on the plain at a height of 3900 feet above sea-level well within sight of our goal, ringed around by the black camps of the *Badawin* ; the air was cold and crisp ; the full moon shed its grateful light on the peaceful countryside, where the shepherds watched their flocks. Irresistibly my thoughts carried me back over nineteen hundred years and more to just such a scene as this, when simple herding folk received the first tidings of an event destined to change the history of the world. Should one come this night with word that 'Isa ibn Miryam had returned to earth to gather the true believers to their God, the 'Ataiba shepherd folk around me would arise and follow him, believing and fearing not.

The temperature was down to 41° Fahrenheit at 4 A.M. when we rose next day to make ready for the long journey before us, for we were determined to reach Taïf by sundown. The baggage we left behind to follow, for there was now no danger of raiders to fear, and I with a dozen of my companions, mounting at 5 A.M., set out at a brisk trot through the chill morning. The coast of Hadhn gradually receded in our rear ; to the south-east the solitary obelisk peak of Ruqba and a hill called 'Ant stood out of the Jarad plain far away ; the cone of Saq in the southern part of Hadhn marked the point at which the Taïf road pierces the range on its way to Turaba; in the south stood the massive Taur al Akhdhar in the Asir mountains; before us lay the saddle-back hill near Taïf and the whole of the Hijaz range.

Three hours later we made a brief halt for a breakfast of cold mutton and girdle-bread near a low rock ridge called Barth; farther on we passed the solitary red granite mound of Hamra, at whose foot lay the wells of Mab'uth. As we approached the edge of the hills the plain began to break up into a gently undulating wold, through which ran a line of bushes on our right, marking the course of the Wadi 'Aqiq. Little groups of palms began to appear in the outer folds of the foothills before us. At length, having covered some five-and-thirty miles in six hours of march, we reached the edge of the *Wadi*, which, debouching at this point into the plain, runs between low banks in a northerly direction to 'Ashaira, situate in its bed, and thence past the wells of Tandhuba, eight miles farther on, to the rock ridge of Bisyan, twenty miles south of Marran. Beyond this point, according to Izmai, who conducted the *Hajj* from a point east of Khurma by way of 'Ashaira, water seldom or never reaches, but at Taïf it is believed that Wadi 'Aqiq runs, or at least sends out a branch northwards to Madina, and that in years of heavy rainfall the waters of the Taïf valley pour down this channel to the city of the Prophet's tomb. If the local view is correct, Wadi 'Aqiq, rising in the hills behind Taïf, must be a tributary of the great westward-draining channel of Wadi Hamdh,[1] whose source Doughty found in his wanderings in the Harra Khaibar, where rises also the Wadi Rima. The width of the Rakba plain was about forty miles along our route.

Thus we passed out of desert Arabia, the long upward sloping wilderness of sand and steppe, into the great hill barrier which fronts the western sea. Immediately opposite us across the sandy bed of the 'Aqiq, about 4000 feet above sea-level, stood a solitary grange, close by a small patch of palms and in the midst of thirty or forty acres of corn land, divided up into little square patches bordered by low

[1] This has been confirmed, on the authority of Sharif Faisal, by Mr. D. G. Hogarth, in a recent paper read before the Royal Geographical Society.

dykes of sand and irrigated from wells. Farther up the torrent bed we saw other palm patches, with a hamlet; the whole of this settlement from the grange upwards is called Ukhaidhar.

We followed the course of the *Wadi* upwards past the palm-groves to a little spring-fed pond, at which we watered our thirsting camels, close by the hamlet, a straggling group of mud and stone cottages built up the slope of a low knoll. The upward slope became steeper as we advanced, now in and now away from the tortuous torrent bed, running down amid a jumble of low hills and rocky ridges. Two miles above Ukhaidhar we passed another small hamlet surrounded by palms and fruit-trees at the foot of a small hill on the summit of which stood a stone-built dilapidated fort, and soon after rose up a long steep boulder-strewn track to a great terrace walled up by a solid dam of stone blocks at its lower end; the descending torrents are here held up to soak into the soil above the dam, on which crops are grown. Passing on, over and round the contours of gently sloping hillocks we left another palm group and hamlet to our left, and reached a small village situated on the right bank of the ʿAqiq, in the midst of a considerable area of orchards, palm-groves and arable land; on a little eminence on the left bank stood a delightful three-storeyed mansion of stone faced with gypsum or white cement, the residence of some local Sharif; very beautiful it seemed to my eyes, long accustomed to huts of clay and mud, as it stood out amid the sombre rocks glittering in the sunlight.

Here Ibrahim was guilty of a serious misdemeanour. It was about the hour of the afternoon prayer, which might well have been made before we reached the village; it would have been no new thing for them to pray unwashed, as they had done time and again in the waterless desert, but now Ibrahim decreed that the prayer should be said after ablutions at the village well and, careful always to avoid interference with their devotions, I made no protest. We couched our camels, and my companions hastening to the well washed and lined up to pray, while I reclined against Himra, seeking shade from the sun. I soon became aware of the villagers, men and children, gathering about me, wondering what manner of man this was that prayed not with his fellows, and I cursed Ibrahim for subjecting me to this unnecessary humiliation. As soon as I saw the prayers ended I mounted in haste and rode from the scene with Tami, Badr, Manahi and a few others. It was not till half an hour later that Ibrahim, Sa'd and their following caught us up, and then I realised the reason for their praying by the well. Their travel-stained garments had been exchanged for others more suitable for a triumphant entry into the town, and Ibrahim, at any rate, was determined to cut a splendid figure before the lads and lasses of Taïf at our entry. He had combed out and curled his raven-black tresses and beard; his raiment was resplendent; snow-white pantaloons protruded from the skirt of his *Zabun*, a striking "creation" of soft green cloth decked out with a red-brown pattern of *Kashmir* loops; over this fell the graceful folds of a pale cream mantle with collar of rich gold-thread embroidery; from his person distilled the unctuous odour of some strong scent; and he was unashamed. The others had donned holiday garb, each according to his means, but Ibrahim was the cynosure of envious eyes; nevertheless I thought that Tami and Badr, the nephew of the Duwish, chief of all the Mutair, in their dirty cotton shifts and worn mantles, were far more beautiful in their simple manliness. The true *Baduwi* seldom decks himself out in gay colours, which are the mark of the slave and the slave-born Bani Khadhir, imitated in this respect by the town dandies of nobler parentage, who think in this wise to ape the citizens of the great cities. Ibrahim often took it upon himself to lecture me on the simplicity of my dress, and could never understand my obstinate neglect of his advice; to him it was a crime that one, who had the means to do otherwise, should arrive at a town from a long journey in travel-stained garments.

We now ascended the torrent bed running down amid hills and boulders until we came to a low ridge parting us from the hamlets of Qaim, and skirting it on the near side entered a narrow passage between high hills. From the top of the pass we looked down on the fair vale of Taïf bathed in a dusty haze and backed by the high-reared

Palace of Shubra in Taif valley.

masses of Barad and Qarnait, monster peaks of the main range silhouetted against the setting sun.

2. Taïf

Right glad we were to see our goal before us, after about forty-five miles of strenuous travel and eleven hours in the saddle with but two short breaks. The sun was now low over the hills and we hastened down the slope and up the valley, past little hamlets girt around by orchards and fields. There was little to arrest the attention of our weary eyes until we came to the great four-storeyed marble palace of Shubra, the palace of 'Ali Pasha, ex-Grand Sharif and cousin of Husain ibn 'Ali, King of the Hijaz, towering above its splendid orchards. I marvelled to see a building so exquisite, with the great steps leading to the front door, and the delicate window-shutters of fretwork, in Arabia, and my companions, most of whom had never been out of the desert, stood amazed at such magnificence. This palace stands about one mile to the north of the town on the highway, which at this point runs through a ragged avenue of mulberry trees.

A few yards farther on we were received by a guard of honour of the local *Shurta* or police force, some dozen men and a sergeant clad in weird uniforms of blue cotton coat and trousers, with rifles and bandoliers to complete their outfit. At the word of command, given if I remember right in distorted English, the guard presented arms after our fashion, and turning to the left preceded us up the road in ragged pairs. With difficulty I resisted a smile at the amazement stamped on the faces of my following, who had not seen the like before. Ibrahim ostentatiously placed himself at my side at the head of our *cortège*, whose train was swelled as we progressed by crowds of children gathered to see the show ; among them I saw one with a skin as fair as my own, maybe some relic of the Turkish garrison. And thus, just before sundown on Christmas Day, we made our entry into Taïf by a gap in the broken wall hard by the barracks, and in a few minutes we couched our camels at the door of a house which had been placed at our disposal, the property of 'Ali Effendi, *Amir* or Director of the *Shurta*, who met us at the door at our dismounting.

From the Qurainat *Sha'ib* we had sent on Zubar of the Harb and the *'Ataibi* Hailan with letters announcing our arrival, but it was disconcerting now to find that this was the first announcement of my visit, of which I had hoped to find the local authorities warned by telegram from Baghdad; indeed I had hoped that a British officer from Egypt would meet me here to accompany me back to Najd. My expectations had been disappointed in both matters, but the local *Amir* had sent to Mecca for instructions, and meanwhile I was received as an honoured guest, being treated with effusive courtesy and the most bounteous hospitality by my hosts.

We were conducted across a narrow open court and along a short passage to the reception hall, a high chamber richly furnished with carpets and *divans* and open on one side to a small court or *impluvium*, in whose midst grew a few bushes and about which were set plants and ferns in pots. Out of this opened a small room for me to sleep in, adjoining which was a larger room reserved for the rest of my party; on the opposite side of the passage by which we had entered was the bathroom, with a floor of stone slabs and a marble basin fed from two cisterns by hot and cold water pipes. A great curtain of red plush hung on rings to one side of the reception hall, to be drawn across for greater warmth at night. Such were the apartments placed at our disposal, complete in themselves and very comfortable; whether they constituted the whole house I was unable to discover, but they seemed to have no means of communication with the adjoining buildings, in which I believe lived the family of our host.

It is no part of Arab or indeed oriental hospitality to leave weary guests arrived from a long journey to themselves; on the contrary it is expected of a guest that he should never arrive at his host's place after a long journey, or in other words that he should so conduct his march as to halt an hour or two short of his destination and arrive the following morning fresh and fit to be entertained. We by our late arrival had transgressed the Arab rule; and

Taïf.

paid the penalty by having to endure vigorous entertainment by our amiable hosts from the moment of our arrival till 11 P.M., when I craved their permission to retire to rest. In all this time I only escaped from them for half an hour, during which I enjoyed the grateful luxury of a hot bath in the *Hammam*.

'Ali Effendi, whose functions as *Amir Shurta* comprise the organisation, training and manipulation of the twenty-seven persons who make up the Taïf police force, was supported in the task of entertaining us by his secretary, 'Abdullah Effendi, and the local revenue officer,[1] Siraj Effendi, a genial hearty person with a rugged countenance and intelligent mind. 'Ali himself appeared to me to be about fifty-five years of age, a tall lank man clad in a long cream-coloured cassock, courtly and extremely hospitable, but not endowed with much knowledge or intelligence. 'Abdullah, who reminded me strongly of Khalil Effendi of Hufuf, was a typical official of the Turkish régime, full of cunning and ill-digested though widely-assorted knowledge. It was he who generally monopolised the conversation, exhibiting to the admiration of his comrades and mine a varied but entirely superficial knowledge of grammar, history, geography, politics, religion and what not. He was a pleasing person to converse with and, when speaking of matters nearer home, imparted to me much useful information about Taïf and its surroundings.

As we sat around on the cushions of the *Diwaniyya* after our arrival sipping coffee and tea, there arrived a representative of the *Amir* of Taïf to welcome me on his behalf. This was Muhammad 'Ali, a well-built, handsome man of middle age, who appeared to be a sort of master of the ceremonies to the *Amir* ; in a few moments he took his leave, apparently to inform his master that we were ready to receive him, for shortly afterwards the latter appeared in person. Hamud ibn Zaid was a pleasant youth of about twenty, grave, silent, somewhat awkward in manner and unintelligent on general matters ; he was, as a matter of fact, not *Amir* in his own right but merely officiating in that capacity for his uncle, Sharif Sharaf, who was away

[1] *Katib Takrijiyya* or clerk of the taxes.

at the wars, I think in the train of Sharif Faisal. His elder brother, Shakir, who was on the staff of Sharif 'Abdullah, was destined to achieve fame or notoriety during the coming year as the leader of several disastrous punitive expeditions against the stout fanatics of Khurma; three younger brothers were with him at Taïf, one of whom, 'Ali, was his junior by two years and the others yet children.

Conversation, as is usual on such occasions, was formal; I apologised for my unheralded arrival only to be assured that I had honoured rather than inconvenienced the authorities at Taïf; I had been without news of the war since my departure from Bahrain six weeks before and received the cheerful tidings of the great victories in Palestine and the capture of Jerusalem. The columns of the *Qibla*, published daily at Mecca and received at Taïf within twenty-four hours of publication, were full of the dramatic changes which the war situation had undergone; the latest issue received discussed the significance of Germany's latest peace note. I had been told in error that at Taïf I should find myself at the end of a telegraph and telephone line; though this was untrue, I felt that my hosts were at any rate not cut off from intercourse with the world as the denizens of Central Arabia; here at least the affairs of the world, though discussed unintelligently, were discussed as contemporary events. My comrades sat round the room silent and awkward as naughty children marvelling at the easy manners and courtly geniality of these men, Arabs like themselves but civilised, *Muslims* like themselves but exercising a reasonable discrimination between the dictates of their creed and those of their comfort. "When," asked Badr of me the following day, "are we going to move on from here? the air of the town is close and cramped; and I yearn for the desert and the camels and the black tents." I laughed aloud knowing why his heart was straitened within him. He was of the *Ikhwan* and had but recently relaxed to join in the frolics of my party; formerly he had ridden apart; a little residence among townsfolk would do him good, for at heart he was of the soundest. The soul within him, warmed by communion with nature in the desert, had been nipped and frozen by a creed. He was yet a young man of five-and-twenty summers with the rich deep voice characteristic of the Mutair; his nickname of Abu Saba', the seven-months child, commemorated the accident of his premature birth. For him these days of companying with an infidel and sojourning in great cities—for on this journey he saw Taïf, Mecca, and Jidda for the first time—were like the warm springtide dissipating the mists about his spirit. For a brief space he appeared to me for what he was, a very child of nature, tottering in his faith before the allurements of filthy lucre and sensual enjoyment. From Jidda he returned only to be engulfed in the accepted faith of his land and I never saw him more.

The *Amir* withdrew, shepherded away by Muhammad 'Ali; 'Abdullah and Siraj slipped away to their dinners and families, while 'Ali, giving the signal to bring in our repast, left a henchman 'Ali, a corporal of the guard, to attend to our wants. Two great circular mats were brought in and spread upon the carpet in the middle of the hall; on each was placed a metal tray with limbs of sheep piled high on steaming rice, whose snowy whiteness contrasted strangely with the brown mess of dusty rice boiled in dirty water to which we had grown accustomed in the desert. Such was our Christmas dinner, to which we sat round, myself and my twelve comrades, and of which little was left but bare bones when we rose to wash our hands and resume our seats round the *divan* for coffee.

For a while 'Ali the corporal entertained us telling us of his Quraish descent, of the siege of Taïf in the early days of the Arab rising, of the pictures on the rocks on the way to Mecca, and of the cornfields tilled by the Quraish and Thaqif mountaineers on the flank and summit of Jabal Kura. In the days before the capture of Taïf by the Arabs, with whom he himself had served, there was, he said, a Turkish garrison in the barracks. I asked if ever he had seen Europeans here before or whether I was the first of whom he knew. "Yes," he replied, "when the Turks were here there came officers to train them from the Germans; some twelve of them there were, but they never went outside the barracks by day and kept to themselves. We seldom saw them, but they were *Kuffar wa la yusallun wa la yukhafun min Allah* (Infidels who prayed not nor feared they God), and when the faithful turned to Mecca for the evening prayer they made a din of music." Later, when I reached Jidda and found the Sharif shocked by my intrusion into the Holy Land, I pointed to the previous incursion of Germans as a precedent, but ʿAli's story was stoutly denied as being without foundation. Maybe the corporal was romancing and had mistaken the pale complexions of Anatolian Turks for those of their allies. I give his story as he told it in the hope that the annals of the German General Staff may rebut or confirm it beyond doubt. In any case mine was by no means the first visit of a European to Taïf, for, to mention but a single case of which I was then ignorant, it was at Taïf that my wanderings first coincided with those of Doughty, who, brought here as a criminal to the judgment-seat, had been hospitably entertained by the Grand Sharif himself forty years before, and sent down to Jidda with honour. My subsequent passage to the coast lay for the greater part over his route. Before him Hamilton and Hurgronje [1] and possibly others had visited the summer capital.

ʿAli, the *Amir*, rejoined us after his evening meal, and ʿAbdullah came in later; with them I sat up talking till nearly midnight, when thoroughly fatigued I retired to rest, after giving orders that I was on no account to be woken in the morning, for a long series of long days and short nights had left me great arrears of sleep to make good. In a few moments I was wrapped in a deep refreshing sleep enveloped in the soft warm quilts of an Arab bed, spread upon the floor of my little room.

It was not till 9 A.M. that I woke to find the world already long astir. Ibrahim was fortunately away shopping in the town and, at my summons, Saʿd brought in my tea with a tray, on which was laid out an alluring spread of delicacies —leavened bread of local baking, cream cheese, fresh honey from the mountains, pomegranates and quinces. Long shall I remember the delicious luxury of that meal, over which I dawdled chatting with Saʿd about the iniquities of Ibrahim. My host hearing that I was awake came in, and I

[1] Yet more recently, and presumably with the approval of the Sharif, it was visited by Colonel Vickery, the British Agent at Jidda, in the summer of 1920.

conversed with him still recumbent on my bed. It was not till 10.30 A.M. that I roused myself for a good hot bath and donned my clothes. The baggage train which we had left behind on the Rakba plain had, I was told, arrived at 8 o'clock in the morning, having halted for about six hours during the night in the foothills and thus covered the distance, which we had traversed in twelve hours, in about twenty. I now summoned the whole party to distribute among them cash presents to each man according to his degree, and this completed, suggested to Ibrahim and Sa'd that they might like to select for themselves each a mantle out of the bundle I had brought to distribute among such as might be our hosts on the way. I did not know that in the bundle was one mantle of superior quality among others less splendid, and it happened by chance that Sa'd taking the first to his hand lighted upon it. Ibrahim, eyeing Sa'd's choice with envious glance, searched through the pile for its fellow, but, finding none like it, coolly turned to me, saying: "*Ma fih shai yajuz li*" ("There is none among them pleases me"). "*Kaifak,*"[1] I replied, utterly disgusted and registering another point in the already long count against him. I added yet another, when I learned next day from Sa'd that he had surrendered his mantle to appease the ill-temper of his friend; yet I held my peace to avoid dissensions in our midst.

Soon after noon a light morning meal of bread and dates with vegetable patties and saucers of meat mince was spread before us. My companions had already breakfasted as I had, but, when we were alone, had no compunction in ridiculing and commenting on the spareness of the spread. At Taïf custom rules that there should be but one square meal a day, namely dinner at any time after sunset. On rising and at midday they partake of light refreshments only; it seemed to me an excellent arrangement.

During the afternoon a messenger announced that the *Amir* was at leisure to receive me for the return call, which I had announced my desire to pay, and accompanied by my host 'Ali I sallied out along the street by which we had arrived. Reaching a fair-sized triangular open space

[1] "As you please."

constituting the camping-ground for arriving caravans or *Baraha*, I saw the low square barracks to the left forming the base of the triangle ; at its apex to our right or eastward stood a mosque with a tall minaret surmounted by a circular *Mu'adhdhin's* gallery and a pinnacle pointed like an extinguisher, strangely unlike the low-stepped platform of *Wahhabi* mosques ; on either side of this ran a broad street leading to a maze of shop-lined alleys constituting the local *Suq*. Round the *Baraha* and facing it stood a number of well-built two-storeyed houses of stone, the most of them plastered over with white gypsum ; one of these opposite the mosque and standing at the beginning of the more northerly street was the *Amir's* residence, at the door of which I found Hamud waiting to receive me. With easy courtesy he conducted me into a large clean room with white-plastered walls, carpeted and set with cushions along the sides. Prominent in an alcove in one corner of the room stood a large iron safe marked in large type with the name of an *Austrian* manufacturing firm ; Austrian matches were still, in spite of several years of war, a conspicuous feature of the local market.

Hamud, seating me by the cushions in a corner, took his place on my right with 'Ali at his own right hand, while his brother, 'Ali, sat on my left ; before long two other persons arrived, one a local merchant and the other a scion of the *Ashraf* clan, Husain ibn Judi by name, obviously a person of considerable influence in the town and second in order of precedence to the *Amir*. Hamud had never been outside the Hijaz and had very little to say for himself. Travel, he said, is not likely to appeal to a citizen of Taïf, who, placed by a bountiful Providence in a veritable Paradise with an ideal situation and a temperate climate, had little to gain by wandering in the pestilent Tihama or arid deserts around ; of the world beyond these again they knew little and cared less, for the Sharif, to whom he always referred by the venerable title of *Saiyyidna wa Saiyyid al jami'* (Our Lord and the Lord of all), did not encourage the *Ashraf* to venture abroad. In summer-time the population of Taïf is ordinarily doubled and trebled with the incursion of *Meccan* merchants and grandees, fleeing from the fierce heat of the stifling plains, but the Sharif had discontinued his annual visits since his revolt against the Turks, owing to his heavy preoccupations in the direction of the war. There had been talk before the war of connecting Taïf with Mecca by telegraph, but the scheme had been suspended for the time being. Most of the grand houses dotted about the town and its suburbs were at the time of my visit untenanted or in the hands of caretakers; only the local families were in residence, and the traders, impoverished by the suspension of the annual incursion from the plains, had for the most part hied to Mecca and Jidda to draw against Fate in the lottery of war commerce. The resident population of the town may be 5000 souls, and of all the surrounding hamlets of the valley and foothills around it as many more. In summer-time as many as 20,000 persons may be collected in the whole area to enjoy the mild climate of the mountains within twelve hours' journey of Mecca by the direct and difficult sheep-track, practicable with care for mules, through the gorges of Jabal Kura, whose summit, possibly the highest in the Shifa as the main range is called, must rise to a height of between 8000 and 9000 feet above sea-level. The elevation of Taïf above the same level is 5400 feet.

The sheep and bees of the mountains and the fruit trees of the valley and foothills are the stock-in-trade of the local population. Taïf honey enjoys a high and well-deserved reputation throughout Arabia; I had already tasted it at Riyadh, where the large store brought back by the returning pilgrims in the summer of 1917 had not been exhausted in August of the following year, what time I left the capital for the last time. It is in great demand in the markets of Mecca and among the uncouth, miserable highlanders of the Hijaz takes the place occupied by dates in the Arab dietary. Honey and sheep's milk form the staple diet of the mountains, as dates and camel's milk constitute that of desert Arabia. Milk, cheese and mutton are the marketable items of pastoral produce. The orchards of Taïf provide Mecca with quinces, pomegranates, peaches, apricots, grapes, melons, pumpkins and vegetables of many kinds; there are date-groves in the lower hamlets such as Ukhaidhar, Qaim and Marisiyya, but not at Taïf itself; orange and lemon trees are found here and there, but never in profusion. In spring and early summer, when the orchards are in blossom, the valley must be lovely indeed, but in mid-winter, when I saw the trees denuded of their foliage, blossomless and sere, it must be admitted that the scene was somewhat bleak; the lofty palaces of the wealthy stood out cold and naked against a grim background of rocky ridges.

The fantastic pinnacles of Qarnait and the sombre saddle-back mass of Barad are all one can see of the main Shifa from the valley; Jabal Kura behind the latter is invisible. I had purposed visiting the summit of Kura, where 'Ali, the corporal, promised to show me the gardens and cornfields clinging precariously to its sheer flanks, but my arrangements took no account of the disposition of the King and my project remained unrealised. The mountain tribes are the Quraish, the Thaqif, and the Thibata branch of the 'Ataiba; the valley is for the most part held by the *Ashraf*, the lineal descendants of the Prophet.

Taking my leave of the *Amir* with his cordially accorded permission to make myself at home in his domains and to see all that I would, I spent the hours remaining before sunset in a short walk with 'Ali, my host, on the outskirts of the town, returning in the evening to the cheerful comfort of our quarters, where both before and after dinner I was entertained in a manner which left no doubt of the cordiality of my new friends. I was more particularly honoured by a visit of the *Imam* of the great Ibn 'Abbas mosque, a jolly, well-nourished monk, who smoked publicly from a jewelled *Narjil* of prodigious proportions, telling me between the deep long draughts the story of his charge, and discussing the affairs of the world in a way which showed that the administration of the mosque and the conduct of the formal services by no means occupied the whole of his time or attention. The mosque stands just outside the south gate, a delicate structure of stuccoed stone colonnades facing inwards to the open court, in midst of which rise two well-proportioned domes, the one standing over the tomb of 'Abdullah ibn 'Abbas,[1] the patron saint of Taïf, and the

[1] 'Abbas, uncle of the Prophet and ancestor of the 'Abbasid dynasty, lies buried at Madina.

other over the graves of two sons of the Prophet, 'Abdullah al Taiyib al Tahir, and Muhammad al Hanafi. At one corner of the square rises a slender minaret similar to the one already described, but somewhat taller. The main entrance to the mosque is on the south side, a simply decorated arch with a central door. The building was apparently erected at the expense and on the initiative of one of the 'Abbasid *Khalifas*, and is much frequented by pilgrims, especially those of the female sex yearning for husbands or children ; the blessing of the son of 'Abbas, it is said, seldom fails the pious barren wife. I did not venture to enter the sacred building, but my *Najdi* comrades told me in confidence that what they called the heathenish practices resorted to therein had shocked their tender susceptibilities ; some of them doubtless saw here for the first time that praying for the intercession of the saints, which they had been taught to regard as the unforgivable sin.

Next morning I was woken to be told that the *Amir* had sent to enquire whether I was awake ; he had received a letter from the Sharif and desired to call upon me to communicate its contents. I dressed with what expedition I could and issued forth to the *Diwaniyya*, where I found Hamud and a few attendants awaiting me surrounded by my own people. After the usual interchange of greetings, he informed me that he had received tidings from the King. Ibrahim and the rest craned forward eagerly to hear ; I gave a sign that I wished them to depart, and, Hamud having given a similar order to his attendants, we were left alone. He then handed me a letter from the Sharif's secretary addressed to myself, which, translated, ran as follows :

Honoured sir, deputy and envoy of the Political and Civil Governor of 'Iraq ! Peace and greeting ! Secondly, the '*Amir* of Taïf has reported your arrival with your companions in the neighbourhood of Taïf to His Majesty, my Lord the King, who expresses his gratification and commands me to send you this letter to welcome you and to express the hope that your journey has been happy and propitious. I am also to inform you that the bearer of this letter, Ahmad ibn Hazza', has been appointed to accompany you from Taïf to Jidda, to provide you with all you may require and to protect you on the road. And if it be that your oriental companions are desirous to visit Mecca the blessed, they are welcome. I close with my respectful compliments. *Rabi' al awwal* 12th, 1336 A.H. From Musa'id, Director of Translations, on behalf of the Deputy-Secretary for Foreign Affairs."

The instructions received by the *Amir* were substantially in accord with the above with the difference that suspiciously heavy stress was laid on the necessity of sending the whole of my following with me. Contemplating as I did to return to Najd by way of Taïf, I was not a little disconcerted at these explicit orders, the motive of which I at once and, as it happened, correctly suspected. I could not, of course, so much as hint at such a suspicion, but I determined, nevertheless, to leave my heavy baggage and the greater part of my following behind. Fortunately the fatigues of the long journey from Riyadh had reduced many of the camels to a state of complete prostration, necessitating a long period of rest and recuperation before they could venture on the return journey. After much protest and argument the *Amir* acceded to my urgent representations, and it was arranged that a select party of us should start on the following morning, leaving the remainder to pasture their camels in the neighbourhood of Taïf.

I had wasted much of the previous day enjoying a much-needed rest in the expectation that my stay would extend over several days at least. There was now no time to be lost, and I spent the rest of the day in a vigorous exploration of the whole valley in the company of 'Ali, the corporal, and three fellow-*gendarmes*, whose untiring energy was admirable. By sunset I had been round and through the town, had visited nearly every hamlet in the valley and had been shown proudly round the old Turkish barracks. Unaccountably and much to my subsequent chagrin, though at the time I was ignorant of their existence, I failed to visit the idols of Al Lat and 'Azza, of which Doughty[1] gives a full description, and by reason of which, conjoined with the shrines before mentioned, Taïf enjoys among the

[1] C. M. D. vol. ii. pp. 515-16.

Wahhabis a sinister reputation as the home of ancient and modern idolatry.

The valley of Taïf comprises two fairly distinct sections, both roughly oval in shape and connected by a passage half a mile wide between the rocks of Dimma and the northern extremity of the Sharaqraq ridge; the smaller oval, in which are the hamlets of Qaim, lies south-east by north-west between this passage and the pass from which we had looked down on to the valley at our first arrival; an extension of the Sharaqraq ridge bounds it on the south and west, and a similar barrier on north and east; through it flows Wadi ʿAqiq, reinforced close by the Dimma hill by the confluence with it of Wadi Wijh, the main drainage channel of the whole Taïf area.

The town of Taïf itself stands almost at the centre of the greater section, which lies nearly due north by south and is bounded on the east by a low bare slope dotted with ridges and hillocks, on the west by the Sharaqraq ridge, and on the south by low hills receding towards the main range and connected with the line of the Sharaqraq by four prominent hillocks called Madhun, Sakhara, Umm al ʿAdam and Umm al Shiaʿ, in that order from north to south. Behind and a little way back from this western boundary rises a yet higher ridge called Ghumair, over whose shoulder to the south-west rises the mountain of Barad. Two or three low hillocks form a line southward in continuation of Dimma; low isolated ridges stand out from the face of Sharaqraq between it and the road, Musarra at the joint of the two sections of the valley, Riʿ al Akhdhar and Akabir to its south, and Umm al Sahfa about a quarter-mile north-west of Taïf, to whose south-east lie the ridges of Riʿ al Shuhada, Majarr al Shash and Qarahin. Such are the hills about the valley.

The Wijh channel rises in the heights of Barad and, dividing into two south of Taïf, descends on either side of it down the valley to coalesce with the ʿAqiq on the borders of Qaim; the ʿAqiq comes down from the flank of Ghumair and, breaking through a gap in the Sharaqraq, flows past Dimma into the Qaim area and onwards as already described. In addition to these three main lines of drainage a stream called 'Ain, having its origin at the foot of Barad in a living spring, runs perennially in a subterranean aqueduct past the town to the gardens of Shubra and the few hamlets immediately north of it, providing uninterrupted irrigation throughout the year to the richest portion of the valley ; whether the aqueduct is artificial or natural nobody of whom I enquired seemed to know ; there was along its length no trace of shafts such as would be found in any *Kariz* system, but I have little doubt that the channel, which emerges to ground level in a rushing burn about two feet wide about half a mile south of the Shubra palace, was constructed by human agency.

The hamlets are disposed in little groups about the northern section of the valley. At the northern extremity and to the east of the main road lie Shubra, Umm al Khubz, Qamla, Hizam and Mulaisa. Shubra, the most southerly of this group, consists of little more than the great palace standing amid extensive and luxuriant gardens, through which the 'Ain channel and its distributary veins babble incessantly ; much of the land here was green with young corn already six inches or more above the ground ; the rest was an impenetrable forest of fruit trees. The caretakers of the palace, which was unfortunately closed and inaccessible to us, live in a clay stableyard, in a section of which behind strong iron bars were four full-grown ostriches,[1] which were fed through the bars for our amusement by a hideous old beldam, who appeared to be in charge. These great bird-animals, two cocks with plumage of sheeny black and two hens of a soft dappled brown colour, had, it was said, been received by 'Ali Pasha as a present from Egypt some years before. The ostrich is still extant in the desert tracts of Arabia, particularly in the northern *Hamad* and in the Rub' al Khali, where it runs with the oryx, but none of my companions had ever looked upon one before, and stood open-mouthed in admiration before the ferocious inane-looking brutes dabbing savagely at the lucerne thrown down to them. Indeed, they said, it is but a camel with two legs, or the camel is an ostrich with four legs ; *La haula wa la quwwata illa billah* (There is no majesty and no might

[1] *Na'am.*

save in God). Close by the palace was a draw-well worked by a wind-vane. The other hamlets to the north consisted of small groups of huts amid cornfields and orchards.

Westward of the main road and about a quarter-mile distant from the Shubra palace lay the solitary hamlet of ʻAqiq amid a considerable area of cornland astride the *Wadi* ; the corn had been but recently sown and the brown soil was only just beginning to be speckled with the new sprouted blades. As I wandered in this neighbourhood an uncouth, aged, ill-clad peasant accosted me somewhat brusquely and began to beg. Having nothing with me to give him, I extricated myself with difficulty from his importunate company. ʻAli told me he was of the *Ashraf*, a resident and petty landowner of ʻAqiq.

At a short distance west of Taïf itself stood a string of suburban hamlets : the most northerly of these is Najma under the cliff of the Umm al Sahfa hillock. Here ʻAun, a Grand Sharif of the past, of whose greatness and grandeur they yet talk with bated breath, had begun to build a palace for himself hard by a spring-fed well ; the project was never finished by his successors, and the naked columns and half-built, roofless walls of masonry look like some great ruin of ancient times. Qarwa, the next hamlet to the south, consists of many stuccoed villas of wealthy Mecca merchants, surrounded by orchards ; immediately south of it lies Salama, of similar character. Still farther south and nestling at the foot of the Sakhara hill is Matina, a collection of mud and stone hovels.

Half a mile or more south of Taïf are the orchards and hamlets of Huwaiʻa and Shahar, the latter at the base of the Qarahin and Majarr al Shash hills. The catalogue of suburbs is completed by the quaint settlement of Yumana on the right bank of the Wijh torrent-bed. It consists of a small group of wretched hovels constructed of mud, stone and kerosene-oil tins and inhabited by a pauper population of *Yamani* immigrants, gypsy-like smiths and tinkers, or merely beggars, stranded here at successive pilgrimages. Close by stood the local slaughter-house well away from the town—doubtless a relic of Turkish times—of common clay.

The town of Taïf itself is four-square, each side being

roughly some 300 yards in length; formerly it was girt around by a wall of mud and stone, whose dismantled ruins contrast strangely with the neat houses and great mansions within. The central part of the town is occupied by the *Suq*, whose extent is out of all proportion to the needs of the permanent population, though doubtless designed with a view to accommodating the summer trade. In its rambling streets and alleys I found no system nor symmetry, the central square is of irregular shape with a mosque at the end, the Masjid al Hadi,[1] and the unpretentious offices and court-house of the *Amir*. Round the *Suq* to south and east are the quarters of the poorer inhabitants; to north and west are the mansions of the well-to-do. At the south-east corner within the walls is an old cemetery long disused; a newer graveyard has grown up round the shrine of Ibn 'Abbas outside the walls. The opposite corner is occupied by a fortress of solid structure perched on a natural eminence, a relic of the *Wahhabi* Empire,[2] for it was the great Sa'ud who caused it to be built after his conquest of the Hijaz. It is a complete square with rounded corners and loopholed walls; on its sides are the marks of much battering, but the guns of the Sharif's forces made little impression on its massive bastions. Though the walls of Taïf are no more, the three gates by which admittance was gained in the past still remain in their surviving fragments, the Bab al Sail in the north face leading out on to the main road, the Bab al Ri' on the west, from which leads the direct route to Mecca through Jabal Kura, and finally the Bab ibn 'Abbas opening on the south side towards the mosque of the patron saint. Near the first-named gate are the charred ruins of the Sharif's residence and his *Bait al Hukm* or court of audience, both gutted and fired by the Turks by way of revenge for the Sharif's rebellion against his liege lord, the Sultan of Turkey, before they surrendered the town to Sharif 'Abdullah.

Of the Arab siege and capture of Taïf 'Ali never wearied of talking; was not he one of those who had staked all on

[1] In all there are said to be eleven mosques in the town and one school.

[2] According to Ibn Sa'ud, though it seems to me that the claim rests on doubtful authority and that the edifice is of much greater antiquity.

Palace of King Husain at Taïf—destroyed by Turks before surrendering the town in 1916.

the *Jihad*, and was he not now corporal of the Taïf guard? In our wandering he explained the details of the siege which, carried on after the desultory manner of all Arab sieges, lasted through three months of the late summer and autumn of 1916. Mecca and Jidda had already fallen to the King's forces, and his son 'Abdullah was despatched to crush the last remnants of the Turkish forces in the south part of the Hijaz, or in other words to reduce Taïf. The Arabs occupied Sharaqraq and the outer ranges, with forward gun positions on Dimma and Sakhara, while the Turks shortened their lines by devoting themselves to the defence of Taïf itself, the barracks and outposts on Umm al Sahfa and Akabir, these latter being connected with the barracks by a deep trench, along which, explained my guide, thinking to impress me with the wonders of modern military engineering, the enemy could provision and communicate with their outposts without exposing a single man to the deadly fire of the besiegers. The latter had certainly no light task in bringing up their siege guns through the mountain passes, and the dishevelled state of the barracks, on which for the most part they concentrated their fire, is a living testimony to the good work of the Egyptian gunners. The barracks consist of a great oblong court surrounded by low masonry dormitories and mess-rooms for the garrison; in the midst of the court is a two-storeyed building of some size, the officers' mess, scarcely a single room of which escaped heavy punishment. I ascended by a mass of *débris* which occupied the position of the old staircase to the upper storey, where I found roofless rooms littered with splinters of woodwork and tumbled blocks of masonry; round the mess were the smaller bungalows of the officers, similarly disfigured amid pathetic imitations of flower-gardens. The commandant had during the siege taken up his residence in a subterranean vault specially constructed for the purpose of massive blocks of stone at one corner of the barrack square, but the Arabs were helped by traitors within the walls of Taïf, and 'Ali pointed with pride to a gaping hole in the vault roof caused by a well-directed shot of the Egyptian artillery. Unfortunately the commandant happened to be elsewhere at the time, and, congratulating himself on his lucky escape, he determined to take no further risks. He removed his quarters to the ground floor of a merchant's residence in the town, and the Sharif's supporters duly reported the fact to the officer commanding the artillery at Sakhara. The merchant's mansion collapsed over the corpses of the merchant's family, but the Turkish commandant was again away from his quarters. The next morning the Turks capitulated, and Taïf ceased for ever to be included in the Turkish Empire.

On the morning of the 28th December, having made all ready for a start and instructed Ibrahim to have the camels led out to the Bab al Sail against my arrival, I was conducted by my host to bid the *Amir* farewell. We found him at the court-house in the *Suq*, seated in a deep window recess overlooking the market-place, in a small room on the upper storey, in which was a seething crowd of primitive humanity apparently waiting with the noisy patience characteristic of the Arab for its turn before the judgment-seat in the window. Hamud was supported by Husain al Judi, seated on his right in the window-seat, while on his left stood a notable *Shaikh*, I think of the 'Ataiba, named Qulaiyil, apparently serving in the double capacity of expert witness and either prosecuting or defending counsel in the case at that moment before the *Amir*. Making my way with difficulty through the crowd, I seated myself at the invitation of Hamud in the recess between him and Husain, begging him to hear the case to an end before paying me any further attention. My request was granted, and I was privileged to watch the proceedings of a *Badawin* law-court. The case before him was apparently a trial for murder; complainant and accused stood before the judgment-seat arguing their respective cases, their voices rising to a pitch of furious wrath, and subsiding as suddenly to a gentle whisper, interspersed at intervals with gruff rumbles of laughter or light cackles of amusement, as one side or the other parried the thrust of his opponent by a quick counter-stroke of brilliant repartee. Here was obviously no matter of life and death, but of settlement on the common-sense lines dictated by *Badawin* custom, and, little as I understood of the uncouth highland jargon in which the case was conducted, it was clear from the smiling acceptance by both parties of the order of the court that the dead man's avenger was well content that his murderer should live to pay the sum at which the dead man's life was valued. An eye for an eye and a tooth for a tooth is no part of the *Badawin* code ; the blood feud brought upon himself by his bloody act permits the offender to choose between paying in kind or paying in cash.

An aged man now pushed his way to the *Amir's* seat and proceeded to recite a long eulogy of his own composition on the excellence of the administration of the province ; the *Amir* meekly submitted to the ordeal, and dismissed the offender with a few coins. I rose to take my leave, and Hamud, preceded and followed by his myrmidons, insisted on accompanying me to the *Baraha,* where I mounted with my comrades to set out for the coast. My expectation of returning to the scene of a sojourn so pleasant and all too short was destined to be disappointed, and I saw Taïf no more. I would have given much to be permitted to revisit it and to wander in the mountains among the wild clansmen, of whom I had but a fleeting glimpse in that crowded court. Arabs they doubtless are, but with little in common with the nomads of the desert ; with their coarse features, their wild hair and bridgeless noses, they seemed to me to be of some primitive savage race descending unregenerated by mixture with higher types from the remotest antiquity ; and these are the Quraish, the kinsmen of the Prophet.

3. Wadi Fatima

We retraced our steps of a few days before down the valley, past the Shubra palace to the first hamlet of Qaim, where we diverged from our inward track, following along the channel of Wadi 'Aqiq, in which at short intervals stood the half-dozen groups of houses which constitute the settlement of Qaim. A short rise over a rough boulder-strewn ridge brought us past the palm-groves and hamlet of Marisiyya, nestling in a mass of hillocks to our right, and a few steps farther on we crossed the 'Aqiq, here about a quarter-mile broad and strewn with boulders, for the last time, under the hamlet of Raghadh, perched on the top of a low ridge on our left. The torrent-bed runs down from here through the foothills to the village, where my companions had prayed on the upward march; at Qaim it receives a small affluent in a *Sha'ib* named after the village, and farther down it is reinforced by Sha'ib Judaira and the surface drainage of the enclosed bush-covered plain, which now lay before us. This plain, gently tilted from west to east, is bounded on the west by the long low ridge of Raihab, a mile away, on the south by the hills encircling the Taïf valley, on the east by the Qunna ridge beyond the 'Aqiq, and on the north, straight ahead of us, by the cross ridge of Wudaira.

Judaira, the last settlement, northward, of the Taïf area, lay back in a coppice of acacia trees, a quarter-mile to our right, shortly before we crossed the sandy bed of the *Sha'ib*, which passes through it to join the 'Aqiq; from here to the south-west we had a fine view of a group of hills of the main range, Qarnait with its knotty fingers pointing upward to the sky, Barad and the great saddle-back mountain which had guided our course in the Rakba plain. Maybe the latter was Kura itself or a part of it, but I was unable to discover its name. We marched on to the Ri' al Wudaira, a steep rough pass over the Wudaira ridge, beyond which lay a confused tangle of torrent-beds, storm-tossed boulders reared up in gigantic heaps and rocky ridges and hillocks. The Wudaira ridge, projecting at right angles from the Raihab to the neighbourhood of Ukhaidhar, constitutes a watershed of some importance; all the torrents which descend from the eastern flanks of the main range to the south of this line discharge into the 'Aqiq, while those to the north flow eastward for a while and curve round to north and north-west within the foothills, until at length they merge into the trunk channel of Wadi Fatima, which is to the southern part of the Hijaz what Wadi Hamdh is to the northern.

Local geographers divide the Hijaz into five easily recognisable longitudinal sections, namely: (1) the sea-board or hot country between the sea and the foothills, the Tiham or Tihama; (2) the western foothills or Sudur; (3) the

Shifa or central backbone of high mountains ; (4) the eastern foothills or Manahi, the extremities ; and (5) the Sharqi or eastern desert.

The rough country before us was well wooded with acacia trees and intersected by two main and countless lesser freshets ; we followed first the ʿAmaiza and then the Rajifa *shaʿibs,* the latter named after a huge mass of boulders piled up like some great temple of former times fallen into ruin ; on our right lay a chain of similar piles known as Al Jilla. Threading this maze of rocks and torrents, we came after about three miles suddenly upon the broad sandy bed of Sail al Saghir, or the lesser Sail, running from west to east, with a gradual northward tendency. Here was a springtime profusion of verdant herbs, budding reeds and purple-flowered thyme, whose fragrance filled the sun-bathed air. We halted for an hour for a delicious midday meal of bread and honey and cheese and pomegranates, after which I basked in the sunshine, reclining on the grassy bank and smoking a peaceful pipe in the company of Musaiyis, our guide and *Rafiq,* the leading *Shaikh* ot the Thibata, to whom is all this country of the foot-hills. A grizzled veteran he was, of not less than three-score years, well preserved in body, grey-haired and full of rough good-humour and kindliness. The Thibata, he claimed, is the parent branch of all the ʿAtaiba, holding to this day the hill country, which gave them birth in the distant past ; thus they are entitled to precedence over the great clans of Ruʿuqa and Barqa, which range the steppes of western Najd. He carried a pipe of rough clay and praised my tobacco, remaining with me to smoke, while my companions, having scraped down at his bidding some six inches into the sand for water and performed the necessary ablutions, lined up to pray. He looked up as the leader had plunged into the simple *formulae* of the opening *Sura* ; "More to your left," he directed simply, "*La tashmilu*" ("Not so much to the north") ; and the *Imam* changed his direction without interrupting his patter, while the line shuffled into position behind him. By my compass the direction was two degrees to the south of west ; we were then about twelve miles north-north-east of Taïf. Hereafter it was a source of amusement to me watching my companions at prayer-time; in the near vicinity of the sacred cube they had lost all sense of direction, and more often than not they turned anxiously to Musaiyis or those who took up the torch after him for guidance before marking out their *Mihrab*. According to *Wahhabi* precepts, prayers must be offered in the right direction, at the right time and after the proper ablutions; direction is all-important, for a mistake nullifies the act of prayer; for the rest time is more important than ablutions, and the latter may be dispensed with altogether, when water is not forthcoming, without vitiating the ceremony. In the matter of time, considerable latitude is inevitably allowed in the combined afternoon prayer; none at dawn and sunset, when devotions must be started respectively at the first flush of the real dawn and when the radiation of the setting sun has ceased. No part of the flaming disc should be visible during the prayer.

The left bank of Sail al Saghir is formed by the low lumpy ridge of Naba', whose summit is from 100 to 150 feet above the level of the torrent-bed. We crossed the ridge by a low pass into a rough hill-tract, which we penetrated in a north-westerly direction, along the narrow beds of numerous torrents until we came to Sha'ib Talh, a sandy, acacia-dotted channel about thirty yards across and running eastward to merge eventually into the lesser Sail. Some way down this we left the *Sha'ib* and struck up a petty tributary ravine, whose upper end appeared to be completely blocked by a cross ridge.

This was Ri' al Manhut, the most formidable pass on the regular caravan route between Mecca and Taïf. The approach to it from either side is a narrow ravine; around it on all sides are the bare inhospitable hills; a few tribesmen, well armed and resolute, could hold it against an army; yet here there is neither blockhouse nor guard. "The times have changed," said Musaiyis; "formerly there was anarchy in these parts, and peaceful caravans could pass this spot only by paying *Akhawa* to my tribe; now we all enjoy peace under the benignant shadow of our Lord and the Lord of all." The natural strength of this pass had not been overlooked by the ancients; the summit of the ridge to our right was strewn with the stone *débris* of a dismantled fortress, whose foundations may still be seen; below it a narrow passage has been hewn or blasted through the solid rock; on either side of it to the ravines below extends the road, paved with blocks of stone and walled in on the sheer side by a stone parapet; the ascent from the south was by an easy gradient, the descent beyond was steep and precarious. The Arabs must have performed prodigies of exertion to bring up their guns by this route for the siege of Taïf; perhaps it was only mountain-guns they brought packed on mules, for the way seemed to me utterly impossible for wheeled traffic of any sort and none too easy for camels.

We now followed the rapid descent of Sha'ib Raqad, thirty to fifty yards broad between cliffs rising to 200 feet or more. Two miles farther down we turned up the bed of Sail Ghurban and, passing a flock of black-fleeced 'Ataiba sheep in a wide circle of acacia trees, turned aside to ascend the steep boulder-strewn pass of Ri' al Zallala. It is, I think, at the head of Sail Ghurban that stands the weird rock-picture which Doughty saw,[1] and which unfortunately I missed, as Musaiyis, anxious to arrive at our destination before sundown, omitted to inform me of its existence until it was too late to turn back. The Raqad is said to flow into the Sail al Kabir.

With much difficulty our beasts, labouring heavily, reached the summit of the Zallala pass, from which we looked down on the broad torrent channel of the Sail running among low downs surrounded by higher hills of the Dimma range and the main range on our left. The descent was steep and treacherous over the slippery boulders, and our camels jerked themselves with stiff joints from step to step, until we reached the bottom and passed out on to a sandy down. The sun was below the summits of the mountains, when we reached the edge of the Sail to be met by the emissaries of the King, who conducted us to a group of lowly stone huts encircled by a rough fence of palm branches on a small island raised a few feet above the bed of the channel. Opposite us on the left bank of the torrent-bed lay the hamlet

[1] C. M. D. vol. ii. p. 528.

of Sail, a wretched group of stone-built hovels inhabited by Thibata shepherds. On our left lay the high hills, from which the greater Sail descends eastward to a low ridge some miles away on our right, over which runs the Najd pilgrim road to 'Ashaira twenty miles distant. The day's march had been about twenty miles, in the course of which we had descended about 1500 feet, for Sail stands at an elevation of 3850 feet above sea-level.

The party, which met us here, consisted of Ahmad ibn Hazza', younger brother of the *Amir* of Madhiq, and his cousin Ibn Sa'd, both of the *Ashraf*, with a following of about a dozen men including a negro of the Sharif's personal following. They welcomed us with warm cordiality and spared no pains to make us comfortable in the wretched little hovels. Ahmad, his cousin, the negro, and Musaiyis accepted our invitation to dinner and the evening passed pleasantly enough in their society. Ahmad had spent some years as a student at Damascus, whence he had returned just before the war, performing the whole journey of forty days' march by camel; he shuddered at the thought of such an experience and had apparently made up his mind to eke out the rest of his existence alternately among the orange-groves of his native village and at Mecca. For the most part the conversation turned on the question of the *Ihram*; my companions had come thus far with the idea that our march to Jidda would be by way of Mecca and that they would be able to pay a formal visit to the holy shrine in their stride. Sail is the traditional spot at which pilgrims from Najd and southern Arabia don the white garments, in which the pilgrimage must needs be performed. From here, after ablutions at the village well near by, they ride down bareheaded and thus they must remain until the essential part of the ceremony, the sevenfold circumambulation of the shrine, is performed, when they may resume their normal garments and go about their business. At the best of times the business is an irksome one, involving much bodily discomfort, cold in winter and heat in summer-tide. Accordingly, it had been resolved that, the *Ihram* garments having been donned early the next morning, we should make a forced march to whatever place near Mecca had been appointed for our evening camp and that thereupon my companions should enter the city, lose no time over the ceremony and return to camp and normal garb by nightfall. The Sharif's dispositions, however, upset their reckonings; we were to march by way of and camp for the night at Madhiq, nearly a day's journey away from Mecca; the wretched fellows were faced with the prospect of inadequate covering for at least two days. Torn between the desire to abandon the pilgrimage scheme and fear of the consequences of such an omission, they loyally declined to consider my suggestion that they should leave me to pursue my journey with the Sharif's men and themselves carry out their original design and rejoin me at Madhiq. Ibn Sa'ud would not forgive them such an act of desertion; yet it was ridiculous that all this fuss should be made on my account. I was as good as many in Mecca itself and, if it lay with them, they would gladly enter Mecca in my company. The Sharif's plans were not known, but Ahmad suggested that he might come out from the city to meet me on the road. Ibrahim had a gleam of inspiration: "Look here," he said, "it is not permitted for one who has assumed the *Ihram* to take notice of or salute any human being until he has made obeisance to God in the holy shrine; should he offend in this respect, his pilgrimage is *batil* (null and void). Yet, if the Sharif comes out to meet us, how can we withhold the salutation from him? Nay, let us give up the idea of the pilgrimage altogether." My suggestion that they should at any rate leave the ceremony to be performed on the return journey from Jidda was then unanimously adopted, and their dreams during the night were not disturbed by thoughts of a cold bath in the chill hours of a winter's morning.

The drainage system of the Sail downs is curiously complicated. The southern section slopes from both sides downwards to the Sail channel which runs east for four or five miles and turns north into and through a mass of low hills until, reinforced at some point on its course by the inflow of the Sail al Saghir, it joins the Haradha tributary of Wadi Fatima. The central section, known as Buhaita, similarly slopes down from both sides to a central torrent-bed, which runs down due west to a great gap in the main range called Insumain and through it into Wadi Yamaniyya, which, approaching the Wadi Fatima in the neighbourhood of the settlement of Saula, turns off again to the west and flows through a gap in the Mudarraj ridge to Mecca—it was by this *Wadi* that Doughty travelled as far as Saula when he passed into Wadi Fatima on his way to Jidda. In it are Zaima and other settlements. The third section, separated from the second by a ridge of low hills called Sunaifira, consists of a small triangle enclosed by hills on all sides and sloping down northwards into the Haradha.

From Sail to the entrance to the Haradha is only three miles over a sandy bush-covered tract, which we traversed early the next morning, crossing the Sunaifira ridge close by its highest knoll, called Sunfara, and nicknamed Jiddat al ʿAbid, grandmother or ancestress of slaves, negroes being familiarly dubbed *Sunafira*. The Haradha is a sandy valley varying from 50 to 400 yards in width and bordered by hills rising to 300 and 400 feet on either side; thus for two miles, when a broad torrent comes in from the right, in reality the Sail channel though locally known at this point as Wadi Baʿsh. Here we passed out of Thibata territory into that of the Hudhail, from all accounts a very primitive pastoral community distantly related to the Harb and living in extreme squalor and poverty in worsted booths of a diminutive type, perhaps not more than three or four feet in height, among their rugged mountain fastnesses. They extend along Wadi Fatima to the confines of the Tihama, tending bees and sheep and doing a certain amount of cultivation on the torrent-irrigated terraces found at frequent intervals in the *Wadi*; they also rear camels of a diminutive and extremely hardy highland breed, of which it is said that they can climb up the steep flanks of the hills as surely as goats. Musaiyis had left us at Sail pleading business; he and his servant had performed the journey from Taïf respectively on a fine she-mule and a broken-down ass, the latter collapsing several times during the day under the prodigious burden of baggage it was expected to carry in addition to its rider.

Barely a mile farther on we arrived at a confluence of

Wadi Shamiyya (Fatima) at mouth of Haradha—Ibrahim, the King's slave and envoy, mounted with servant behind.

Wadis, the Haradha, in which we had been marching, and the Birri, a broad torrent-bed descending from due east, merging at this point with Wadi Fatima or Wadi Shamiyya, as its upper reaches are more commonly called, by which the stream of Syrian pilgrims has flowed down year after year through the ages to the House of God. The alternative coast-route, passing from Madina to Mecca by way of Rabigh, is avoided in the summer season owing to the fierce heat of the Tihama lowlands, but at times the exactions and depredations of the Hudhail on the inland route have compelled the official *Hajj* to make a virtue of necessity, risking the dangers of the fever-ridden littoral rather than the savage importunities of a human scourge. In no problem have the Turks failed so signally as in the management and understanding of the Arab tribes ; on the Hai, on the Euphrates, in the Hasa, in the Yaman, in the Hijaz, to mention only a few outstanding examples, the Turkish flag has ever flown precariously over a scene of anarchy, rapine and disorder. Peace now reigns where it never reigned before ; everywhere there is a silent savage joy, deep-rooted in the hearts of men, that the Turks are gone and with them the grinding tyranny of their official rapacity. Wadi Fatima is as safe for the traveller as the roads of the Hasa ; in 'Iraq the savage hastens to forge his sword into a ploughshare ; in the Yaman alone the canker still remains, though its days are numbered.[1]

At our point of entry into Wadi Fatima we were about eight miles distant from Sail and somewhat less than thirty miles practically due north of Taïf ; henceforth the general direction of our march was westward with slight variations to north and south. The valley varied in width from 200 to 500 yards and the hills on either side rose steeply to a height of anything between 400 and 1000 feet above its bed. Three miles lower down we reached the first signs of cultivation at Umm al Khair, a hamlet of three or four wretched stone huts with roofs of mud, situated on one side of a con-

[1] These lines were written in 1919 before the drafting of the Peace Treaty which has withdrawn the Yaman from Ottoman jurisdiction, and before the rebellion in Mesopotamia which temporarily disturbed the peaceful development of the country under the protection of Great Britain.

siderable tract of alluvial soil, terraced by human industry into cornfields, in which among the stubble of last year's crop grazed a herd of sheep. These terraced fields depend entirely on torrent irrigation, the descending flood being diverted from the storm-channel by flimsy barriers of earth and brushwood into the embanked square plots. With one or more such flushings the soaked soil is ready for the seed, which is scattered upon it broadcast and left to germinate and grow until springtime, when the harvesters descend from their mountains and garner in the corn. Several torrent-beds run down into the *Wadi* at this point, Kharan from the south, Namra and Umm Takhr from the north, and Tala' also from the north descending sheer from a high hill, on whose summit, they said, stands the small hamlet of Haliana among its palm-groves.

Less than a mile lower down the *Wadi* curved round a conspicuous basalt hummock, appropriately named Khashm al Ghurab,[1] and ran in a south-westerly direction past frequent patches of terraced cornfields, in one of which I saw the work of embankment-construction in progress. A pair of diminutive oxen are harnessed to a heavy wooden plank, by means of which they drag up the loosened earth to pile it up in the required spot ; the embankment is then trodden down until it forms a solid *glacis*. For six or seven miles we continued thus ; here and there a tributary torrent ran down into the *Wadi*, Ghulwa and Izh'al from the left, Sammu from the right, in whose upper course are the hamlet and palm-groves of Sufaiya, then Qirdha and Qutba from the left, beyond which a high projecting ridge from the left deflects the *Wadi* somewhat more to the west. From this point, which marks the end of Wadi Shamiyya and the beginning of Wadi al Laimun, as the next section of Wadi Fatima is called, we saw the first palms of the village of Madhiq.

A few steps brought us to an orchard, at whose edge we watered our camels at the babbling brook of 'Ain Bardan, a perennial stream rising in the hillside on our left and providing the whole of the Madhiq settlement with water. Continuing we found the valley straitened by sheer

[1] The crow's beak.

THE OASIS OF MADHIQ IN WADI LAIMUN (FATIMA).

precipices on either side to a narrow neck, beyond which the tropical beauty of Wadi al Laimun burst suddenly upon our admiring gaze; orange and palm groves, banana plantations, and fields of young corn and lucerne blended their different shades of green in a wild highland setting; on either side the mountains reared their rugged heads to a height of 1000 feet and here and there stood lesser knolls of rock crowned with hamlets of rough-hewn stone. In the whole breadth of Arabia I had not seen beauty such as this; in all my wanderings thereafter I saw not its like or equal. Such might be Taïf in springtide, but here was nature unadorned and perfect.

We were welcomed here by an imposing cavalcade headed by Sharif Haudhan, *Amir* of Madhiq, and Shaikh Musa'id, the King's secretary, the latter mounted on a sleek, fat mule. After the interchange of cordial greetings they led us down the valley to the foot of the knoll on which stood the main hamlet of the settlement. We ascended by a steep rough path to Haudhan's house on the summit of the hill, where, dismounting, we were conducted into the *Madhif* or guest-chamber, an oblong apartment set about with cushions and carpets and tastelessly decorated with a profusion of European tinsel and *bric-à-brac*. Haudhan, a courtly patriarch, entirely unlettered and sparing of his words, was an older counterpart of Ahmad. A number of their younger brothers and certain of the elders of the village joined the party in the *Madhif*, where conversation, as usual on such occasions, was somewhat stiff and formal; the field was monopolised by Musa'id, who, as the only educated member of the party, was by common consent conceded the place of honour by my side and the task of entertaining the European guest. A plebeian to the finger-tips, a demagogue to the core, his squat well-nourished body, his beaming self-satisfied face, his voluble patter of ill-digested learning, his sigmatic Syrian speech and his hearty patronising manner contrasted strangely with the easy restraint and deep rich tones and courtly manners of the aristocratic peasants of the village. From a small leather handbag, which seemed to be his inseparable companion and in which, he gave us to understand by the air of mystery which he adopted when examining its contents, reposed state papers of the utmost importance, he produced for my delectation the latest Reuter telegrams and a French newspaper or two of ancient date. He discoursed learnedly on the latest developments of the war situation, and it was from him that I first learned of the death of General Maude. The main topic of conversation was, of course, the capture of Jerusalem and events subsequent thereto in Palestine.

I soon wearied of Musa'id and sought a brief respite from his company by proposing a visit to the orchards. Ahmad was deputed to accompany me, and until sunset I wandered in Wadi al Laimun. The valley extends to a length of about two miles from the garden, at which we first entered it, to a conical hillock called Luwaiya, beyond which lay two higher ridges, Mudarraj and Haradh, somewhat to its left and right respectively, between which Wadi Yamaniyya descends towards Mecca through a narrow gap. The valley extends to an average breadth of half a mile; through it runs the pebbly storm channel, to one side of which the stream of 'Ain Bardan runs through green fields and orchards until its waters are exhausted. The chief feature of this tract is its groves of oranges and sweet limes, which are everywhere in profusion though they had suffered severely two years before from a serious visitation of locusts. Groups of palms and patches of banana plants were interspersed among the orange-groves; gardens of chillies, egg plants, beans and other vegetables alternated with long strips of lucerne[1] and wheat. Here and there we saw stubble of recently harvested millet crops. We passed through pleasing hedgerows of *clematis* or some similar creeper, and I saw cotton-bushes in plenty. Cotton could doubtless be cultivated here as a regular crop, but there is so little demand for it and so great a demand for fruit at Mecca that every space and all the energy of the people are devoted to the latter. For irrigation they depend normally on the 'Ain Bardan, whose capacity is limited, and in seasons of favourable flood terraced fields farther down are flushed and sown with corn as in the upper reaches of the *Wadi*. It seemed to me that the population of Madhiq might number some

[1] Here called *Barsim*; in Najd the usual word is *Jat*.

1000 souls, composed of *Ashraf*, to whom the gardens and fields belong, and their cultivating tenants, negro freemen, tribesmen and others. The climate of the valley, which lies at a height of 1900 feet above sea-level, is sub-tropical, mild in winter and unhealthy and enervating in the summer heat. Popular belief has it that there are no less than 300 hidden springs in Wadi Fatima, of which but a few, twenty-seven I think they said, had been brought to light, but Musa'id informed me that the King was devoting his earnest attention to the question of the agricultural development of the Hijaz. An agricultural department had recently been constituted, whose investigations and labours may yet convert the barren acres of Wadi Fatima into rich corn-lands and fruit gardens.

An ample meal was spread before us on our return, rice and mutton with vegetables and some delicious Mecca pastry, which Musa'id had brought with him. After coffee had been served round, Musa'id and I were left alone in sole occupation of the *Madhif*. For a while we discussed politics in general and the politics of Arabia in particular. He talked of the Sharif alternately as *Jalalat al malik* (His Majesty the King) and *Saiyyidna wa Saiyyid al jami'*. I then plunged into the telegrams and papers he had brought, while he penned his first impressions of me to his master; and in due course we rolled ourselves up on our beds and slept.

It had been decided that we should camp the following night at Waziriyya, where, according to Musa'id, we should find all arrangements made for our entertainment. Accordingly soon after 8 A.M. we took our leave of Sharif Haudhan and set out on our journey down the *Wadi*. Passing two torrent-beds, Sha'ba and Luwaiya, coming in from the left, we turned westward along the foot of the Luwaiya hill and came to a wide circular bulge in the valley in which lay the cornfields and scattered stone huts of the settlement of 'Ain Jadida, so called after one of several newly discovered springs, on which the tract depends for irrigation. This spring, at which we halted to water our camels, bubbles up at the upper end of the bulge into a small clear pool, walled round on three sides with a gentle slope downwards on the fourth for the approach of animals. On our left over the low shoulder of the Luwaiya hill appeared the palm-groves of the hamlet of Saula in Wadi Yamaniyya, in whose upper reaches lies the settlement of Zaima. Our onward march lay along the foot of the Haradh ridge westward. Behind Saula to the south extended an endless vista of high mountains towards Jabal Kura. The *Wadi* from this point runs under the name of Wadi Zubara, being some 200 yards wide beyond the 'Ain Jadida settlement and dotted here and there with patches of terraced fields and an occasional stone hut.

Three miles farther on we came to the high cone hill of Abu Khasaf, from whose summit, they said, a view can be obtained of Mecca, and along whose foot the valley turned north-west towards a long low flat-topped ridge of basalt called Widhaf. Here the *Wadi* was joined by Wadi Dhara'a, and again turned westward; up the Dhara'a I saw three great mountain masses called Suda, whose shy denizens bring down the best honey obtainable in the Hijaz. The name suggests that they are of volcanic formation and belong to the great *Harra* system which extends northward to Madina and beyond. To the right and nearer at hand the peak of 'Aqar towered above a tangle of lesser hills.

The valley now ran some 500 yards broad between the Widhaf and the Naba' ridges to 'Ain Mubarak, where we halted to partake of a delicious repast of pastry and fruit produced by Musa'id, to whose disgust I insisted on all my companions joining us. Leaving them to rest, I strolled round the settlement to see the spring, walled round like that of 'Ain Jadida, and the extensive vegetable gardens, in which I saw melons, parsnips, beans and other plants in profusion; here and there was a little group of stone houses and a small group of palms.

Resuming our march, we left the *Wadi* to run somewhat to the north of west, and struck south-west into a maze of low hills, at whose edge nestled the stone-built hamlet of Raiyan; beyond this we passed a small encampment of the Lahiyan, a highland section of the Harb, in whose diminutive tents were a few wretched women and children. We now passed along a narrow neck called Riʿ al Luwab into the Shawatin, an extensive group of low hills stretching without a break from here to the left bank of the *Wadi* as far as Waziriyya. On our left ran a basalt range called Samra, ending in a peak called Laslusiyya. Our march had already been longer than we had been led to expect, and we hastened on through wide bushy openings in the hills as the sun sank to westward. A halt was called at sunset for prayers, after which we resumed in the gathering gloom until at length we re-entered Wadi Zubara. We searched in vain for the arrangements, of which Musaʿid had talked with such confidence, and eventually camped on the edge of the apparently deserted settlement of Waziriyya, after sending out a search party to look for shepherds and purchase a sheep for our dinner. Musaʿid without shame suggested that he and I should share the scanty remnants of our lunch, but I declined the invitation, saying that I would feast or fast with my companions; with that I retired, utterly weary with a long day's march, to sleep until dinner should be ready, leaving him much perturbed at the complete breakdown of all his arrangements. At 10.30 P.M. I was roused by the announcement that dinner was ready, and it was well after midnight before the camp was wrapped in slumber preparatory to an early start on the morrow, when I had announced my intention of making the coast without fail. Of my own companions I made sure by announcing that to every man who reached Jidda by nightfall next day I would present a mantle. At Waziriyya, less than 700 feet above sea-level, we were perhaps not more than ten miles to the northward of Mecca and some twenty miles as the crow flies from Madhiq.

"Each man for himself," said I as we started off down the valley, "and as fast as possible; remember Jidda and the mantles." Himra answered to the heel and I led the way at a swinging trot in company with our guide, a Meccan mounted on a speedy lightly-built *Qaʿud* or male dromedary, I think of *ʿArqi* breed. We were the best-mounted pair in the company and soon left our fellows stringing out in the rear, but gamely following. Between us there was little to choose and, as we rode, I bethought me of bargaining for the purchase of the *Qaʿud*, whose master would as lief have sold his head ; he had bred him himself from a youngster. The extreme rear was brought up by Musa'id still riding the mule and labouring heavily.

For some miles the valley was very broad between indeterminate chains of low hills, gradually converging to a point near the village of Jumum, where the *Wadi* narrowed to a width of less than a mile between a low range on the left and the mountain of Sadar towering above Jumum on the right. At this point the coastal pilgrim track crossed the valley roughly from north to south, marking the end of Wadi Zubara and the beginning of the next section of Wadi Fatima, called Wadi al Murr. This part of the valley was lined on the right by the three great mountain masses of Sadar, Mukassar and Dha'f, parted from each other by the two low passes of Faqq al Rumaidhi and Faqq al Karimi, while the western extremity of Dha'f ran down to the low ridge of Shaiba at a point north of Hadda ; on the left ran the low outer rim of the Meccan hills. The villages of Jumum, Abu 'Arwa, Humaima and Muqawwa, with their *'Arishes* or groups of reed huts and extensive palm-groves, extended along the foot of Sadar and Mukassar, while in the midst of the valley lay the scattered wells and corn-lands of Murshidiyya, whose main section, consisting of stone-built hamlets encircling white stucco villas of the *Ashraf*, lay at the confluence of Wadi Shumaisi, coming in from the hills on the left, and Wadi al Murr.

Having marched some twelve or thirteen miles from our starting-point we halted at an imposing villa, the property of Sharif Muhsin, whose brother, a courtly old gentleman, and other relatives entertained us to a delicious breakfast of pastry and sweetmeats, tea, coffee and fresh milk, using their best endeavours the while to persuade us to stay for a more substantial meal. To our left front lay the Shumaisi hills, through which runs the Mecca-Jidda road past the village of Shumaisi, in which was a small garrison of the Sharif's troops ; to our right in some low hills under Dha'f were the moribund palm-groves of Rikani, once a flourishing settlement but reduced to its present state of decay by the failure of the subsoil water ; between these two points the valley, nearly a mile broad, was choked with sandhills, through which the narrow storm-channel meandered uneasily. The sand was covered with a thick undergrowth of bushes.

From this point begins Wadi Fatima properly so called, running south-west down to the sea between ridges and hillocks rapidly diminishing in elevation. On our left, at about a mile from Muhsin's villa, the Mecca-Jidda road and telegraph line, the first sign of modern civilisation I had seen since landing on the east coast of Arabia, issued from a gap in the Shumaisi hills, and a mile farther down we were on the main road. Hadda was soon reached—a large grove of palms with a few stone huts, an imposing mosque and a few poor shops. On we went without drawing rein, past the four stone pillars set round the well of Umm al Qurun. Two miles on we reached the fort of Bahra, perched on a solitary eminence in the midst of the valley and still wearing the scars of a vigorous bombardment by the Sharif's artillery. Here we halted for half an hour to let our lagging companions come up; I spent the interval in the company of the telegraph master and inspecting the considerable local garrison, which turned out of the little stone huts, which served as barracks, for my benefit. Musa'id, hot and dusty, now came up and set the wires buzzing to Mecca and Jidda with bulletins of our progress. I suggested sending a telegram to Baghdad, but he met me with the objection that it would never do for an infidel to send a message over the wires of the Holy Land; eventually, with much demur, he consented to my doing so, and I left a telegram to be sent; whether it ever arrived at its destination I do not know.

Just beyond the fort lay the large reed village of Bahra, through whose main street we passed; everywhere were shops doing a brisk business, for the streets seemed to be full of buyers, presumably caravaners and travellers on the way between the coast and the sacred city. It was a motley throng of *Badawin* from the hills, Arab carriers, negroes of every shade from Abyssinia and the Sudan, and occasional Indians. A masonry mosque appeared to be the only solid building, the rest being shanties of reed-mats and wooden boards.

As we passed out of the village I called for a great effort for the last lap of our journey. Musa'id had discarded his mule for a *Dhalul*, and we paced out to the tune of *Badawin* songs, slanting across towards the right bank of Wadi Fatima; again the guide and I led the way and behind us streamed the rout. The block-house of Sudaiyan, inhabited by a small garrison, flitted past us, and about a mile farther on we reached the post of Bijadiyya guarding the entrance to the coastal group of hills, through which we now marched over a broad gently-undulating track, ever and anon passing a string of laden camels labouring towards Mecca. Here, as in the hills about Taïf, I noticed that the caravans move not in the open order in vogue in the desert, but in long strings, each animal tied to the one in front, nose and tail.

Next we passed a small circular guard-tower called Nuqtat al Baidha on account of the white stucco facing of its masonry walls, and came to a high rock called Kathana, surmounted by a watch-tower, at a narrow pass, from the top of which we descended to the cave of Ghar al Sauliyya at the foot of a *Wadi* of the same name, which runs down through the hills to Wadi Fatima. Here in former times among the ledges of rock, which they liken to a cave, brigands used to lurk, preying on the pilgrims; now, as we saw indeed with our own eyes, solitary travellers and even unescorted women moved from stage to stage of the pilgrim road without fear.

We followed the *Wadi* to its highest point, at which stood the guard-post of Ri' al Ahmar on a knoll, round whose base were disposed booths for the sale of refreshments to passers-by. A party travelling from Mecca had just halted here and was remounting as we passed; one of them, who was evidently a *Sharif*, urged his camel to my side, where for the moment I rode alone, and in mild tones enquired: "Whence art thou come, O *Shaikh*?" "I am come from Najd," I replied equivocally, leaving him to draw his own conclusions, for in the sacred way it were far from wise to proclaim one's identity to the chance questioner. For a while we rode together conversing: "It is indeed a long way thou art come," he continued, "and what is the news from those parts?" In reply I assured him

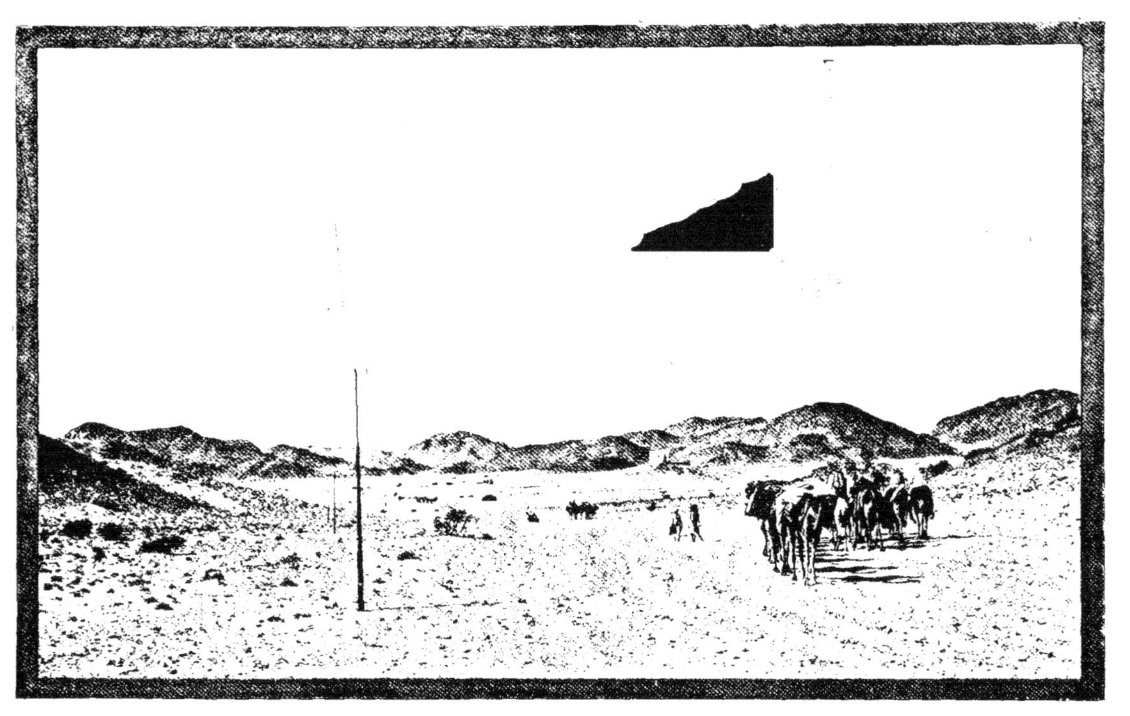

Telegraph line and Mecca-Jidda caravan route at Nuqta Baidha in hills of coastal fringe.

that Ibn Sa'ud was in the best of health, and that the rains had been bounteous, and he left me, for all I know to the contrary, unaware that he had parleyed with an infidel in the sacred way.

A broad upward-sloping glade led us to Miz'al, a watch-tower in ruins perched on the summit of a low ridge; the hills now thinned out before us to a steppe-like plain ending in a low rocky chain surmounted by the guard-tower of Raghama. Beyond the tower out of nothing rose a narrow strip of blue; our eyes, long wearied by the endless desert of sand and steppe and rock, rested on the soft horizon of the western sea, and our hearts were glad within us as we hastened on. Among us were a few, including Badr, who had never seen the sea before. "*La ilaha illa 'llah,*" they cried out, "*La haula wa la quwwata illa billah.*"

From Raghama, where a goodly crowd was gathered about the coffee-booths, we looked down upon the coral palaces of Jidda, enveloped in the midday haze; a vast sandy beach shelved down before us. We were but half-a-dozen who led the van; the rest were far behind. "More songs," I said to Tami, "that we may ride the faster," and Tami opened with the Song of the Camp, to which the weariest camel will respond, scenting repose and plentiful fodder at the couching. At length the weary march drew to an end, and at mid-afternoon on the last day of the year we streamed through the Mecca gate, our goal attained and Arabia crossed from sea to sea.

4. Jidda

Of Jidda,[1] the seaport of Mecca and, as its name suggests, the traditional burial-place of Eve, the ancestress of the human race, there are many more competent than I to write, but the record of my wanderings in Arabia would not be complete without some account of my fortnight's sojourn within its walls, of my doings during that period, and of the impressions I carried away with me of that city on the shores of the Red Sea, so well known to countless generations of *Muslim* pilgrims, who have hailed the first sight

[1] The word means "grandmother."

from seaward of its haze-bound mansions and minarets as the very portal of the House of God.

We had looked down from the Raghama ridge upon the city silhouetted against the azure of the sea, rejoicing that our course was run, and now, as we drew near, we found ourselves amid a litter of *débris* characteristic of the approach to so many cities of the East—gaping pits of huge extent whence building material has been quarried through the ages, piled-up heaps of rubble and refuse, and here and there in the midst of them shops and booths of the poorer kind established within convenient reach of an extensive open space, where caravans halt to deposit or take up their loads of merchandise. On the edge of this great camping-ground we were met by a very stout man riding a very small pony, which scarcely bore him along by the side of our fast-pacing camels. His name I failed to note and have forgotten, but he was a cheerful, prosperous individual, occupying in the municipal scheme of Jidda no less a post than that of Superintendent of Sanitation, and appropriately enough he met us amid the monuments of his activity—that line of rubbish-heaps so high that for the moment the city walls were blotted from our view.

Through a row of dingy shops we passed to and through the solid masonry arch of the Mecca gate and thence through the manifold ramifications of a vast and busy bazar, which recalled to my mind the business quarters of the great cities of India ; and as we passed along following our guide we were hailed from an upper lattice of a great mansion. Our guide checked and there followed the familiar tapping of a score of camel-sticks upon the necks of as many camels as we couched. We entered the great doorway of the mansion whence we had been hailed and ascended two flights of stairs, to be met at the top by no less a person than the governor of the city, Sharif Muhsin, at whose country house of Murshidiyya we had been entertained to breakfast that morning.

Taking me by the hand he saluted me with a kiss upon the forehead and led me into the room, his private reception chamber, where, seating me by his side on the cushioned window-seat and motioning my companions to seat them-

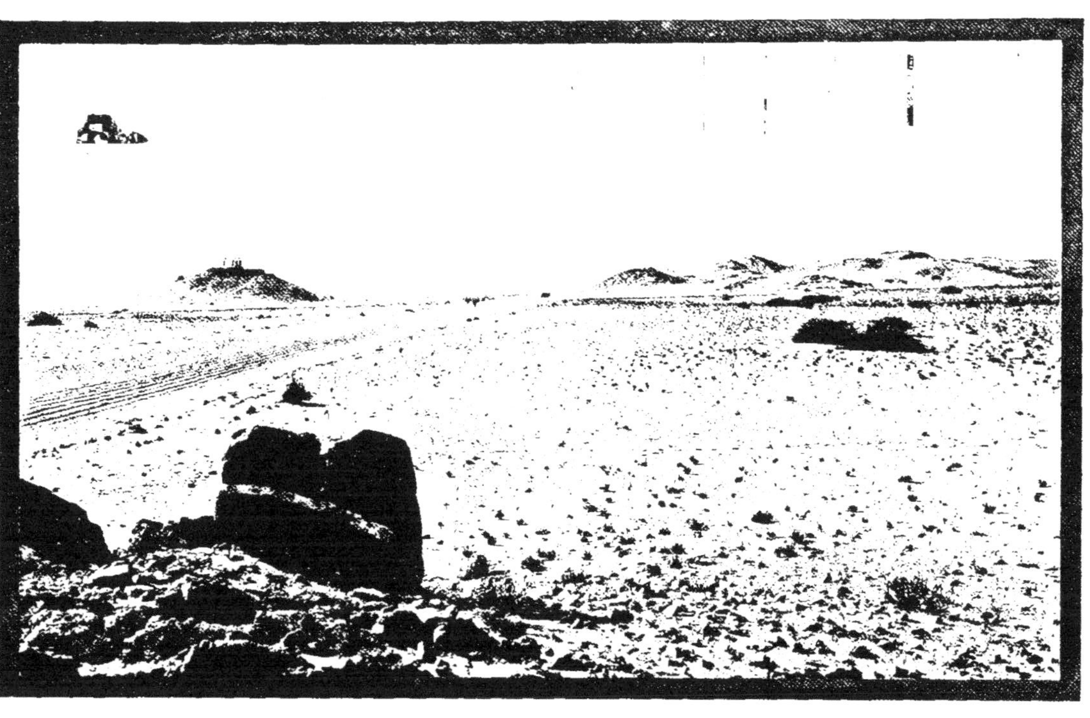

First view of the sea at Raghama.

selves round the walls, he called for coffee, and plied us with questions and the formal compliments of Arab meetings. A full beard, slightly touched with the grey of advancing years, and a kindly countenance gave him a venerable appearance scarcely in keeping with the reputation he appeared to enjoy of being a strong man, ambitious and astute, and withal a tiger to rule the unruly *Badawin* of the Hijaz mountains. He went into raptures over my appearance: "*Wallah chinnak ʿAbdullah ibn al Sharif*," he said. "Forsooth, you might be the King's son, ʿAbdullah; even so does he wear the dappled red *Kafiya* and the white head-band, and even as yours is his beard—all except the eyes; for his skin is as fair as yours." He then strode to the telephone, on which he announced to the King closeted at Mecca the news of our arrival, and received his greetings for us in return. Again the coffee passed round, and we went forth to our own beasts and, mounting, took the road to the British Agency, which lies within the northern wall close by the seashore.

British hospitality is the same the wide world over, and for that reason rather than for any lack of appreciation of the entertainment lavished on me during the next fortnight at the "Pilgrim's Rest," I leave the details of my sojourn beneath the roof of Major Bassett, the acting chief of the British Mission, and his companions, to the imagination of my readers. The days passed by all too rapidly; there was much work to be got through, much to think about; and I was anxious to get back to Ibn Saʿud without undue delay. Sharif Muhsin made provision for the housing and entertainment of the companions of my journey, whom from time to time I visited with some member of the British Mission.

The old year yielded to the new, whose first days were fraught with momentous possibilities for the future of Arabia. I had arrived fresh from strenuous conversations with the *Wahhabi* ruler in the land of his chief rival and much would depend on such negotiations as might take place during these days between the British authorities on the spot and the Sharif. Commander D. G. Hogarth, then on the staff of the High Commissioner for Egypt, was to come to Jidda to conduct those negotiations, and arrived on the morning of the 6th January, but the King, after keeping us on tenterhooks of expectation whether he would come or not in spite of a preliminary promise that he "would try and overcome all obstacles, especially those of his health, to come down to meet his guests coming by land and sea," did not arrive till two days later, when the real business in hand began.

The King, having apparently no palace at Jidda—for the public building known as *Bait al Hakuma* consists only of the court-rooms and other government offices of the local administration—had taken up his quarters in a splendid mansion belonging to one Sharif Taha eastward of the Agency, whither on the morning of the 8th January Commander Hogarth, with a shrewd little Persian interpreter called Ruhi[1] in attendance on him, Major Bassett and I repaired for our first formal audience with His Majesty. There was little pomp or circumstance about the ceremony, for the King received us in an upper chamber as any Arab chief might have done in the circumstances—not without a kingly jest at my appearance, "*Najdi*" he called me, and even "the Lawrence of Najd," and on several occasions "*Ibni*" ("my child"), an endearment which for some reason he did not lavish on my companions. Coffee was more after the Turkish manner than the Arab, and I think we had some sweet, cool beverage as well, while we sat on chairs and not on the floor. The proceedings on this occasion were of a purely formal character and controversial topics were not touched upon. Commander Hogarth opened with a financial announcement which cannot but have given pleasure to his royal hearer, who graciously accepted also a miniature American flag sent by an American admirer in token of his appreciation of the King's services to the world. In reply, the King declared that in heading the Arab revolt as he had done he had nothing in mind but to serve the interests of the whole world and particularly those of *Islam*, whose prosperity, he felt convinced, would ever depend on the assistance and goodwill of Great Britain.

[1] He was a native of Tabriz and, I think, of the *Bahai* persuasion; his services to the British Government had been of very great value.

PART OF AUTHOR'S ESCORT MOUNTED AT JIDDA.

The conversation passed on to Faisal's plans, already well in train, for an advance northwards. Damascus, said the King, would rise in his favour and communication could then be established with Baghdad. We spoke too of Ibn Rashid, who was supposed at that time to be practically a prisoner in the Turkish camp at Al Hajr, this in turn being besieged by a Sharifian force, which, however, owing to unfavourable weather conditions and lack of fodder, had been compelled to withdraw to a better vantage-ground. The audience closed in an atmosphere of goodwill and amity after I had presented the compliments of Sir Percy Cox and we had discussed the details and fatigues of the King's journey from Mecca to Jidda during the previous night. For all his years—he must at that time have been not less than sixty—the King still retained the bodily vigour of a man in his prime, and, though he preferred to ride a mule as being more comfortable than a camel, he made light of the journey which he had made in one stage almost without a break.

Though he has had a full share of *Badawin* life and showed himself at times to have an intimate knowledge of the details of *Badawin* occupations—of camels, of the herbs of the desert, and the like, subjects on which he conversed with evident delight and in the most delightful manner, King Husain, both in appearance and deportment, reminded one rather of a Persian *Mujtahid* or Turkish *Mufti* than of an Arab. Polite and polished of manner, gentle, slow and somewhat hesitating of speech, he only betrays his pure Arabian descent in moments of strong emotion, when, throwing to the winds the clumsy honorifics he has borrowed from a Turkish education for ordinary purposes, he launches forth into the resonant periods of Arabian eloquence and the full-throated accents which can only be heard in *Badawin* assemblies. He addressed us collectively as "*Hadhrat al Afadhil*"[1] or "*Hadhrat al 'Aïzza*,"[2] and had already trained his court to address him in public by the horrible appellation of "*Jalalatukum*,"[3] though such as Sharif Muhsin and others of the old school could not forget the more pleasing and more appropriate "*Ya Sidi*."[4] Such out-

[1] Noble Sirs. [2] Honoured Sirs. [3] Your Majesty. [4] O my Lord.

landish words as *adabsiz*[1] occurred frequently in his conversation.

In recognition of his revolt against the Turks the British Government had conferred on him the style and title of "King of the Hijaz," but, not considering this an adequate description of the *rôle* he aspired to play in the affairs of Arabia, he had arrogated to himself the more comprehensive title of "*Malik Bilad al 'Arab*" or "*Malik Diyar al 'Arabiyya*"—the "King of the Arab Countries"—and all attempts to argue him out of this position were met by the complete and sufficient retort that it would be much easier to become King of the Arabs by dint of being so addressed than to earn the right of being so addressed by becoming King of the Arabs. The vicious circle did not distress him, but he did object to the British authorities in Egypt and elsewhere addressing him as "King of the Hijaz" in reply to communications signed by him as "King of the Arab Countries," and he objected still more to Ibn Sa'ud answering to the Sharif of Mecca letters received from the "King of the Arabs." The dream of an Arabian Empire under his own rule was in those days a pet obsession of King Husain, but he has lived to realise that those castles were built in the air to be shattered not so much by those who resisted his ambitions from the beginning, as by the son, to whom he had entrusted the command of his northern army, and who from the day of 'Aqaba, if not before, had determined to carve out a kingdom for himself independently of his father's schemes. In those days the ideal of Arab unity, on which the late Sir Mark Sykes had set his hopes, still loomed large on the political horizon, but the phantom was already beginning to fade away before the hands outstretched to grasp it. Of all that mighty fabric there remains now nought but a royal title and the barren kingdom of the Hijaz, and, now that all the bickering and argument are over, one cannot but sympathise with King Husain and reflect that he might well have secured the substance of his dreams had he not of his too great ambition grasped at the shadow beyond his reach.

Our first formal audience of the King was followed the

[1] Mannerless—a Turkish word.

same afternoon by a long preliminary conference with him for the discussion of the business that had brought us together, and similar audiences followed on the next two days. By that time it was clear that all immediate hopes of a satisfactory understanding between the King and Ibn Sa'ud were vain, and I abstained from further attendance at the ensuing audiences until the day before my departure, when somewhat unwillingly I attended the last conference to bid the King farewell.

That at this period he regarded, and probably rightly regarded, Ibn Sa'ud as the chief obstacle to the realisation of his ambitions seems to admit of little doubt, and it is not surprising in the circumstances that he should have regarded me, formally accredited as I was to the *Wahhabi* court with the enlistment of Ibn Sa'ud's assistance in the Allied cause as the main object of my mission, with suspicion and coldness. Unfortunately news of my coming had not reached the King until I had actually arrived at Taïf, and it was perhaps excusable that he could not divest himself of a suspicion that my descent upon his territories was the result of a deep-laid scheme on the part of the British Government to force his hand. At any rate he had no reason to be pleased with me for showing that the plea, on which he had refused to allow a British officer to go from his territory to Najd, was untenable, and he showed his irritation in the uncompromising attitude he adopted at these conferences whenever Ibn Sa'ud's affairs came under consideration.

He made little secret of his objection to the utilisation of his rival's services in any form for the furtherance of our designs or of his conviction of Ibn Sa'ud's untrustworthiness or, again, of his fear that our dealings with Central Arabia might involve a modification of the undertakings into which we had entered with himself. He seemed to have a more grandiose conception of those *Muqarrarat*,[1] as he termed them, than was justified by the facts, and to all arguments that Ibn Sa'ud's services might be advantageously used for the furtherance of the common cause he replied that he already had his own schemes matured and completely sufficient for the attainment of the objects in view, and

[1] Agreements or promises.

begged us to trust him and leave matters to him in the assurance that all would be well in its own proper time. Of the details of our discussions it is unnecessary here to speak; suffice it to say that, in face of the King's attitude, the negotiations, so far as the objects of my own mission were concerned, broke down completely and left me with no alternative but to ask the royal permission to return whence I had come.

Now, when I had set out from Taïf at the King's invitation to come down to Jidda, I had taken the precaution of leaving half my escort with all my heavy baggage there, with strict injunctions to the man in charge of the former to remain there without fail until my return. The more weary of our camels would thus enjoy the rest they had earned, and my return to Taïf would be assured; but my shrewdest calculations were of little avail in the face of events over which I had no control. My suspicions of the King's designs were first aroused by the tenour of his instructions to the *Amir* of Taïf and confirmed by a casual hint from Musa'id, the secretary, when I met him at Madhiq, that I doubtless did not contemplate returning to Najd by the land route and that it would be more comfortable to return by sea. He had actually suggested on that occasion that I should send for the rest of my party, but I had assured him in reply that my intention was indeed to return by land as I had come. There the matter rested until the third day after my arrival at Jidda, when Ibrahim informed me casually that Sharif Muhsin had received telephonic intimation from Mecca to the effect that the King had written to my people "giving them the choice" of remaining at Taïf or paying him a visit at Mecca, and that, bag and baggage, they had arrived at Mecca that day. That communication could have but one meaning, and my suspicions were confirmed by a conversation on the following day with Musa'id, in the course of which he suggested that, now that the party was at Mecca, it would be best for them to join me at Jidda. I protested against the action which had been taken without my knowledge and pressed Musa'id to arrange for their immediate return to Taïf to enable them to rest their camels before our return journey,

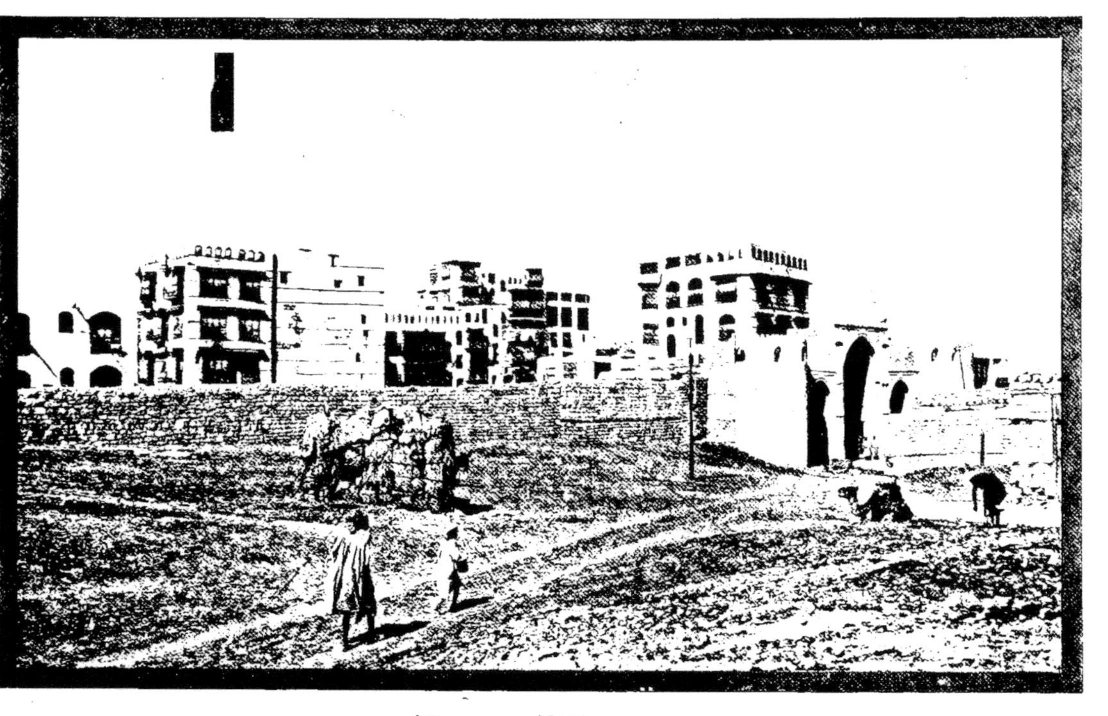

JIDDA—THE MECCA GATE.

and at the same time I wrote a letter to the King thanking him for his courtesy in inviting my men to Mecca, expressing the hope that they were not giving any trouble and begging that they should be sent back to Taïf as soon as possible to be ready for the return journey.

At Mecca, however, they remained in spite of all my representations, and it was clear that the King had no intention of allowing me to return through his territory; but the climax only came at the close of our third business conference, when, seeing that no good could possibly come of further negotiations, I asked the King's permission to depart on the ground that I had already unduly prolonged my sojourn at Jidda. He then showed his colours: he could not possibly think of letting me go back through his territory; my arrival in it had already created much comment and criticism and people were saying that he had sold his country to the English. "That," I replied, "is exactly what the *Wahhabis* say of my being in Najd, but Ibn Sa'ud silences them by declaring that the presence of an Englishman in Najd will prove advantageous to him." It was vain to argue with one whose motive[1] was so obviously to slight Ibn Sa'ud, and the conference terminated somewhat abruptly, with a feeling of high tension all round. I need dwell no longer on a scene so distasteful, after which I saw the King no more until I went to say good-bye to him on the day before I left Jidda by sea. On that occasion, politics having by common consent been eschewed during the audience, the King expressed the hope, as we rose to take our leave, that we would come in due course to accept his view of Ibn Sa'ud's unworthiness. "I was sent to Najd," I replied, "by the British Government to see things there with my own eyes, and it is my misfortune that I have arrived at conclusions widely differing from those of Your Majesty." This remark seemed in danger of precipitating another "scene," which, however, Commander Hogarth tactfully averted with the result that, as we went forward to

[1] Lest it may be thought that the King was inspired by any other motive it is, perhaps, necessary to state that not only had he himself invited British officers to visit Taïf the previous summer, but actually allowed one to visit the same place during the summer of this year (1920).

shake hands with the proud old tyrant, he singled me out for the honour of a kiss upon the forehead. "I am very sorry" I said, "that my visit to Your Majesty has produced no good results."

The heavy official preoccupations of these first days had left me but little leisure either to explore the city and its surroundings or to make the acquaintance of its chief residents and visitors, but the culmination of the royal audiences in the anti-climax I have just described left me free to roam about during the last few days of my sojourn. The lofty mansion, in which the British Mission was accommodated, lies somewhat westward of the northern gate of the city, looking out over the wall and a small bay towards a group of three of four hamlets of reed huts, known collectively as Ruwais, a settlement with an unsavoury reputation as a den of smugglers and slave-traders, who not only resent visitors but have been known to repel them with violence. On a small promontory jutting into the bay the officers of the British Mission had constructed a golf-links, whose eastern side marched with a maze of trenches made by the last Turkish garrison, and the scene on this side was completed by the local barracks, over which the Sharifian flag of the four emblematic colours now flew in place of the Ottoman ensign, and the great walled cemetery whose most conspicuous feature was the green cupola of Eve's tomb.

A short avenue of struggling trees leads out from the northern gate to the front of the barracks, a modern white building of considerable dimensions, before whose doors were disposed a number of serviceable or unserviceable guns. Within are the quarters of the local garrison and the Sharifian general staff, presided over by *Yuzbashi* Kaisuni, once an officer in the Egyptian army, but now Minister of War in the Hijaz administration. I had the pleasure of taking coffee with him in his rooms and of conversing with him in English, a language he spoke very fairly. Whether he was an efficient War Minister I cannot say, but I had no reason to complain of his very cordial reception or of the interest he took in the political difficulties of the time, a subject on which he talked with an independence of judgment, which was both surprising and refreshing in a

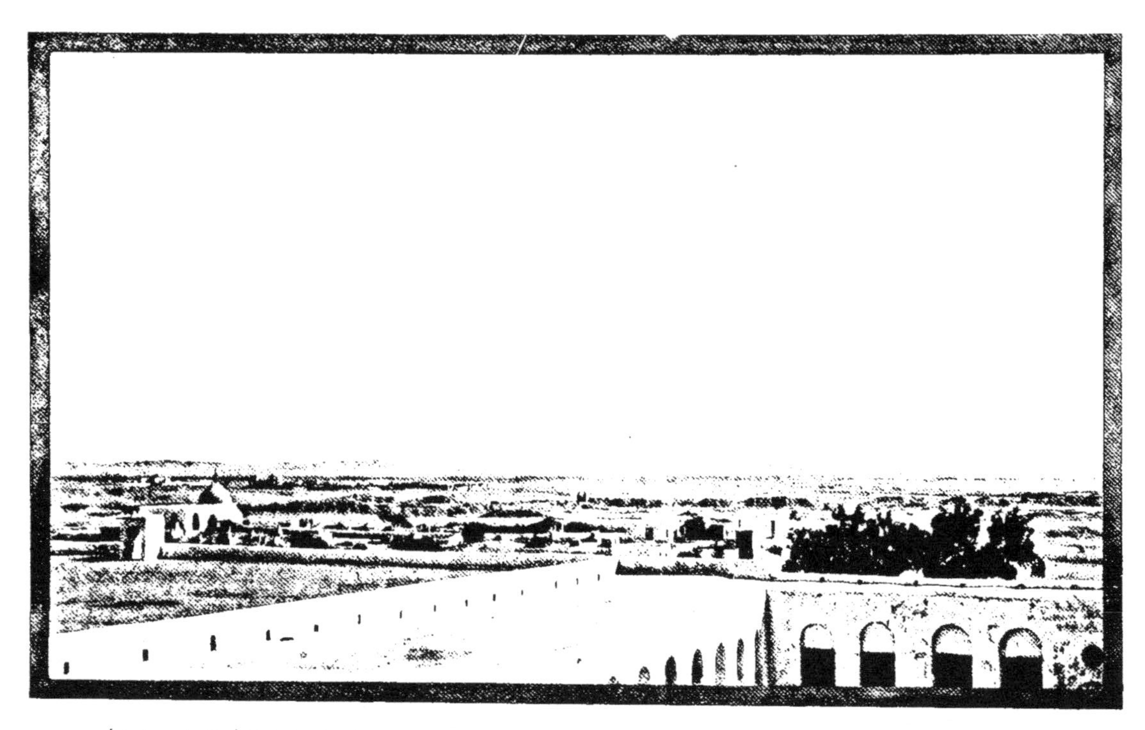

JIDDA.—THE SHARIFIAN BARRACKS IN FOREGROUND AND THE TOMB OF EVE IN CEMETERY BEHIND.

member of the King's cabinet. He was good enough to give me some excellent photographs of Mecca and its surroundings and to conduct me on to the roof of the barracks, that I might the better see Jidda and the mountains which shut in its beach on the east. I left him with a request that he should use his good offices with the King to procure a reconsideration of his verdict regarding my return overland to Najd, but when I next saw him on my way to my last royal interview he whispered hurriedly in my ear that he had tried and failed. Altogether he seemed to me a man of great parts and promise, and if he is typical of the products of the Egyptian army the British authorities in Egypt are to be congratulated on the success of their methods. Another of the Sharifian officers I met on the occasion of my visit to Kaisuni in the barracks was Munir ibn 'Abdullah, a native of Baghdad, who had fought against the British forces in Mesopotamia at Kut al Zain and been taken prisoner subsequently at Nasiriyya. From the Prisoners of War Camp in Burma he had been released to fight for the Sharif, in whose service he seemed to be more than content with his lot.

The roof of the barracks overlooks the cemetery, which also I visited to have a near view of Eve's tomb, the only structure of any merit in the whole enclosure. It comprises a long and narrow rectangular enclosure surrounded by a low white-plastered wall, perhaps seventy or eighty feet in length and but a few feet wide; in a central position astride the enclosure, which is supposed to cover the remains of the mother of the human race, stands the shrine itself, surmounted by the greenish dome and covering a double slab of stone with a marked indentation representing the *Surra* or navel of Eve and covered over by a tawdry square canopy of the kind common to *Muslim* tombs. At the door stood the guardian of the tomb, a woman, of course, who with one or two others, including a saucy wench—apparently a casual visitor—were not backward in claiming their share of the contributions expected of all visitors to the shrine, and who in return for my mite vouchsafed me a glimpse of the venerable relic.

The city of Jidda is hemmed in by solid walls on the three

land-faces to north, east and south, and these are continued along the sea front, on which side, however, the customs houses and other official and commercial buildings, for the most part of modern construction and without elegance, reach right down to the wharves along the fringe of the sea. Here in the town hall Sulaiman Qabil, the mayor or *Raïs Baladiyya*, and his officers carry out their official duties; and here too lie the great hostels in which pilgrims from all parts of the world are accommodated, each according to his nationality, by enterprising agents from his own country, during the days they spend at Jidda on the outward and return journeys. Jidda is indeed a busy port with a floating population, whose numbers I cannot conjecture.

Outside the south-eastern corner of the city lies an extensive *Takruri* settlement of reed huts, the haunt of labourers and artisans come from the African coast in search of a living; and beyond it on the seashore is the *Kanisa*, as the Arabs call the little cemetery in which are interred such Europeans as from time to time death has overtaken during their sojourn on the inhospitable coast of the *Muslim* Holy Land.

Within the city is a truly eastern jumble of wealth and poverty: great mansions of the captains of commerce and enterprise, with their solid coral walls and wide expanses of woodwork tracery, side by side with hovels broken and battered by age; mosques great and small, with pointed minarets tapering skyward amid masses of vast square buildings; and crowded bazars, with their lines of dark shops, protected from the sun by central roofs, here of wood and canvas much the worse for wear, and there of corrugated iron. Everywhere a contrast of light and shadow, splendour and squalor, dust and dirt; and above it all flew the flags of many nations [1] amid the countless emblems of an united Arabia.

At length my sojourn at Jidda came to an end, and on the afternoon of the 14th January the companions of my desert journey from Riyadh accompanied me to the wharf-side, whence, with their last words of farewell ringing in my ears and with but slender hopes of seeing them again,

[1] Great Britain, France, Italy and Holland.

I launched out in a steam-cutter to embark on H.M.S. *Hardinge,* lying in the outer harbour to take Commander Hogarth and myself to Egypt. It was not for this that I had come forth from the *Wahhabi* capital; but there was no appeal from the King's decree.

CHAPTER VI

THE HINTERLAND OF EUPHRATES

1. Al Batin

My farewells to Ibn Sa'ud in December were accompanied by the assurance that I should, *Inshallah,* be back in Riyadh by the end of January at the latest, but Fate decreed otherwise, and weeks grew into months of suspense, as I sought to console myself among the fleshpots of civilisation for a disappointment, bitter enough in itself and doubly embittered by the knowledge that the prospect of an early return to Arabia depended on circumstances entirely beyond my control. I had seen enough of the desert and its strange society in the six weeks of a sojourn so untimely ended to make me yearn for a further opportunity of studying them more closely with the eyes of one already, as it were, initiated into their mysteries by a preliminary blooding, and to fill me with that restless longing for the vast spaces and pure air of the wilderness which only those can know who have had the good fortune to pass for a while beyond the thronged vistas of the modern world into the throbbing silences of endless sand and rock, where Nature rules without the aid of man, as she has done from the beginning and shall do to the end. But, " past regrets and future fears " notwithstanding, I had little cause for complaint, for did I not see for the first time Cairo in all its glory, its myriad pinnacles, its mighty Nile, its ancient pyramids? and I came, too, for the first time, to Jerusalem, newly released from the long tyranny of the Turk. But the call of the desert was strong upon me, and the melodious chant of the *Muadhdhin* calling to prayer in the Temple of Solomon seemed but to mock my treasured memories of the full-throated discord which at the appointed hours rends the still air of Riyadh and the desert settlements, even as the howl of the wolf at eventide recalled to the exiled *Dausari*, tending his sheep in the pastures of 'Iraq, the sweet music of a beloved voice in his homeland :

> *Sahibi Wadi al Dawasir maqarruha*
> *Bidhila' al asmar min wara al ramal min ghadi.*[1]

Fortunately my fears proved groundless, and in due course, the edict having gone forth that I should return forthwith to Riyadh, I took ship for Bombay and Basra, landing at the latter on 24th March to prepare for my onward journey. Winter had already passed into spring; spring would be passing into summer by the time I could arrive at my destination; and the prospect of spending the whole summer in "one of the hottest and driest countries in the world," where "the sky is generally cloudless and the sun pours its rays on plains of burning sand,"[2] and, what is more, of spending it in the open, was far from reassuring; nevertheless, into Arabia I had to go—fortunately to discover that the description, which I have quoted, was far from just.

On my arrival at Basra I was informed that Ibn Sa'ud, having heard of my coming, had left his son, Turki, in command of his camp of exercise in the 'Arma uplands and had come down to the Hasa to meet me. I accordingly laid my plans to journey by land from Kuwait to the southward, but my calculations were upset by the arrival of emissaries from Dhari ibn Tawala, chief of the Aslam Shammar, who, having received conflicting reports of my whereabouts and intentions, had thought it high time to make enquiries on his own account and incidentally to explain to the authorities at Basra that his monthly subsidy, for the payment of which I was responsible, had fallen seriously into arrears owing to my erratic movements. Great, therefore, was the surprise of the *Shammari* messengers, Dhaidan and Hamdan ibn Sultan by name, at finding their quarry preparing to evade

[1] "My love, in the valley of the Dawasir is her dwelling,
In the black crags beyond the sand far away."

[2] *Arabia and its Prophets*—a pamphlet (1909) of the Christian Literature Society, London, Madras and Colombo.

them even as they arrived, but greater still was their delight when I proposed that, instead of taking back to their master a letter in answer to his, they should return to his tents in triumph with me and the missing money-bags. The chance of spending a few days among the redoubtable Shammar and in a *Badawin* atmosphere as yet untainted with the dour puritanism of Central Najd was too good to be missed, and I squared my conscience with the reflection that I should reach Ibn Sa'ud as soon by way of the Batin as by any other route, and that a conference with Dhari was necessary to the prosecution of my plans.

Prior to November, 1917, when I started off on my mission to Arabia, the ever-present though remote possibility of an attack on the railway line between Basra and Nasiriyya, either by Ibn Rashid or the Muntafiq outlaw, 'Ajaimi al Sa'dun, who between them controlled the desert west of the Euphrates in the interests of the Turks, had imposed on the British military authorities in Mesopotamia the necessity of cultivating political relations with the border tribes, who, by reason of their intermediate position between ourselves and the enemy, were not only able to put their services up to auction, but in practice sold their good offices to both sides and kept faith with neither. The capture of Baghdad and the subsequent consolidation of our position beyond it had relieved us of all serious anxiety for the safety of our line of communications south of Nasiriyya, but it was only when we found ourselves in secure possession of practically the whole of the food-producing area of 'Iraq that any serious attempt could be made to establish an effective blockade of the enemy's borders, and the tribes which had enjoyed the profitable sinecure of the defence of the railway were now called upon to form part of the economic cordon with which we hoped to strangle Turkey, in return for the continuation of their subsidies and for preferential treatment in the matter of permits to draw the supplies necessary for themselves from the markets under our control. Short of dissipating our military resources by the establishment of blockhouses manned by troops at frequent intervals on an extended and tiresome desert frontier, there was no alternative before us but to secure the co-operation of the friendly Arabs in the enforcement of the blockade, and how exasperating and unsatisfactory that co-operation was may be judged by a single instance, in which Ibn Saʿud himself was indirectly the culprit. A Shammar caravan of 3000 camels from Haïl itself had boldly come down to Kuwait in September ; goods recently landed from British ships were openly purchased by the enemy's agents, and the formal enquiries of the *Shaikh's* blockade-officials were without difficulty satisfied by equally formal lies assisted, doubtless, by more substantial evidences of goodwill, and, the formalities over, the caravan set forth not, as one might suppose, by the direct but more precarious route to Haïl, but by way of the Qasim. Arrived at Buraida, the caravan leaders repaired to the presence of Turki, whom Ibn Saʿud had left in command of the blockading force in the Qasim, paid their respects, presented their credentials—to wit the clearance certificate of the Kuwait authorities—and not only demanded but received permission to depart in peace. Thus was a rich consignment of British goods pioneered through the British blockade to Haïl, and thus did our Arab allies acquit themselves on one occasion of the task imposed on their goodwill. The explanations of and apologies for an error due to misconception of our wishes came too late to remedy the damage which had been done. But let it not be supposed that this was an isolated case or that Kuwait enjoyed a monopoly of supplying the enemy's requirements, for do not the chronicles of the merchants of Syria betray the peccadilloes of their brethren of Ezion-Geber and others who should have known better ?

But to return from this digression to the affairs of Dhari. At the time of my departure from Baghdad in October doubts had begun to arise regarding the honesty of our tribal agents for the prosecution of the blockade on the Kuwait-Basra-Nasiriyya line, and my instructions were to take advantage of my stay at Basra to meet the *Shaikhs* concerned with a view to revising the existing arrangements and to co-ordinating their operations if possible with those which it was hoped Ibn Saʿud might be induced to undertake in furtherance of the common object. A race-meeting at

Basra, to which the leading Arabs of the locality had been invited, coincided luckily enough with my arrival and gave me an opportunity of consultation with those concerned with one important exception, for Sa'ud al Salih al Subhan, a chief of the 'Abda Shammar, and by common consent the premier "friendly" *Shaikh* of the Euphrates marches since he had abandoned Ibn Rashid and thrown in his lot with us nearly a year before, had of recent weeks made himself so conspicuous in the profitable business of blockade-running, which he was handsomely enough subsidised to prevent, that he judged it more appropriate to be represented at the races by an unimportant younger brother than to risk the consequences of a personal appearance. He stood condemned by a guilty conscience and henceforth, shorn of his subsidy and deserted by the friends who valued their friendship at a higher price than he could afford to pay, cut but a sorry figure in the desert, a proved traitor to both the causes he had served. The mantle of Ibn Subhan fell on Dhari ibn Tawala, whose reputation for open-handed hospitality had crowded his camp with more mouths than he could feed on his modest pittance, and who, seeing in the downfall of his rival an opportunity of realising his own ambitions, hastened to contract with the British authorities for a display of greater activity in support of the blockade in return for an increased salary—with what results I shall record in due course. A minor *rôle* was assigned to the Dhafir tribe under its chief *Shaikh*, Hamud ibn Suwait, who had done good but unostentatious work in connection with the protection of the railway line in the earlier days of the campaign, and the desert alliance in this sector was formally completed by the inclusion of Ibrahim, *Shaikh* of Zubair, as the guide, philosopher and friend of all parties concerned.

Dhari was the pivot of the whole arrangement, the link between the desert and the sown, and, though he had achieved no substantial results in the four months which had intervened between my departure for Arabia and my return to Basra, he could at least claim that he had fulfilled the letter of his contract by collecting and keeping a large gathering of friendly elements at his camp by the wells of Al Hafar, and it was in the hope of spurring him into

Group of desert chiefs; from left to right: Muhammad ibn Salih al Subhan, Shaikh Ibrahim of Zubair, Dhari ibn Tawala and Hamud ibn Suwait.

something like active co-operation with our blockade that I conceived the idea of visiting him in his den. My preparations for a start were completed by the afternoon of 28th March, when I drove to the terminus of the Basra-Nasiriyya railway and took my seat in the Nasiriyya express. The barren plain between Basra and Zubair station is too well known to need description: the winter rains had reduced the country-side to a morass wellnigh impracticable for motor traffic and the landscape to the southward towards the head of the Khor 'Abdullah creek was a network of muddy lagoons. Through the tumbled remains of old Basra, the first town of purely Muhammadan origin, we passed laboriously to the station of Shu'aiba, where I alighted to find after diligent enquiry that some weary camels couched by the permanent way were intended for my baggage, and a dilapidated victoria outspanned in the station-yard for my conveyance to Zubair. A thin coating of grass, with here and there a patch of young wheat or barley, adorned the ragged undulations of the way, and by nightfall I was deposited at the door of the Assistant Political Officer of Zubair, Lieutenant A. H. Roberts, with whom I proceeded at once to the *Shaikh's* residence, whither we had been bidden for dinner.

It was good to be on the threshold of the desert once more, and Shaikh Ibrahim is an excellent host, at whose hospitable board many a British officer, nay, many a lady of our race, has been initiated into the mysteries of Arab fare and admitted into the brotherhood of Arab society. In him the British cause has a friend who has never wavered in his allegiance since the fateful day when, lying between two fires, he saw the supremacy of Britain finally established on the field of Shu'aiba; than him there is none who studies more anxiously the movements of the political barometer, and none who has a clearer idea of what he regards as the ideal settlement of the affairs of 'Iraq. Short of the ideal there are many alternatives, between which he hesitates to express a preference lest experience prove him wrong, but why experiment? Simple and direct are the arguments of the Arab, but always *ad hominem*; by his own prosperity or adversity alone, regarding not the case of his fellows, he judges the success or failure of the system under which he lives; there is indeed no other possible criterion in a community whose primitive social standards are yet far from envisaging the ideal of the common weal. Thus, while many deplore, cloaking their regrets under the guise of religious sentiment, the passing of the good old times, when a host of petty officials battened on the helpless public and the lawless tribes could defy the tax-gatherer with impunity, there are many—and of them is Ibrahim—who allow no sickly sentiment to moderate their unbounded satisfaction with the gifts of the new order. "In the days of the Turks," Ibrahim would say, and his brother, Hamad, would echo his sentiments, "there was no justice and no security; as for myself, sometimes I was prosperous and sometimes not, for everything depended on the whim of the *Wali* for the time being—and the *Walis* were changed very frequently; some liked me and some did not; but since your occupation matters have changed, praise be to God I have that which I have and your Government is one. Whoever may be the officer at Basra or here in Zubair itself, my treatment does not vary. If you remain permanently, every one who has anything to lose will be content, and of one thing we are particularly glad; you will not compel us to serve in the army as the Turks did or as the Sharif would do if he were our ruler, or any other Arab government. We want but peace and freedom from interference. As for the future, we want no more of the Turks, that is certain, while of the possible claimants among the Arabs, the people of 'Iraq would select the Sharif on account of his religious pre-eminence—but with misgiving; Ibn Sa'ud is out of the question outside the limits of the desert, where he in turn will never acknowledge the overlordship of the Sharif." Of Saiyid Talib,[1] the accomplished villain in the drama of Basra politics before the war, he spoke freely at my prompting, and it was clear that there was a link of tenderness between the two. "He is not so bad," said Ibrahim, "as people now say, and most of the ruffianism attributed to him was the creation of lively imaginations; he did

[1] Appointed November, 1920 Minister for the Interior in Mesopotamia; deported to Ceylon in April, 1921.

indeed compass the assassination of Farid Bey, but his victim would have dealt with him in like wise had he had the chance; there is no doubt, Saiyid Talib exercised extraordinary influence over the affairs of Basra, both in the law-courts and over the successive *Walis*, but the fault was rather of the Turkish system, for Talib did not scruple to act the spy on the doings of high officials for the benefit of Constantinople, whence many an order of summary dismissal came in consequence of his secret reports. No wonder then that he could control the administration in his own interests by blackmail threats to report its patent shortcomings to the central authority. No, the people of Basra want no more of him except he return as a private citizen like any one of themselves." He was interested to hear that I had seen something of the redoubtable *Saiyid* in Cairo, where he was consoling himself for his enforced absence from home with the lighter diversions of a great city.

I retired to rest that night, reconciled beforehand, in spite of Ibrahim's promises, to a belated start on the morrow and the customary *Tabriz* of short duration in lieu of a full day's march, but the *Shaikh* was as good as his word, and it was I who kept the caravan waiting while I broke my fast and completed my packing. At 9.40 A.M. on the 29th March we mounted, a goodly company of thirty-three persons, and the march began, Shaikh Ibrahim and his brother accompanying us some way along the dusty streets until I insisted on their turning back; and so we came to the south gate of the desert town and passed through it into the wilderness. At first we fared over a rough bare upland, varied here and there with ragged patches of corn. Behind us, as we steered slightly south of west, lay the town of Zubair, with Basra and the palms of the Shatt al 'Arab receding slowly into the mist; to our right northward lay Shu'aiba, on our left rear the palms and *Ithils* of Rafidhiyya, and away to the southward the solitary limestone mass of Jabal Sanam, the "hill of the hump," conspicuous in its desert setting but no longer deserted, for a branch line of the railway has been laid to its foot and its flanks are pierced with quarries for the service of the permanent way. Two years before it was a far cry to Jabal Sanam, when Ibn Rashid himself camped at Safwan but was deterred from further adventures by the activities of the cavalry detachment at Shu'aiba; and now the Arabs of the desert, marvelling at our industry, find it a source of innocent merriment. "Does it still stand?" they ask of travellers from the east; "and how long will it be before it is levelled to the ground?"

An hour's march brought us to the crest of the downs, whence the land slopes easily down to the dark *Ithil* coppices and green corn-lands of Barjisiyya, an extensive but straggling plantation in a shallow bottom, possibly the extremity or one of the extremities of the Batin channel. Here it was that the Turks in April 1915 fixed their headquarters for the battle of Shu'aiba, and traces of the trenches they then dug were still visible among the melon beds—for Zubair and the surrounding settlements are above all famous for their melons—and cornfields, by which we passed as we descended the slope. At length, having marched about five miles from Zubair, we came to the southern extremity of the settlement and halted for a brief space among its outlying cornfields to water the camels at one of its many *Jalibs* or draw-wells. The mud huts of a small hamlet lay among *Ithils* at some little distance to the north, and Jabal Sanam appeared afar off due south.

Soon after noon Mr. Roberts, who had accompanied us thus far on our way, left us on his return to Zubair, and we resumed our march in the opposite direction, steering a few degrees to the westward of Jabal Sanam, over a dreary, gently rising plain, which they call Al Raha, until the thickets of Barjisiyya disappeared behind us into the mirage, and all that met our gaze was wilderness before, behind and on either hand, with only the familiar "hump" to guide our course. Nevertheless, the Arabs divide the featureless waste into smaller pastoral units—Najmi they pointed out, and Quraitiyya, though I could not distinguish between them, and Baniyya, where they gather brushwood, between us and Jabal Sanam. The plain was sparsely covered with young grass and little flowering plants and a low shrub called *Idhris*. The only break in the monotony of that march was the slaughter of a viper which sought refuge in vain in a derelict kerosene tin by the wayside.

Thus we marched for seven miles, when a perceptible rise in the ground marked the termination of the flat plain of Raha, and we passed into a tract called Al Mafrash or the delta of the Batin, a wide area of gently swelling downland intersected by a network of depressions, which once upon a time no doubt were the channels along which the flood-waters of the Batin found their way to the Euphrates or the sea ; for in ancient times, before the process of desiccation had created the deserts of northern Arabia and the alluvial deposits of the two great rivers had formed the fertile flats of Mesopotamia, a great river descending from the Harra of Khaibar in the far west along the bed of Wadi Rima and the Batin, which are in reality a single channel, must have flowed here into the Persian Gulf, whose head must have reached far to the north of the point at which we had now arrived—even to the neighbourhood of Ur of the Chaldees, the home of Abraham. The Mafrash downs, presenting a contrast of pebble-strewn ridges and grassy hollows already beginning to be decked with the little desert flowers of spring-time, white and yellow and purple, extended for some six miles from the edge of the Raha plain, converging gradually to its apex in the extremity of the Batin channel proper, which is marked by two low rounded hillocks, one on each side of the opening, Al Ratak al Shamali and Al Ratak al Janubi. Here, finding profusion of the hardy grey-green *Arfaj* shrub which the camels like so well, we decided to camp for the night, well content with the progress we had made during the day. Afar off and behind us now the lonely peak of Jabal Sanam, disappearing into the gloom of night, reminded us that we were yet in touch with civilisation, while before us ran the broad shallow trough of the Batin, with the bare desert on either bank, beckoning us towards the mysterious beyond. Behind our camp the Mafrash channels extended their fan-shaped tentacles towards what was once the sea.

The good Shaikh Ibrahim had warned us that it was generally unwise to spend the night where one halted for the evening meal, lest the camp-fire should betray one's position to a prowling foe, but his wise counsels were forgotten in the weariness induced by a long day's march, and we remained where we were, feasting comfortably on rice and chickens provided by the *Shaikh*, and gathering afterwards round the fire for coffee and converse. Dhaidan did most of the talking, which turned largely on the virtues and exploits of his master, Dhari, and on the doubtful services of the *Shaikh* of Kuwait, who, if my informant was to be believed, was doing exceedingly well out of the contraband business, and was supposed to harbour too friendly feelings towards the Turks. Another member of our party, ʿAbdulʿaziz, had been in the service of a former Political Officer of Zubair, Captain R. Marrs, who was well known to many of my companions and had endeared himself to the Arabs of the Euphrates hinterland during his wanderings in the desert in the early days of the war. The evening wore on as we discoursed pleasantly of the past, the present and the future, and our conversation was brought abruptly to an end by the sudden irruption into our midst of a group of shepherds with a caravan of asses, who, having gone down to Safwan to fetch water and been overtaken by night on their return, had mistaken our camp-fire for that of their fellows. Amid much confusion and shouting their mistake was explained to them, and they steered their flock clear of our camp to search for their own ; the voice of a woman, loudly grumbling at their misadventure, was conspicuous in the hubbub, which slowly died away in the distance and left us to our rest. It transpired that our visitors were of the great grazier tribe of Juwarin, which winters along the right bank of the Euphrates, and moves during springtime into the pasture lands of the desert.

We were astir betimes the following morning and lost no time in starting off on our march up the monotonous and almost featureless valley of the Batin. From rim to rim of the gently sloping banks on either side of the bed of the channel the valley varied in breadth from one to four miles, and our course lay for the most part either just within or just outside its right bank, which was broken at frequent intervals by little *Shaʿibs*, little more than drainage rills, running down the slope to the main depression, whose bottom of clayey loam was lightly covered with grass or the salty *Rimdh*, and dotted at intervals with *Raudhas* or small patches of *Sidr* bushes. At about 10 A.M. we halted for our midday meal in the bed of a nameless sandy *Sha'ib* halfway between two of these *Raudhas*, Mutriba and Hulaiba, where the valley was scarcely a mile broad, and beyond which we passed out of it into a somewhat tumbled tract of low downs. In the afternoon, having threaded a maze of depressions draining this tract into the Batin, we found ourselves again on the right bank of the latter at a point where a low tumulus called Jirishan lay athwart the middle of the valley, and the well-marked ridge of Mitiyaha formed its left bank. Here we descended into the depression towards the *Raudha* of Sufaiya, where, having covered about twenty-five miles during the day, we halted to let our beasts derive the fullest advantage from the *Rimdh* and other luscious herbage which covered the valley.

All day long we had been in sight of scattered shepherd encampments up and down the valley, and from time to time had passed flocks on the move from pasture to pasture —mostly groups of the same Juwarin, whose donkeys had stumbled into our camp during the night, with an occasional sprinkling of the Albu Salih, while at Jirishan we encountered representatives of the Shuraifat, from whom after some haggling we managed to purchase two fine sheep for the sum of twelve dollars for our evening meal. On one occasion during the afternoon we were coming up in the rear of a party on the move, when one of their number, doubtful of our intentions, fired a shot over our heads, apparently only to warn us that they were armed, for no further notice was taken of us, though the flock was hastily driven off our line of march to be out of harm's way. Contrary to expectation the spring season was further advanced at this higher level—our camp at Sufaiya was rather more than 400 feet above sea-level—than we had found it on the Mesopotamian border, and the profusion of spring flowers amid the rich grasses which covered the slopes and bed of the valley afforded me some compensation for the monotony of the scene. For every plant the Arab has a name and for most of them praise or blame in proportion as they serve or not as fodder for sheep or camel. First on the long list come the *Arfaj* and *Rimdh*, which seldom appear together but alternate in extensive patches, as though Nature itself recognised that no animal could exist solely on the dry tasteless tufts of the former without an occasional taste of the brine, which makes the latter in too great quantities harmful. The succulent *Nussi*, favoured above all grasses, was not here to be found, but its place was taken by a herb like wild barley called *Sam'a*. Then there were the flowering plants, on which our beasts browsed as they marched, with a nice appreciation of the advantages of a mixed diet—the yellow *Haudhan*, like a dandelion, the white *Jahwiyan* or desert daisy, the yellow and succulent *Kahil*, the purple *Shiqara*, a yellow mustard-like plant called *Sufara*, the *Dhanab Nab* or wild mignonette, the creeping *Hambaiz*, the *Niqq*, and many others.[1] It was delightful to march thus on and on into the desert over a rich carpet of flowers and grasses, amid which the grazing sheep and the black tents of the shepherds seemed as much in place as the quails and hares, which rose up at our feet to disappear in tremulous haste over the low rim of the valley, or the flights of sand-grouse which sped over our heads on their way back from their morning watering by Euphrates' banks, or the swallows and hawks that darted or hovered over the scene. The familiar landmark of Jabal Sanam had now sunk below the horizon for ever, and the cool winds of the desert spring lulled us to sleep under a clouded sky, which gave welcome promise of more rain ere summer should overtake us.

The promise was soon fulfilled, for a few drops of rain were falling from a leaden sky when I awoke at 5 A.M. on the following morning, and though we had no repetition of the downfall during the march, which was as featureless as that of the preceding day, the evening closed in on us in our camp, some twenty-five miles farther on, with a gentle drizzle which persisted through most of the night. We saw but little of the sun during the day, and the great patches of purple-flowered *Shiqara*, which stretched across the valley, produced the illusion of a heather moor in more temperate climes. As on the previous day the scene was dotted profusely with the tents and flocks of herding Arabs,

[1] *E.g.* the purple-flowered *Karish* (pronounced *Charish*), the *Raghal*, the *Kharit*, a red variety of *Kahil*.

but herds of camels tended as we advanced to predominate over the flocks of sheep, and the progress of our desert march was emphasised by our entry into the *Badawin* sphere, the sphere of the lordly camel owner, the lord of the desert, as opposed to that of the humbler shepherd. We passed during the morning by the last groups of the Juwarin, the Nubhan section of the tribe, into the range of the Dhafir, whose leading *Shaikh*,[1] Hamud ibn Suwait, was reported to be not far distant in the desert behind the hillock of Ruhail, which with the raised ridge of Adhaiba broke the low monotony of the left bank of the Batin towards the end of our march and near which we found encamped the 'Araif section of the Dhafir and the Tawatha section of the 'Anaza, which is numbered among the clans owing allegiance to the *Shaikh* of Kuwait. Near Adhaiba we sought in vain certain pools or *Thamaïl* [2] reported to be full of water at this season, and passed on to our camp in time to pitch my tent before the rain began. During the march Dhaidan had found the nest of a *Hubara* or Lesser Bustard with three eggs,[3] which were now brought to me as an appetiser before our dinner, but their taste was somewhat coarse and too redolent of *Saman* to be pleasing.

The fact that we were now well within the *Badawin* area, where the desert code of chivalry was in full force and passing strangers were liable to be treated as pawns in the noble game of raid and counter-raid unless they observed its rules, was signalised by our *Rafiqs* in the customary way —our identity and peaceful intentions being proclaimed from the four corners of our camp at intervals during the night. For the moment we were in Dhafir territory and could count ourselves their guests, but they were ever on the look-out for the attentions of hostile bands of Shammar or Mutair,

[1] This news was given us by a member of the Dhara'an section of the tribe who visited us in our camp during the evening.

[2] Sing. *Thamila.*

[3] The following day we found a solitary egg of a plover-like bird called *Smaqq*, and passed a nest, possibly of some finch, perched on the top of a *Rimdh* tuft. A common bird in these parts is the *Ras Maridhan*, a grey and white bird of the hawk type though said to be useless for hawking purposes. The *Umm Salim* with its curious tumbling flight and staccato piping note also deserves mention—its plumage is white and grey with some black about it. The *Smaqq* is eaten by the Arabs.

and it behoved us to look after ourselves in case of accident from those directions. The Mutair indeed were believed to be far distant beyond the wells of Al Hafar, but the Shammar are intermingled with the Dhafir without very definite boundaries, and it would have been far from pleasant to fall in with a hostile section.

Dawn of next day, 1st April, dispersed the last clouds of the night, and we set forth on the next stage of our journey under a clear sky and a sun bereft of his wonted power with a steady drying wind from the north-west blowing across us. The surface of the valley, broad as ever, became more and more broken up as we ascended; the slopes on either side ran down more abruptly than before to the central depression, which zigzagged more sharply from side to side and into which, more especially during the later portion of the march, little rough tributary *Sha'ibs* ran down at frequent intervals from the uplands of the left bank, to which on this account they give the name of Shuqaiyat.[1] Apart from these, the only noticeable features of the day's march were a long low eminence on the right bank called Abraq al Hibari, a low sandy tumulus in the bed of the valley known as Hiss wa Dhabi, and a striking little eminence of blackened rock on the left bank, which from its colour derives the name of Al 'Ubaid, or the Little Negro.

In the neighbourhood of this hillock we came upon the tents of the notorious Sa'ud al Salih al Subhan and his 'Abda following, and I turned my *Dhalul* towards the great black tabernacle of the chief in the hope that I might find him at home and force upon him an acquaintance, which he had evaded in the previous November. My luck was out, however, as Sa'ud had gone off some time back to Kuwait—I suspect to wheedle provisions out of the *Shaikh* to pass on to Haïl—and was daily expected back by his young brother Muhammad, the dull-witted, silent boy whom I had met before at Basra and who now entertained me to coffee amid a full gathering of his retainers. These latter numbered not more than some seventy men, who with those in attendance

[1] Each of these *Sha'ibs* is called Shuqaiya; apart from them we passed two others known as Shiqq al Wasi'a on the right bank, and Sha'ib Aqfa issuing into the valley from the left bank beyond Al 'Ubaid.

on the chief might be reckoned at one hundred men-at-arms in all, a number which, as Dhaidan did not fail to point out to me, was eloquent enough evidence of the decay of Sa'ud's power since the days, not so long ago, when he was by far the most important of the Shammar chiefs on friendly terms with the British. The house of Al Subhan played an important and honourable part in the stormy history of Haïl between the years 1906, when the reigning *Amir*, 'Abdul-'aziz ibn Rashid, fell in battle against the *Wahhabi* forces in the Qasim,[1] and 1908, when a series of dynastic murders culminated in the assassination of an usurper by Hamud al Subhan[2] and the restoration of the *Amirate* to the present ruler, Sa'ud ibn Rashid, the ten-year-old son of 'Abdul'aziz and the sole survivor of the legitimate line.[3] Hamud's place as regent and adviser to the young ruler was taken on his death in the following year by Zamil, another member of the same family, but his wise direction of affairs was terminated by his assassination in 1914, and Sa'ud al Salih, the chief in whose tent I was now sitting, was one of those who involved the Shammar power in hostilities with Great Britain and deserted it to come over to us for his own ends at the end of 1916. Of his services to the Allied cause I have spoken, but it is a matter of regret to me that I never had an opportunity of meeting him. The opportunity will never recur, for since I left Arabia the hand of an assassin or an enemy has laid him low, and his name will only be remembered as that of a traitor to both the causes he served so ill.

This visit to the camp of Sa'ud was the event of a day which was full of human interest. Earlier in the day we had seen a black mantle spread out in the valley over a tuft of *Rimdh*, and my companions had explained that this was the *Badawin* manner of bespeaking a site for a camp. When the pastures around them are exhausted they send out horsemen to seek another suitable spot, which being reserved in the manner here indicated, the signal is given for a move

[1] At Raudhat al Muhanna.

[2] *Vide* p. 383 *infra*.

[3] Sa'ud was, however, murdered in the spring of 1920 and succeeded by a cousin, 'Abdullah ibn Mit'ab.

to the new quarters. On this occasion we had the pleasure of seeing the whole of the Afnan[1] section of the Dhafir on the move, lock, stock, and barrel, down the valley—a striking procession of hundreds, nay, of thousands of camels, for the most part milch animals and young stock representing the material wealth of the section, while here and there rode groups of men directing the march which centred round a long line of baggage animals carrying the womenfolk, children, and camp *impedimenta*. Near the van rode the head *Shaikh* of the section, Darwish ibn Ridan by name, though better known by the familiar sobriquet of *Ra' al Buwait* or "He of the little tent," a title whose origin and exact significance my party could not explain though they supposed it to be a pet diminutive applied to the ancestors of the present bearer of the title in the days when they lorded it over all the Dhafir. Another prominent person in this group was 'Ajaimi ibn Shuhail, first cousin of Hamud ibn Naïf ibn Suwait, who for some reason, probably a family quarrel, had temporarily joined the Afnan. But by far the most striking feature of the procession was the weird panniers, in which rode the consorts of the tribal chiefs and their children. They were of two distinct types —the *Qin* or comparatively unadorned *howdah*-like equipage set apart for the servants and women of lesser rank, and the extraordinary *Kitab*[2] of the important wives, a sort of rocking carriage poised on the camel's hump with two great wooden crescents front and back, whose horns protruded outwards on either side to a distance of several feet, and a galaxy of gaudy tassels descending from it almost to the ground. So far as I could gather the design of these carriages was purely ornamental, and the more ornamental parts served no purpose but to increase the discomfort of the unfortunate beast which bore them—that they were not too comfortable for the vain but unfortunate passengers who rode in them was obvious at a glance.

My party, drawn largely from urban or semi-urban

[1] The Dhuwaihi section of the same tribe was encamped in the neighbourhood of Hiss wa Dhabi, at which place during our midday halt we were visited by one of the sectional *Shaikhs*, Hamdan ibn Dhuwaihi.

[2] Pronounced *Chĭtăb*.

elements, was not a particularly interesting one, but by this time the restraint natural (in a townsman) amid strange company was beginning to wear off and the tedium of the day's march was beguiled by a most entertaining exhibition of voice mimicry by one of my companions. While I was riding ahead my attention was arrested by the high-pitched tones of a querulous feminine voice behind, and reining back to see what was passing, I found that it was only one of our servants giving an imitation of the ordinary speech of a queer race or tribe, which according to him inhabits the country beyond Sham (presumably Syria) and is known by the name of Sukun or Bani Yakhlib. He stopped abashed when he saw that I was included among his amused audience, but on being pressed by me to continue the entertainment, he did so with much zest, but, try as I might, I could get no further information either from him or the others regarding the subjects of his imitation beyond the fact that their manner of speech, which is a sort of vulgarised Arabic, is known as *Sikni*, and that both sexes of the tribe dispense with all clothing but a loin-cloth. The imitation, sustained as it was, rang true enough, but I am not prepared to say that he was not pulling our legs or that he had not himself been deceived in taking the high-pitched effeminate speech of a party of eunuchs for the speech of a tribe. I remembered at the time that the late Captain W. H. C. Shakespear had recorded from hearsay the existence in Jabal Radhwa and the neighbouring mountains of the Hijaz of a primitive branch of the 'Ataiba whose men and women did without clothes until marriage, but my questions failed to connect these in any way with the squeaky-voiced Sukun.

Our intention had been to camp for the night by the water-pools of Riqaï situated at the edge of the right bank of the Batin, but our delay at the 'Abda camp made this impossible and darkness overtook us, when we had already covered about thirty miles during the day and were still in the Shuqaiyat tract somewhat short of our goal. Here we camped, consoling ourselves with the reflection that at this season our camels could never be in serious need of water, while we ourselves had at least enough to drink and to cook our rice in, as well as a single hare, the solitary victim of many chases, for hare and lesser bustard had been seen in plenty during the day.

The night was clear and cold and my thermometer recorded less than 45° Fahr. at 5 A.M. next morning, when we rose for what was to prove our longest and dullest march since leaving Zubair. At first the surface of the valley retained the rough character of the Shuqaiyat tract, being bounded by the Kharja [1] and Adhariyat ridges to right and left of us respectively, but thereafter, until within a few miles of the Hafar wells, the scene was bare and desolate, a broad clay bottom dotted with rare patches of thin grass and screened off from the desert on the north by the long, broken ridge of Dharabin.[2] We were, however, now approaching what must in former times have been the cultivated portion of the valley, for close by the upper end of the ridge we came upon extensive remains of a number of wells connected with a series of masonry reservoirs by stone-lined conduits. The whole system, together with the seeming remnants of a few buildings, was in a dilapidated state and choked with earth and *débris*, and must have fallen into disuse many generations ago, for there remains no tradition of its past, and not even a name to know it by, though doubtless it was constructed at about the same time as the grange or fort called Qusair Ballal, whose ruins, now but a heap of rubbish whose outer design alone is traceable, we stopped to view nine or ten miles farther up the valley. Of this little fortress it is said that it was built by one Ballal, a slave of the chieftain who excavated the wells of Al Hafar in the dim past, and it is not improbable that it was built as an outpost to defend those wells from invaders from the north.

Beyond the ruined fort the valley resumed something of the rough undulating character of the Shuqaiyat tract and the grassy uplands were dotted with the flocks and tents

[1] Close by this ridge we passed the remains of some disused water-holes (*Jalta*, plur. *Jalat*) of a former age.

[2] Opposite this ridge on the right bank lies a ravine called Jalta Hissu, containing water-holes; behind it to the southward but out of our sight runs the ridge of Musanna, which is said to extend between the depression of Shiqq al Wasi'a and that of Fulaiyij al Janubi, which runs down to the Batin near Al Hafar.

of the following of Dhari ibn Tawala himself, who, we learned from passers-by, was encamped far ahead of us up the valley. On we sped determined to arrive at our destination at all costs before nightfall, and it was not until the sun was very low over the horizon that we espied the great tent, which Dhaidan recognised as his master's *Madhif* or pavilion of audience.

Despite the earnest entreaties of Dhaidan to be allowed to go ahead to announce my coming, I insisted that we should arrive unannounced and leave our unsuspecting host no time to prepare for my reception. But the noble Arab is too habitual an entertainer of unexpected guests, always too ready with the simple desert entertainment, which is all that rich and poor alike can offer, to be flurried by or to exhibit surprise at the arrival of a party however big or distinguished. By the manner of my arrival I possibly escaped the formality of a reception by my host and his retainers on horseback and in full war-paint, but I was compensated therefor by the fact that I was able to dismount at the doorway of Dhari's tent as any Arab might have done, and to enter with the common salutation on my lips before he knew who his visitor was. Among a race, whose standards of courtesy and gentleness are so high—and in this respect the Shammar are perhaps second to none but the noble 'Anaza—Dhari ibn Tawala stands out in my experience in the front rank, though at times in the course of my later dealings with him I found him somewhat effusive even to obsequiousness; on this occasion the scene was as impressive as I could have wished, as Dhari rose from his seat in a corner of the tent and the great assembly of his friends and retainers rose to their feet at the same time to greet the stranger. When I was seated at his side in the place of honour and had been presented to the chief of those present I was able to look around while coffee and great bowls of sweetened camel's milk were served. The great black tent-cloth covered an enormous area which was divided into two apartments by a screen of similar worsted, that in which we sat, a gathering of men alone numbering close on 200, and the private apartment of the womenfolk, who gathered together behind the flimsy partition excitedly whispering and doubtless prying through the veil to get a glimpse of so unusual a visitor. Thus we sat conversing until our baggage came up and my tent was pitched, when I was allowed to retire to wash and rest until dinner should be ready—and such a dinner it was when it came. For my benefit it was served in the open close to my tent and Dhari himself joined us at it—great dishes of rice and excellent mutton on which my companions made amends for any shortage we had endured during the march, and for the meatless meals which would be their lot on the return journey, for, having accomplished the task entrusted to them by Shaikh Ibrahim they were to return homeward on the morrow. Meanwhile having dined well we retired at an early hour to the rest which we had earned by a march of about forty miles during the day.

Our march up to this point, about eight miles short of the Hafar wells, had covered some 150 miles from Zubair, and I decided to spend the following day, 3rd April—my birthday incidentally—and its successor in leisure amid the tents of the Shammar, for I had much business to transact with Dhari, accounts to settle, plans to make for the future, and, last but not least, much to learn about the dispositions and attitude of the tribes which occupied this section of the desert. My tent had been set up about a hundred yards from the great *Madhif* and next door to a great white tent, presented to Dhari by the British authorities in 'Iraq, which served partly as the chief's office and partly as the residence of his secretary, Mulla 'Abdullah, a native of Mausal, who had visited Egypt, had been in Haïl quite recently, and had but a few months before entered the service of Dhari. He was neither a very clever secretary nor a very pleasing character, but on the whole I found him harmless enough and often a useful intermediary between myself and his master, and it was in his tent that we held conferences of a nature too delicate to be held in public assembly.

I had instructed Dhari at our last meeting in November to collect as large a gathering as he could with the funds at his disposal and to take up his position in the neighbourhood of Al Hafar with a view to cutting off all contraband traffic between Kuwait, the weakest point in the British blockade cordon, and the hostile Shammar elements based on Haïl and the mobile camp of ʿAjaimi ibn Saʿdun. He had made the necessary dispositions and had certainly succeeded in drawing a considerable following to his standard, as the variety and importance of the sections and *Shaikhs* encamped round him testified, but I was somewhat disappointed at his inability to produce more substantial evidence of his activities than statements that he had captured a number of caravans, which had attempted to evade his vigilance, and that the contraband traffic was now compelled to adopt the Qasim route through Ibn Saʿud's territory. The Arab is an elusive and difficult person to deal with when it is a question of a distasteful task, but in the course of my conversations I made it clear to Dhari that, while I was ready to let bygones be bygones and to pay him according to our agreement for the past months, which had been empty of achievement, I would expect him to earn the future instalments of his subsidy by vigorous action. He in his turn was prolific of promises for the future, but we shall see in due course how he proved himself a broken reed.

The gathering of the clans about Al Hafar at this time exhibited a variety of elements, chief among which were: Dhari's own clan, the Aslam section of the Shammar, comprising the whole of the premier subsection of Tawala under the lead of his cousin, Satam ibn ʿAjil, and some of the Masʿud and the ʿAïsh clan of the Tuman under Jumail ibn Rudhaimi and the Faid subsection under Fuhaid ibn Jifan; the Zumail subsection of the Sinjara Shammar under Fahad ibn Thunaian, who was supported by four lesser *Shaikhs*;[1] and finally the Dahamsha section of the ʿAnaza, or a considerable part of it under its astute old chief Muhammad ibn Mijlad, who brought his ten-year-old little son, Kida, to see me. The news of my coming lost no time in getting abroad, and I had the pleasure of meeting all the above-mentioned chiefs, who came in to see me and incidentally to receive cash presents, each according to his importance, as earnest of the goodwill of the British Govern-

[1] These were Sultan ibn Nuwaishi, Husain abu Qiran, Subaih ibn Nuwaishi, and ʿAïs ibn Dhawi. Fahad's cousin, Baïq ibn Thunaian, who did not come in, was with him in his camp near Al Jalt to the northward.

ment. Spread as their camps were over a considerable area, it was impossible for me to form an idea of the man-power at Dhari's disposal, but I estimated that he could probably rely on the services of some 600 or 700 men. He had received a present of 300 rifles from the Mesopotamian authorities about a year before, but I was unable to encourage his further demand now made for 700 more, though I allowed him to think that he might get everything he could desire in return for substantial achievements in the direction desired by us. Dhari, like all Arabs, lost nothing for want of asking for it, and the only hope of getting anything out of him and the rest was to dangle an attractive bait before their eyes to be won by action.

While Dhari was at Al Hafar responsible for the economic blockade of the enemy, Ibn Sa'ud was reported to be at the wells of Hafar al Ats or at Shauki, whither he had gone with a considerable following for his annual spring camp of exercise, which on this occasion was, we hoped, to be the prelude to a vigorous offensive against Jabal Shammar; it was, however, rumoured that he himself had gone on to the Hasa, by which route he expected me to return, and had left his main force behind under the command of his valiant son, Turki.

The Allied desert line was completed on the north by the 'Amarat section of 'Anaza under its aged but still active leader, Fahad ibn Hadhdhal, whom some months previously I had had the pleasure of attending during his visit to Baghdad, when he saw for the first time something of our military preparations by land, air and water, and made no secret of his amazement and uneasiness, when he suddenly realised that he was sipping coffee under one of the big guns of one of our gunboats — the *Mantis*, I think. He was now reported to be at Lasaf, some seventy miles south-west of Najaf with Colonel Leachman, watching the movements of the redoubtable 'Ajaimi, who was reported to be at Qaisuma with a following of Dahamsha 'Anaza under Muhammad ibn Turki[1] and the Shilqan subsection of the

[1] Another Dahamsha chief, Jazza' ibn Mijlad, brother, I think, of the Muhammad who was with Dhari, was in attendance on the Turks farther to the north.

Sinjara Shammar under Abaqili ibn Falih. 'Ajaimi was perhaps the greatest, if not indeed the only, military genius produced by Arabia during the war and his qualities deserved better inspiration and a happier issue. Enemy as he was, we cannot withhold our admiration of the manner in which, serving a lost or losing cause, he held out through all the years of the war in the deserts behind the Euphrates—always a thorn in our side and a factor to be reckoned with. But the Turks and Huns had no Lawrence to direct his operations and, fortunately for us, they always expected him to do the best he could with the minimum support in arms and funds which they could place at his disposal instead of encouraging and enabling him to carry out his operations on an imaginative scale by lavish provision of the necessary materials. At the time of which I am now speaking—and I must confess to wild dreams of inducing Dhari to undertake a flying raid in the direction of Qaisuma —'Ajaimi was too well provided with artillery and small arms to be attacked without preparations on a prohibitive scale, and the hope of taking him by surprise was discounted by the fact that he had organised an excellent intelligence system throughout the Euphratean desert—at least so said Dhari when I broached the subject with him, and I have no doubt he was not far wrong.

Farther westward towards Haïl the wells of Lina, about 110 miles north-west of Al Hafar, were occupied on 'Ajaimi's behalf by hostile elements of the 'Abda[1] and Tuman sections, while Ibn Rashid's outpost of Haiyaniyya was held by Ibn Khamsan of the Sinjara. Ibn Rashid himself was still with the Turks at Al Hajr or Madaïn Salih on the Hijaz railway, but according to Dhari's information a letter had recently been received from him announcing

[1] The 'Abda is perhaps the premier section of the Shammar and comprises the following sections: Al Ja'far under Wadi ibn 'Ali and 'Abbas ibn 'Ali, lineal descendants of the 'Ali dynasty which ruled Haïl as vassals of Ibn Sa'ud until the *Amirate* was transferred by Turki ibn Sa'ud to 'Abdullah ibn Rashid in return for services rendered; Al Fadhil under Matni ibn Shuraim; and Al Mufadhdhal, whose allegiance is divided between Ibn Rashid and Ibn Sa'ud—the leading *Shaikh* Mulbis ibn Jabrin and another Barjas ibn 'Ubaid having joined the *Ikhwan* while 'Aqab ibn 'Ajil was with 'Ajaimi.

his early intention of returning to his capital, which was garrisoned by Arab troops and could count on the active assistance of the local Shammar, some 4000 strong and all armed with Turkish rifles, to say nothing of four or five guns and a few machine-guns. It rather looked as if the Turks were detaining the chief himself at Al Hajr as the only way of ensuring the provision of camel transport of which they were in sore need and for which the letter in question made an urgent appeal.

The southern borders of Jabal Shammar were held by the Ghufaila subsection of the Shammar under Ghadhban ibn Rimal,[1] while the country between Thamami [2] near the edge of the Dahana at the head of the Batin and ʿAin ibn Fuhaid on the borders of the Qasim was occupied by various sections of the great Harb [3] tribe, whose allegiance is divided between the Sharif and Ibn Saʿud according as it is for the time being in the territory of the one or the other, the tribal range extending from the Dahana to Madina. Finally the Mutair, comprising an able-bodied male population of about 1000, among whom the *Ikhwan* movement had made great progress, were based on the new settlement of Artawiyya and extended thence over the desert eastward towards Kuwait.

The differences, which made the relations of Ibn Saʿud and the Sharif somewhat strained at this period, were of course common talk in the desert, and independent chiefs of the subordinate standing of Dhari experienced no little difficulty in maintaining an appearance of friendliness to either party behind the back of the other. He was certainly making a bid for a share in the Sharif's ample funds, but he told me frankly that, in spite of his admittedly ancient and respected lineage, the King of the Hijaz enjoyed such allegiance as he commanded in Arabia by virtue of British

[1] Lesser *Shaikhs* with him were ʿAiban ibn Maïq and ʿAiyada ibn Zuwaimil.

[2] Water is said to be found here at a depth of only three fathoms, and again at Ajibba beyond the Dahana at four fathoms.

[3] According to Dhari the sections now in Ibn Saʿud's territory were: the Bani ʿAmr under Nahis ibn Dhuwaibi; Bani ʿAli under Muhsin al Firm; Al Frida under Ibn Hammad and Ibn Hudaib; Bani Salim under Ibn Nahit; Al Wuhub under Ibn Saʿda, and other fragments.

support and not of any natural or personal title, while at the same time he admitted Ibn Sa'ud's title to be Ruler of all Central Arabia, not, however, I think, without a mental reservation in favour of himself in the event of his realising his rapidly growing ambition to sit on the throne of Ibn Rashid.

It was not altogether a sinecure being an honoured guest in Dhari's camp, for at meal-times my host—who, I noticed, always ate with his left hand, as he had lost the use of the other owing to a bullet-wound in the forearm, which had been dressed, I believe, by the British medical authorities at Basra and was held together by a tightly strapped leather splint—insisted on handing me all the daintiest morsels in the dish with his own fingers and on serving me personally with every cup of coffee I drank. In spite, however, of his somewhat overdone obsequiousness I found him a pleasant enough companion, not too richly endowed with intelligence, for which he made up by his easy bearing and distinctly good looks. Of his subordinates I thought Fahad ibn Thunaian too dull and stupid to deserve the confidence of his host or the position of second-in-command which he appeared to occupy, while Muhammad ibn Mijlad always struck me as being a little ashamed of himself for having allowed the temptation of Dhari's fleshpots to inveigle him from the natural allegiance he owed to 'Ajaimi.

The day following my arrival with the long-expected bags was a busy one in the camp, and Mulla 'Abdullah was fully occupied in settling his master's debts to his following, who were paid partly in cash and partly in the necessaries of life, and in drawing up lists of stores to be sent for from Zubair and Kuwait—one such list which was shown to me being an order on a Kuwait merchant for the supply of 110 *maunds* of rice and 107 *maunds* of dates, while I was somewhat unconvincingly assured that orders already placed accounted for a further 800 *maunds* of food-stuffs. It was, of course, to Dhari's advantage to make a big show of his responsibilities to impress me with the size of his following, but it did not take me long to become familiar with the rapacity of my new-found friends, who in this respect were not unlike their compatriots everywhere. Two of the lesser chiefs on receiving their presents made bold to ask in mysterious whispers for more — the one because he had recently taken to himself a wife and the other because he had a father to support; a little later Dhari's own coffee-maker appeared to express a hope that I had not forgotten his existence or his excellent coffee; none of these met with the success they hoped for, but a little naked boy, who appeared at my tent door without ceremony and with the single word *Dirahim*[1] in lieu of other greeting went away happy as a lark with two dollars, while double that sum was the generous portion of a fellow who insisted on my taking charge of a wounded *Smaqq*[2] and grinned from ear to ear when I suggested that it was probably money he was looking for.

So passed my stay in Dhari's camp, which was all astir when I was woken up between 4 and 5 A.M. on the morning of April 5 to make ready for my onward journey; it had been decided that Dhari himself and a large following should accompany me to Ibn Sa'ud's camp in case further discussion of our plans should prove necessary, and that the remainder of the camp should move to fresh pastures at a spot already marked out about ten miles to the southward. While I waited till all should be ready for a start I found much of interest in watching the process of the striking, rolling-up, packing and loading of the great black tents and the household furniture—a task which fell entirely to the womenfolk, who set to work in the most business-like fashion to the music of snarling, groaning camels and bleating sheep, while their lords and masters were gathered round the camp-fire drinking coffee and discussing the prospects of the future.

At length all was ready and the signal was given for a start; we mounted and set our faces to the south-west along the rough slope of the right bank of the valley. We were a goodly cavalcade of over sixty camels, and my companions included besides my host, his cousin, Sultan ibn Tawala, Dhaidan and Hamdan, who had been with me on the march from Zubair, and the indispensable Mulla 'Abdullah, while Fahad ibn Thunaian rode with us for

[1] Sing. *Dirham*=money. [2] *Vide* p. 247, note 3, *supra*.

THE WELLS OF HAFAR AT BATIN, WITH CAMEL DRAWING WATER.

half an hour and Muhammad ibn Mijlad set out with the declared intention of accompanying us to Ibn Sa'ud's camp, but took his leave after about an hour's riding, pleading indisposition.

It took us two and a half hours to reach the wells of Al Hafar, where we made a lengthy halt to draw water for the long march before us. The wells, some ten or more in number and descending to a great depth — thirty-five fathoms the Arabs say—are scattered about an extensive circular basin, which forms a nodal point in the drainage of the surrounding country, for on the Batin channel at this point converge from either side the two important channels known respectively as Fulaiyij al Shamali [1] and Fulaiyij al Janubi, along which descends such rain-water as is not absorbed by the uplands on either side; these abut on the valley round the basin in a circle of low cliffs, broken by the wide delta-like mouths of the two channels. The main trough of the Batin enters the basin from the south-west and flows through it to the north-east down the channel, which we had followed up to this point almost from the neighbourhood of Zubair. The basin, which for generations has been the resort of the *Badawin* from every side—for in this tract the waterings are few and far between—is bare of vegetation except for a thin covering of *Sam'a* grass and occasional patches of a purple-flowered thyme-like plant called *Qaisum* [2] and is dotted with the conical mounds, which time has piled up round the mouths of its wells, three of which are distinguished among their fellows as containing the sweetest water, namely, the two at the northern end and that on the extreme south, which is known by the special name of Al Barzan. Each well is surmounted by a wooden post [3] slanting forward over its

[1] About five hours' march up this channel are the wells of Dulaimiyya, beyond which in the same depression to the northward are the waterings of Rukhaimiyya and Tuqaiyid among others; the Fulaiyij al Janubi is without wells, though the Arabs spoke as if it formed part of the same depression in which lie the wells of Al Safa—but I am doubtful of this.

[2] This plant has medicinal qualities and is only sparingly browsed on by camels—once in twenty mouthfuls as they told me; it is heating.

[3] Every part of a well has its name: *Bir* or *Jalib* = well; *Maqam* = post; *Mahala* = pulley; *Mukhtar* = iron pin; *Jaru* = trough; *Dalu* = bucket; *Araji* = cross-piece of bucket; *Arsha* = rope; *Mijarr* = inclined slope.

mouth with a simple wooden pulley fixed to its top by an iron pin and is surrounded by earthen troughs, into which the water is poured as it is drawn, and at which the animals are watered and the water-skins are filled. These are the permanent fixtures of the wells, while the buckets and ropes necessary for the drawing of water must be provided by each party for itself. The rope, to which the leather bucket held open by a cross-piece of wood is attached, is lowered into and drawn up from the water by a camel ascending and descending an inclined slope extending from the mouth of the well to a distance equal to its depth; the drawing of water at wells of such depth is a picturesque but laborious process, which is accepted by the Arabs philosophically enough as a time-honoured institution of their pastoral life.

At length we were done with the watering and continued our march up the centre of the valley across a small *Sha'ib* called Rijlat al Dhaba' to a fairly large patch of *Sidr* bushes known as Hulaiba, which marked the limit of our progress up the Batin, for we now turned abruptly to the southward and, crossing the trough up its sloping right bank, soon stood on its summit at the edge of the vast stony wilderness of the Dibdiba. Turning back for a last view of the Batin, I saw the mouth of the channel of Fau Shamali,[1] where it joined the valley far away to the south-west and traced the bed of the old channel of the Batin backward to the north-east by its narrow band of dark green vegetation forming a noticeable contrast to the lighter green of the slopes on either side. We then set our faces to the southward, and the Batin merged behind us into a featureless desert.

2. The Dibdiba and the Summan

Arabia is rich in desolate places and it would be invidious to single out the Dibdiba for special condemnation, but as

[1] This channel, like Fulaiyij al Shamali, to which it runs parallel, drains the northern section of the Dibdiba into the Batin; opposite its point of entry into the latter is the mouth of Fau Janubi, the counterpart of Fulaiyij al Janubi, to which it runs parallel into the Batin from the south. The two Faus are collectively spoken of as Al Fiwan; there are no wells in either channel, though those of Qubba and Jalt (water-holes only) appear to lie in tributaries of Fau Shamali.

we passed beyond the gentle undulations, which mark its descent into the Batin, on to a boundless arid waste of stone and gravel, thinly dotted here and there with patches of grass and low bushes, it seemed to me that I had never seen anything so utterly dismal. My companions must have experienced something of the same feeling, for we had not made any considerable progress, when they began to evince a desire to discontinue the march and, as Dhari himself joined in the clamour, I had no alternative but to acquiesce in a halt, though I should have preferred to march for another hour or two in the welcome cool of the late afternoon after a somewhat breathless day.

The camels having been driven out to graze, we settled down for the evening, and after the sunset prayer, at which Mulla 'Abdullah officiated as *Imam*—and he certainly had the qualifications of a very pleasing voice and a beautiful enunciation—I was introduced to a luxury of the desert, for during the latter part of the march our people had collected a number of truffles [1] and these were now served up to Dhari and myself by the versatile Mulla, who in addition to being a good *Imam* and an indifferent secretary now showed that he really did excel as a cook. As a matter of fact I must confess that I did not find the truffles very exciting, but, nevertheless, they provided a welcome change of diet, and the Arabs regard them as one of the blessings of springtide, for they are found all over the desert at this season.

A strong dust-laden wind made our long thirty-mile march of the following day over country without a single feature to relieve its dull monotony weary and irksome in the extreme; about seven miles out from camp we crossed the depression of Fau Janubi, slightly to the south of the watershed which divides its drainage to north and south. Just before reaching it we espied in the distance to our right front a group of camel riders, whom our experts guessed—correctly as it turned out—to be of the Wahab subsection of the Aslam and, therefore, part of Dhari's following. Two of our number were detached to pay them a visit and we continued our advance, but had not gone far when we

[1] *Faq'a* pronounced *Faj'a*.

saw another party ahead of us, who, having apparently not noticed our envoys going forward to fraternise with their fellows, fired three shots into the air as a warning both to us and their friends, for in a moment the horizon was covered with black specks and some more shots were fired, one of which whizzed over or through us uncomfortably near. Some of our number then rode forward rapidly, holding out their mantles as a flag of truce and in token of our friendly intentions, while at the same time we saw a group of five horsemen gallop out towards us from the opposite side. The firing now ceased, and the five horsemen, wiry rough-visaged individuals, all riding bareback and armed with long quivering spears with heavy points, were soon in our midst, hailing their chief in the manly and confident manner of the sons of the desert. When we reached the edge of the Fau we found the whole of the Wahab on the march down the depression to the southward with all their panoply of *Qins* and *Kitabs* and grazing milch camels ; our track lay through the midst of them across the trough, but it took us some time to extricate ourselves from them, for not only did the inevitable desire of both parties to exchange news and small chat delay us, but my companions found the temptation of a free drink from the heavy udders of the milch camels too much to resist and were out of their saddles in a trice. The great beasts accustomed to such demands on their indulgence stood still as, two at a time, my companions milked them into a bowl and each in turn emptied the bowl until he could manage no more. It was a curious scene—an exhibition of primitive greed—but the Arab is always ready for a feast, be it milk or meat, as indeed he is ready for the lean days, which in his country are all too many. But what struck me as more remarkable than the greed of my own party was the philosophic calm with which the Wahab camel-owners watched their animals being drained by their unbidden guests, and I was told afterwards in answer to my queries that I had good reason to be surprised at their hospitable indulgence, as the practice of the desert varied greatly from tribe to tribe, the Shammar standing by common consent at the very top of the scale of open-handed generosity, while the next tribe on our way, the Mutair, are accounted churls ; and they told me tales of how the latter tribe would come out with their weapons against a thirsty traveller who ventured to touch their cattle, while a *Shammari* would run a great distance to force his hospitality on a passing stranger, and would regard him with unfriendly eyes if he declined to drink.

We were fortunately able to return the chance hospitality of the Wahab at once, for we halted for our midday rest some three miles beyond the Fau and were visited by three notables of the tribe representing its three leading clans, our guests being Dhahir ibn Shamali, the head *Shaikh*, in person, Khunaifis representing his father Hailim ibn 'Aqab and the son of 'Awwad ibn Badr. They had little news to give us except that the country ahead of us was occupied by the Mutair and that nothing had occurred recently to disturb the tranquillity of the desert ; they were anxious to improve the occasion by wheedling permits out of me to buy provisions at Kuwait, but I parried their importunity by telling them that all such arrangements were in Dhari's hands, and I think they went away satisfied with the doles of cash I made in the name of Government, exhorting them at the same time to join actively with Dhari in the suppression of contraband traffic.

Some eight miles beyond this point we passed out of the stony Dibdiba into a well-marked and still more dismal division of the desert, a vast area of smooth firm loam or clay [1] very scantily covered with grass and diversified at rare intervals by small patches of bushes ; they call it Juraiba and regard it as the dividing line between the Dibdiba and the downs of the Summan, four miles short of whose edge we camped for the night in a pleasant bush-covered depression, which formed a veritable oasis in the wilderness, but seemed to be of no great length.

The bare plain before we reached camp seemed to be alive with herds of gazelles, but our efforts to secure meat for the pot ended in failure and we had no better luck with

[1] The soil was of a reddish-brown colour ; the grass covering it was mostly *Sam'a*, with a considerable proportion of a yellow-flowered prickly plant called *Niqt*, a small green succulent weed called *Hathara* and a low dry bush called *Khadhdhar*.

a *Hubara*, which flopped lazily away out of our track, but we picked up two eggs of this species in the neighbourhood. Our dinner was delayed by the discovery that Dhaidan's *Dhalul* was missing when the animals were rounded up for the night after a short period of grazing. A search party went out at once but without success, and it was a glum party that sat down to a meal which had grown cold and nasty, for Dhaidan could do nothing but pour his woes into our ears; only a few months back he had bought the animal for £T.8 in cash, a camel worth £T.10, and four goats valued at £T.1 each. Fortunately the animal was found and brought in by a search party next morning. During the day I had ridden Dhari's own *Dhalul*, a big light-coloured beast with a beautiful swinging trot which I greatly enjoyed. He told me he had captured it on a raid against the 'Abda and that it was worth £T.50, but Dhaidan, not having heard his master's tale, informed me that it had been purchased quite recently from an Arab for £T.25—I do not know which was telling the truth.

The passage of what remained of the Juraiba was enlivened next morning by an alarm; a *Zaul* or moving body was seen far away on the right just before we sighted the edge of the Summan; "Bushes," said one; "Arabs," said another, meaning graziers; "*Badu*," said another, meaning raiders; and so on until the glasses put an end to the discussion by leaving no doubt that the suspicious apparition was a party of mounted men marching towards us. We had passed the last of the friendly Shammar and had not yet reached the Mutair marches, so the probability was that it was a party of 'Abda or other hostile section of Shammar. Rifles were unslung and loaded and scouts were sent forward on the right flank, but the party, which was not a large one, appeared to become aware of us and relieved us of further worries by turning tail and making off in the direction whence it had come.

The incident, however, served to put us on our guard, and we entered the gently undulating stony downs of the Summan with our scouts well in advance, for in such a country an enemy might be lurking in any fold of the undulations. As we approached the first ridge several shots rang out ahead, and it was clear that our scouts were in action. Amid much shouting of orders and counter-orders we pushed forward helter-skelter through a narrow opening in the ridge which disclosed a wide circular basin surrounded by a ring of low mounds. Shots were still being exchanged, and some of our scouts were seen moving about in the open beyond the water-hole of Barjisi, which occupied the centre of the clearing. The enemy, whoever it was, appeared to be beyond the farther mounds and we now gathered behind one of those nearer at hand, couched our camels under cover and proceeded to make dispositions for the battle; ammunition was dealt out and the line of heights in front of us was picketed, while Dhari, myself and the main body remained in the hollow awaiting events. The general opinion was that we had come upon a body of the 'Abda, whom our scouts seemed to be defeating on their own, but, as suddenly as it had begun, the firing ceased and the report came in that we were in contact with a party of Suluba—a strange gypsy tribe of the northern desert—who, being engaged in drawing water when they were surprised by what they took to be a raiding party, retired into the downs behind, letting off their rifles as they went, more to attract their own folk than with any idea of contesting the ground.

Peace having been established, we ascertained that our late enemy was a small party which had come down to Barjisi for water from an encampment of some 200 tents in Sha'ib Makhit, a depression not far distant which drains the northern part of the Summan into the Batin. Dhari at once entered into negotiations with them for the hire of some camels, of which we were in need, and it was decided that we should halt here till midday, while he went off with a small following to the Suluba camp to complete the deal. The camp must have been close at hand, for we had scarcely settled down to a long rest and loosed the camels to browse among the downs, not forgetting at the same time to picket the surrounding heights to guard against surprise, when we were visited by two Suluba *Shaikhs*, Huwaidi ibn Badi and Suwaidan ibn Muharib, nephew and cousin respectively of Mahdi and Khalaf, joint chiefs of the Ghunaiman clan of the Jamil section, with which we were in contact. Suwaidan wore no clothing but a long smock of deerskin reaching to his knees, but his companion affected linen and coarse worsted like the *Badu*.

The Suluba are a race apart, assimilated by environment to the Arabs, but not of them, a sort of lost tribe, whose origin is veiled by the mists of antiquity. Despised and patronised by the Arabs, to whom they pay a mild tribute in cash, kind or service for the right to breathe the desert air and for the complete immunity from molestation which they enjoy by the unwritten law, they are conscious of their low status in the social scale and are not ashamed of the current myth, which regards them as the surviving relic of some Christian tribe of the past, though at the present day they comport themselves in every respect as *Muslims* even to the practice of circumcision, with which they probably dispensed until comparatively recent times. Whatever their origin may be, there is no doubt that they owe their privileged position in the desert to crafts of which they enjoy a practical monopoly, for in addition to being unrivalled hunters and expert guides—they are credited with knowing the positions of waterings in the desert unknown to any one else—they are the tinkers and smiths of the nomad community and as such indispensable. In this respect indeed they remind one strongly of the Sabaean community of the Euphrates valley and the Jews of Najran in the far southwest, who owe their continued existence in the midst of wild and intolerant *Muslim* tribes to the special services which they alone are capable of rendering to their neighbours in peace and war. The Suluba are organised into sections and clans like the Arabs around them, the two main sections at any rate in this neighbourhood being the Jamil and Majid, and they combine pastoral pursuits with their other activities, having amassed by their industry considerable numbers of camels and sheep, to say nothing of a peculiar breed of large white asses,[1] of which they seem to have a monopoly and which enjoy a wide reputation for speed, carrying capacity and endurance of thirst and fatigue.

Soon after the departure of our guests with a present of ten dollars each we received a visit from two lesser per-

[1] *Vide* p. 12 *supra*.

sonages of the same community, who had come frankly for money and whom I tried in vain to inveigle into conversation, one of them being Khulaifa, a younger son of Mahdi. My companions began to exhibit some impatience at their presence, but I ordered coffee and persisted in my attempts to draw out my guests, who did nothing but fidget as if they were in a hurry. "Why have you come here?" I asked at last in desperation. "To greet you," was the laconic reply. "Have your *Shaikhs* gone home?" I tried again. "Yes, they told us they had seen you, and we came along, leaving our camels at the water, and there is nobody there to look after them." At length coffee being disposed of and all further attempts at conversation ending in failure, I gave them five dollars each and they leaped to their feet and were off without further ceremony. My companions remonstrated with me for the consideration which I had shown them. "It is not necessary to give money to such folk," said Mulla ʿAbdullah, "they are not like the Shammar or other *Badu*."

It was well past noon when Dhari returned and we were able to resume our march into the heart of the Summan, which, though part of the same belt of downs which extends unbroken to the southward down the centre of the Eastern Desert across the track I had followed on my journey from the Hasa to Riyadh, was here much rougher and more accidented than I had found it in the south. We now passed through a succession of short valleys and more or less circular depressions, lined or encircled by low ridges of dull-grey limestone exhibiting occasional patches of whiter colouring, the whole being much weathered by wind and rain. The general character of the country was bleak and bare[1] enough, but the Muhaqqaba and other nameless ridges, which limited our view as we passed from valley to valley and from depression to depression, provided a welcome variation on the endless desert horizon of the preceding days.

This northern part of the Summan is sometimes spoken

[1] The vegetation in the valleys included *Samʿa* grass, a plant called *Rutha*, much relished by camels and resembling the *Arfaj*, and patches of *Sidr*.

of as Al Duhul in reference to a curious natural phenomenon which differentiates it from its southern section; the whole tract for miles around is honeycombed by a network of natural subterranean galleries to which access is obtained in widely scattered localities by what look like well-shafts but are in reality natural cracks in the surface which descend to a depth varying from twenty to thirty feet and are attributed locally to meteorites or falling stars. The term *Dahal* (plural *Duhul*) is applied properly to those perpendicular shafts at the bottom of which, as one might expect, the rain water tends to collect and form pools, as it also does along the galleries which ramify from the base of the shafts sometimes to a great distance; whether all these passages are so connected as to form a regular system of underground drainage—the *Badawin* certainly believe that they are—I am not in a position to determine, but the frequency of the shafts would seem to suggest that this is the case, and I have heard tales of these galleries being used by Arabs passing underground from one *Dahal* to another to escape an enemy, and of venturesome individuals disappearing [1] in the same way, to be heard of no more. More usually, however, it is in search of water that the Arabs descend into the subterranean maze and, when the exhaustion of the supply at the shaft-base renders exploration of the interior necessary to tap its hidden supplies, they take the precaution of tying a rope round their waists to guide them back again to the shaft when they have filled their water-skins, for it would not be difficult to lose oneself in the darkness below.

The Barjisi shaft was the first of the *Duhul* which we encountered, and during the day we passed another in a wide depression named Umm al Dhian, while the neighbourhood of the Muhaqqaba ridge was said to be full of them, as also was the country we traversed on the following day. The country was full of game—gazelles which eluded us; hares, one of which was knocked on the head by one of our party as it lay asleep in a bush; *Hubara*, one of which was annexed after a long patient pursuit; while our bag also included a *Smaqq*.

One of our *Dhaluls* distinguished herself in the evening by

[1] *Vide* p. 47 *supra*.

deserting ; she was seen moving off at a rapid pace into the desert just at the moment when our party was lining up for the evening prayer ; the prayer was forgotten and a pursuit was hurriedly organised, but the renegade had a good start towards a ridge which closed in the distance. For a brief while we enjoyed the unwonted spectacle of a camel-hunt, until quarry and pursuers passed beyond the ridge and the shades of night blotted out the scene. It was not till late in the evening that the four men who had gone off in pursuit returned—but on foot ; the defaulting *Dhalul* had taken refuge in an outlying encampment of the Mutair, and its inmates, surprised at the sudden apparition of four armed men of the Shammar and a runaway camel in their midst, decided after hearing explanations, which did not convince them, to retain all five camels as hostages against disturbance during the night and to dismiss the men with their blessing. This necessitated the despatch of a second expedition, accompanied by the *Mutairi Rafiq*, Sa'ud, who had been with us from Al Hafar, and the animals were duly reclaimed and brought back to the camp in triumph.

Early next morning we passed without incident through the scattered encampments — the tents were of unusually small size—and grazing herds of the Mutair, who, being aware of our identity and having had our news from their overnight visitors, ignored us entirely, and came in for much adverse comment on the part of my companions as they cast longing glances at the milch-camels about us without daring to help themselves to a drink ; but their patience was presently rewarded, for we came upon a man of the Harb who was sojourning temporarily with the Mutair and insisted on our partaking of the milk of his own animals. These Mutair were of the Abassifa subsection of the Buraih section, many of whom had joined the ranks of the *Ikhwan* ; among them we also noticed some Suluba tents.

Shortly after this we halted for a few moments at the mouth of Dahal Suqur in the hope of finding water in the shaft, but in this we were disappointed and, as no one seemed anxious to explore the subterranean galleries branching out from its base, we continued our march after killing a snake which had issued from one of the many shallow rock-clefts [1] which encircled the *Dahal*. Other shafts pointed out to me hereabouts, but somewhat off our line of march, were those of Fudhaili, Abu Nakhla and Raqqas, while some distance farther on we passed near by Dahal Hamad and Dahal Shayib, beyond which we passed into a tract called Rubaida, which though to all appearances of very similar character to the Summan differed from it in its more sandy reddish-brown soil and in the reappearance of *Arfaj* in place of *Rutha* in its vegetation. It was also less broken in character—the latter part of the Summan had been covered with outcrops of hard red sandstone [2]—and more gently undulating without marked ridges; away on the right an arm of the Juraiba tract seemed to extend between the Summan and the outer ridge of the Dahana, of which we now had our first view.

Almost immediately there was another slight change in the character of the country and we entered the Hatifa tract, a gently swelling plain of sandy loam, with frequent grassy depressions full of *Arfaj* and other vegetation, including a thistle called *Samna*. The largest of these depressions was one called Faidhat al Rutha, near which is another *Dahal*, that of Umm al Qurun, and beyond which we came to a small coppice of well-grown *Sidr* trees; here there had of late been much felling of timber by the *Ikhwan* of Artawiyya for the building of their city.

We were now rapidly converging on the 'Araiq Duhul, an outlying ridge of the Dahana but popularly not reckoned as being of it though of the same general character, and the landscape resumed the name though not the broken character of the Summan just before we reached the Manshariha or main caravan track from Kuwait to Zilfi and the interior. We struck the road about two miles east of the point at which it crosses the 'Araiq near a group of *Sidrs* known as Sufaiya, but our course lay southward past one or two other *Sidr* patches, and it was not till some three miles beyond the road that we came to rest for the night

[1] These are called *Kharqa* or *Khariqa*.

[2] The term used for this is *Salbukh*, a word also used for the curious cylindrical (coral ?) stones which I had met with farther south on the journey to Riyadh—*vide* p. 49 *supra*.

at the edge of the sand-ridge and stood once more on the threshold of the Dahana.

3. The Dahana

To travellers from the east arrival at the edge of the Dahana marks a welcome turning-point in a weary journey; the naked wilderness of the Eastern Desert is behind them and they stand before the lofty barrier of sand which almost encircles the inner core of Arabia. As a matter of fact the ʿAraiq Duhul is not part of the true Dahana, whose eastern edge was still some six or seven miles distant behind the sandy plain of Jandaliyya, but it is of identical formation with the main mass, which it resembles both in colour and in its vegetation, and should probably strictly be regarded as an offshoot of it. In breadth it does not exceed half a mile, but it extends without a break from the north-eastern angle of the Dahana in a south-easterly direction to a great distance, though it does not reach the Hasa-Riyadh track. Our camp was pitched in the first fold of the ʿAraiq, and it was pleasant to lie on the soft warm sand watching the great silhouettes of our camels browsing among the billowy dunes as the short twilight faded away.

Next morning, just before we broke camp, a party of four Suluba mounted on two *Dhaluls* arrived in our midst; the bounty which I had distributed at Barjisi had produced a flutter in the Suluba camp at Makhit, and our new visitors had set out during the previous morning and ridden all night on our tracks with the object of paying their respects to me; the party comprised Mahdi ibn Khalaf and Khalaf ibn Muslab, the joint *Shaikhs* of the Ghunaiman clan, the latter's son, Mubarak, and another. They were obviously anxious to return without delay to their own folk with such gifts as their enterprise in coming so far might procure them, but I was equally anxious to profit by the unexpected addition of so representative a group of their tribe to our party, and common politeness compelled them to accede to my suggestion that they should join us in our march across the Dahana, though half-way across Khalaf made a determined but unsuccessful attempt to obtain an honourable dismissal by confiding to me his anxiety about the folk they had left behind without adequate protection from the dangers to which they were exposed, as he put it, "from north and south." Earlier in the day he had told me that their camp numbered no less than 1000 tents, and I think he actually appreciated my point when I suggested that the absence or presence of four individuals could scarcely prejudice or secure the well-being of so large a community. However that may be, they marched with us all that day and part of the next and proved a never-failing source of merriment and instruction.

The day's march exactly coincided with the crossing of the Dahana, whose width, by our somewhat southerly course from ʿAraiq Duhul to our evening camp near the similar outlying Batra ridge on the other side, I reckoned at about twenty-five miles, though the true Dahana barrier was only some fifteen miles across. The sand barrier is traversed at irregular intervals by a number of recognised tracks connecting the waterings on either side by the shortest possible lines; one of these, the Manshariha, leads from Kuwait *via* the wells of Safa across the Dahana in a south-westerly direction to Artawiyya, while another, known as Baihis, is formed by the junction[1] of the roads leading from the wells of Haba and Qaraʿa, strikes the sand at a point south of our camp, crosses it parallel to the Manshariha at a distance of seven or eight miles, and branches out again on the other side into two paths leading to the wells of Qaiʿiyya and Dijani. In the spring season, however, travellers need not hasten over the waterless interval on account of their camels, which find sufficient moisture in the vegetation, and we made ourselves secure on this score by sending a small party ahead to the Qaiʿiyya wells to bring water to our evening camp for ourselves, and were thus enabled to strike across the Dahana on the line most convenient to us—a line which took us diagonally from our camp near the Manshariha road on the east to the point at which the Baihis emerges from the sands on the west. Even so, however, though the going was occasionally a little heavy for the laden camels, we experienced no serious difficulty in crossing the successive

[1] At a patch of *Sidr* bushes called Al Khamma.

sand-ridges, which trend at this point from north-west to south-east and were everywhere intersected with the tracks of sheep and camels, which we found grazing in great numbers throughout our march, for at this season the *Badawin*, in this instance the Mutair of Artawiyya and the surrounding country, spread over the Dahana to regale their flocks and herds on the rich herbage which a little rain brings to fresh life each year out of the sand. The last occasion on which I had crossed the Dahana was in November, when the surface was bare or thinly covered with withered weeds and bushes, but now my eyes encountered a very different scene, for the sand, except where it lay in steeper slopes, was covered with a richer profusion of plants and grasses than I have met with anywhere else in Arabia. Among the more conspicuous and plentiful herbs I counted thirteen varieties,[1] which number might have been multiplied many times if I had had the leisure for a proper survey.

The invasion of sheep had of course driven all game from the scene, but at other times, as the Suluba told me, these ridges teem with gazelle. "Do you ever nowadays meet with the oryx or the ostrich in these parts?" I enquired of Mahdi as he was speaking of the days he had spent here in the chase. "Long ago," he replied, "these animals were certainly plentiful everywhere in these sands, and then the Arabs came"—I presume he referred to the greater traffic which has been developed in comparatively recent times with the growth of Kuwait as a seaport—"and then the oryx and ostrich scattered to north and south, where alone they are found now in the great sand wastes; I have hunted both near Jauf, and next time I go in that direction I will try and get some young animals for you." "What is the ostrich like in the deserts?" I asked. "*Wallah! ya Sahib*, seeing them afar off you would say they were a *zaul* of camels and they move like the wind; the hen

[1] *Arfaj, Arta, Qirdha, Alqa, Adhir* among the shrubs; *Nussi, Qasba, Musaï, Sabat* among the grasses; and *Hamat, Karrath, Hambasis* and *Kharshaf* among flowering plants. Snakes seem to be very plentiful in this tract for we killed three, two of the class called *Hanish*, and the other a diamond-headed viper which they called *Haiya*; the term *Dab* (plural *Diban*) is used generally of all snakes.

lays from twenty to thirty eggs, which we often find and eat, and the young when hatched are as big as a *Hubara*." But it is mostly after the gazelle that they go, and it is a common thing for a *Sulubi* on a single expedition to lay low some twenty or more of these animals, whose flesh with the help of a little salt and the blazing sun he converts into *Jila* or dried venison for home consumption and for the market; very excellent it is, and there is no better provision one can make for a long march, for if the meat has been cured by skilled hands it lasts for a month and even more in the winter and retains its delicious flavour.

I was riding ahead with Mahdi across the Jandaliyya plain when my attention was arrested by sounds of merriment in the rear. Khalaf, the other Suluba *Shaikh*, was declaiming a poem in honour of Dhari, and the murmurs of approval which punctuated the couplets showed that he was having a great success. A roar of laughter from the audience greeted the concluding couplets, which contained a demand for a *Dhalul* as the reciter's reward, and Dhari had no alternative but to promise the gift. The poem was a long one, and I was amazed and even a little sceptical when they told me that it was an *extempore* production, but I believe the claim was perfectly genuine; at any rate Khalaf immediately repeated it from beginning to end for my benefit, with the addition of a few couplets suggesting that a *Dhalul* would be little good without a Mauser rifle to go raiding with, and the same evening the whole poem was repeated again to Mulla 'Abdullah, who took it down in writing at my request.

It took us but a few minutes to traverse the 'Araiq Duhul, but a good two and a half hours to cross the Jandaliyya plain, a great sandy valley as it were with occasional dunes and ridges, one of which lying to southward of our course runs for a considerable distance down the centre of the depression and is important enough to have a name—Haraba. The surface of the plain became rougher and exhibited occasional outcrops of rock and gravel as we approached the farther side and ascended the first slope of the true Dahana, on which we found a small Mutair encampment of thirty tents. Some of our party were bold enough to enter one of these in search of hospitality, for our water-supply was fast running out and a drink of milk would have helped to conserve it to the end of the march; they spoiled their chances, however, by their own folly, for the Mutair took offence at the humming of a secular melody and bade them begone lest worse should befall. I did not witness the occurrence, but Dhaidan assured me that their host actually took up his rifle to hasten their departure. During these days I certainly heard no good of the Mutair and, though perhaps some allowance should be made for Shammar jealousy of their nearest neighbours and for some exaggeration of their defects natural in such circumstances, it was clear enough that those portions of the tribe with which we came in contact were conspicuously lacking in the qualities of open hospitality one is accustomed to associate with the *Badawin*. Dhari often declared that he did not like being in their country, while Dhaidan never lost an opportunity of gibing at the churlishness and morosity, which he attributed partly to natural defects and largely to the rapid spread of *Ikhwan* tenets through the tribe. Their little praying enclosures neatly marked out with stones and often approached by narrow causeways similarly marked out from the encampments, to which they belonged, were a frequent source of ridicule and resentment; after all, who were the *Ikhwan* that they should arrogate to themselves all the favours of the Almighty? and Dhaidan delivered himself of a striking epigram on the subject, which doubtless did justice to the sentiments of his fellow-tribesmen in general about the hated sect: "*Ma hum jaïyin min Allah wa chinnahum chilab*" ("They be not come from God but like unto curs").

The first section of the Dahana, a gentle down very lightly covered with grasses but changing abruptly to typical sand billows of deep orange colour, is known as Jaham; about two and a half miles in width, it is separated by a narrow depression or *Khabb* of sand-covered loam from the next section called Murait, whose breadth across is about two miles. This in turn is marked off by a similar depression from the third section. This section and the next, the one nameless and the other named Mukhaiyit and each about two miles broad, are separated by the wide depression of Khabb al Naum, more than a mile across, and constitute by far the most striking part of the Dahana. Their sands are of looser texture than those of other sections, and their deeper billows give the effect of a storm-tossed sea, while the summits of their ridges are marked at intervals by immense cones of pure sand rising to a height of perhaps 200 feet above the general level of the ground. From our midday camp in the Khabb al Naum I counted eight such cones on either section, extending like the summits of mountain ranges from north to south, but doubtless I could have counted many more from a loftier point of view. Such sand peaks are known as *Ta'S* (plural *Tu'us*), *Niqa'* (plural *Niqyan*) and collectively as *Gharamin, Barakhis, Haumat al Niqyan* or *Majlis*, the last term being derived from the grouped arrangement of the peaks — as it were some assembly of desert giants. Individual peaks, again, are honoured by special names, of which the most striking is Niqa' Mutawwa', a cone somewhat to south of our course, which some desert wit has nicknamed "The Proctor" in allusion to a prominent feature of the ecclesiastical system of the *Wahhabis*. These lines of peaks seemed to me to trend from north-west to south-east, which is the general direction of the Dahana belt in this sector; how far this peculiar feature is reproduced to north and south of the farthest limits of our view I cannot say, but in the latter direction it certainly does not occur as far southward as the Hasa-Riyadh tract, and so far as I could ascertain it ceases at about the latitude of Shauki.

From the ridge-summit of Mukhaiyit we saw the dark line which marks the plain beyond the Dahana, but we still had three sand-belts to cross, the first nameless and separated from Mukhaiyit by a narrow *Khabb*; the second called Ardh 'Aqal after one 'Aqal, a hunter who used to frequent this tract; and the last nameless and separated from Ardh 'Aqal by the broad depression of Khabb al Radhm, the appearance in which of scattered limestone outcrops bore witness that we were not far distant from more solid ground. The total width of these sections and the depressions between them was less than five miles, and they call for no remark except that in their general characteristics they resemble the earlier sections of the Dahana.

It was with a feeling of relief that we descended from the last slope on to the Baihis track where it passes into the Lughaf, a narrow sandy strip dividing the Dahana from the ʻArma plain, at the very edge of which we pitched our camp near the outlying sand-ridge of Batra, the counterpart of the ʻAraiq Duhul on the other side. The Dahana had again disappointed me, but I was glad to have seen the seven-ridged formation, which is peculiar to and the main feature of this alone of the sand areas of Arabia.

CHAPTER VII

RIYADH REVISITED

1. The 'Arma Plateau

The pastures round our camp were dotted with grazing camels and sheep, the former by their black colour betraying the presence of either 'Ataiba or Harb *Badawin*, who seem to enjoy a monopoly of dark-skinned cattle, though why this should be so when black sheep seem to predominate in all *Badawin* flocks in contrast to those of the Euphrates shepherd tribes, which are almost invariably white, it would be difficult to say. We soon discovered the camp of our neighbours, who proved to be *Ikhwan* elements of Ibn Rubai'an's section of 'Ataiba, now settled with the Mutair at Artawiyya.

The men we had sent on to fetch water did not succeed in finding our camp till late in the night, when we had given them up and retired supperless to bed, for the last foul dregs of Hafar or Barjisi water remaining in our skins had been used up by the ever-thoughtful Dhaidan in brewing me some tea, which I had to drink, disgusting as it was, with some pretence of enjoying it. In justice to myself, however, I should mention that during the march Ghazi, a member of Dhari's own clan, who was our guide during the journey and often beguiled me with tales of how he and his father before him had served in the same capacity on many a Shammar raid of the past, and had thus acquired an intimate knowledge of all this country, had drained the contents of my water-bottle. When the water party arrived it was found that one of its number was missing, and, a search for him next morning ending in failure, it was assumed either that he had lost his way and would now make straight for Ibn Sa'ud's camp or, as the more pessimistic would have it, that he had been the victim of foul play on the part of the treacherous Mutair, for it so happened that the missing man was one of the very few habitual smokers of our party—the habit of smoking seems to be dying out rapidly in the desert, largely no doubt under the influence of puritan propaganda. There was, however, nothing to be done but to write him off as missing for the time being, and it was not till we found him safe and sound in Ibn Sa'ud's camp two days later that the Mutair were acquitted of responsibility for his untimely end.

The northern part of the 'Arma, a bare gently-undulating plain over which the Baihis highway runs to the wells of Qai'iyya, with a branch to those of Dijani farther north, is sometimes spoken of as Al Jalad or simply Al Safra,[1] a common term indicating a waste or wilderness, though it differs only in having a smoother surface from the southern parts. Generally speaking, the 'Arma tract is a plateau sloping gently down to the edge of the Dahana from an escarpment of varying elevation and abruptness trending from the neighbourhood of Artawiyya in a south-easterly direction parallel to the sand-belt and at an average distance of ten miles from it ; it is in fact the first and lowest of a succession of steppes, which form the Tuwaiq system and rise by easy gradients until they culminate in the high ridges which run along the summit of the western cliff of that mountain barrier.

The wells of Qai'iyya lay some ten miles away to the south-west, their position being rendered unmistakable by a profusion of cairns erected on every eminence for miles around to direct the thirsting wanderer to their waters ; one of these, on the edge of the Baihis road about three miles out from our camp, is popularly known as Rijm al Mufarrih or " the cairn that makes glad," for it is when they see this that travellers coming from the east may know that they are very near their goal ; afar off we had a glimpse of the dim coast of Mujazzal towards Tuwaiq.

[1] Another name for this tract from its northern extremity to the Ats valley in the south is 'Uraima or the little 'Arma, but I did not myself hear this name.

The wells, some thirty in number, though some of these are fallen in or not in regular use, are situated in a shallow circular depression at the base of a gentle slope descending from the outer rim of the steppe, beyond which again lies the Butain valley ; they are sunk to a depth of from fifteen to twenty feet in the hard limestone and lined with cut blocks of the same material for about two-thirds of the way down ; the water is abundant and excellent, and our camels, which had last been watered at Al Hafar five days before, drank of it inordinately, much to the surprise of their masters, who confessed that they did not expect such eagerness for water in the spring season.

Groups of shepherds were watering their flocks at the time, but we had two or three wells to ourselves and our business was soon finished. The supposed position of Ibn Sa'ud's camp was now, owing to the detour we had made, well to the south-east, and it was in that direction that we now headed, frequently, however, deflecting our course to a more easterly direction, with a view to hugging the Dahana, whose lofty sand-cones—now a beautiful pink—soon came into view.

Here and there soon after leaving the water we passed small groups of tents, mostly of 'Ataiba *Ikhwan* of the Qurainiyya subsection ; pretty scenes they made of pastoral peace, with the black flocks scattered about them or lying huddled together between the tents, and at one of them we halted for a draught of delicious *Liban*, butter-milk of sheep, watching the while a woman shaking the goatskin *Samil* or churn in which it is made.

The bare wilderness was varied at times by patches of *Aushaz* bushes and occasional trees of *Talh*, the gum-bearing acacia, while *Rimdh* and spiky *Sih* and *Arfaj* strewed the depressions ; towards the end of the Jalad tract we halted for a midday rest in a shallow *Sha'ib* scarcely three miles distant from the Batra ridge, behind which I counted as many as twenty-one sand-peaks ; farther south the Batra sands come to an end in a ridge of rock called Abwab, through which there is a narrow passage to carry away the drainage of the 'Arma to the edge of the Dahana itself ; the Abwab in turn yields farther south to the sand-ridge of

'Araiq Khalaf, beyond whose southern extremity the 'Arma reaches to the flank of the Dahana; opposite the Abwab ridge the western extremity of the plateau is marked by a pair of prominent cairns, Al Dhirain, doubtless marking a practicable descent from the ridge to the plain beyond.

Late in the afternoon our eyes were gladdened by the sight of a long line of trees stretching across the plain at right angles to our course, and we were soon couching our camels by the banks of Sha'ib Asal, a narrow sandy meandering torrent-bed, which, rising near the watering of Shahama, about twelve miles distant to the south-west on the fringe of 'Arma, courses down the slope to the edge of the Dahana, where its flood-waters sink into the ground in a depression called Haira in the Lughaf. The acacias bordering its banks were grown to lofty trees thirty feet high—sure sign of plentiful water, as also were a number of apparently recently excavated water-holes, not more than three feet deep, in the bed of the channel; at the time of our arrival, however, the holes were dry, but the trees were the first real trees we had seen since leaving Zubair behind us nearly a fortnight before.

The long march of thirty miles had tired us and Dhari complained of a headache, which I treated with phenacetin pills, prescribing at the same time absolute rest and abstention from evening prayers. The latter injunction he complied with implicitly, somewhat to my surprise,—for the Shammar though not excessively religious are always punctilious in the observance of the formalities of their faith,—and in spite of occasional exhibitions of restiveness under the ban of silence and inactivity, I had the satisfaction of seeing the headache vanish and Dhari sitting down to his dinner with a hearty appetite. Lack of medical skill is a serious defect in one who would travel in Arabia, and I often had occasion to regret that I was so inexperienced in the art of healing that I never dared to administer anything but the commonest pills or tabloids, and those not without trepidation and in weak doses; and on the only occasion on which I ventured to apply zinc ointment to a cut finger my victim remained for some time in such obvious agony and complained so of creeping pains all up his arm that I thought I must have poisoned him. We were now without our Suluba visitors, whom I had dismissed from our midday camp with suitable gifts and with the promise of more when they returned with the ostriches and oryx they had undertaken to procure for me—needless to say I never saw them again.

We set out early next morning resolved to reach our goal by nightfall, but only achieved that object by increasing our pace to a swinging trot of five miles an hour during the afternoon. The going was easy enough over the broad rolling plateau, which degenerated, however, as we approached the line of Sha'ib Shauki into rolling downs shading off to the westward along the outer edge of the plateau into rough weather-worn ridges, in which the *Sha'ib* rises and from which it descends in a winding course north-eastwards, to be absorbed in the depression of Faidhat al Tanha at the edge of the Dahana. In the latter, in line with the depression, rises what appeared to be the last of the sand-cones, a solitary peak named Nuqai'at al Tanha.

The march was marked only by incidents of a minor character: the passage of small camps of 'Ataiba and other *Ikhwan*, at some of which we enjoyed hospitality in the shape of *Liban* ; the discovery of a *Hubara's* nest with four eggs, an unusual number according to Dhaidan, who averred that the bird seldom lays more than three ; a group of well-grown *Talh* trees in a small *Sha'ib* called Wudai' ; but most interesting of all, a scarecrow, or rather something very like one though used for a very different purpose—it was just an *Aba* or common mantle set up on a pole to do proxy for a shepherd, who was doubtless asleep or coffee-bibbing in his tent, for the Arab shepherd, naturally lazy like all his kind, has invented the device of the *Khaiyul*, as they call it, to prevent the straying of his flock without inconvenience to himself, having found by experience that lambs and kids—though apparently not grown sheep and goats—will remain in one spot for hours placidly grazing round the dummy in the belief that it is their master. At this season they were weaning the youngsters and herding them together to play at being sheep and goats, and very pretty did the flocks of little ones look.

At length we reached the tree-lined channel of Sha'ib

Shauki and, being uncertain of the exact position of Ibn Sa'ud's camp, followed its meandering descent. The rich vegetation of the valley exhaled sweet odours into the evening air, and here and there a pool of standing water was evidence of the recent passage of floods, but a little way down our progress was checked by a chain of regular lakelets extending from bank to bank, some twenty or thirty feet across and fully a hundred yards in length, with a depth of perhaps a foot or more. We halted to give our beasts a well-earned drink of the sweet torrent water, into which they waded knee-deep, and then continued our march up the slope on the left bank until, on reaching its summit, we came into full view of a veritable city of canvas, for far and wide over the depression in front of us stretched the tents of the *Wahhabi* camp, in whose midst rose the great white pavilion which we readily recognised as the headquarters of Ibn Sa'ud.

2. The *Wahhabi* "Gom" in Camp

Gathering our mantles about us—for in the desert during warm weather the Arab rides with his cloak thrown back on the hinder part of his saddle, though he would never dream of entering a town or encampment thus—we closed our ranks as we moved down the slope and entered the outskirts of the camp in two serried lines, with Dhari and myself in the midst of the foremost. An imposing spectacle we must have made too with our sixty odd strong as we threaded our way past outlying tents towards the central group with all eyes—at least so it seemed—on us. A curious feeling of oppression weighed upon us, and I know that Dhari and his followers felt not a little uneasy as to how their appearance thus uninvited might be received by the *Wahhabi* host. We halted at a respectful distance from the royal pavilion in the open space which surrounded it and it was some minutes before our suspense was relieved by the sight of a man coming out of the tent towards us, and the man was Ibrahim.

The familiar features of the one man among those who had accompanied me to Jidda for whom I had conceived a strong dislike roused in me in the somewhat cheerless circumstances of our arrival a sense almost as of home-coming, and the greetings we exchanged were cordial and even affectionate; we couched our camels at his bidding, and Dhari, Sultan and the more important members of our party having been introduced, he led the way without further ceremony towards the large tent. Among the guards on duty at the door I recognised Sa'd al Yumaini, who seemed somewhat disturbed at my insistence on exchanging a few words of greeting and a handshake before we passed into the interior of the tent. The floor was covered all over with carpets, while on one side was placed a settee of carpets and cushions about a foot thick, in the midst of which was set a decorative camel saddle, against which Ibn Sa'ud was reclining as we entered. He rose from his place as I entered with Dhari at my side and the rest of the party behind, came forward and greeted each one of us with the simple greeting of the *Badawin*, whereupon we ranged ourselves along the tent sides, my host and I reclining on either side of the saddle, while Dhari was next to him on the other side. Coffee was served round immediately, and after a few moments of formal conversation Dhari and his folk withdrew on the pretext of preparing for the evening prayer and Ibn Sa'ud and I were left together till sunset, when he too went off to take his place in the long double row of worshippers, who had gathered for the Friday[1] evening prayer outside the tent, where I remained pending the pitching of my tent. The prayer was followed by a long *Khutba* or sermon, declaimed in harsh fanatical tones by the presiding priest and conveying to me the impression—though I could not hear what he was saying—that he was denouncing all unbelievers and their wicked works.

After prayers Ibn Sa'ud did not return, but I received a visit from one who was to be hereafter one of my closest friends and was incidentally a member of the deputation from Central Arabia which visited England in the latter part of 1919; 'Abdullah al Qusaibi introduced himself to

[1] Thursday even by our reckoning, for Muhammadans regard the day as beginning at sunset; in towns the main Friday service is held at the hour of midday prayer, but in the desert at the preceding sunset.

me as Ibn Sa'ud's business agent at Bahrain, where he and his four brothers constitute a flourishing company of pearl and general merchants with branches at Hufuf and Bombay. Ibn Sa'ud had gone down some time before to the Hasa, he told me, in expectation of my coming, but about five days since news of my having set out by way of the Batin had reached him and orders had been issued for an immediate return to Shauki, where they had only arrived a few hours before us — travelling rapidly by way of Mount Judi. 'Abdullah had accompanied his chief, with whom he had a great deal of business to discuss, and proposed to come on to Riyadh and spend some months there before returning to the coast *en route* for Bombay. In due course it was announced that my tent was ready and I retired to wash and dine, but, weary as I was, I was summoned soon after my meal to Ibn Sa'ud's tent, where I remained for two hours, letting him do most of the talking, before I retired to bed. Our conversation was of a very general nature and we did not touch on the more important matters, which I begged him to reserve for the morrow, when I should be fresher.

My sojourn at Shauki extended from the evening of the 11th to the morning of the 16th April, five days of pleasant camp-life, during which I devoted myself to business connected with my Mission and made the most of the limited social amenities which came my way. Expeditions into the surrounding country were out of the question as all the camels, including those of Dhari's party, were away grazing, and indeed there was little temptation to wander in a country whose general character obviously varied little if at all from that of the downs we had already traversed and of those which lay before us on the forthcoming march to Riyadh. The *Wahhabi* forces had spent the earlier part of the spring round the wells of Hafar al Ats to the southward, but had come up here on account of the superior grazing facilities of the neighbourhood as soon as the floods had deposited sufficient water for so large a host in the depressions of the *Sha'ib*, for for some reason there are no wells in this locality. The whole country from somewhat southward of this point to the line of the Baihis road is regarded as the *Dira* or range of the Subai' and Suhul tribes, who hold in common the grazing rights of a considerable area extending from the line of Wadi Hanifa eastward over the 'Arma and Dahana into the Summan steppes beyond.

My own little 40-lb. tent was set in the royal enclave, a dwarf among surrounding giants, at a convenient distance from the reception pavilion, but a larger tent was placed at my disposal to serve as occasion required as bathroom and dining-room. In spite of all that had passed on the way to Jidda, Ibrahim was again in charge of my arrangements and of the small staff of servants detailed for my service; he was, therefore, my constant companion from the time that he brought in my morning tea and biscuits to the time that I lay down again to sleep and was present at all meals. Sa'd al Yumaini, now preoccupied with his duties on the personal staff of Ibn Sa'ud, visited me as often as he could for a clandestine smoke and on such occasions my little tent, with flaps close drawn for fear of attracting the attention of passers-by and with the three of us huddled together in its narrow space, resembled a den of vice amid the tabernacles of the elect. Thus forgathered we had little to fear from chance intruders, but once my guests had reason to congratulate themselves on a narrow escape. They were smoking with me while I was still in bed after my morning tea when a messenger announced the approach of no less a person than Ibn Sa'ud himself. Ibrahim and Sa'd scarcely had time to stuff their pipes under my bedding and bundle out of the tent to salute their master when the latter appeared at the door and entered without ceremony. He had fortunately come to consult me at so unusual an hour—indeed his visits to my quarters whether in camp or at Riyadh were rare events—on a matter of great importance, and, though my eyes assisted by my imagination detected cigar-boxes, tobacco-tins, pipes, and matches in every corner, I consoled myself with the reflection that, if in spite of the urgency of the matter in hand he was aware of them or of the thickness of the atmosphere, he did not connect these things with my companions. At any rate the matter went no further.

Of the sequel of our journey to Jidda these two had a sad tale of woe to relate in answer to my enquiries about other members of the party. No sooner had they waved me farewell from the pier than they went to the Sharif requesting permission to depart *via* Mecca, and the Sharif very naturally took advantage of their proposed visit to his capital to ask Ibrahim to convey thither a sum of £4000 which he wished to despatch without delay; at the same time he handed him a further sum of £62 for division among the members of my escort as bounty. On arrival at Mecca the latter sum was duly distributed, but it began to be whispered that Ibrahim and Sa'd had not acted fairly by the rest and had misappropriated the greater part of the Sharif's donation. It may be that the pair had given grounds for the suspicions, on which this accusation was based, by their extravagance and loose living in the holy city, but, whatever be the rights and wrongs of the case, a conspiracy against them was organised by Izmai, Badr abu Saba', and Shaya, in pursuance of which letters were secretly despatched to Ibn Sa'ud from Mecca and again from Quai'iyya during the return journey, in which the two leaders were formally accused of squandering money due to the rest on harlots, smoking, and other forms of vice. On receipt of these letters Ibn Sa'ud, who also told me the story from his point of view, determined to exact the utmost penalty of law and custom from the miscreants who had abused his confidence—they were on arrival to be publicly arraigned before the congregation at the conclusion of the *'Asr* prayer, shorn of their moustaches, beards, and eyebrows, and either flogged or executed; fortunately he had time for reflection before the arrival of the culprits and resolved to give them an opportunity of clearing their reputations. The charge of embezzlement they had no difficulty in refuting while Izmai and his fellow-conspirators failed to produce any evidence of loose living or even to substantiate the charge of smoking. The tables were turned on the accusers who were made to realise that it was a mistake to trifle with Ibn Sa'ud; they were publicly stripped of their weapons and banished the country, a sentence to which Badr and Shaya submitted by withdrawing to their *Badawin* kinsmen, while Izmai took sanctuary [1] in Ibn Sa'ud's

[1] *Dakhal ila baiti*, as Ibn Sa'ud put it, *i.e.* "took refuge in my house."

private quarters in the palace and thus not only evaded the sentence of banishment but lived for some months as the guest of his judge, until by conspicuous devotion to his religious duties he earned a reprieve and was allowed to resume his position in the bodyguard. I met him but once again but he passed by on the other side without a word or any sign of recognition ; the other two I never saw again. It was not without a shudder that Ibrahim and Sa'd told me the tale of their narrow escape from justice, for guilty they were without a shadow of doubt, and it was not without a grim smile that I heard Ibn Sa'ud profess his conviction of their innocence on all the counts, but it was no business of mine to interfere with the course of Arab justice, while my sympathies in this instance were all against Izmai and his fellows in spite of the friendly feelings I had developed towards them on the journey we had made together. It was also on this occasion that I heard of another instance of the taking of sanctuary for which I was indirectly responsible. I have already related how Izmai had been compelled by Ibn Sa'ud to accompany me to the Hijaz in spite of his violent prejudices, but I now heard for the first time that another of the *Ikhwan*, Ibn Huwair by name, had flatly refused to obey a similar order and had fled to the Hasa where he took refuge with 'Abdullah ibn Jiluwi and remained in sanctuary enjoying complete immunity though Ibn Sa'ud threatened to put him to death without mercy should he ever be caught in the open. On the occasion of the chief's recent visit to Hufuf, 'Abdullah had interceded for his uninvited guest and Ibn Sa'ud had no alternative in the circumstances but to grant him a free pardon, but in doing so he seized the opportunity of making a remarkable statement of his own attitude : "See, thou dog," he said, addressing the reprieved sinner, "see these clothes I wear, nay, the very food I eat—all these I have from the English ; how darest thou then abuse them ? Go, dog, the pleading of Ibn Jiluwi has saved thee from death."

The weather during these days was erratic in the extreme ; the temperature was pleasant enough ranging from an average of about 69° Fahr. at 7 A.M. to an average maximum of 93° in the afternoon and back again to an average of 67°

about 11 P.M.; on one occasion only I recorded a reading of just over 100°, and the lowest reading I obtained was 65° though it is probable that the temperature fell some degrees below this point in the early hours when I was asleep. But, though the thermometer behaved throughout in a normal manner, the wind went from one extreme to the other in the most remarkable way, and clear skies became overcast with thunder-clouds, light breezes changed into gales with the most bewildering suddenness. On one occasion I returned to my tent from an interview with Ibn Sa'ud just in time to secure the flaps before half a gale broke upon us and clouds of dust blew through the camp for half an hour leaving a thick layer over my coverlet and everything in my tent, to be cleared away when the wind dropped and light rain fell to clear the atmosphere. On another occasion I was less fortunate, for I was deep in some book when an ominous rumble warned me that a storm was upon us. I rose in all haste to secure the flaps of the tent, but no sooner had I got hold of them than the storm burst in all its fury and all I could do was to hold them with all my strength against a furious gale, which filled my mouth and ears and hair and clothing and everything in the tent with sand, and dashed my thermometer—fortunately I had another in reserve—to pieces against the pole to which it was attached, while with my hands full I watched the disaster helplessly. Luckily everything of a volatile nature was under something too heavy to be moved by the wind, but when the storm was over the interior of my tent was a sorry spectacle indeed, with a thick covering of fine red sand over everything; even so I had just cause for self-congratulation for my little tent was one of the very few which weathered the storm upright, and the rest of the camp was a litter of fallen canvas. This was the more pleasing to me in that only a short while previously Ibrahim or some other well-meaning visitor had taken upon himself to criticise the small dimensions of my abode and I was now able to point to an advantage which it enjoyed above more pretentious tabernacles. But little rain fell at Shauki itself though localities not far distant in the uplands of Tuwaiq seemed to be getting their fair share of precipitation, to judge by the storm-clouds which worked up towards them almost daily from the south-west; we were somewhat out of the direct line of such storms.

Among my regular visitors during this time were ʿAbdullah al Qusaibi and Ibrahim al Junaifi, the latter one of Ibn Saʿud's chief secretaries, a scion of Bani Tamim stock with all the virtues and defects of his ancient lineage, and a veneer of western knowledge, whence acquired I know not, which made him an interesting but not altogether agreeable study. At an early stage of our acquaintance he objected to my clothes as not being sufficiently showy, and even offered to make good the deficiencies of my wardrobe out of his own stock—an offer which I declined with the remark that I had not time to worry myself about such a matter. In point of fact I had long since devoted much thought to this subject, and had deliberately decided to steer a middle course between the simplicity of the better-class *Badawin* and the magnificence of the slaves and myrmidons of the royal household, with the result that I wore white under-clothing, as simple a coat as I could procure, a mantle of black or brown, a head-kerchief of red check by day and a lighter white one in the cooler hours, and a head-band of simple type given me by Ibn Saʿud himself.

These two with Ibrahim, a cousin of the latter named Hamud, and either Dhaidan or some other member of Dhari's suite generally joined me at meals, which were simple enough—seldom anything but mutton, rice, and bread, though occasionally varied by sweet concoctions of milk and vermicelli or little cakes, and on one occasion by a dish of dried prawns, *Rubiyan*, from the Hasa coast. Camel's milk and *Liban* there were, of course, in plenty, and the royal cooks know how to make delicious broth. In addition to these things Ibn Saʿud had got in a supply of various kinds of biscuits from India, but these only appeared with my morning and afternoon tea and were much appreciated by Ibrahim and Saʿd. The cost of all imported provisions had risen very considerably during the war, partly owing to the enhanced prices demanded at Bombay, and largely owing to the greatly increased cost of camel-transport in Arabia. For instance, during this period Ibn Saʿud sent an order to Kuwait for 1000 bags of rice, estimating the cost thereof at eighteen dollars per sack containing one and a quarter Basra *maunds* on account of purchase price and fifteen dollars per sack on account of camel freight—a total charge of thirty-three dollars equivalent to Rs.78 per sack delivered in the Qasim. In camp and in the field Ibn Saʿud is responsible for the maintenance of his whole force to the extent of providing the necessaries of life—dates, flour, and rice—while at Riyadh the average number of people catered for daily in the palace is over a thousand when he is in residence and not less than two-thirds of that number in his absence; indeed, the maintenance of his household, his army and his guests accounts for the greater part of his regular expenditure.

In conversations with me Ibn Saʿud never tired of talking about the state of his finances. "*Wallah,*" he said to me one day, "all I have at the present moment is—*Khalli ahachik,*" he persisted impatiently brushing aside an interruption on my part deprecating the carrying of his confidences to such lengths, "let me tell you, all I have at the present moment in cash is £3000 and 4000 dollars; what can I do with that but restrict my military activities? See I have 1500 men out with me now"—I do not think the total could have exceeded 1000 all told—"I would have more but that I am compelled to economise by mobilising my forces by relays, each division on duty with me and at my expense for a month at a time, after which it is disbanded while others take their turn." The treasury at Riyadh derives its revenue from three main sources. Firstly there is the *Zakat* or tax on sheep and camels levied at the rate of one sheep or five dollars on every full tale of forty sheep, and one goat or five dollars on every complete tale of five camels, —thus an owner of seventy sheep or eight camels pays but five dollars like the owner of the minimum taxable number, the owner of thirty sheep pays nothing, and the owners of ten and fourteen camels respectively pay alike. This clumsy and unevenly distributed system of taxation is reckoned to yield about 20,000 dollars a year. Secondly the *Zakat al Arudh* or land tax, levied at the rate of one-fifth or one-tenth of the main crops, dates and cereals, on flow and lift irrigated lands respectively, yields in the Hasa and at Qatif alone about 190,000 dollars *per annum*, and elsewhere very considerably less though he could give me no definite figures. And lastly there is the *Qumruk* or customs duties, levied at the rate of one-eighth per cent *ad valorem* at the Hasa ports, yielding Rs.4,60,000 during the past year of restricted trading. These figures work out roughly[1] at an annual income of some £70,000 only—perhaps £100,000 would fairly accurately represent Ibn Sa'ud's total annual income from taxation or it may be somewhat more. "But until quite recently," he would tell me, "I had regular opportunities of adding to my resources by the capture of live stock and other booty in expeditions against recalcitrant tribes, but now God has blessed my territories with peace and that source of revenue is lost to me."

I enquired whether he derived any income from the passage of pilgrims to and from Mecca through his territories. "By our religious law," he replied, "it is *haram* to take anything from *Muslims* going to Mecca as Ibn Rashid and the Sharif do; I therefore get nothing from this source except from *Shia'* pilgrims, whom we regard as infidels and are at liberty to tax in return for the protection we assure them; true *Muslims* merely pay the expenses incidental to the journey." It is extraordinary how the rigid precepts and prejudices of religion accommodate themselves to circumstances, for the number of foreign pilgrims, other than those of the *Shia'* sect, who use the Najd routes is negligible and the *Shia's* are taxed as infidels. A similar amenability of religious prejudice to political circumstances is apparent in the matter of marriage: "I should have no objection," Ibn Sa'ud confided to me one day, "to taking to wife a Christian or Jewish woman, and she would have full liberty of belief and conscience though her children would necessarily be brought up as *Muslims*. The Jews and Christians are both peoples of a book; but I would not marry a *Shia'* or a woman of the people of Mecca on any account." "But are not the Meccans and *Shia's*," I objected, "also people of a book?" "No," he replied, "it is true that they accepted the Prophet and his doctrines, but since then they

[1] Counting 6 dollars and Rs.15 (the current rates at this time) as the equivalent of £1 sterling.

have been guilty of backsliding and of *Shirk*, the association of mere creatures with God in their worship, for do they not pay divine honours to Muhammad, 'Ali, Husain, and other saints and seers ? " Thus is religion made to pander to political and personal jealousies and the distant, inaccessible stranger is given preference over the cousin and neighbour, because these are rivals in the struggle for existence.

The reasoning of Ibn Sa'ud, for all its covering of rhetoric and real eloquence, was often threadbare enough and transparently directed *ad hominem*, but let it not be supposed that he was devoid of political acumen and the qualities that go to make a leader of men ; on the contrary, while railing in season and out at the backsliding and sins of his *Muslim* neighbours, none was more acutely alive to the necessity of exercising a judicious tolerance towards the black sheep in his own flock and the history of the Hasa and the Qasim under his rule is a striking tribute to his political wisdom. " The faith," he told me, meaning of course the *Wahhabi* conception of the *Muslim* faith, " is making steady progress in the Hasa, but I am not pressing matters there ; *Shia'* and *Sunni* I leave them all to their own modes of worship and to their own mosques on condition that they make no parade of their ceremonies and ornaments ; by degrees, I hope, they will all come to be as we are." He did not mention that smoking is tolerated though not encouraged, that even the unostentatious sale of tobacco is winked at in both these provinces with the result, as I believe, that the use of tobacco has become appreciably less common than it was some years ago in both places.

Deeply convinced of the absolute truth of the doctrines of his creed and uncompromising in the enforcement of its precepts within the fold, Ibn Sa'ud looked out nevertheless on the affairs of the world with a vision unclouded and far-seeing, and his tendency to allow his interpretation of doubtful points of principle or practice to be influenced by political motives led me often to wonder whether his domestic policy was dictated less by his religious convictions than by political ambition and the desire to weld the centrifugal human forces of Arabia into a mighty empire for himself and his descendants. The circumstances of his career, however, would seem to supply an adequate answer to the riddle, for it must not be forgotten that the whole period of his childhood and adolescence was spent in the comparatively enlightened atmosphere of the Persian Gulf ports and particularly of Kuwait in the good old days of Mubarak—an environment which could not have failed to imbue a lad of such parts with a deep interest in politics as such—and that on the other hand he was never allowed by his father to forget that he was but a homeless exile and that, so long as he remained such, the heritage of his ancestors and the temples of the true God would continue in the hands of the ungodly, for it was in full middle-age that ʻAbdulrahman, born and bred in the stifling puritan atmosphere of Faisal's court, chose exile rather than dishonour at the disruption of the *Wahhabi* empire, and carried away with him into foreign lands the flame of fanaticism which had warmed his own youth, and with which he hoped and ever sought to fire the ambitions of his son. It was in exile, too, that father and son first came to regard the British Empire with friendly feelings, which rapidly developed into a more intimate relation, and finally, when all obstacles had been removed by the outbreak of war between Great Britain and Turkey, into an open and formal alliance. The origin of this alliance we must, therefore, seek in an obscure event in the eighties of last century, the battle of Judi, which flung the decadent *Wahhabi* dynasty from its throne into exile to purify it through its misfortunes, and to prepare the way for the recovery of its birthright by a younger and more vigorous branch. Had it not been for the turn of fortune which for a time riveted the yoke of Jabal Shammar on the territories of Najd, ʻAbdullah, the son of Faisal, would have been succeeded in the ordinary course of events by the offspring of his ill-fated brother and rival, Saʻud; ʻAbdulrahman and his promising sons would never have passed into exile to develop the keener political vision and broader sympathies which now control the destinies of Najd, and it is more than probable that Riyadh would have followed the example of Haïl by throwing in its lot with Turkey at the outbreak of the Great War. The Turks at any rate would still have been in occupation of the Hasa and probably also of the Qasim, threatening our flank in Mesopotamia, and under other auspices it is unlikely that the *Wahhabi* peoples would have developed the uncompromising hatred of their *Muslim* neighbours, which is to my mind their most remarkable characteristic.

Ibn Sa'ud never tired of holding forth on the details of his organisation. For the purposes of internal propaganda he had recently gone to much trouble and expense in arranging for the printing of a comprehensive survey of *Wahhabi* history, the work of one Ibn Ghannam, and of various religious text-books, including the original treatise of Muhammad ibn 'Abdulwahhab himself. His own preoccupations in other directions and the dilatoriness of the Bombay printers had, however, somewhat delayed progress in the education of the masses, for whom he was catering in the meanwhile through human agency. The direct descendants of the founder of the *Wahhabi* sect, whom it was always an important part of Ibn Sa'ud's policy to bind to himself and his dynasty by marriage ties,[1] constituted a recognised state hierarchy with its headquarters at Riyadh and with ecclesiastical functions practically independent of all control. Under their general direction the instruction and religious administration of the country was entrusted to a body of *'Ulama* or Vicars, of whom there were at this time six at Riyadh, three in the Qasim, a similar number in the Hasa, and one in each of the other districts or provinces of Najd—some twenty or more in all. Besides their administrative functions these Vicars are responsible for the administration of the *Shar'* law, and their decisions are binding on the provincial *Amirs*, who merely sign and execute them, subject of course to a discretionary power of reference to higher authorities—the *Shaikhs* at Riyadh and Ibn Sa'ud himself—in cases of great interest and importance. They are also responsible for the training and direction of the *Mutauwa'in* or Deacons, who enjoy no administrative or judicial functions but are entrusted with the religious instruction of the *Badawin*, among whom they are distributed

[1] For instance the young Faisal, who visited England in 1919, is the son of Ibn Sa'ud by a daughter of Shaikh 'Abdullah, the present head of the *Wahhabi* family.

apparently in the proportion of one for every fifty men. Beneath these again is a body of *Talamidh* or candidates for orders, who, under the guidance of the *Mutawwa'*s aspire one day to be enrolled among them, and so to take an active share in God's handiwork among men.

The rank and file of the populace fall into three categories by the application of a religious test—the *Hadhar* or townsfolk, who profess the *Wahhabi* creed as a matter of course, having been born and bred in it ; the *Badu* or general mass of ignorant, unthinking folk, whose tendencies are *Wahhabistic* by association with their neighbours, though their practice is not altogether in conformity with the precepts of the true faith ; and lastly the *Ikhwan*, a recent creation of Ibn Sa'ud himself, who about ten years ago conceived the idea of diverting the surplus energy latent in the nomad masses into channels subservient to his own general design of founding a powerful homogeneous state on a religious and military basis. By the end of the first decade of his reign and the present century he had found himself the acknowledged ruler of vast territories, every part of which had suffered grievously during a long period of war and internal disorder ; at the same time he had made a careful study of the history of those territories in the hope of finding therein lessons for his own guidance, and he could not have failed to remark the significance of its two most salient points. In the early days of the *Wahhabi* movement, that is to say in the last half of the eighteenth century, his ancestor, the great Sa'ud, had built up a mighty empire under the inspiration of a strong religious impulse, but that empire was founded on the shifting sands of the desert, on a heterogeneous association of *Badawin* elements, and it needed the constant attention of the architect to keep it together. When Sa'ud was gathered to his fathers, his throne crumbled rapidly to pieces under the machinations of Ibrahim Pasha, who knew only too well how to play on the rivalries and jealousies of tribal communities hitherto welded together in an unnatural alliance by the fear of God. In more recent times Muhammad ibn Rashid, the greatest of the *Amirs* of Jabal Shammar, attained to a position in Arabia comparable to that of Sa'ud in past times, by the skilful manipulation of a single but powerful and united tribe deeply attached by sentiment and interest to a common centre, the town of Haïl in the mountains of Jabal Shammar; but, when the master-hand was withdrawn, the military ardour of the Shammar cooled for want of inspiration, and the frontiers of Muhammad's empire shrank rapidly back to their old positions in the natural course of disruption and decay. Sa'ud had failed because the fanatical devotion of his people was nullified by the want of a disciplined standing army, and Muhammad had failed because his standing army was without any real incentive to fight, but from their failures 'Abdul'aziz ibn Sa'ud culled the secret of success, and proceeded with characteristic courage and rapidity to put his theories to the test of experiment by laying at Artawiyya, an insignificant watering-place on the Kuwait-Qasim track, the foundation-stone of a new freemasonry, which, under the name of *Ikhwan* or the "Brothers," has in the course of a decade transformed the character of *Badawin* society and caused a flutter of anxiety throughout Arabia.

The *Ikhwan* movement, which is nothing but a *Wahhabi* revival in an intensified form, is the result not of accident but of a well-considered design, conceived with no less a purpose than that of remedying the shortcomings of the Arab race, of checking before it is too late the insidious processes of decay, and of rebuilding on the wreckage of past prosperity a better and more permanent structure than the old one. As history supplied the designs for the new order, so history must judge in its proper time of the measure of credit due to and success achieved by Ibn Sa'ud, but his contemporaries may anticipate its verdict to the extent of congratulating him on the rapid fruition of so bold and novel an experiment, and even perhaps of predicting the realisation of the ideal to which he has devoted himself—if fate spares him to attain the natural limit of the human span. He found his country devastated by war and civil strife—in ten years he has founded twice that number of colonies [1] to repair the damage, and no year passes but

[1] Some of these are Artawiyya, Ghatghat, Dakhna, Dahina, Mubaïdh, Furaithan, Sajir, Dhaba'a, Silh wa Ruwaighib, Saih, Khuff, Rain, Nifi.

he adds to their number. He recovered the heritage of his ancestors with the help of a handful of adventurers—his new colonies are but cantonments of his standing army of 30,000 men or more, and every man-child born therein is a recruit to his forces from the day of his birth. He found the *Badawin* homeless, poor, without religion, and cursed with a tribal organisation which made united action impossible and strife inevitable—in the new colonies he has settled them on the land with the fear of God and hope of Paradise in their hearts, substituting the brotherhood of a common faith for that of a common ancestry, and thus uniting in common allegiance to himself as the vicegerent of God elements hitherto incapable of fusion. At the same time he has made war unsparingly on the old tribal practices, the old game of raid and counter-raid is forbidden in his territories, and many a tribe has felt the crushing weight of his wrath for transgression of his laws; peace reigns where peace was known not before, and it is only on the borders of Wahhabiland that it is disturbed by foreign alarums and excursions.

Apart from the *Ikhwan* colonies organised as such, Ibn Sa'ud reckons in the same category for all practical purposes the whole of the Subai' and Dawasir tribes, the Najd section of the Qahtan, and considerable portions of the Ataiba, Harb and Mutair, apart from those who have been absorbed in the colonies. Such elements, however, while subscribing in a general way to the *Ikhwan* tenets, retain in great part their tribal organisation and prejudices, and can only be regarded as an irregular force not always available or liable to be called out and not always reliable; while the towns and villages are only liable to contribute fixed quotas for active service in proportion to their population and to the importance of the occasion—the full contingent, for which such communities are responsible, being called out only for a *Ghazu 'Am* or general muster in full force to repel a serious danger, while half only or less than half the full number is called out for a *Ghazu Khas* or territorial muster for minor purposes, and on such occasions only the localities within the area of operations are in practice called upon. Formerly, before the institution of the *Ikhwan*, the

Hadhar element was always regarded as the backbone of the army and the fighting-men of 'Aridh the *élite* among the *Hadhar*, but of late Ibn Sa'ud has evinced a tendency to rely more and more on the *Ikhwan* contingent, which always marches under the royal banner, and, though time alone will show how the experiment works, it gave very successful results in the last two important campaigns in which it was tried—the campaign against Ibn Rashid in the autumn of 1918 and that against the Sharif, which culminated in the decisive victory of Turaba in May, 1919. These, with Ibn Sa'ud's own bodyguard, composed of mixed elements, constitute the *Wahhabi* army or *Gom*,[1] as it is called when mobilised for active service.

The *Wahhabi* creed is of the simplest structure, uncompromisingly dogmatic and puritanical and contemptuous of the theology which has overlaid and obscured the simple doctrines and precepts of the Prophet with an unwieldy mass of interpretative literature, which has misled the faithful into the paths of heresy. It is based primarily on the *Quran*, but recognises as authoritative six collections of *Ahadith* or *Traditions*, of which the most important are those of Al Muslim and Al Bukhari, and only two books of *Interpretation* or *Tafsir*. These, with the concise digests or rather extracts of Muhammad ibn 'Abdulwahhab, constitute the reference library of the *Ikhwan*, and in them they seek the guiding principles of their life. It is unlawful, according to Ibn Sa'ud, for the faithful to study the Pentateuch or the Bible, or either to admit or challenge the truth of any statement purporting to emanate therefrom; it is better to preserve silence, for the Jews and Christians are "people of a book," though they have allowed their texts to become corrupted, and no one can judge whether their quotations from modern editions represent the original texts or not. But this tolerance towards Jews and Christians, or rather towards Christians alone—for Ibn Sa'ud in his more confidential moods will readily confess to an intense dislike for the Jews—is a recent growth, not to say an invention

[1] This word is a corruption of *Qaum*=tribe, a word used by the Arabs exclusively in the sense of a military body (tribal or other) on the war-path.

of Ibn Sa'ud himself, though one he can justify by chapter and verse of the *Quran*. The *Shia's* are frankly condemned as infidels or polytheists, but it is for the orthodox congregation of the four *Sunni* churches—Turks, Egyptians, *Hijazis*, Syrians, Mesopotamians, Indians and the like—that the *Wahhabis* reserve the undiluted venom of their hatred. The respect they pay to the memory of Muhammad and other leaders of the church is condemned as an exhibition of polytheistic tendencies, their different attitude towards the problem of the names and attributes of God is denounced as *lèse-majesté*, while their interposition of saints and prophets as mediators between Man and God is regarded as heresy. The people of Mecca are singled out as an epitome of the orthodox *Sunnis* and their crimes are these: *yaznun, yakhunun, yashribun, yatalawatun, yashrikun*—fornication, fraud, smoking and drinking, sodomy and polytheism, the whole *gamut* of crimes against God and Man. *Shirk* or polytheism is the great unforgivable offence, the rest are minor though serious misdemeanours, which it rests with the Almighty to chastise or condone at his discretion.

Religion was, however, but one of many subjects which we discussed during these days in the great pavilion of audience, reclining against the camel-saddle on the daïs of carpets and cushions and looking out over the camp and boundless desert beyond, for the side awnings of the tent were always drawn back on the side farthest away from the sun to give the monarch the full benefit of the cool desert breezes. On these occasions he would always have his binoculars at his side, and ever and anon, often breaking off our conversation abruptly in the middle to do so, he would scour the horizon with his glasses or take them up to examine some new arrival in the camp, for in these days there was much coming and going of visitors from far and near.

"Is it true," he asked me once, "that the British have had trouble of late in Palestine?" "Not unless it has occurred in the last fortnight since my departure from Basra," I replied, "for I was myself in Jerusalem scarcely two and a half months ago, and since then our troops have captured Jericho and crossed the Jordan." "It is well," he said, "for the rumour I heard referred to more than three months back; nevertheless it will be better when you have advanced to Haifa and Nablus, for those are the important points." "And how long, think you," he asked again, "will the war last and how will it end?" "It may be another five years," I replied, little dreaming of the turn of events which was to bring the enemy to his knees almost within as many months, but I was happier in my prediction of the manner of its ending: "I do not think that we shall ever have peace with Germany by agreement, for no agreement would amount to more than a temporary cessation of hostilities, and we want not a peace that must end again in war. No, both sides will fight to the end, and in the end the victory will be ours by force of arms—*Inshallah*." "I tell you the truth," he said to me, "I foresaw the outbreak of this war and, when Shakespear passed through my country a few months before,"—this was in the spring of 1914—"I told him that before long the Germans would be at war with you and that the Turks would be with them, for I had had the information from reliable persons in high quarters,"—possibly from the Turkish commandant and officers who fell into his hands at the capture of Hufuf—"and at the same time I told Shakespear of a plan I had conceived to attack Basra itself provided I were guaranteed immunity *min sharrkum*," *i.e.* from interference by the British, "but he told me the British could never entertain such a proposal and I abandoned the scheme. But it is well as it is for you occupied Basra soon afterwards, and my anxieties are over so far as the Turks are concerned."

Nevertheless he was at that time, as he still is, beset with enemies on every hand, the Sharif on the west, Ibn Rashid on the north, the *Shaikh* of Kuwait on the north-east, and the rebel tribe of the 'Ajman on the east. For the time being, however, the parochial rivalries of the Arab states were overshadowed by the greater issues at stake in the world-war, and the Hijaz, Najd and Kuwait maintained a semblance of friendship under the aegis of the British alliance, while Jabal Shammar stood alone in the ranks of the enemy and received fitful assistance from the outlawed 'Ajman, or such sections of them as had not subscribed to an agreement recently drawn up between the tribal authorities and the British, by which the former undertook to settle quietly in the neighbourhood of Zubair under British protection for the period of the war and to leave the territories and tribes of Najd alone. This agreement was, I found, a source of unbounded satisfaction to Ibn Sa'ud, who was further mollified by the assurances I was able to convey to him regarding the matters at issue between himself on the one hand and the Sharif and the Kuwait authorities on the other. Unfortunately, mere assurances were not enough to stem the tide of troubles which were destined ere long to involve our Arab allies in mutual recriminations and almost in active hostilities, which were as a matter of fact limited to operations of a tribal character and did not develop into anything more serious until the great war had come to an end.

Ibn Sa'ud had but a poor opinion of Shaikh Salim of Kuwait. He regarded him as the unworthy son of a father, who by common consent was accounted among the greatest personalities who have passed across the stage of Arabian politics in modern times. Mubarak, for all his broad-minded tolerance of every shade of opinion, had always been a special friend of the *Wahhabi* dynasty in adversity as well as in happier times; to him Ibn Sa'ud owed in large part his training in the affairs of the world and constant assistance and encouragement in the efforts which resulted eventually in his restoration to the throne. "I always regarded him," he said, "as my father, and in his days our close friendship did away with all need of fixed frontiers, for my people were as much at home in the territories of Kuwait as were his in my country. To him I always went for advice in my difficulties, and on one occasion, before I drove the Turks out of the Hasa, I went to Kuwait primarily to approach Colonel Grey [1] with a view to arranging an alliance with the British; but I went first to Mubarak, and he advised me against such a step. Then I asked him whether I ought to make advances to the Turks, and he advised against that also. I was much puzzled at his attitude and thought that perhaps he might

[1] Then Political Agent at Kuwait.

be jealous of my growing power and wished to keep me out of direct relations with the Great Powers ; however, I was in too great difficulties to listen to him, and I made peace with the Turks, who gave me a decoration and the title of *Wali* of Najd, together with assurances that they would never interfere in my domestic affairs." Jabir succeeded Mubarak on the latter's death in 1915, but his sudden death left the throne of Kuwait in the hands of Salim[1] the following year, and Salim was of a very different mould. The laxity of his predecessors was replaced by a bigoted and fanatical enforcement of *Muslim* precepts according to *Maliki* doctrines, and the austerity of the *Malikis* found in that of the *Wahhabis* a natural enemy. Ibn Sa'ud having already adhered to the British cause, Salim developed Turkish sympathies, and though his position made it impossible for him to defy the British, there can be little doubt that he connived at, or at any rate was aware of, the smuggling of supplies from his territory to Haïl and that the enemy had his agents at Kuwait. This at any rate was the view of Ibn Sa'ud, who regarded the ruling *Shaikh* of Kuwait as unworthy of British confidence and friendship, and denounced his harbouring of the outlawed 'Ajman as an act of hostility towards himself. "If you want to make the blockade effective," he told me, "you must construct a barbed-wire fence round the town of Kuwait, with British troops to guard it." I replied that such a scheme was scarcely practicable, but that if he could prove the complicity or connivance of his rival in the contraband business by capturing a caravan on the way from Kuwait to Haïl, the British authorities would know how to deal with the situation. The patient indulgence of the British authorities towards the delinquencies of Salim exasperated Ibn Sa'ud beyond measure, for, apart from the religious differences which divided them, the commanding position of Kuwait constituted a serious obstacle to the free economic development of the interior, which he was ever seeking to overcome. Kuwait and Bahrain are under existing conditions the only important commercial outlets of the *Wahhabi*

[1] Salim himself died in February, 1921, and has been succeeded by Ahmad ibn Jabir, his nephew.

territories, and neither is under *Wahhabi* control, with the result that all imports of the interior are taxed at entry for the benefit not of the *Wahhabi* treasury but of foreign communities; goods passing from Bahrain to the Hasa ports are taxed again at the latter by Ibn Sa'ud's customs officials, so that, in order to avoid such double payment of duty, trade tends to select the Kuwait route, where desert conditions make the establishment of a customs cordon between the port and the interior impracticable, and where in consequence duty is levied but once, but for the sole benefit of the Kuwait treasury; thus Kuwait prospers at the expense both of Bahrain and Najd, and the latter at least has a grievance with which one cannot but sympathise. To remedy this unsatisfactory state of affairs is Ibn Sa'ud's main preoccupation, and he naturally looks to his own ports on the Hasa coast for a solution of the problem. In Jubail, Qatif and 'Uqair, to say nothing of the apparently derelict site of the ancient port of Gerra south of the last named, he has excellent natural harbours awaiting development if the requisite funds are forthcoming for deepening their approaches and for providing the necessary warehouses and other facilities to cope with a largely increased volume of trade, and last but not least, for reducing the distance between the coast and the interior by the construction of railways. Funds are unfortunately not available for the realisation of such ambitious projects, or at any rate of the railway scheme, but there is no reason why much of the trade of the interior should not find its way direct by the Hasa ports, if the improvements contemplated therein are of a nature to attract the attention of British and Indian shipping. Ibn Sa'ud did not evince any enthusiasm for my suggestion that, when Kuwait is, as it inevitably must be, connected by rail with Basra, he should endeavour to secure the continuation of the line to the Hasa as a first step towards linking up the towns of the latter with their ports by branch lines; in such a scheme he foresees the perpetuation of his own economic and financial dependence on Kuwait; nevertheless, it is in my opinion only in some such way as this that railways are ever likely to make their appearance in eastern or central Arabia, and it should be feasible enough to devise some arrangement satisfactory to both parties for the division of customs receipts accruing at Kuwait between the port of entry and the ultimate destination of imported goods. In any case, it always seemed to me that, in speaking of railway projects, Ibn Sa'ud was looking too far into the future and, in doing so, was losing sight of a far more practicable proposition, whose advantages had become more and more obvious during the Mesopotamian campaign, for motor traffic had been shown to be eminently suitable for desert countries; the introduction of such traffic into Arabia for commercial purposes offers at any rate the advantage that it can be proceeded with on an experimental scale for an insignificant initial outlay and developed steadily in the light of actual experience until it takes the place of the laborious camel-caravan on the Hasa-Riyadh route and elsewhere. "How would you," I asked Ibn Sa'ud one day, "view a project for the construction of a railway from Suez to Kuwait or Basra across part of your territory?" "*Wallah! ya Sahib,*" he replied, "*ahna aminin min taraf wa ghashin min taraf; aminin min taraf al Inqlis walakin al Turk wa 'l Jarman—la.*"[1] There was certainly no question in those days of his trustful confidence in British honour or of his determination to cling to an alliance which he dated, with undisguised pride, back to the days of his grandfather, Faisal, and to a "treaty" which the latter had made with Colonel Lewis Pelly in the early sixties of last century. Pelly's own account of his interviews with the fanatical old monarch did not, however, suggest that their conversations had resulted in anything like a formal agreement, and I was curious to know whether the archives of Riyadh contained any document purporting to be the *Wahhabi* account of what had passed. I accordingly asked him if he had a copy of the treaty on record, as I had never seen it. "No," he replied, "but the Government of India must have a copy, and that is enough for me; I know they will abide by its conditions." On another occasion he silenced apprehensions voiced regarding the attitude of the British in a council he had summoned

[1] "By God, O Sahib, we trust on one side and are apprehensive on the other; we trust the English, but the Turks and Germans—no."

to consider the Sharifian situation by saying: "Philby *'atani qaul min taraf hakumatu*"—I had given him the assurance of my Government and that was enough. He told me, too, that some day he would invite English engineers to examine the mineral resources of his country and to advise him regarding the sinking of artesian wells for agricultural purposes. Water there certainly is in abundance throughout the deserts if it can only be tapped, and there is no reason why the mountains of Najd should not be made to yield their hidden ores as those of Midian did in the distant past and may yet do again; and besides these there are the sulphur springs and mineral waters of the Hasa and other provinces, which may yet prove to have some economic value, to say nothing of the oil sources which have yet to be discovered. The *Wahhabi* territories are yet on the threshold of development, which civil war and foreign incursions have retarded and *Wahhabi* bigotry may check for ever; but Ibn Sa'ud is not blind to the possibilities of his desert kingdom or to his own urgent financial obligation to make the most of them, and if he remains for a prolonged period at the helm, the ship of his state should make rapid progress towards the goal he has marked out for it.

While the difficulties which confront him on the east are largely of an economic character, those which encircle him on north and west are rather political and strategical. Up to the outbreak of the war the Turks had maintained a more or less effective dominion over the Hijaz through the agency of the Sharif of Mecca and had been content to assert without enforcing in practice a vague hegemony over the two central states of Jabal Shammar and Najd, which enjoyed complete and equal independence under their respective *Amirs*; the war, however, one of whose early events was the Arab rebellion of the Hijaz under countenance of the British, created a great disturbance of the Arabian balance of power, and the two central states, which had for so long and with varying success contested the primacy of the peninsula before the averted eyes of an effete Turkish suzerain who seldom dared to interfere, found themselves confronted no longer by the harmless

Turks but by one whom they regarded as an upstart, and who, by proclaiming himself to the world as the "King of the Arab Countries" in virtue of his recognition by the British as "King of the Hijaz," made no secret of his pretensions to the overlordship of all Arabia. This new development of affairs was naturally enough little pleasing to either of the central states, but while Ibn Rashid as the ally of the Turks could openly deride and defy the Sharif's pretensions, Ibn Sa'ud was in the difficult position of having to hail the new monarch as a welcome addition to the ranks of the Allies and of seeking at the same time assurances from the British Government that his proclaimed pretensions were in no way intended to affect the independence which he himself enjoyed and would never forgo. The fact that Ibn Sa'ud was in independent treaty relations with ourselves and showed an evident disinclination to respond to his patronising advances was a source of annoyance to the Sharif, while Ibn Sa'ud was galled to the quick by the knowledge that his rival, by reason of his being in a position to play a more prominent part in the Allied campaign, was able to influence British policy to an extent to which he could not possibly hope to aspire, and matters were not improved by the fact that neither party could divest himself of an uncomfortable suspicion that the British might be in secret agreement with the other in a sense disadvantageous to himself.

Up to this time, however, nothing in the nature of an open breach had occurred between the two, and though the British authorities were well aware how matters stood, there was nothing particularly incongruous in their expression of a pious hope that both parties would maintain an attitude of mutual goodwill essential to the successful prosecution of the campaign against a common enemy. To Ibn Sa'ud they were further able to convey the assurance that they were not privy to the Sharif's assumption of the title which had offended him; that they appreciated his anxiety to maintain the independence guaranteed to him in the treaty of 1916, and would never press him against his will to accept the suzerainty of the Sharif; and that, when released from the preoccupations of a world-wide war, they would be glad to place their friendly offices at the disposal of both parties for the settlement of any points on which they might find themselves at variance. A friendly letter from Sir Reginald Wingate, the High Commissioner for Egypt, in which graceful reference was made to the *Wahhabis'* traditional enmity towards the Turks, paved the way for the announcement of the assurances I was authorised to convey to Ibn Saʿud on behalf of the British Government, and I found him favourably enough disposed to listen to proposals for an offensive against Haïl, which I assured him was the only direction in which he could hope to acquire a reputation comparable to that which the Sharif had made in his operations against the Turks.

This brought us to the knotty problem of ways and means. My long delay in returning to him had prepared him for disappointment in this direction, and it would be idle to pretend that he was not bitterly disappointed at the whittling down of the programme I had communicated to Government on his behalf in the previous December; but, to his credit be it said, he realised that further discussion of the matter would be useless and immediately set himself to consider the practical aspect of the situation. "The capture of Haïl," he told me, "is an object I have had at heart for many years, and do you think that I should have left it till now had I had the means to do otherwise? Haïl *ajdar wa nar*—Haïl is walls and fire, Ibn Rashid is safe behind its fortifications and guns, and God has blessed him with an united tribe which would flock to a man for the defence of their capital; what can I do?" "You know," I replied, "that 'Cokas'[1] and I have done our utmost for you, but in the eyes of the British Government Haïl is but a small pawn in the great war. For you it is a different thing; war conditions enable you, with British assistance in money and material, to seize it and make yourself master of all Central Arabia, but, if you miss the present opportunity and the war comes to an end with the Arabian situation unaltered, you will not be able to count further on British

[1] Major-General Sir Percy Z. Cox, G.C.I.E., K.C.S.I., K.C.M.G., then Civil Commissioner of Mesopotamia, and subsequently H.B.M.'s Minister at Teheran, and now High Commissioner for Mesopotamia.

aid. Now is your opportunity or never, and I have told you the extent to which we can help you." So we argued on a matter which was beyond argument; for him it was no light matter to decide on action which might involve him in war with inadequate resources, but it was harder still to let the proffered bait slip from his hands for want of courage to hold it. "*Wallah wa billah wa tillah!*" he broke out at last, "see, it is not for your Government that I do this thing, but for you and 'Cokas.' I will move, and by God I will make your faces white. My intention was to disband my forces and go up to the Qasim to see to my affairs there, but now I will send my troops off to their homes for a month only to get the mange[1] out of their camels; after that I will call them up again, and by *Ramdhan* I shall take the field to harry the tribes of Jabal Shammar; but, mark you, Haïl cannot be attacked; however, I will give the Shammar no respite and, *Inshallah,* Haïl itself may be ours in two months."

Little time was lost in proceeding with the programme thus decided on. The same day it was submitted to a council of prominent persons in the camp and approved by them after a free and open discussion of the respective merits of an offensive against Haïl and an attack on the Sharif, which the more fanatical element would have preferred. Next day messengers were sent to Kuwait and 'Uqair with large orders for provisions, and it was decided to call in the grazing camels and break up the camp without delay in order that everything should be in train when Turki was ready to put himself at the head of the army at the beginning of *Ramdhan*; for on second thoughts Ibn Sa'ud decided to spend that month in attending to religious and administrative duties at Riyadh, while his eldest son opened the ball with a preliminary foray across the Dahana into the Shammar country. I did not altogether relish the idea of spending the interval in inactivity at Riyadh, but it was with some trepidation that I broached the matter to my host. "Well," he said, "I do not wish it to be thought that my operations against the enemy are inspired by the British; the *Ikhwan* would not like that; it would certainly

[1] *Jarab.*

be better that you should not be present during the preparations. Perhaps you would like to go and stay at Kuwait until we are ready, and then you can rejoin me in the field." Now Kuwait was the last place at which I wished to make a prolonged sojourn. "I cannot possibly do that," I replied, "for if I go back with tales of your forthcoming operations they will laugh at me. I cannot go back except to announce your victory, and, as you want time to prepare for it, I must remain in your country, but I agree that your people should not see too much of me. Why should I not spend the interval in an expedition to your southern provinces, to Wadi Dawasir? I could go there on the pretext of hunting the oryx." To my surprise he agreed to the plan. "Certainly," he said, "by all means I will send you to the south, and on your return you shall join me in the Qasim and be a witness of my operations." "Would it not be better," I asked, "if I started straight away from here to give your people the idea that I am returning to the coast by way of the Hasa?" But he did not agree to that, for such an expedition demanded some preparation and the necessary escort could not be supplied except at Riyadh; however, I was well content that he had given me his word—indeed, I could scarcely credit my good fortune in having obtained his acquiescence so easily, for I knew that there were not a few in that very camp who regarded me askance and questioned the wisdom of Ibn Sa'ud in treating me as an honoured guest; but he had deliberately made up his mind to strengthen the British connection to the best of his ability, and he was not the man to waver in face of criticism. "*La,*" he said to me on one occasion, when I asked him whether he thought there was any real objection to my remaining in his country, "*istiqamatak mufid lina*" ("Your staying is to our advantage"). He always looked ahead, and in doing so he saw that if the war came to an indecisive end the Turks would help Ibn Rashid to attack him, for they had promised him the *Sultanate* of Central Arabia; in a British alliance, therefore, he foresaw the best guarantee against such a contingency.

"You know," he said, "that I have never forgotten that it is my duty to bring Jabal Shammar and its people back to their allegiance to the house of Sa'ud,[1] but I have never yet felt myself strong enough to attack them. We are always fighting, but the issue ever varies; nevertheless, I have long been undermining the position of the house of Rashid by *siyasa*—by diplomacy—and now there are several sections of the Shammar who are openly with me, as Ibn Jabrin and those whom he has drawn with him into the *Ikhwan* fold, or have a secret understanding with me to support me in the event of my making good. And now that I have fully determined to deliver a sustained attack on their country I propose to issue an *ultimatum* to the Shammar, informing them of my intentions and calling upon those who wish to avoid hostilities with me either to move northwards into the 'Anaza country or to accept my hospitality within my own borders and well behind my line. Whoever remains thereafter in the war arena knows that he does so as an enemy, and I shall harry them far and wide without compunction."

Ever and anon in the course of such conversations he would recur with manifest concern to the theme of the Sharif and his pretensions. The presence in the camp of certain *Shaikhs* of the 'Ataiba reminded him of the Sharif's somewhat gratuitous intervention in the Ghatghat affair of the previous December. In the first instance a party of 'Ataiba, under one Ibn Humaidi, had attacked a body of *Ikhwan* while engaged in prayer near Ghatghat; the *Ikhwan* retaliated by slaying Ibn Humaidi, whose relatives, apparently despairing of obtaining satisfaction at the hands of Ibn Sa'ud, had arrived at Jidda while I was there to lay their complaint before the Sharif, who in his turn, unable to do anything, made rather heavy weather of the incident by reporting it to the British authorities as an instance of *Wahhabi* ferocity. This availed the plaintiffs nothing, and

[1] In this connection recent events (1920) at Haïl have a special interest. Ibn Rashid was assassinated in the spring of this year, whether for private or political reasons it is not easy to say; and rumour has it that the new ruler, or rather his regent—for he is a minor—has entered into a treaty with Ibn Sa'ud, the effect of which is to make Jabal Shammar revert to its original status of dependence on the *Wahhabi* state. Later information (1921) discredits the rumour of such an alliance and indicates that Ibn Sa'ud is gathering his forces for an attack on Haïl.

they took the law into their own hands by raiding the *Ikhwan* and lifting some of their camels. The *Ikhwan* replied by attacking the offenders in force near Nifi on the western borders of the Qasim and slaying no fewer than thirty-three of them with slight loss to themselves. It was only at this stage that it occurred to the ʻAtaiba to appeal to Caesar, with the result that representatives of both parties were now amicably engaged in settling accounts under the guidance of Ibn Saʻud on the basis of an ordinary blood-feud. This involved a payment of 400 dollars for every man killed, and as the Ghatghat people had undoubtedly had the best of the exchanges with their opponents —no less than twenty-seven scalps on the balance—the ʻAtaiba were declared entitled to a sum of 10,800 dollars in full and final settlement of the account. Negotiations for the payment of this sum by instalments were now proceeding without a hitch, and Ibn Saʻud was soon to reap the reward of impartial justice. At this time, however, he was not unnaturally a little annoyed at receiving a letter from the Sharif—who had further taken upon himself to send copies of it to the ʻAtaiba *Shaikhs* for their information, copies which their recipients immediately forwarded to Ibn Saʻud—in which there was much trite and superfluous criticism of the conduct of the *Ikhwan* and of Ibn Saʻud's policy.

In this connection he had drafted, and now showed me, a long and dignified reply to the animadversions of the Sharif, in the course of which he took strong objection to the latter's tendency to address communications direct to *Shaikhs* of the Najd tribes and even to Ibn Saʻud's own officials, as if they owed him allegiance and obedience, for it was at this time too that Fahad ibn Muʻammar, the governor of Buraida, had received—and naturally sent on to his master—a letter from the Sharif announcing the establishment of an embargo on caravan traffic between the Hijaz and Najd on the ground that *Najdis* had of late been guilty of abusing the facilities accorded to them by smuggling goods into enemy territory. No evidence of the truth of this charge was vouchsafed in the letter, and it was held—possibly with justice—by Ibn Saʻud that it was but part and parcel of a policy of oppression recently adopted by the Sharif against those who professed allegiance to his rival. Only recently a case in point had occurred; two natives of 'Anaiza, the son and nephew of one Salih al Fadhl, long resident at Jidda as the representatives of their family firm, had some time before been seized and thrown into jail on the ground that Salih himself was at the time residing at Madina, where he happened to be at the outbreak of the Sharifian rebellion. Ibn Sa'ud had already refused to intervene in the matter, when approached by a relative resident in India, on the ground that the continuance of Salih at Madina was in itself sufficient justification of the suspicions entertained about his family. Salih had now, however, arrived at 'Anaiza, but his son and nephew remained in durance, and I may anticipate matters by saying that there they remained until after the armistice, in spite of frequent representations made by myself and the British authorities in Egypt with a view to obtaining their release. It was by such acts that the Sharif multiplied quite unnecessarily the points of friction between himself and Ibn Sa'ud, and alienated the sympathies even of the more enlightened parts of Najd, such as the Qasim.

"The limits of Najd towards the Hijaz are well known," he told me, and proceeded in typical Arab fashion to name a series of vague landmarks which would satisfy no regular boundary commission, "from Bisha to Ranya to Khurma and the Hadhn—that is my frontier, for did not the Prophet —on whom be peace—declare '*Man raa Hadhnan faqad anjad*' ('When you see the Hadhn you are in Najd'). But let an assembly of Arab chiefs be called together, Ibn Subah, Ibn Thani,[1] Shaikh 'Isa of Bahrain, and the like; they will have no difficulty in fixing a line satisfactory to all. After that let those of the 'Ataiba, Harb and other tribes, who settle permanently *bi-ahlhum*—with their families—on either side of it be accounted subjects of the respective rulers. Just as many people of Najd have passed out of my ken by settling permanently in 'Iraq, so it may be with those who elect for the Hijaz; but let the British Consul at Jidda act on my behalf for those who settle there only temporarily

[1] The ruler of Qatar.

for business. The Subai' belong to me, and parts of them reside in these districts towards the Hasa, but even so let those of Khurma and Wadi Subai' choose for themselves, and, if they declare for the Sharif, let them be counted to him."

The greater part of my time during these days was taken up in conversations with Ibn Sa'ud, who was indefatigable in his attention to the affairs of state, but I did not neglect to make the most of intervals between such audiences to pay occasional visits to the tents of other members of the royal family present in the camp. Second only to his father, and commander-in-chief of the army in his absence, was Turki, the heir to the throne, who appeared to be the only member of the royal family permitted to have a definite share in the administration of the country, for the history of his own dynasty had taught Ibn Sa'ud the danger of entrusting executive functions to others than those who had a natural right to aspire to the throne, lest the pretensions of younger brothers and collaterals, who had had administrative experience and opportunities of ingratiating themselves with sections of the populace, might plunge the country into civil strife. Turki had his own bodyguard and suite of tents, in one of which was lodged a girl, whom he had taken to wife, of the *Badawin*, and whom incidentally he divorced on the day when the camp broke up. Women had not the same attraction for him as for his father, and he told me that it was only for war and the chase that he had any real passion. He had struck me, when I first made his acquaintance at Riyadh, as being exceedingly delicate—as a matter of fact he had been far from well in the Qasim, whence he had recently come, but now in the dim light of his tent I thought he showed a great improvement, and he was certainly exceedingly handsome. Shorter by a good deal than his father, but with several years of growth before him, he was of lighter build, and his thin pale face and dark eyes, set in a framework of plaited locks drooping on either shoulder from beneath his silk headkerchief, betokened a physique little suited to the rough environment in which he had been born and bred. A stout heart had, however, surmounted the disadvantages of a delicate constitution, for already, though barely in his nineteenth year, he had given ample proof of his qualities in a dozen campaigns, and seemed destined to prove a worthy successor to his father. But, alas, he was rapidly approaching his appointed hour, for the young promise of his youth was cut untimely short, ere twelve months were out, by the influenza epidemic which raged through Najd in the winter of 1918–19 and took a heavy toll of the royal family. In rapid succession Turki and his brothers, Fahad and Saʿd, and Ibn Saʿud's favourite wife, the Queen of Najd, were laid to rest in the royal cemetery at Riyadh. But I am anticipating events. Turki received me with boyish cordiality and talked with splendid enthusiasm of his favourite pastimes—war and sport—as we sat upon the carpet in his tent sipping coffee. "I hope," I said, "that some day in the near future you will visit us at Basra and Baghdad, and perhaps even go on to England to see our King." "Fain would I do so," he replied, "and I count on you to persuade my father to let me go, for I would like of all things to see the countries of the world, of which I hear so much. Here we are but simple folk, with nothing to do but eat and drink and fight, but your world is, they say, very different." He had, of course, known Shakespear, for, young as he then was, he had taken part in the battle of Jarrab, and he had met Hamilton in the Qasim a few months before, but he had never himself been out of Arabia.

Turki's younger brother, Saʿud, a lad of perhaps sixteen, was also present in the camp; he had the same delicate, handsome cast of countenance as his brother, than whom, however, he appeared to be less mature in manner and, if possible, even less robust in physique, while in intellect he was at that time a mere child. He is now, of course, the heir to the throne, and I have heard that he is shaping very well in the military and civil duties which have devolved on him since the death of Turki. They say, too, that he is grown exceedingly tall and bids fair to emulate his father in stature. I spent a pleasant half-hour with him one evening in his tent in the midst of his retinue. He had just acquired—I know not whence—a new Mannlicher sporting rifle, but had omitted to procure suitable ammunition at the same time, and his eyes lit up with unfeigned delight when I promised to let him have my own stock, for I had a rifle of the same pattern, though I generally carried a ·303 service rifle for ordinary use. Sa'ud, like Turki, had never been beyond the limits of Arabia.

Another part of the royal enclave was occupied by the tents of 'Abdullah ibn 'Abdulrahman, who, though only twenty years of age, represented an older generation than the royal princes, being a younger brother of Ibn Sa'ud himself. He was a young man of considerable intellectual distinction, being unusually well read for a *Wahhabi* in the poetry of the ancient Arabs and in the history of his own country. In appearance he approached nearer to the type of his father than to that of his handsome brother, being somewhat short and squat ; like many of his family he was beardless, and a curious diffidence of speech, which made him muddle and invert his sentences, lent a peculiar charm to his conversation. He spoke enthusiastically of Shakespear, whom he had met on three occasions, the last time he saw him being at Khufaisa in the upper Butain, just before the battle of Jarrab ; he spoke warmly, too, of the existing friendship between Britain and Najd, which Shakespear's personality had done so much to cement. I was greatly impressed by his cordial entertainment of myself : when coffee was served he begged me to take the first cup, and when I insisted, as I always did with members of the royal family, on his drinking first, he yielded only after much deprecation of the honour. "*La tatakallaf,*" he said when I rose to depart, "*saiyir alaiya*" ("Stand not on ceremony with me, but visit me again") ; and I took him at his word, for not many days had passed when I stood again before his tent-door. On this, as on the previous occasion, I found 'Abdullah closeted with my old friend, Ahmad ibn Thunaian, who by reason of his birth and long residence at Constantinople, where he had acquired an excellent knowledge of French, stood on an intellectual plane above his fellows, and enjoyed the intimate confidence of Ibn Sa'ud in matters of foreign policy. The carpet on which we reclined was strewn with books, which the cousins had obviously been reading together at the time of my entry. One of the books was an

Arabic history of the war compiled in Egypt by a contributor to the *Muqattam* journal—Hasan Ridha by name, if my memory serves me—and the others were volumes of poetry, one being an anthology which ʿAbdullah, after pointing out and reading to me some of his favourite poems, insisted on presenting to me, saying he had another copy. When I rose to go they insisted on my remaining a little longer, and I spent some time in describing in broad outline something of the British constitution and our parliamentary system. ʿAbdullah was born at Kuwait, where as a boy he remembered seeing the British flag at half-mast and wondering what such a phenomenon might portend, until he was told that it had been lowered as a token of respect to the memory of King Edward on receipt of the news of his death.

Dhari and his suite remained with us, resting their weary camels and making the most of Ibn Saʿud's hospitality until the camp broke up. I had hoped, and indeed suggested soon after our arrival, that I might be permitted to remain in their midst for the period of their stay, but Ibn Saʿud had different ideas on the subject, and I judged it expedient not to press the matter lest they should suffer. Nevertheless I made a point of visiting them in their quarters as frequently as possible and of inviting Dhari himself and others of the party to share my meals, though I could not fail to notice that Dhari accepted such invitations with obvious reluctance and perhaps misgiving as to the effect it might have, for on the first occasion of his dining with me he stipulated that I should myself explain matters to Ibn Saʿud. Arab hospitality is not often open to the reproach of clumsiness, but Ibn Saʿud's treatment of Dhari was an exception to the general rule, and was the more inexcusable for being almost ostentatiously deliberate. It was also, however, instructive, and augured ill for the scheme of co-operation on which I had set my heart, for while Dhari, secure in an independent alliance with the British and assured of the subsidy resulting therefrom, was ready enough to be friendly on even terms, Ibn Saʿud was too proud to receive him otherwise than on a basis of inferiority. It must also be admitted that he was in part actuated by doubts of Dhari's loyalty, and in this respect at least the subsequent course of events justified him.

Nevertheless, I did not at this time give up hopes of so arranging matters as to bring about a measure of co-operation between the two, and, though Ibn Sa'ud could not bring himself to include Dhari in our councils, I found him ready enough to discuss ways and means of including the "friendly" Shammar in our programme of action, and he did not disdain to have private conversations with Dhari himself with the same end in view, while in frequent conferences with Dhari and Mulla 'Abdullah I never ceased to point out the necessity for active co-operation in the enforcement of the blockade if they hoped for the continuance of British favour. It was accordingly arranged that on our departure from Shauki he should return to his camp in the Batin and that he should send a messenger to me once a month, reporting the progress and results of his activities. He was to raid the 'Abda whenever occasion arose, and, above all, to prevent the passage of enemy caravans, sending such prisoners and camels as he might capture to Basra as practical evidence of the energetic prosecution of his duties; meanwhile Ibn Sa'ud was to maintain an inner line of blockade, and it needed little argument to convince Dhari that the fewer the caravans that reached that second line the better for his own reputation.

I reinforced my exhortations with a substantial sum of money for distribution among his retinue, and a further sum was received for the same purpose from Ibn Sa'ud; but Dhari was not going without a determined effort to get more, and in the course of the last evening of our stay at Shauki, Mulla 'Abdullah brought me a bill for 514 dollars, representing on a scale decidedly liberal the cost of feeding the unnecessarily large escort which they had seen fit to provide for our journey hither. Incidentally I had during the journey begged Dhari to let me pay for any sheep or other provisions purchased on the way, but he had held up his hands in horror at such a suggestion; nevertheless, the bill now presented included the cost not only of sheep purchased and camels hired during the march itself, but also the value of rice, coffee, *Saman* and other articles brought with us from

Dhari's camp. However, I raised no objection to the demand and, pointing to a box containing 1500 dollars, told the *Mulla* to convey it to his camp and to distribute the balance—986 dollars in lieu of 1000 which it had been my intention to give—among the retinue with my blessing; at the same time I asked him to give me a distribution list in respect of the latter sum for inclusion in my accounts. "Many thanks for your generous present," said Dhari to me at one of our last interviews, "the *Mulla* has the list you asked him to give you; I have given every man a present of twenty dollars out of it." This reference to the matter seemed somewhat pointed and at any rate his arithmetic seemed a little at fault, for the company numbered some sixty persons, so I sent for Mulla ʿAbdullah, who without a blush produced a list showing the distribution of 1510 dollars as largesse purporting to come from me. "I do not quite understand," I said, "and what of the bill?" "That is no matter," he replied, "this is what Dhari told me to do as there was not enough to give every man his proper share, and as for the bill, Dhari says he will pay that himself; that is quite all right." "That is not quite all right," was my reply; "over there is a box of money; go and take 524 dollars out of it; good-bye." He went off murmuring excuses, to which I made no reply. "Good-bye," I said to him when he came back to announce that he had received the money, and I never saw him again. My parting with Dhari was also a little strained in view of this little incident, which served to illustrate at its worst the worst trait in the Arab character—the lust for gold—and I consoled myself with the reflection that the next penny I should pay to Dhari would be dearly bought with the sweat of his brow.

3. The Pillar of Cloud by Day

"To-morrow we march," Ibn Saʿud told me when I was ushered into the presence on the morning of April 15, "the *Bairaq* starts at dawn." For even as the Semites of old marched through the desert under the guidance of their Lord, who "went before them by day in a pillar of cloud, to lead them the way; and by night in a pillar of fire, to give them light,"[1] so do the hosts of Wahhabiland direct their marches and halts to this day by a symbol of their God—the banner of the true faith by day and a lamp raised aloft in its place by night; behind it they march and round it they encamp; "and when the cloud was taken up from over the tabernacle, the children of Israel went onward throughout all their journeys: but, if the cloud were not taken up, then they journeyed not till the day that it was taken up."[2] The ways of the desert have changed but little in three thousand years.

That day there was much stir and bustle in the camp as the camels came in in snarling, gurgling droves to be sorted out and distributed among the companies to which they belonged, and the gear and packages were laid out in rows ready for the lading. On the morrow I was woken betimes and issued from my tent to watch the dawn creep over a scene of indescribable confusion; on every side tents were being levelled to the ground and rolled into bundles, while a *crescendo* of piteous groans betokened the loading of the camels. All eyes were on the centre of the camp, whence, even as I watched in the dim twilight, a dark mass rose as by a single impulse and lurched forward as the light green standard of Wahhabiland at its head fluttered free in the gentle breeze—signal to all the camp that Ibn Sa'ud himself was on the move. And, as the royal bodyguard moved through the camp and across the brook of Shauki to the bare downs beyond, there was a thrill of movement through the mighty host, and company after company wheeled into position behind it, each behind its own banner, and the column was on the march. "And in the first place the standard of the camp of the children of Judah set forward according to their hosts . . . and the standard of the camp of Reuben set forward according to their hosts . . . and the standard of the camp of the children of Ephraim set forward according to their hosts . . . and the standard of the camp of the children of Dan, which was the rearward of all the camps, set forward according to their hosts . . . thus were the journeyings of the children of Israel according

[1] Exodus xiii. 21. [2] Exodus xl. 36, 37.

to their hosts: and they set forward."[1] Thus, too, with little changed but the names of the contingents, was the journeying of the *Wahhabi* host that day before my eyes, and my thoughts went back to the Old Testament narrative as standard after standard took its place in the line at the head of its cohort—the cohort of Washm with its standard, light green with white inner fringe like that of Ibn Sa'ud himself, but of smaller dimensions; the cohort of Sudair with its standard of red with green border all round; the cohort of Mahmal with a banner like that of Sudair, but with the colours reversed; the cohort of Hauta, whose standard was white with red border; and that of the Aflaj with a banner of simple white: these were the contingents that marched that day—perhaps a thousand strong.

It had been arranged that I should march independently of the "*Gom*," and it was not till the column had made considerable headway that, with a small suite of attendants, which included Ibrahim, his cousin Hamud and one Hamdani, I mounted and threaded my way through the camp, deserted now except for a certain amount of stores and heavy baggage which was to go direct to Riyadh, in the direction indicated by stragglers of the main body, baggage trains, servants leading horses and the like accompaniments of an army on the march. Not being obliged to conform in detail to the movements of the main body, I had an excellent opportunity of observing the ways of an Arab force in motion; the serried column of companies, which had marked the outset of the march, soon degenerated into successive sinuous waves of men and camels extended along as broad a front as the nature of the ground permitted, for, as we advanced, the downs on either side of us became too rough to negotiate without discomfort to the beasts and restricted our line of march to an ever-narrowing plain. We had scarcely been marching an hour when I observed the leading wave swerve abruptly to one side into a bay in the downs, whence a minute later a column of smoke rose skyward to announce that Ibn Sa'ud had halted for his morning meal. The example thus set was catching—wave after wave turned aside for the same

[1] Numbers x. 14, 18, 22, 25 and 28.

purpose, each company pleasing itself as to the time and place of its breakfasting—but the standards marched ever onwards on their course to avoid a break of continuity, for none but Ibn Sa'ud himself and the princes of the blood might pass ahead of the royal standard, and the royal tent at least should be ready pitched before their arrival at the appointed camping-place.

I rode on past scattered groups, breaking their fast or sipping coffee as the case might be, and at one of them I was very courteously invited to halt for refreshments, my would-be host—for I only drank a cup of his coffee without dismounting—being a chief of the Sudair contingent, Sulaiman al Hamad ibn 'Askar, nephew of 'Abdullah ibn 'Askar, *Amir* of Majma'a. One of his followers had met Shakespear during his passage through the uplands of Sudair, and it was doubtless to that circumstance that I owed the cordial greetings of the young *Shaikh*.

There was little to remark in the country through which we passed during the early part of the march ; the downs were bare except for occasional patches of *Arfaj* in the hollows and merged gradually to the westward in a distinct ridge, which seemed to be of greater elevation above the mean level of the plateau than anything we had seen to the north of Sha'ib Shauki ; but, when we had covered about five miles, the scene changed suddenly, as it so often does in the Arabian deserts, and we emerged from the monotonous downs on to the edge of a mile-broad valley running at right angles across our path between well-marked and for the most part continuous ridges rising to a height of 50 or 100 feet. The direction of our march now changed abruptly from south-east to south-south-west, and for the rest of the day we ascended the valley in that direction, the standards, which had now closed in on the royal banner, marching in line at the head of the procession, while the rest of the host followed in the rear, company by company, in extended order across the valley, interspersed here and there with groups of baggage animals and led horses. It was a splendid and inspiring scene, of which I made the most by hugging the higher ground along the foot of the ridge on the left bank.

Sha'ib al Ats, as the valley is called, is or was one of the six principal "rivers" of Central Arabia and the most northerly of them with the single exception of Wadi Rima, whose lower reaches I have already described under the name of Al Batin and whose mid-course in the Qasim I was yet to see. Formed by the convergence of drainage channels from Western Mahmal and the Hamada plain at the oasis of Qasab under the steep western escarpment of Tuwaiq, the Ats cleaves its way through the great plateau barrier along a line which forms the boundary between the province of Sudair on the north and the district of Mahmal proper on the south, and emerging on to the Butain strikes immediately into 'Arma by a gap in its western wall and cleaves through it in like fashion—its course throughout lies from W.S.W. to N.N.E.—to the edge of the Dahana, just short of which it ends in the wide shallow basin, in which lie the wells of Hafar al Ats,[1] so called to distinguish them from those of Al Hafar in the Batin, a dozen miles or so eastward of the point at which we entered the valley.

Our view was now circumscribed by the low ridges on either side, occasional breaks in which brought down the drainage of the uplands into the valley, which was bare and flat and splayed out about five miles above our point of entry into a broad bulge, at whose entrance two detached

[1] The wells of Hafar al Ats are said to descend 30 fathoms to water, while those of Abu Jifan farther south, which I had passed earlier on the way from Hufuf to Riyadh, were barely 2 fathoms in depth. Between these two points the 'Arma plateau is full of waterings, the positions of which and the depth of each to water are shown roughly (from information collected during the march) in the accompanying diagram:

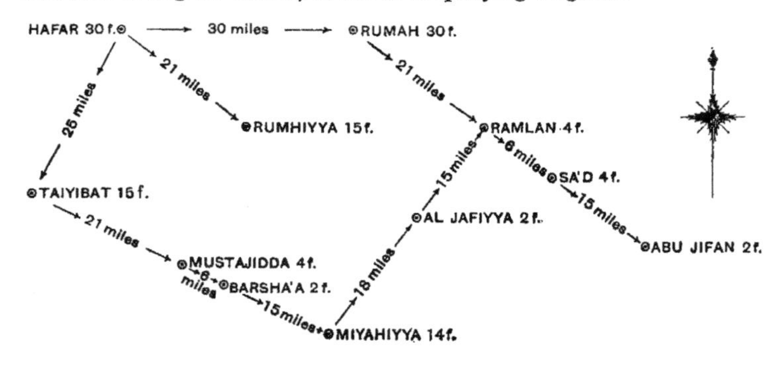

conical hillocks called Al Hanadir stood out in mid-valley like guardian sentinels. Beyond them the ridge of the right bank assumed a serrated form and at the same time the name of Al Khanasir, indicating the finger-like appearance of its little pinnacles, while at the point where I called a halt for breakfast, the downs of the north seemed to have overflowed the left bank and deposited an extensive group of low hummocks beyond it in the valley itself. Here and there in bays among these hummocks and between them and the ridge they pointed out to me occasional *Raudhas* or *Sidr*-clumps, only two of which—and those not visible from our position—appeared to have acquired names, Raudhat al Haqqaqa on the near side of a fairly prominent headland of the same name, and Raudha Nura between it and the Ats valley. We were now approaching the end of the march appointed for the day, and as we resumed our ride after breakfast we saw the standards and the vanguard of the army come to rest some distance ahead, and by the time that we drew near the pitching of tents had begun, the place selected for our camp lying at the mouth of a tributary of the Ats, Sha'ib Abu Ramal as it was called by reason of the drifted sand which had piled up against and almost obliterated the ridge on the right bank of the valley. Nearer to the other bank and perhaps a mile distant from the camp lay a large clump of bushes called Raudhat Abu Rukba, in which was said to be a *Ghadir* or water-hole now run dry.

As soon as my tent was up Sa'd and Ibrahim joined me for a smoke and in the course of conversation mentioned that Ibn Sa'ud would probably not require my attendance during the day as he was to be married in the afternoon to a girl of the Damir section of the 'Ajman, who had been expected at Shauki, but, delayed for some reason, had only just arrived. Almost as they spoke a messenger came in from the royal pavilion begging me to excuse his master on the ground that he was overwhelmed with important business. The marriage ceremony took place, I was afterwards told, that afternoon in the presence of Ibn Sa'ud himself, two representatives sent by the girl's father to give her away in due form and the officiating priest—an informal affair occupying no more than five minutes; but according to the custom of the country it would not be till after the evening prayer that he might repair to the bridal tent and see his bride. That evening after dinner I was sitting in my tent with Ibrahim when Sa'd appeared. "*Dakhal al Shuyukh?*" asked Ibrahim, eager for the latest gossip from the court, "has the chief gone off to his bride?" "*Ba'd*—not yet," he replied, "all day he has been working and he is still at it with Al Junaifi and Ibn Suwaidan"—the two chief secretaries—"writing for all they are worth." I had to leave them gossiping, for to my amazement and theirs I received a summons to the presence and, entering the royal pavilion, found Ibn Sa'ud seated by the old camel-saddle with a secretary on either side of him, dictating letters on different subjects simultaneously to both with a rapidity and precision that astonished me. He greeted me with a genial smile but scarcely rising, and, beckoning me to a place at his side, which Ibn Suwaidan vacated to take up a kneeling position in front of his master, apologised for being so busy and continued the double dictation, conversing the while with me. Even that was not all, for in the midst of it a case was called on, and, with scarcely a check either in his conversation with me or in the composition of the letters in hand, he elicited its salient facts from the plaintiff—a suppliant for redress in respect of camels, sheep and money taken from him by 'Ajman raiders in the territories of Kuwait—and, having sworn him to the correctness of his estimate of the loss involved, proceeded, as soon as one of the letters was finished, to dictate another to Shaikh Salim of Kuwait inviting him to accept responsibility for the loss suffered within his jurisdiction and to make it good, failing which, he said, he had instructed his own agent at Kuwait to pay the claim and would consider it a debt due to himself. I had never seen Ibn Sa'ud in the throes of transacting his ordinary business of state before; this was by no means the last time I did so, but it was a memorable experience. It must have been about nine o'clock in the evening when I first went to him and it was not till about 10.30 that the work in hand was disposed of and the clerks dismissed; I deemed it tactful to rise at the same time, but he stayed me to discuss certain letters he had just dictated—one in answer to the High Commissioner's letter and others to the authorities in Mesopotamia—and it was not till 11.30 that night that I took my leave of him. "I march to-morrow morning two hours before daybreak," he said; "you will not rise so early and can follow me when you are ready." No word was said of the young wife so patiently awaiting him, and I went back to my tent wondering what she would think of being deserted at 2 A.M. on her bridal night; it was her first experience of marriage.

One day during our sojourn at Shauki, Turki and 'Abdullah had been boasting in the royal pavilion of the merits and speed of their respective mounts, as fine specimens of *'Umaniyya dhaluls*, I was told, as could be found in all Arabia, and Ibn Sa'ud clinched the discussion by offering a prize of 200 dollars to the winner of a race from the camp to Riyadh on the condition that the time occupied in covering the distance was not more than twenty-four hours from the start. The challenge was accepted and about a dozen competitors, including Turki, 'Abdullah, Sa'ud and Salman al 'Arafa, offered themselves for the contest, which began with the break-up of the camp. The distance to the capital was some eighty miles by the route which I followed and perhaps somewhat less, about seventy miles, by a more direct track, which branches off from the Ats valley at the Hanadir hillocks and runs behind the Khanasir ridge to Khafs, where it rejoins the ordinary route. The race started quietly and the competitors followed the standard to the beginning of the short cut, where Ibn Sa'ud witnessed the beginning of the real struggle. It was a test of endurance rather than speed until nightfall, when the competitors supped and rested for a while together before entering on the last lap and the race for home. There was much interested speculation in the camp that night as to the result of the contest, many favouring the *dhalul* which 'Abdullah had recently purchased from the Murra for 1000 dollars, while Turki came in for much confident support. "*Wallah! Khayyal!*"[1] somebody remarked to me—a sentiment which sounded strange on Arab lips, for perfection of horsemanship is taken for granted in Arabia,

[1] "By God, what a rider!"

where they ride from birth, and even Doughty in all his long and intimate acquaintance with the Arabs never heard one praise another for his riding. I thought I had found an exception to the rule, but was soon apprised of my error, for the words did not bear the meaning I suspected and referred rather to the boy's courage and skill in battle than to his seat on a horse. It was Turki who won the race—a very popular success—with Salman second, the winner arriving at Riyadh just before dawn on the following day, having, as they reckoned, spent twelve hours in all in the saddle. There was nothing remarkable in Turki's performance as a speed-test, for a rate of six miles an hour represents little more than a good swinging trot, but the earlier part of the march was done at an ordinary marching rate and the speed attained during the last lap must have been at least ten miles an hour and that over none too good going, which included a two-mile stretch of heavy sand in the 'Arq Banban. I myself covered the longer route in just over twenty-five hours of actual marching spread over four days, and Ibn Sa'ud covered the forty-six miles between Khafs and Riyadh in thirteen hours, halts included, but these were feats of no account. Zubara and Mutailij of my Jidda escort had done the distance from Mecca to Riyadh *via* Marran and Sha'ra in eight days, riding post-haste on camels which had already undergone the fatigues of the march from Riyadh to Jidda—this was an excellent performance, though perhaps not to be compared with the brilliant feats of Lawrence's camelry in the Hijaz campaign and other instances of amazing speed and endurance recorded on good authority.[1]

I was woken at 3.30 A.M. the following day to find that Ibn Sa'ud, true to his word, had already departed, leaving the camp in a state of bustle that rendered any attempt at further sleep impossible. It was still dark when I issued from my tent; Venus shining brightly in the midst of a perfect halo paled by slow degrees as the metallic sheen of the morning twilight, the false dawn[2] as the Arabs call it, gave way step by step before the yellowish tints of approaching dawn. Ibrahim, who overnight had drained a bowl of

[1] *Vide* Vol. II. p. 126. [2] "*Subh Kadhib.*"

camel's urine to cure him of an attack of constipation which had made him miserable for four days, gave thanks to God for his deliverance and assembled our small party for the dawn prayer, whereafter, all being ready, we mounted to follow in the tracks of the army, whose stragglers and baggage trains we passed at frequent intervals during the march.

And it so happened that one of the parties we passed was that of last night's bride and her attendants, one of whom was her nephew, a child of ten, Muhammad ibn Mani' ibn Jima', who, may be, had been one of the sponsors of his aunt at the wedding ceremony. More inquisitive and enterprising than the others of the party, which was riding parallel to us but at a little distance, he rode up to us gaily with an attendant riding postillion behind him on his *Dhalul* to see who we might be, for the dangling tassels of our saddle-bags proclaimed us to be of the better sort. Without bashfulness or awkwardness he exchanged greetings and entered into conversation with Ibrahim with the ready assurance which is the natural heritage of the Arab—to the best of my memory I never saw one of that race, however young, timid in the society of his elders and I marvelled often at the finished grace of their deportment in all circumstances, whether in public assembly or in private. His curiosity, however, got the better of him when he noticed me, and I could not fail to observe the whispered asides that passed between him and Ibrahim until, apparently satisfied with the information he had elicited, he urged his camel to a quickened pace and left us abruptly—doubtless to tell his aunt about the infidel. But what particularly struck me about the young man was his contribution to a discussion of the merits of a fine mare, which happened to pass us, led by a groom on camel-back, at the moment of his arrival; there was certainly little he did not know about the points of a horse. I noticed that the horses belonging to Ibn Sa'ud and other members of the force were all shod with shoes of curious pattern,[1] consisting of a nearly heart-

[1] Shaped like this 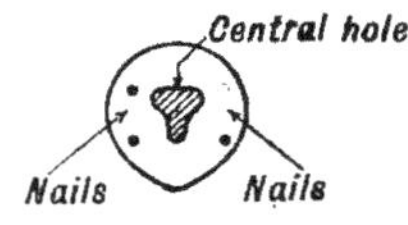

; the unshaded portion represents the metal plate.

shaped piece of metal pierced in the centre with a small and—so far as Ibrahim knew—purely ornamental hole, but otherwise covering the whole of the under side of the hoof, to which it is attached by two nails on either side. The use of such a shoe is rendered necessary in Najd by the rocky character of the ground, against which the pattern used in this country would be but poor protection; but horses are not shod until they are actually required for daily use, and in the stables and grazing-grounds no attempt is made to check the growth of the hoofs.

For about three miles our course lay close along the right bank of the valley, whose containing ridges diverged gradually in wide semicircular sweeps to north and south as we approached the Butain, the surface over which we marched becoming more and more sandy, with occasional patches of low, bush-covered dunes at the same time. Far away on our right front appeared the long coast of Mujazzal, while straight ahead of us the ridge of Khazza marked the farther extremity of the Butain and the beginning of the uplands of the Tuwaiq system. A headland called Khashm ʿAli Dairab, by which a track descends into the Butain from the direction of Shaʿib Asal, stood to north-west of us at the junction of the left bank of the valley and the western escarpment of ʿArma, while on our side the right bank joined the southward extension of the escarpment in a projecting shoulder of crumbled hills, between whose folds the twin *Shaʿibs* of Silh and Ruwaighib, generally known together as Shaʿib Taiyibat Ism, or the channel of the excellent names, run down into the Ats at its crossing of the Butain. Out of sight and higher up these gullies lay, they told me, the watering of the same name, converted since my departure from Arabia into an *Ikhwan* village-colony.[1]

From this point the trough of the Butain assumes the name of Sahlat al Khafs—the plain of Khafs—its drainage flowing not into the Ats but southward into the Khafs depression, and the escarpment of ʿArma, steep and rugged, runs in a south-easterly direction without a break to the neighbourhood of Abu Jifan and beyond. On the right hand lay the Khazza ridge already mentioned, with the upper

[1] *Vide* p. 299 *supra.*

portion of the Ats valley ascending to the uplands between its southern extremity and a low, nameless and indeterminate slope, whose southern end impinged on the high sand-ridges of 'Arq Banban. In the uplands they told me of scattered villages—'Ashaira, Hassi and Daqala, outliers of the prosperous settlements of Sudair, and here and there *Badawin* groups were seen grazing their sheep, those of one small Suhul encampment we passed being mostly white. The cliff along our route rises sheer to a height of 300 or 400 feet above the plain, its summit is worn by wind and weather into weird outlines, in the carving of which Nature has hurled down the crumbled rocks in a sheet of *débris* to lie piled up in fan-shaped heaps about its base, and into the far distance recedes an endless echelon of frowning headlands, to each of which the Arabs have given a name. We decided to halt and break our fast after some four hours' marching in Sha'ib Khafs, a sandy torrent-bed with bush-strewn banks and a wonderful profusion of well-grown *Talh* trees and broad-leaved *Sharr*, whose source lay somewhere on the summit of the plateau amid a jumble of fantastic boulders, one of which, a slender pinnacle of rock standing upright on a huge boulder, they call Al Usba' or the finger, while in others of them my fancy pictured fallen columns or pediments of some vast temple, in the midst of which reposed a colossal rock carved by no hand of man in the image of a Sphinx. The appointed camping-place was not far distant, there was no need for haste and it was very pleasant to lie under the cool shade of the acacias devouring the meal of cold rice and meat which had been provided by the royal kitchen for our refreshment, and to smoke and sip coffee at our ease when the meal was over.

During these days I frequently came into contact with old acquaintances, mostly friends of the Jidda journey but friends who had forgotten me, for the most of them passed by on the other side without so much as a greeting or any sign of recognition, while none came out of their way to visit me in my tent. Ibn Nassar, the cook, came one day to see Ibrahim on business and, finding me with him, murmured some feeble excuse about his excessive work in reply to my reproaches; Jarman and Zubara meeting me

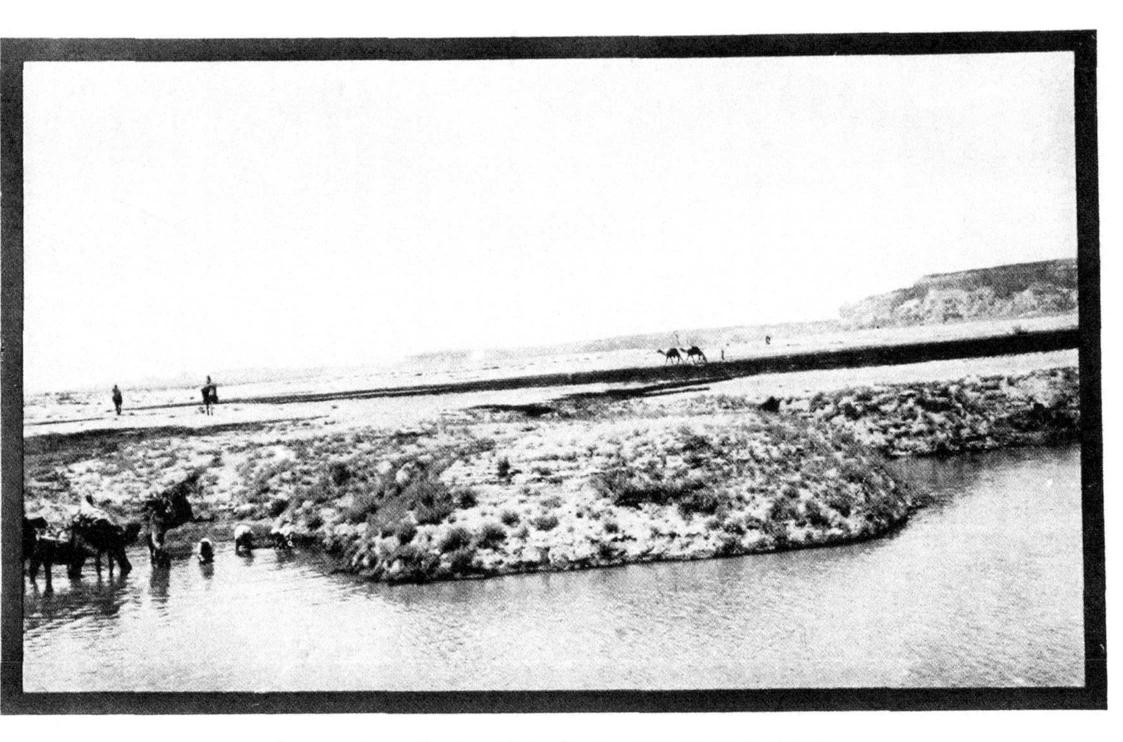

The pond of Khafs with 'Arma cliff in background.

face to face were as curt as possible in their greeting; Dhaifallah, Minwar the camel-herd and Abu Nura averted their eyes as they passed me during this march, in the course of which I also passed 'Abdullah al Nafisi, the warrior *Amir* of Dhruma, who had entertained me under his own roof during my visit to his village but now made no sign of recognition. They are churlish folk, these *Wahhabis*, in their own environment however much they may unbend in other circumstances; one has but to claim their hospitality in their own houses or hold out some hope of reward to discover the underlying amiableness of the Arab race. Of all my friends two only had stood the test of separation or had the courage to flout the criticism of public opinion, and those two salved their consciences with my tobacco in the discreet privacy of my tent.

Resuming our march we soon came to Ibn Sa'ud's camp, pitched about midway between the cliff and the edge of the 'Arq Banban sand-ridge in an extensive patch of bush-covered sand-dunes known as Dakakat al Khafs; at the foot of the cliff, where it rises in a steep precipice of limestone surmounted by a thick stratum of black and red sandstone to a height of nearly 500 feet, lay the *Ghadir* or pond of Khafs, with another but quite shallow sheet of water[1] in a depression close by to the northward. The pond itself, attributed by the Arabs like all clefts of a similar character to the fall of a star, is a permanent feature of the landscape, being a deep crack in the ground some 80 yards in length and 50 across, with two slender, claw-like extensions, which give it the appearance of a crab and by which the drainage of the surrounding slopes finds its way into the reservoir. Last year when the "*Gom*" was encamped in this locality, the basin was full to the brim, thanks to excellent rainfall, but at this time the water-level was perhaps 2 or 3 feet below the brink, the depth of water in the centre of the pond being, they said, about 3 fathoms. The water, of which I drank while Arabs and camels bathed and wallowed in the shallower parts, was as clear and sweet as any I have met with in Arabia, but both the pond and the

[1] This was about 40 by 20 yards in superficial area with a depth of only a few inches.

whole plain about it from the Ats to well south of our camp constitutes a crown reserve or "*Hima*," as they call it, for the grazing of the royal herds and flocks, and all trespassers thereon are rigorously prosecuted before the tribunal of Ibn Sa'ud himself. The result of this restriction, very necessary in a tract so dependent on rain as the environs of Riyadh, is a rich profusion of herbs—*Arfaj*, *Rimdh* and the valued *Ribla*—on which from time to time the royal camels are sent to gorge themselves in the intervals between *ghazus* and other excursions.

"Have they told you about it?" asked Ibn Sa'ud a little bashfully, I thought, as I entered his tent soon after my arrival in the camp. Fortunately Ibrahim had accompanied me to the presence and, not knowing whether the fact of his having gossiped about his royal master might prejudice his position, I was able to prevaricate and give him time to answer for himself. "By God!" he said, "I forgot to tell him about it." I assumed an air of proper mystification. "Why," said the chief, "I married a wife last night; did you not know of it?" "By God!" I replied, "I knew not of that, but Ibrahim told me that you had received news yesterday of the birth of a daughter at Riyadh; I congratulate you on the fortunate event"; the widow of his luckless brother Sa'd had indeed borne him a daughter. He then told me that his new bride had pleased him not overmuch, that he had left her in the early hours and that, as he was proceeding without delay, indeed immediately after his interview with me, to Riyadh and would not there have leisure to attend to an extra wife, a *Baduwiyya* to boot, he proposed to divorce her without further ado. So ended the poor girl's romance; a queen she had been indeed, though for but few hours, and now she would go back to her father's tents; her little cavalcade with the curtained *Qin*, which concealed her from our view, had passed us while we lay breakfasting in the *Sha'ib*, and Rushaid akhu Hasana, who had been made responsible for her well-being, rode up to us to crack a joke with Ibrahim at the expense of the bride. "See you this man?" said Ibrahim by way of introducing him to me, "do you know why he has been placed in charge of the girl? Why, his own wife wants to divorce him on the ground of his impotence; so Ibn Sa'ud can trust him in such matters." "The curse of God be upon you," he replied with a merry laugh, "he is a low fellow, sir, and a liar"; with that he was gone, pursued by ribald laughter.

Our camp had been pitched among the sand-dunes for a special reason, for in these parts in springtime one can never count on the weather, and a brisk shower in the uplands might be followed without warning by the descent of a flood sufficiently strong to sweep everything before it into the pond; it was not therefore considered safe to pitch on the open plain. But the sand was very disagreeable when, as often happened, a gust of wind swept over us, and our troubles culminated towards mid-afternoon in one of the blackest sand-storms I have ever witnessed. At first it seemed like a low cloud trailing over the 'Arma plateau from northward towards us; then the cloud was transformed into a high wall of swirling sand, which obliterated the escarpment as it advanced directly upon us. I rushed into the tent for my camera, and was just in time to snap the advancing storm when the hurricane burst upon us in a perfect tornado of wind and dust which turned day into night; in a moment it had gone as it came, to be followed by frequent gusts of wind until towards sunset a sharp shower laid the sand, while over the uplands of Tuwaiq the heavy clouds banked up for a deluge accompanied by much thunder and lightning.

"Last night," Ibn Sa'ud told me, "I dreamed a dream, and it has frequently come to pass that God has vouchsafed me visions of the future in such dreams. Many years ago I saw in a dream a lofty minaret which the *Sultan* of Turkey —it was 'Abdulhamid—was trying to climb; he failed at each attempt, and at length he gave it up murmuring that he had not the strength to reach the top. Soon after that I heard that he had been deposed. Again, about six years before the war I dreamed and saw the present *Sultan*, Muhammad Rashad, walking in a flourishing garden; again I looked and the garden was in ruins. 'Who art thou?' said the *Sultan* seeing me, and I replied, 'Ibn Sa'ud.' And last night I saw a lofty minaret, as it were the minaret of the mosque at Damascus"—incidentally he had never visited that city—"and a crowd of people were firing at it without avail; then I came up with my people and we fired at it and it fell. Assuredly this dream means that the British will capture Damascus, but not without my help."

At Khafs the "*Gom*" broke up; Ibn Sa'ud himself had departed post-haste to his capital; the territorial contingents had gone to their various homes; and we were left with the *impedimenta* to make our way to Riyadh at our leisure. The first stage, a march of thirty miles to Sha'ib Makharr, was a little wearisome. For twenty miles we marched south-eastward along the continuation of the Butain valley with the long ridge of 'Arq Banban on our right and the cliff of 'Arma on our left, with its endless succession of headlands—Khashm al Khafs, the first of them, by the great pond; next Al Mufaikh, by which a track leads up to the wells of Rumah on the plateau; 'Amya next in order, with a *Jalta* at its foot; then Tauqi, Humaiyim, Hamama and Thamama in succession, beyond the last of which ran the long ridge of Buwaibiyat, with the wells of Barsha'a and Buraishiyya tucked away somewhere in its gullies. The valley itself was of a gently undulating character and was divided by low ridges into a series of crater-like depressions without drainage connection. The first and most important of these was that of Khafs itself, whose reservoir was fed by the *Sha'ib* of its own name descending from 'Arma, and Sha'ib Balham issuing from the uplands of Mahmal past the northern extremity of 'Arq Banban; the next was the waterless depression of Raudha Tauqi, lying, unlike the rest, at the foot of the sand-ridge and fed by a *Sha'ib* descending from the headland, whose name it bears; next came a small basin under Khashm Thamama, and, finally, at the point where the valley bifurcates and we left it, Raudhat Umm al Salam, a large patch of low bushes. Here and there the surface of the valley is disturbed longitudinally by outcropping rocky ridges—that of Hishat Umm al Salam in the vicinity of the *Raudha* of that name and Muwaika over against the Tauqi headland.

After a short halt for a midday repast and a siesta on

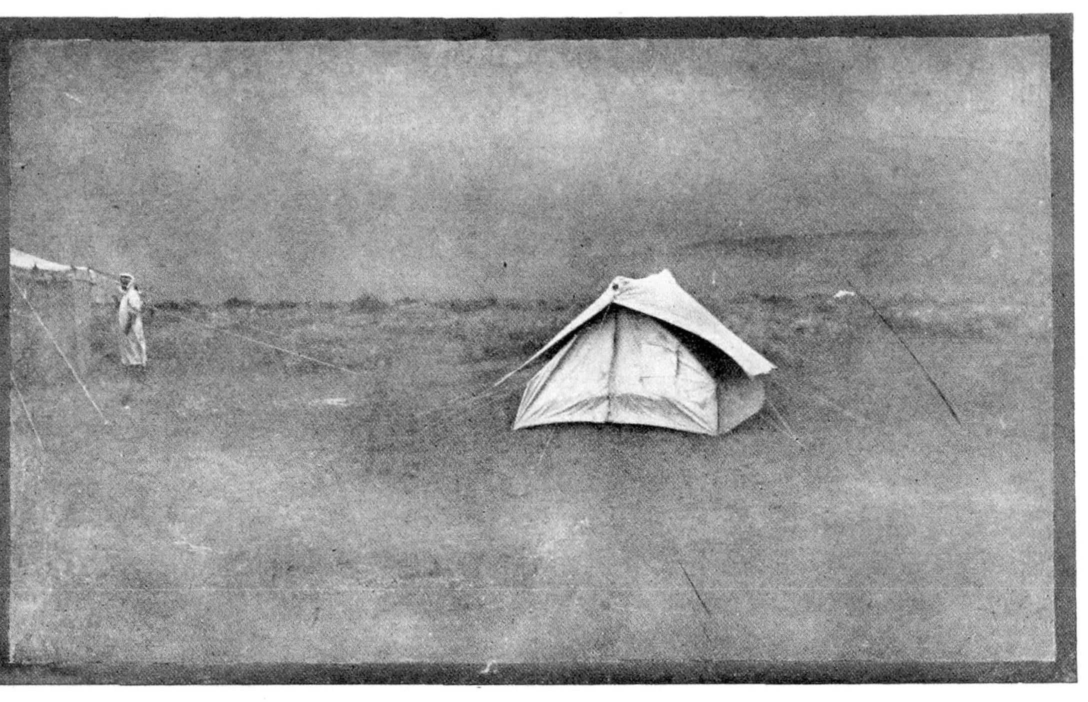

Sandstorm sweeping over camp near Khafs – 'Arma cliff dimly visible in background.

the soft sand we tackled the 'Arq itself, which ascends from the valley in four steep waves of heavy sand, each higher than the one before, which it took us a quarter of an hour and much urging of our beasts to negotiate; the summit reached, we found ourselves on a narrow tableland of sand raised about 100 feet above the plain and perhaps half a mile across. From here we had a good view of the 'Arma cliff on one side, with the dome-shaped hill of Bruma perched on the summit of the Buwaibiyat ridge over the watering of Barsha'a, and on the other side a wide stretch of low sand-hills,[1] among which the lofty sand-cones of Niqa' Shamali and Niqa' Janubi stood out prominently at some distance apart. Beyond the sands lay the valley of Sha'ib Banban, in whose upper reaches is the *Qasr* of that name in the midst of well-irrigated corn-fields; and beyond again rose, ridge upon ridge, the desolate rock-wilderness of Mahmal and 'Aridh.

The descent from the tableland to the lower sands was steep and the going was heavy among the sand-hills, but beyond them we experienced no difficulty as we padded on over the dismal landscape. At intervals we crossed *Sha'ibs* running from north-west to south-east—Sha'ib Thumaiyila, Sha'ib Tulaiha and, finally, Sha'ib Makharr, in whose bed we halted for the night—all of them tributaries of Wadi Sulaiy, which is formed by their confluence near Raudhat Umm al Salam, where, as already noted, the Butain valley bifurcates on either side of the Jubail[2] upland, Wadi Sulaiy running along its western escarpment to the confines of Kharj, while the branch which follows the trend of the 'Arma cliff becomes the valley or plain of Turabi. I was back again among the familiar names and landmarks of my first journey in Arabia, and it was with a thrill of pleasure that I descried afar off the great buttress of Khashm al An frowning upon my return as it had done on my first coming. So we spent the last night of a long march under the shade of the tall *Talh* trees, pitched amid a thick undergrowth of *Arta* and other shrubs by the side of the pebbly torrent-bed winding between low banks set twenty or thirty yards apart. Storm-clouds beat up over the broad back of Tuwaiq,

[1] Known by the name of Ma'aizil. [2] Also called Jibila.

sprinkling us with a few drops of rain ; and around us reigned the silence of the wilderness.

Bare stony slopes, rising by easy gradients to a never-ending succession of ridges, exiguous torrent-beds traversing our course in the direction of Wadi Sulaiy—such was the Hishat al Bilad, as they call the undulating wilderness, which lay between us and the capital as we marched next morning ; away on our right front towards Banban lay the similar tract of Muannisiyya, while our eastward horizon was bounded by the Jubail cliff. Two miles or so from the start we came to a solitary acacia tree, dignified by the name of Talhat al Maqil in virtue of the shade it might afford to the weary traveller ; it stood in a small branch channel of Sha'ib Abul Jurfan, which we crossed shortly afterwards. The loam surface of the depression, in which it ran, was soft from recent rains, and here and there in its bed were pools of water not yet absorbed, one of them forming a narrow lakelet not less than 200 yards in length though but a few feet in breadth. Here the camels slaked their thirst and on we went, crossing *Sha'ib* after *Sha'ib*, among them the 'Aqula and the Abul Masran, in which, on the top of a spreading *Talh*, we found the nest of an eagle, *Nasr* they called it, with two young birds, over which the anxious mother wheeled round and round watching our movements. The ridges now became rougher and in places degenerated into disconnected groups of rounded hillocks, one group of which to the right of us formed the Mugharrizat, while those on the left and directly in front of us were known as Abu Makhruq. Through the scattered *tumuli* of the latter we wound our way towards a ridge higher than the rest, from whose summit, when we gained it, we looked down through a vista of barren hummocks on the dark oasis of Riyadh. *La ilaha ill' allah!* our haven was in sight and the long journey was over ; east and west lay the long black line of palms before us amid the bleak uplands of Tuwaiq.

But ere we could cover the interval that separated us from the city gates it would be time for the midday prayer and the gates would be barred against us, for my second coming to Riyadh fell, like the first, on a Friday. It would be better, we decided, to halt in some shady nook until a more convenient moment, and a suitable spot was near at hand, for a few steps brought us to the foot of Al Makhruq, the grotto hill, from which the surrounding hillocks derive their name; the scene of many a royal picnic in the cool of a summer evening. Here we halted and, couching our camels on the road, ascended on foot, perhaps 100 feet, to the mouth of the grotto itself, a strange freak of nature, which has tunnelled through the summit of the hill, creating a cavernous gap open to east and west and arched over by a natural roof of rock. In the recesses of this rock-walled chamber, in which was ample room for a large party, we disposed ourselves upon our rugs in perfect comfort for more than two hours, eating, drinking coffee and sleeping, as the humour took us, secure against sun and wind. Ibrahim, anxious to create a good impression on the ladies of his household and the city gallants, spent most of his time trimming his beard and otherwise adorning his person before a pocket-mirror, which some of the others also borrowed for a like purpose, but I was obdurate to all suggestions that there was room for improvement in myself and spent some time with my glasses on the summit of the hill surveying the landscape. Below us, all around, the plain was scored with countless tracks converging on the great oasis from every direction; along them was a constant going and coming of camels—a caravan arriving from the Hasa or the royal camels going out to the pastures on their return from camp. Above us, a pair of crows circled round our rock, cawing reproaches at our intrusion and words of parental advice to their chicks in a nest perched on a ledge of the grotto wall.

At length it was time to resume our march. The track led us past the outlying grange of Murabba' and along the palm-groves of Shamsiyya to the gate, by which I had entered Riyadh at my first coming nearly five months before. The gate was open and I passed along the familiar street to the palace square, where the greetings of Ibn Musallim, the chief steward, and others of the household testified that I was no stranger to the palace. During the twenty-three days which had elapsed since I said good-bye to Basra I had journeyed some 400 miles, and I was glad that a few days of rest awaited me before I should resume my wanderings.

4. Riyadh in Spring-time

I was immediately ushered into the presence of Ibn Sa'ud, whom I found busy as usual in his work-chamber on the first floor. "Wait yet a moment," he said, detaining me as I rose to go after a few minutes of conversation over the coffee-cups, "I have sent for the children to greet you. Ho, fellow, tell the boys to come quickly." He could have paid me no prettier compliment; to be welcomed to the palace by the children of the queen, the little princes whom their father loved so dearly for their mother's sake, was more than an honour paid by host to guest; it was an outward and visible sign of my admission into the family circle, a public acknowledgment that our relations had passed from the official to a personal stage. Henceforth I was at home in the royal palace, where before I had sojourned as an honoured guest. In a few moments the little princes appeared—Muhammad and Khalid, aged nine years and six respectively—and, as they entered and I rose to greet them, they came forward without prompting and, with the prettiest grace, put up their little faces to be kissed. I made much of them and asked them how they did before rising to take my leave of my host, whereupon I was conducted by the attendants to the same apartments that I had occupied in December. A much-needed bath and a change of raiment obliterated the stains of long travelling in the desert, and, with occasional interruptions by old acquaintances come to greet me, I was left in peace for the rest of the day to set my house in order

On this occasion I remained at Riyadh until the 6th May—seventeen days, during which I had better opportunities of seeing something of the ordinary life and surroundings of the capital than the heavy official preoccupations of my first visit had allowed. These were the last days of the dying spring, ideal days of sunshine and storm, which succeeded each other with the ordered precision of day and night themselves. The dawn would bathe the world in a flood of cheerful sunshine cooled by a northern breeze;

the breeze would drop as the forenoon hours wore on till the sun from its meridian in a cloudless sky poured down its blazing rays upon the shadeless streets ; the wind would change with the sun's decline to a gentle southerly breeze ; a puff or two of woolly cloud would pass over us before it ; then a gust to herald the coming storm ; afar off to the southward a dark cloud ominously rumbling and about us a sultry, dusty stillness of the air ; and the sun would sink below the ragged edge of the tilted plateau in a blaze of glory, its flaming shafts piercing the advancing storm. Then chaos reigned ; wind and dust blew shrieking through the town ; the heavy black clouds rolled on over the broad back of Tuwaiq, growling angrily as they passed on to the northward and lighting up the deepening gloom with brilliant flashes ; a heavy splash or two of rain or a smart shower to lay the dust and the storm was gone, suddenly as it had come, leaving behind it a trail of stars brightly shining in a cloudless sky. The nights were calm and clear. Such was our daily, or almost daily, experience during this last period of the spring ; some few days were fine throughout, but they were few, and two days out of three the storms rolled up. Riyadh itself, lying as it did out of its direct path along the summit of the uplands, enjoyed but a scanty share of actual rain—perhaps not more than one inch in all during the fortnight—but reports from the province of Kharj told of heavy falls, while the racing torrents of Wadi Hanifa from time to time testified to heavy deluges in the northern area.

The wheat and barley crops were by now well advanced, and harvesting [1] was in full swing throughout the oasis ; fields of waving corn ready for the sickle alternated with stubble patches, where the harvesters had done their work and arranged the sheaves in circular heaps to be trodden out by the oxen before winnowing.[2] The local labour supply seemed unable to cope with all the work in hand, and the uncertain weather conditions necessitated a system of rotation by which the crop of each field in a particular area was cut, garnered and winnowed before work was begun on that of the next, lest a heavy deluge might ruin

[1] *Hasad, yahsidun* = to cut (a crop). [2] *Das, yadusun* = to winnow.

the whole crop on the threshing-floor. Standing crops might be safely left against the unlikely hazard of a hail-storm—no such calamity occurred during this period—and would suffer but little from the dropping of the grains from the ripened ear. Women played an important part in the process of harvesting, their hire for a day's hard work being a sheaf of corn as large as they could carry away, and it was no rare sight in the evenings to see groups of these women wending their way towards the town from some distant corn-field, each with her day's earnings poised upon her head. On one occasion I was out with Manawar and 'Ata'llah on the Dara'iyya road when a gang of them passed us on their way homeward from harvesting in the Maidhar plantation a few miles out. At sight of us an old hag of the party stopped and, with scraggy arm uplifted to heaven, intoned a solemn prayer for my long life and prosperity. Scarcely realising the purport of her words until it was too late to make a suitable response I passed on, and it only dawned on me afterwards that she had mistaken me for a prince of the royal house owing to the presence of the royal slaves. These were, of course, women of the poorer classes, for the ladies of Riyadh were seldom seen abroad, and then only so heavily veiled that nothing of their persons might be seen. At times on a hot day one might, when turning a corner, see such an one hastily draw across her face and body the dark, generally black, mantle which she had perhaps allowed to fall open for a breath of air, but such glimpses were fleeting indeed. The poorer women, however, were frequently seen abroad, both in the streets and in the fields, the outer garment or mantle, generally of coarse brown cloth, being worn over the head so as to cover the whole body down to the knees within the precincts of the town itself, but discarded in the open, where the requirements of convention and convenience are sufficiently met by a long, full smock, generally of red colour, reaching to the ankles, and a clinging veil of black muslin covering the head and the upper part of the body; beneath the smock they wear a pair of baggy pantaloons of black or red cloth. A common sight during these days was bands of women gleaning where the harvesters had passed, and their labours were not in vain, for in Najd custom forbids the gleaning of a field, from which the crop has been harvested, by its owner ; the fallen stalks are God's provision for the needy.

Next in importance to wheat and barley among the agricultural products of Riyadh, and indeed of most of the oases of Najd, is the lucerne crop, perhaps the only crop grown exclusively for the supply of fodder, needed in the large caravan centres not only to supplement the sometimes precarious supply of desert herbs, which are daily brought in on camels to the markets, but also to provide a salutary and strengthening diet for camels and horses jaded by long journeys over lean deserts or by prolonged periods of drought and scarcity. At Riyadh considerable areas are reserved for this crop, which is not only exceedingly profitable to the grower, but appeals to his innate love of ease by the slight demand it makes on his attention, the rapidity with which it grows and the long period during which a single sowing will yield a rich produce in return for no more than regular watering ; once sown, they say, a field of lucerne will remain productive, yielding crop after crop during the year, for as long as seven years, provided it is watered afresh after every cutting. For some reason, which I did not succeed in fathoming, the male and female plants are generally grown separately in alternating strips, which give the fields the pleasing effect of a green carpet with broad purple stripes, the male flower being larger and of a deeper hue than its mate. I did not discover whether the separation is effected at the sowing or by subsequent transplanting.

Under the shade of the palm-groves I found a rich profusion of vegetable crops, onions and lady's fingers and saffron, the last called *Khirriyya* by the townsfolk and *Samna* by the *Badawin*, among the most prominent, with cotton-bushes grown as border plants along the irrigation runnels : among fruit-trees I noticed mulberries and a sort of crab-apple, vines and pomegranates, figs, peaches, apricots and the like. There is little science in the market-gardening of Riyadh, which falls short of the Qasim in this respect, but the rich soil yields its fruit in abundance in response to light manuring and regular waterings, whether from wells, rain-water or the flow of torrents, whose supply is skilfully distributed over the gardens by a maze of channels entering each in turn by rough temporary breaches in the base of its protecting wall.

For the first few days of my stay I was left to fend for myself as regards companionship. Hamdani, a youth of little merit and a hang-dog countenance, was allotted by Ibrahim for my personal service to accompany me on my walks abroad and otherwise dance attendance on me, but the wretched fellow made no secret of his shyness of being seen with me in public, and spent most of his time herding me along byways and little-frequented alleys, and ever heading for home with a persistence that exasperated me. Conversation in such circumstances was impossible, and finding that I enjoyed his company as little as he did mine, I determined to shake him off by doing exactly the reverse of what he suggested. I led him as often as possible through the crowded *Suq* and past the mosques just as the faithful were wending their ways towards them for the sunset prayer. I would sit down patiently while he prayed and, protesting that I was not hungry when he suggested that it was time to return home for dinner, would lead him off to the Manfuha ridge or in the direction of the Batin to watch the sunset or the coming storm. The crisis came on the fourth evening. I had told Hamdani to call for me at five o'clock, as I contemplated a longer excursion than usual; he failed to appear at the appointed hour, and I waited patiently till dinner-time, when Ibrahim, coming in to share my meal, found himself the innocent victim of my pent-up wrath and was told that I never wished to see Hamdani again. Next morning I scandalised Riyadh by walking abroad alone; through the *Suq* I went and out by the Dhuhairi gate, whence I wandered round the whole circuit of the walls, compass and note-book in hand. My conduct —for I was not supposed to leave the palace without escort —must have been reported to Ibn Sa'ud, for the same afternoon two of the royal slaves, armed to the teeth with sword, rifle and bandolier, appeared in my room to inform me that from that moment, by the special command of their master, they were at my disposal morning, noon and night, to accompany me wherever I would go; that I only had to call and they would appear; and that, should I wish to do so, horses were always ready that I might ride. They were as good as their word; whether I rode or walked, one or other of them or both accompanied me, and they were untiring in their devotion. Henceforth my excursions reached to the farthest limits of the oasis and its surroundings regardless of time and distance. Unlike the Arabs, my new friends vied with me in feats of endurance, which provoked the wonder and admiration of Ibn Sa'ud, and most evenings it was dark before we returned to the palace for dinner. Their conversation, moreover, was a source of unfailing interest to me, for they loved to regale me with stories of their own experiences from the days of their childhood in darkest Africa, of the domestic side of the palace life, of persons and things in general.

Manawar and 'Ata'llah were their names, the one a *Nubian*, the other a *Takarini* from Sindar on the Upper Nile, both of about the same age—perhaps about twenty years old—but full of ripe experience in many lands. "My original home," Manawar told me, and I give his story in his own words without comment, "is a land called Abbisha, a year's journey or more beyond Khartum as slave journeys are reckoned, for the convoys are mostly of little children, for whose sake it is necessary to make frequent halts lest the hardships of the way should rob their pirate owners of the profits of their enterprise. We have a *Sultan* in that land and his name is Jarma; the people are *Muslims*, at least they pray and fast as we do here—*yasallun wa yasumun*—and practise circumcision, and their tongue is as the tongue of the Arabs, not the *Takarina* which is spoken by another race far off, whence also come slaves and of which is 'Ata'llah. Beyond us was another race called Janagua, who are not of our creed, whose men go naked and whose women wear nothing but a *Farwa* of sheepskin about their loins; they sleep on the bare earth, and if they see one circumcised they ask why the top of his *penis* is cut off. In those days I was a child and was tending our sheep in the desert when a band of robbers—they call the slave dealers Jallaba—came suddenly upon me and carried me off; never again did I see my three brothers or my mother, who was left to mourn me. With others in the same plight, lads and lasses of my own people, I came riding upon a donkey to Khartum and on to Suakin, whence I was carried across the seas to Jidda. May be that was fifteen or sixteen years ago. The man who brought me across took me first to Mecca to sell me in the slave-market, but none would buy me—for fear of the *Daula*, I think—and my master returned with me to Jidda, where I was circumcised and grew up in his service. He was a merchant, and in due course I was made to work as his salesman; but he accused me of appropriating his profits and beat me. Then he took to doing his own selling but prospered not, and one day I taunted him for his lack of success. He beat me again, and I sued him in the Turkish courts, but without avail; he won the case, and the next time I took the law into my hands, gave him a sound beating and fled to Mecca. He pursued me, vowing to have his revenge, but the Sharif protected me, eventually insisting on buying me from my master Thus came I into the possession of the Sharif and abode in Mecca three years, at the end of which—that is about three years ago—my lord sent me, among other slaves, as a present to Ibn Sa'ud. In fifteen days I came *via* Sha'ra to Riyadh, and ever since I have been happy and prosperous in the palace service, accompanying Ibn Sa'ud in his military expeditions—once, two years ago, against the Murra south of the Hasa, and a second time against the Shammar last year, who fled when they saw afar off the dust of our coming. Slaves are well treated and held in high esteem here; never a foray goes forth but a slave goes with it, partly as a mark of royal authority and partly as a check on the leader, for Ibn Sa'ud trusts no man very far except the royal slaves, whose fidelity is above suspicion. Why, it is his ambition to have sufficient of us to give us a standard of our own in battle. Were it so, we would fight to the last man; but at present his male slaves number but thirty-eight, and a few others there are in Riyadh in the possession of the well-to-do. My uncle"—*'ammi*, as the slaves affectionately address their master—"gives me twenty or twenty-five dollars every month, and he gave me one of the slave girls to wife, who has borne me a little daughter. I am well here and the palace folk treat me well; but the best of them is Ibrahim, the usher, who is not too proud, as some are, to eat and talk with the *'Abid.*" Such was the life history of one of my new companions. 'Ata'llah, filched away from his home at a tenderer age, had little to tell of the country on the Upper Nile, where he was born.

It will be remembered that the League of Nations covenant, to which both Great Britain and the King of the Hijaz have put their signatures, enjoins upon its members the necessity of doing everything in their power to put down slavery and other recognised abuses; and it will be interesting to see what the practical effect of this injunction is in view of the fact that, while Great Britain effectively controls the Sudan and its ports, the route by which the slaves come down from Africa to Arabia, the King of the Hijaz has his capital at Mecca, probably the greatest slave-mart in the modern world. As I have indicated, slaves are well treated and for the most part exceedingly happy in Arabia, but that fact alone cannot be held to justify the operations of the slave-dealers, the worst part of whose business is the terrible mortality involved among the unfortunate children, filched away from their parents and compelled to make that long and arduous journey from the heart of Africa to the coast.

On the afternoon of the day following my return there was a great feast given by Ibn Sa'ud in the palace by way of farewell to those members of the "*Gom,*" who had accompanied him to the capital; the scene of the entertainment was the courtyard of the building, of which my apartments formed part—to wit, the north-eastern block of the palace. In the great quadrangle were set some sixty or seventy trays of steaming meat and rice, each raised a few inches above the ground on a wicker stand; around them, in groups of seven or eight, sat a vast concourse of *Badawin,* tackling the good viands with appetites sharpened by long and frequent repression. Along the walls stood others ready to take the places of those who had had enough. There were perhaps not less than 500 men who feasted that day, and their host with all his family sat at meat with them in a corner of the yard. As each man rose with words of thanks on his lips—"*In'am allah 'alaik, ya Abu Turki*" ("May God requite thee, O father of Turki")—he passed into the little yard on to which my rooms looked out, in the midst of which was set a great pot of water at which he washed his hand and rinsed his mouth before departing.

I was summoned down from my room to see the feast, from which I went on to pay my respects to Ibn Sa'ud's father, the *Imam* 'Abdulrahman. The old man was not in his hall of audience when I arrived, but came in after a few minutes with a genial greeting, whereafter we seated ourselves—he between the cushions in the corner of the room and I at his left hand—and coffee was immediately served. He was in a somewhat taciturn mood, and I found myself forced to do most of the talking, which centred mainly around the war and the changes which Baghdad had undergone in the forty years which had elapsed since he visited that city in the days of his youth. Periods of silence interrupted our conversation, and I was beginning to wonder when the second passing of the coffee would leave me free to take my leave, when the *Imam* called out to the servitor, who had conducted me thither, and in a few words bade him lead me thence. With that he rose and held out his hand; I did the same and faded away with a feeble "*Fi aman illah*" on my lips, to which he made no reply.

Outside the house I met Hamdani, to whom I suggested that we should visit Junaifi, whose house was in the street leading from the *Imam's* residence past the fort to the Shamsiyya gate on the north side of the town. The door was ajar and we entered, Hamdani announcing our presence by calling out the name of our host, who immediately appeared in the hall to conduct us into his parlour, a narrow little apartment without window or other means of ventilation than the door, but cosy enough and stylishly furnished with carpets and cushions. In one corner was the hearth, sunk into the floor and plastered over, with a cupboard behind it, built into the wall, to hold the coffee-cups and other utensils and a store of coffee, tea, sugar and the like. Nine beaked coffee-pots of Damascus manufacture, brightly burnished, graced the back of the hearth, whose front portion held the fire and the pots in actual use besides the usual accompaniments of tongs and bellows. Junaifi, who had two guests besides ourselves, presided at the hearth, dispensing tea and coffee while we discussed the merits of tea without sugar—as I drank it—and other topics until a diversion was created by the entry of two little boys, aged six and five respectively, as charming children as one could wish to see. These were ʿAbdulmuhsin and Saʿd, the children of ʿAbdullah ibn Jiluwi by a *Qasimi* lady, married in the days of his governorate of the Qasim, but long since divorced and now about to be married to Junaifi. He would thus assume paternal responsibilities in respect of the boys, who had never known their own father, for they were but infants when he left them to go to the Hasa. When we had had enough of tea and coffee, incense was passed round and the party broke up, Junaifi accompanying Hamdani and me for a stroll outside the town, and returning with me for dinner in my apartments.

Next day there was a royal garden-party at the Shamsiyya grove, which Ibn Saʿud had recently purchased for himself from a private citizen of Riyadh; the function lasted from about seven o'clock in the morning till sunset, and was combined with the important annual ceremony of camel-doctoring, for the rich fodder of the spring season brings on the *Jarab*, a sort of mange, in the beasts, which will spread in epidemic form with disastrous results if steps are not taken at an early stage to localise the outbreak. All the affected animals were now driven to the scene of the picnic, the people of Riyadh, high and low, turned out in force to assist in the work, and those who were accounted skilled in the veterinary art directed the proceedings under the control of Ibn Saʿud himself, who mingled freely with the workers, chiding here and praising there as occasion demanded. About noon the kitchen tents poured forth a stream of steaming dishes, mutton and rice galore, which being set upon the ground on palm-mats the assembled company gathered round in relays to fortify the inner man for the work that remained to do. The royal family acted as hosts during the meal, and it was not till the workers had had their fill that Ibn Saʿud, taking me by the hand and followed by his kinsfolk, led the way to a mud-built shed within the garden, where lunch was to be served. It was an interesting and representative family party—Turki, Sa'ud, Muhammad and Khalid of the royal line; Muhammad and 'Abdullah, brothers of Ibn Sa'ud; Salman and others of the 'Araïf branch; 'Abdulmuhsin and Sa'd, the little sons of Ibn Jiluwi; Faisal ibn Rashid of the royal house of Haïl; and a host of others. At first we sat round along the walls conversing while coffee was passed round; this was followed by the arrival of trays of dates—a Riyadh variety called *Ambaut*—and bowls of camel's milk by way of appetiser; and last of all came the meat and rice, deliciously prepared with spices, on trays around which we sat in groups of half-a-dozen, Faisal and I squatting as the chief guests on either side of Ibn Sa'ud. The proceedings were marked by a complete absence of formality, and the chief was in his best vein. "Slowly there," he said to one of the family; "have you eaten all the dates?" "Yes," was the prompt reply, "to the last one." "And none left for me?" "Not one, except only this," and a shrivelled date was solemnly extended towards him. "Come, what's this?" said Ibn Sa'ud to one of the workers who happened to be idle as he passed, "why are you not working?" "I am, O father of Turki," replied the culprit with a grin, "and God give you a good morning." The camel-doctoring was a simple, rough-and-ready affair: one by one the beasts were couched in position by a large tub containing a bluish wash—a compound of *Nura* or lime and a drug called *Zarnikh*. They were then securely bound fore and aft and rolled over on their sides, their heads being at the same time drawn right back along their spines and secured by ropes; the wash was then applied all over the skin with the butt of a stripped palm-frond and the business was over, the camels, looking pathetically miserable with their coating of moist dull-blue paste, being herded together and left till the morrow, when the treatment would be completed by cautery and greasing of the affected parts.[1] Before the war, they told me, a Jewish leech, famous for his skill as a

[1] The wash entirely depilates the skin, and the first greasing with *Dihan* is followed by a second a few days later.

camel-doctor, used to come down to Najd from Damascus every spring season to cure the camels; but of late he had not been at Riyadh, with the result that last year there had been a very heavy mortality among the camels, Ibn Sa'ud himself losing as many as 500 of his own beasts.

The same evening, after a short stroll in the gardens, I turned aside on my way home to visit Ibrahim, whose house stood at the head of a somewhat dingy blind-alley in the southern part of the town. The door was opened by Hamud to my knocking, and I ascended by a winding flight of earthen steps to the first floor, where was the parlour facing inwards on to an open balcony overlooking the courtyard, from which it was screened by a flimsy lattice of mat-work. I was expected and found a goodly company assembled in the diminutive chamber, which, what with the heat of the fire in the hearth and with tobacco-smoke—for Ibrahim opened his doors only to the discreet—was incredibly stuffy and made me wonder, as I sat gasping and perspiring under the influence of alternate tea and coffee, how the Arabs could endure such discomfort when they had but to step outside to enjoy the rich warmth of those perfect evenings of spring. But the Arab will never sit in the open air if he can sit over the fumes of a coffee-fire, though Ibn Sa'ud and a few others are exceptions to the rule, the former notably never allowing a fire to be kindled in his audience-chambers, to which coffee and tea are brought by slaves from the kitchen. Besides Ibrahim and Hamud, who keep joint house, the company included Sa'd and Tami, the latter newly arrived from the Qasim, and Ibrahim's two little children, a pretty little boy called Hamud and a daughter, Nura, about six years old. The boy was not at all happy in the atmosphere and company in which he found himself and was soon led howling back to his mother's arms, but little Nura was much more sociable and nestled up at my side while we drank and talked and smoked. From Jidda and Mecca, Tami, weary of wandering and fearing that he might be sent off on another mission on his return to Riyadh, had taken the law into his own hands and gone straight off to his home at Buraida. There his wife presented him with an infant daughter, who, however, succumbed to smallpox a few days later, being the fifth of his children—three daughters and two sons—to die in infancy, and leaving him as before with three daughters, two of whom are still children while the eldest is married and has a baby son. Ibn Sa'ud was far from pleased with Tami's desertion, and orders were sent to the *Amir* of Buraida, in pursuance of which Tami found himself in jail, whence he had only been released ten days before with peremptory orders to appear at once before Ibn Sa'ud—hence his coming and the nervousness he exhibited as to the outcome of his interview with his master on the morrow. Having duly sympathised with Tami on his approaching chastisement we turned on Sa'd to chaff him on the better fortune that awaited him, for he was engaged to be married to a young lady of Dhruma, a relative I think of the *Amir*, and in a few days he was to go for his bride. "But, you dog," I said, "you already have one wife ; is not that enough for you that you want another ? and where will you keep her for you have but one house ?" "There is room enough," he replied, "in my house for the two of them and for my old father and mother, who live with me. The wife I have now is too small and has borne me no children ; so now I want a big woman with large haunches to bear me sons ; and if my wife doesn't like it, she can leave me." "But what of the other girl ? perhaps she may not be such an one as you desire, for you have not seen her." "Oh no," said Tami, "do you mind the day we rested at Dhruma—well, he saw her then, and there it was he made a proposal of marriage to her people ; they say she is fat and beautiful." "*Ai billah*," said Ibrahim with a sigh of envy at his friend's good luck, "he is fortunate." That evening the three of them, Ibrahim, Sa'd, and Tami, dined with me, and when they took their leave, Sa'd lagged behind to whisper in my ear that his wedding was likely to involve him in considerable expenditure. "Look, Sa'd," I replied, "I have given you much already and how have you treated me in return ? Why, you have not even invited me to coffee in your house, as the others have done." "You know," he said, "what people think and say, and my old father is exceedingly bigoted ; it nearly broke his heart when I was sent with you to Jidda, and on my return he told me he would leave my house for ever, if ever I invited you inside it." "Then ask me not for money," I replied, and he departed disappointed.

Another day, Junaifi having again invited me to coffee, I sallied out with Hamdani—it was before our rupture—but, finding our host not yet at home, decided to walk in the gardens rather than await him in the stuffy parlour. As we issued from the town by the Shamsiyya gate we found ourselves almost on the heels of Ibn Sa'ud and a family party strolling out in the direction of the Hauta garden ; so we turned aside and followed the wall round to north and east past the Hassi well and palm-plot and the 'Id-prayer enclosure, by which we found Sa'ud, brother of Ibn Sa'ud, meditating in solitude. The third son of the *Imam*, he was reputed to be something of a hermit in his habits and a fanatic at heart and was seldom seen in any company but his own, but, as I approached, he came forward with an almost effusive greeting, shook me by the hand and detained me for some minutes in conversation, which left me with the impression of a nervous, excitable creature, intensely shy of society but anxious to be sociable, and perhaps a little unbalanced. Physically he was somewhat ill-favoured and certainly entirely without the good looks that distinguished so many members of the family. We passed on, leaving him to his meditation. Re-entering the city by a little doorway at the north-eastern corner, we pursued our way past the stable where Ibn Sa'ud's brother, Muhammad, keeps his horses, along a broad street leading southward—perhaps the filthiest street in the whole city, for it appeared to have been in long and regular use as a public latrine and refuse-heap, and had certainly never been cleaned for years. From it we passed through a gate into some of the richest gardens of Riyadh, the Jiri and Wusaita, both the personal property of the *Imam* 'Abdulrahman, who is in all agricultural matters at once the most progressive and most enlightened member of the whole family, and takes a strong personal interest in the development of his estates. While wandering here under the deep shade of the palms amid saffron-beds and vegetable plots we fell in with an acquaintance of Hamdani, one Ibrahim ibn Muraikan by name, superintendent of public works in the *Wahhabi* administration and acknowledged chief of all the builders and masons of the capital. We gladly accepted his friendly invitation to his house in a neighbouring palm-grove outside the city walls, where in a parlour of the common type, comfortably furnished with rugs and carpets, we spent half an hour drinking and talking with our host and his coffee-maker, Ibrahim al 'Id. It was hot and stuffy indoors and I was glad when the *Muadhdhin* of a neighbouring mosque called all but myself to prayers, and left me to wander in the shady palm-lanes until Hamdani should be free to conduct me home; but my walk was spoiled by the sour glances of passers-by hastening to the service and wondering why I did not the same, for it was clear that they did not know who I was, when one fellow, a lad of not more than twelve or fourteen years, himself belated and passing me going in the opposite direction, addressed me as he hurried by; "*Musallat?*" ("Have you already prayed?") was all he said. I murmured something unintelligible and passed on, wondering whether he meant to censure me for not having prayed or merely to enquire whether he himself was too late for the regular service; Tami, to whom I reported the incident, was of opinion that he had probably intended no more than to suggest my praying with him as he was obviously too late to pray in other company.

So the days passed placidly enough and without any striking incident, but one day there passed through Riyadh on his way northward one who gave himself out to be a wandering *Darwish* from the south. Quite casually, it appeared, the matter was mentioned to Ibn Sa'ud, whose curiosity being aroused to know whence he came, with what news and for what purpose, the man was pursued—he had already been gone a day or two—and brought back to the capital, where a searching cross-examination elicited the fact that he was in reality a Turkish officer of the Yaman garrison, *Qol-aghasi* Qudsi Effendi by name, who had assumed the disguise of a *Darwish* in order to make his way on foot through Najd to Madina and would certainly have won through but for the unfortunate accident which directed the attention of Ibn Sa'ud to his movements. He carried concealed about his person a sum of £T.341 in notes, ten official despatches from the military authorities in the Yaman and Asir provinces to the commandant at Madina and the authorities at the Sublime Porte, and more than thirty private letters from the troops in those far-distant outposts informing their relatives in Turkey that they were still alive. The letters, which I examined with the assistance of Ahmad ibn Thunaian, were of no great importance from a military point of view except that they contained mention of the departure from Ibha, the capital of Asir, two months before Qudsi, of another officer in similar disguise with letters for Madina; he was to have gone by a more direct route through the 'Ataiba country, and the fact that nothing had been heard of him left us to draw the inference that he had either reached his destination or perished in the desert. Qudsi himself had been court-martialled at San'a on a charge of misappropriation of funds intended for the payment of the troops, but had at his own request been given the opportunity of redeeming his misconduct by undertaking the precarious mission which had been terminated by his capture; he had accordingly travelled from San'a to Ibha and thence by way of Wadi Dawasir into Najd. The letters mentioned the privations which the force had to suffer owing to the complete severance of communications between the Yaman and Turkey. Some were statements of accounts and demands for money, while the most interesting of all was a schedule showing the distribution of 1920 rifles among the local tribesmen for the prosecution of the *Jihad* in the neighbourhood of Lahj. Qudsi was now lodged in the fort more like a common felon than a prisoner of war, so far as I could gather from Ahmad, but at my request he was henceforward treated with greater consideration, being provided with more comfortable accommodation, food and clothes from the palace and a servant to attend to his wants, though he was never allowed to leave the fort, where he remained until after the signing of the armistice. I expressed a desire to see him, but on being informed that I proposed to visit him, he replied that, while he was powerless to refuse obedience to Ibn Sa'ud's orders in such a case, he would prefer to have no commerce with an infidel. Thus did he requite my solicitude for his comfort; however, I deemed it best to leave him to his solitude and I never saw him.

My thoughts during these days were ever directed towards the speeding up of operations against the Shammar. Although Ibn Sa'ud had given me his word to attack them in due season I was always apprehensive lest much valuable time might be lost in preparing the ground for action, and I was accordingly much gratified to hear one day from Ibn Sa'ud that envoys had arrived at Riyadh to negotiate an alliance on behalf of Majid ibn 'Ajil, brother of 'Aqab who was at the time with Ibn Rashid at Al Hajr. Majid with a following of his own section, the 'Abda, and elements of the Tuman and Sinjara was in charge of an enemy outpost at Lina in the Euphrates hinterland and was beginning, it seemed, to feel the effect of the recent tightening up of the Kuwait blockade. "I have told you," said Ibn Sa'ud to me, "that I am in honour bound to warn the Shammar of my intention to attack them in order to give friendly elements an opportunity of moving out of the way; now is my opportunity of doing so. What answer shall I give their envoys to take back? shall I tell them I want none of their friendship or shall I invite them to adopt a neutral attitude and settle down well out of my way—say in the Tawal al Dhafir?"[1] I objected to the latter alternative as not affording adequate security for their abstinence from hostile action in the future, and declared that in any case the British authorities would never consent to the provisioning of enemy elements in any locality where they could not be effectively controlled and prevented from supplying their friends, but suggested at the same time that, if Majid and his following could be induced to settle within the sphere of Ibn Sa'ud's effective control, it might be advisable to receive them on that understanding, if only as a means of lessening the numbers of the enemy in the forthcoming campaign. He suggested the Tawal al Mutair, that is to

[1] *I.e.* the well groups round Rukhaimiyya in the tribal range of the powerful Dhafir tribe.

say, the line of wells extending southwards from Safa in the Eastern Desert, and I agreed on the condition that they should not be allowed access to Kuwait, and should be effectively debarred from all communication with Haïl. Ibn Saʿud immediately proceeded to dictate a letter on these lines to Majid and his fellow-*Shaikhs*, and three days later it was handed over to the envoys on the occasion of a public audience, which I was specially invited to attend. It was an imposing scene. Outside the great audience-chamber the stairs and corridors were thronged with retainers, while, inside, it was filled with a great company seated on cushions and benches set along the four walls. In the centre stood Ibrahim in his capacity of master of ceremonies, directing new arrivals to their appropriate positions—each according to his rank—in the assembly; at the farther corner of the room diagonally opposite the entrance sat Ibn Saʿud. Two or three seats on either side of him were left vacant for guests of high position, and I was ceremoniously conducted by Ibrahim to one of these immediately on the monarch's left hand. Turki and young Saʿud I noticed far removed from the places of honour, while by one of the central pillars, that nearest to the throne, were ranged four men sitting on the floor, all ready to start on a long journey. Two of these were the envoys from Majid, fine-looking men of the Shammar, well stricken in years, but sturdy and obviously responsible persons though not of *Shaikhly* rank; the other two were men of Ibn Saʿud's own following, Nasir the *Harbi*, who had been of my escort to Jidda, and another—these two being selected to escort the Shammar envoys back to Lina. To the envoys Ibn Saʿud now proceeded, with frequent side-glances towards me and occasional more direct references, to deliver a spirited and eloquent harangue on the subject of the blockade and the Shammar demand for peace. "If you want my friendship," he said, "here it is, come and settle between me and my tribes and enter into my bosom—*Idkhalu fi chabdi*; but see," he continued, pointing to a man of the Harb, who had been turned away from Kuwait recently in connection with the blockade operations, "how your hostility to the English has involved me and my people in trouble. You all know my hostility to the Turks; *wallah!* you know that formerly I hated the Sharif well enough, but see—since he is now fighting against the Turks I am friends with him. What has your master, Ibn Rashid, done? He has sided with the Turks and I am, therefore, his enemy; I declare to you now that I will assuredly go forth against him as I have agreed to do with this man here"—he clutched at my sleeve as he said this. "If you wish my friendship, do as I bid you or, *wallah!* I will fight you; I will not embroil myself with the English on your account or let you profit by the supplies which they command, for unto them has God given ships and guns and dynamite to blow up their foes with." It was a most inspiring address, and at its conclusion the letters were brought in and handed over. "You see," he added, "I warn you of what is to come for I cannot attack you without warning according to our law." He bade them begone, and so went forth the declaration of war against the Shammar for which I had worked so hard.

After three and a half years of war, during which no serious attempt had been made to watch or control the inward trade of Arabia, a study of statistics had recently revealed the disconcerting fact that exports from Kuwait into the interior during this period, and particularly during the last few months of it, had greatly exceeded their normal volume for corresponding periods previous to the outbreak of war. That this should have been so is not surprising when we consider that on one occasion in the previous September a Haïl caravan of 3000 camels had loaded up and obtained clearance from the local officials in spite of all the efforts of the Baghdad authorities to stop it; that caravan had been chased in vain by Colonel Hamilton and had reached its destination safely, and it was unfortunately not the only one which succeeded in defying the blockade. At the same time insufficient allowance was made for the fact that before the war the interior had drawn its supplies from a number of centres now no longer accessible—Damascus, Madina, Baghdad and Basra, to say nothing of Mecca recently closed to Najd by order of the Sharif, and the Hasa ports, which had suffered from the world-wide shortage of shipping—and the orders issued by the British authorities restricting the volume of inward exports to the pre-war average of Kuwait alone constituted somewhat of a hardship for Ibn Sa'ud's people, *Hadhr* and *Badu.* But the individual who objected most to the new arrangement, was Shaikh Salim of Kuwait, who, deprived of the large revenues accruing to him from the increased trade of his port, legitimate and contraband, sought to console himself for his losses by imputing responsibility for the new and very unpopular measures to Ibn Sa'ud and making the latter's subjects the chief sufferers. While at Shauki I had discussed blockade matters very fully with Ibn Sa'ud, and had arrived at an arrangement with him whereby, with effect from *Sha'ban* 1st (about May 12th), all caravans authorised to proceed from his territories and vouched for by his representatives should be accompanied by special envoys, or provided with certificates stating their business and other necessary particulars, the number of camels, etc. Letters were accordingly issued to all persons concerned enjoining careful observance of the new restrictions on pain of refusal of supplies at Kuwait, and I wrote explaining the new arrangements to the British authorities at that port, hoping that, so far as Ibn Sa'ud and his territories were concerned, the blockade policy now adopted might be carried out without undue friction. But, before my letters arrived, a crisis had been precipitated by drastic action on the part of the blockade authorities amid loud murmurs of wrathful indignation, whose confused reverberations reached Riyadh in the shape of almost incredible rumours and insistent demands for the exaction of satisfaction from Shaikh Salim by force of arms for the insult he had offered to the whole of Najd. According to these tales a proclamation had been issued in the name of Salim ordering all *Najdis* to leave the city by the following morning, and there being then a large number of Mutair in the place who had come down to buy provisions, their chief, 'Abdul'aziz al Duwish, a lad of fifteen, had gone to the palace to demand an interview with the *Shaikh* and had been refused admittance. The boy then left Kuwait with his following and fighting was said to have taken place between them and the

Kuwait tribes. The affair looked very unpleasant, but I begged Ibn Sa'ud to suspend judgment until the receipt of further information. Next day, having received confirmation of the rumours in a letter from the young Mutair *Shaikh,* he came towards evening to the courtyard below my apartments and there, sitting without formality on an earthen bench built out from the wall, we had a long and intimate conversation on things in general. "*Abahachik bil hurriyya,*" he began, "I want to speak quite frankly with you ; I see the hand of Salim in this affair of Kuwait and if, indeed, it is his doing I must demand reparation, but if it is a mistake on the part of one of the British officers, it matters not, for I know it will be rectified as soon as your letters are received." The embers of his hatred for Salim were smouldering ready to burst into flame at the slightest stirring, and I took advantage of the glimpse he thus gave me of the fire within to impress upon him the need for very delicate handling of the situation. "I have already sent orders," he assured me, "to the Mutair to take no action without my sanction and have told them I am taking up the matter myself with you." The following day, no report of the alleged occurrence having been received by me, I was inclined to think that the *Badawin* had unduly exaggerated some petty affair, but that was not the view of the people of Riyadh. The matter was raised in a formal council attended by Ibn Sa'ud, his father, and the chief *Qadhi,* 'Abdullah ibn 'Abdulwahhab, and the monarch's pro-British policy, which he had always defended with assurances of practical benefits to follow from it, was now seriously called in question in the light of the disastrous results it had produced—an interesting demonstration of the truly democratic spirit of the Arabs, whose rulers must hearken to public opinion if they would have public support and confidence. When I saw Ibn Sa'ud in the evening he was evidently worried, and next day the rumours assumed a more fantastic and alarming form. I was still without information, but Ibn Sa'ud had received letters from Shaikh Salim and his own agent at Kuwait, 'Abdullah al Nafisi, the former assuring him that his refusal to see the Mutair chief was due to illness, while the latter stated categorically that he himself had seen Salim looking remarkably well soon after the occurrence. Rumours also became current, though from what source I know not, that British troops had been landed at Kuwait to give effect to the blockade measures above described, that panic had ensued among the *Badawin*, to allay which 'Abdullah al Nafisi had sought an interview with Salim—but in vain—and that the British officer in charge of the operations had been relieved of his post by orders from Baghdad. I knew not what to make of the situation. "What has become of British *Siyasa*?" Ibn Sa'ud asked me, and I could only reply that, if the facts were as stated, somebody must have blundered. The following day I was summoned to the presence, and introduced to two men just arrived from Kuwait with the latest news of the blockade affair. "See," said Ibn Sa'ud, "here is Ibn Mandil, a reputable man of Zilfi; hear from him what happened at Kuwait; what he says I believe to be the truth." The man's account not only confirmed the general tenor of the previous rumours, but added lurid details regarding which they had been silent. The occurrences complained of had been preceded by a conference between the British Political Agent, the Blockade Officer, Shaikh Salim, and an American doctor of the local mission; the *Najdi* leaders had then been summoned and ordered to quit Kuwait the same day, the *Hadhr*, but not the *Badu* element, being subsequently allowed a respite till the following morning; and finally a detachment of troops had been landed from a ship in the harbour to superintend a baggage inspection intended to prevent the smuggling out of contraband goods and carried to the extremity of probing the *Mirkas* or shoulder-pads and camel-saddles for hidden articles, while the martial aspect of the proceedings was enhanced by the mounting of machine-guns on the roof of the bungalow at Shuwaikh. Confident that these details and the story as a whole were greatly exaggerated I assured Ibn Sa'ud that if any mistake had occurred in the prosecution of the blockade policy it would be rectified, and guaranteed that, if the elements who had been ejected from Kuwait returned thither accompanied by a representative of his own, they would be able to make such purchases as they desired. This guarantee, which appeased the hostile feeling daily growing more apparent around me, was in due course made good at Kuwait in response to my representations, but when the full official reports of the affair came in, I could scarcely believe my eyes. The rumours, which had reached Riyadh through prejudiced channels, were true in all essential details and, as I had surmised, somebody had blundered grievously. However, all's well that ends well; I was greatly relieved when the cloud passed by with so little harm done, and having in one sense served a very useful purpose inasmuch as it brought home to the people of Najd and to Ibn Sa'ud himself the fact that the British authorities were very much in earnest over the blockade.

Complaints had reached me from the Political Agent at Kuwait that two Syrian merchants or *'Aqail*, as they are commonly styled, Qasim [1] ibn Rawwaf and Muhammad ibn Dukhaiyil by name, had been making suspiciously large purchases of goods in the name of 'Abdul'aziz ibn 'Uthman, the son of the *Amir* of Zilfi, a person who had wormed himself into the good books of the Agency by giving Colonel Hamilton and his party a hospitable reception at Zilfi on their passage to the Qasim. I mentioned the matter to Ibn Sa'ud by way of sounding him as to the reliability of his subordinate, and was somewhat surprised at his immediate expression of grave doubts about the man's honesty. "He is a scoundrel," he said, "and I am not well with him, but Hamilton, when he was here, spoke very well of him; for long I have been intending to dismiss him, and maybe these agents of his are working in his name for the Turks, for they are Syrians. I will dismiss 'Uthman at once." Next day he showed me a letter about to be sent to the offending *Amir*. "From 'Abdul'aziz ibn 'Abdulrahman al Faisal," it ran, "to 'Uthaimin.[2] Verily God Almighty has not endowed thee with grace, neither thee nor that which thou hast begotten. Did I not, O enemy of God, O ass, forbid thee on oath and thou didst swear by God? and then thou didst send thy offspring with a letter to Hamilton saying that thy son wished to purchase food and goods, and then thou didst sit down, thou and he, to profit thereby.

[1] Pronounced Jasim. [2] Contemptuous diminutive of 'Uthman.

Thou knowest not evil from good, until by reason of thy deeds occurred what has occurred to the people of Najd. This, thy evil conspiracy, will remain in my memory. Thou art dismissed; not again shalt thou be ruler, thou or thy house, at Zilfi for ever. Go forth to any country that may be in thy mind except to my countries unless I give thee permission, or else repent and settle under my eye in 'Aridh. See, if thou delayest, by God! though it be an hour, or there remain any of thy house—verily, I am not ruler of this land if there remain a trace of thee; beware and sue for pardon. Be it known to thee." I never heard what was the ultimate fate of the recipient of this remarkable document—he was not at Zilfi when I passed through six months later, having been succeeded by one Salman ibn Baddah of *Ikhwan* propensities.

On the last day of April, having seen the surroundings of Riyadh fairly thoroughly, and being somewhat weary of waiting for the completion of arrangements for the promised southern excursion, I took Al Qusaibi into my confidence, complaining that, whether intentionally or otherwise, the circle of my acquaintance was unduly restricted and declaring that I could not be expected to stay indefinitely at Riyadh unless I was permitted a freer entry into its society. I had made similar though unsuccessful attempts with Ibrahim, who, I am convinced, was too timorous to broach such a delicate subject to his master. Qusaibi, however, was a man of different mould, and must have gone forthwith to Ibn Sa'ud to lay the matter before him; at any rate, the same afternoon, being summoned to the presence, I found Ibn Sa'ud and several of the royal family about to make a tour of inspection of the new rooms and buildings under construction in the palace. Inviting me to accompany them, he turned then and there to Ibrahim, rated him in public for his failure to introduce me to a wider range of society, and gave orders that henceforth I was to visit whom I wished. Shilhub, the treasurer, being present to conduct the party round the buildings, was ordered to invite me to coffee that same evening, and I felt somewhat abashed at being the cause of all this trouble, but thereafter I found life much more tolerable than it had been before.

Ibn Sa'ud took a great personal pride in his new buildings; in every part of the palace the builders were busy demolishing here and constructing there, and from what I have heard since I left Arabia I should scarcely be able to find my way about the building now, so many are the changes which have taken place, including, I regret to say, a straightening of the frontage, which always seemed to me, as it stood, the best part of the palace, and as good a bit of architecture as any in Najd. I was taken now to see the new hall of public audience—a vast oblong apartment of simple design with only three small windows, and those set so high in the outer wall that they were of no use except for the purpose of ventilation. The roof was supported by a row of plastered pillars set at intervals along the central line of the room; the floor was covered with carpets, an amazing mixture of good and bad ones; the ceiling and main beams of palm-wood were completely covered with gaudy cloth and large square cushions of the same material in a variety of colours lined the walls. The chamber was practically ready for use, and a similar apartment below it on the ground floor had already been made over to Turki as his public reception-room, for he was now taking an ever-increasing share in the work of administration and was entrusted with the disposal of all business of secondary importance; it was an excellent training for him and relieved Ibn Sa'ud of a great burden of work. I was also shown over various other rooms not yet completed, including a suite of rooms intended for occupation by distinguished visitors; "*Imthal Janabakum*" ("The likes of yourself"), as Ibn Sa'ud explained. Personally I thought these rooms ill suited for the purpose as being too near the public rooms and approachable only through crowds of servitors waiting on their master, while the apartments I was actually occupying seemed to be in every way more convenient. I did not, however, voice my opinion, and was left to my original suite during the whole period of my stay, though it is now, I fancy, finally relegated, together with additional rooms then being built in the courtyard, to the domestics of the household and their families. Stables and a guest-room were also in course of construction in the western wing of the palace, from whose roof Ibn Sa'ud pointed out to me the directions in which he purposed eventually to enlarge the city—a process which appeared to involve the levelling of some of the best palm-groves outside the south corner of the capital.

After a short walk in the gardens I hastened back to Shilhub's house for coffee. It was, he explained, the house of his favourite wife, a lady of some taste, to judge by the neat little parlour on the first floor, well provided with carpets and cushions of decorative Indian cloth. In the hearth were eight brightly burnished coffee-pots, and by it a cupboard from which my host produced for my admiration an atrocious *Midkhan* apparently made at 'Anaiza, its frame of *Ithil*-wood being ornamented with brass studs, fragments of a mirror, and four strips of tin, one on each side and each bearing the painted image of an eight-oared racing boat with the legend "Made in Austria." Qusaibi, Ibrahim, Hamdani, and a few others made up the company, and the conversation turned mainly on the marriage of the first named to the widow of one of Ibn Sa'ud's deceased retainers, which, having been celebrated that afternoon, was to be consummated according to custom after the evening prayer. The conversation was somewhat coarse and obscene. As I returned home a heavy shower came on and I was drenched to the skin before I reached the palace.

The village and oasis of Manfuha, which, though separated from it by a low ridge, form an integral part of the Riyadh oasis and to which I made several visits during these days, lie about three miles S.S.E. of the capital and are approached therefrom by two tracks. One of these follows the flood channel of the Shamsiyya past the royal cemetery, lying on its left bank about half a mile east of the city, and through the ridge mentioned above, from which it emerges in a wide, shallow trough between it and the Duraibat al Khail slope. A small patch of cultivation with a few wells stands well back from the road about two miles out, and one soon thereafter enters a ruinous area marking the beginning of what once used to be a great city, comparable with if not indeed greater than Riyadh. The other track passes from the south gate of the capital in a southerly direction through the palm-groves, and turning out of them, about a mile on, strikes across a plain studded with ruins of an old outpost or suburb and up the dividing ridge from whose summit one has an excellent view of the palms of Riyadh to the north, those of the Batin to the west, and Manfuha itself and its extensive groves to the south.

The ruins of old Manfuha surround the modern village and extend in a long line along the eastern side of the palm-belt, but there is so little left of them that it would be difficult to reconstruct a picture of the old city, which flourished when Riyadh was no more than a hamlet. Its princes, Daham ibn Dawwas and his predecessors, were rivals of the Sa'uds of Dara'iyya. From the broken remnants of one of its old towers, I looked down on the village which has replaced it, while Manawar after a fruitless attempt to stalk a fox, which dodged him up and down the depressions of the broken ground all round, composed himself for the evening prayer, and the westward sky growing blacker every moment with the heavy thunder-clouds of an approaching storm warned us not to dally. It is a wretched, ragged little village of mud hovels, for the most part of a single storey, surrounded by a mud wall. Its seven gates were with few exceptions mere breaches in the wall and its towers were mostly in a state of decay. The uncomely minaret of the chief mosque stood out high above the low huts in the midst of the settlement, whose background was a dense forest of well-grown palms stretching out in a line nearly three miles in length, with an average breadth of perhaps a quarter-mile. Before turning homeward I paced the greater part of the circuit wall, which forms an irregular hexagon with a diameter of about 350 yards, enclosing a population of perhaps 2500 souls, among whom, they say, no trace can be found of the old ruling house.[1] Passing the southern gate I noticed one good street with a few shops leading from it through the village, but the remaining thoroughfares appeared to be narrow, crooked lanes. The population is mixed like that of Riyadh and none too prosperous. For some reason the royal treasury is entitled to a quarter of the gross out-turn of dates and

[1] The *Amir* of the village is Ibn Kharashi, I think of the Bani Tamim.

corn in the oasis, perhaps because it lies in the direct path of the Hanifa torrents and taps their water by an excellent system of irrigation ducts, but it appears that in practice Ibn Sa'ud contents himself with a levy of only 5 per cent in kind as at Riyadh and in other parts of Najd where perennial irrigation is absent. The road to Riyadh across the ridge is dotted with derelict guard-towers, relics of a time which wrought on both sides the havoc to which their ruins still bear witness. A narrow glade divides the palm-belt into two parts, the northern groves being counted to Manfuha itself, while the southern contain in their midst the village of Masana', a small settlement of 400 souls under a separate *Amir*, Ibn Zaid, and at their southern extremity a large fort called Miz'al, apparently built during the stormy times of 'Abdullah's reign half a century ago to guard the approach to the capital from the south.

While the main stream of the Shamsiyya torrent sweeps past the north side of the capital trending in a south-easterly direction past the Manfuha oasis to join Wadi Hanifa at the southern extremity of the latter, a subsidiary branch thereof runs through the groves west and south of Riyadh itself to join the Hanifa channel at a point, where, debouching from its rock-bound course through the heart of the Tuwaiq plateau, it makes a sharp bend to the southward along the outer slope of the uplands. The pent-up flood of the Hanifa, rushing down at intervals during the winter and spring in great volume and with an eastward impetus, would, in the natural course of things, sweep with destructive force over the wide area now covered by the southern groves of Riyadh and the Manfuha palm-belt before steadying down into the broad valley between the Tuwaiq uplands on the one hand and the Duraibat al Khail on the other, had not man interposed to restrict its course within reasonable limits for his own advantage. The left bank of the channel has been artificially strengthened to meet the first shock of the torrent's issue from the uplands by a long curved dam of rough but massive stonework, by which the stream is checked and forced into a southward channel along the base of the Tuwaiq slope. About a mile farther down a dam of similar masonry has been thrown out from the slope at right angles to the stream, and across it to a point well beyond its left bank to serve the double purpose of a dam and weir; a parapet, raised a foot or somewhat more above the level of the bed, diverts the waters of a normal flood into a side channel, from which distributaries radiate in various directions towards the Manfuha palm-belt, while at the same time it allows any excess over a normal supply to escape over it into the main channel, between whose upper and lower sections there is a fall of about four feet. The foundations of this dam reach down to the solid rock underlying the pebbly torrent-bed, which has been laid bare by scouring for some distance immediately downstream of the obstruction, and is pitted with great cavities, in which water is to be found for the greater part of the year and which were brimful at the time of my visit. As a matter of fact I was unfortunate enough on this particular occasion to miss by only a few minutes the magnificent spectacle of Wadi Hanifa in full flood. I had walked out with Manawar and 'Ata'llah to Manfuha and thence to the lower dam, where I had spent half an hour examining its cunning workmanship, while my companions performed their ablutions and devotions; in the gloaming we had wandered slowly up the channel to the upper dam and thence hastened homeward by the direct route through the palm-groves. Just as we reached the city gates, we were overtaken by a man on a pony who must have passed the dam—he came from the Batin—about ten minutes after we left it. "Didst see the *sail*?" quoth he. "*Wallah!* God has been bountiful; I crossed the *Wadi* just in time, when behind me it flowed in a great swift stream." The news he brought was confirmed by an arrival from Dara'iyya, who had got his camels across the channel at that spot just in time to see it obliterated by the flood; had he delayed a few moments in starting, he would have had to wait till the morrow, for, when the *Wadi* is in flood, no man will venture to cross it. It was the greatest flood of the season and the last.

Within the folds of Tuwaiq and for about a mile up the torrent-bed from its exit, the valley of Hanifa, here designated Al Batin, is dotted with rich palm-groves on either side of the flood channel, a narrow strip of fine sand and pebbles lined by terraces of silt and *detritus*. This rich soil, renewed yearly by fresh deposits brought down by the torrents and left behind in every bay and cranny of the winding channel, supports some of the finest groves in the whole oasis as well as patches of corn, vegetables and melons, but there are no permanent settlements in this area except a few huts occupied by tenants of Ibn Sa'ud and the other owners of the groves. The Batin is a favourite resort of the citizens of Riyadh and particularly of the royal family on high days and holidays, when they hie thither in great numbers with their horses to make merry with shooting matches, mounted displays, and other sports the live-long day from early dawn till evening, feasting and coffee-bibbing and praying at proper intervals.

No sooner had the Shammar envoys left on their return journey with letters for their chief than I heard of the arrival of an imposing deputation from no less a person than 'Ajaimi himself, bringing letters from their principal and a present of horses—four mares and a fine stallion—from his chief lieutenants, Muhammad ibn Turki ibn Mijlad, the leading *Shaikh* of the Dahamsha 'Anaza, and Fahad ibn Dughaiyim, the rival of Fahad Beg ibn Hadhdhal for the headship of the Amarat section of the 'Anaza. The envoys themselves were persons of consideration, Naïf ibn Dughaiyim, brother, I think, of Fahad, and Badr ibn Mijlad, cousin of Muhammad. There was clear evidence in the letters, which were couched in the politest and even in affectionate terms, that the writers were already feeling the effects of the rigorous enforcement of the blockade, but the Arab will part with his last breath rather than his pride. As one free man to another 'Ajaimi wrote that his presence in the Euphrates desert—he was apparently in the neighbourhood of Rukhaimiyya though he did not say so—was due solely to grazing considerations, and that he would be glad to be allowed access to the Qasim markets. His lieutenants wrote in the same strain but with clearer indications of their personal weariness of the long struggle and with pointed references to the blood-tie, which made their real interests identical with those of Ibn Sa'ud himself, the natural leader of the *Muslimin* against all heretics and infidels. "Do you see?" said Ibn Sa'ud to me during our discussions as to what reply should be made to these emissaries, "for many years now I have been applying all the resources of diplomacy to detaching the adherents of the enemy to my side and now my efforts are beginning to bear fruit. You saw the reply I sent back to Majid and the proclamation I have issued to the Shammar *Shaikhs*. Now I will send a similar reply to 'Ajaimi and his fellows, but remember that the time for action is drawing nigh and I want to be assured that the British Government will not withdraw their support from me once the die is cast. If left to myself I would work by diplomacy and, if God wills, all the tribes would be with me in a few years; but now you ask me to hasten matters by active operations. When I start, there can be no drawing back." "I have given you my word," I replied, "and from that there is no drawing back, but remember that the British Government will only judge by actions and results and not by words and promises." "Well," he said, "I will do with these people as I did with the Shammar. I will say to them: 'If you desire my friendship, you are my cousins and welcome, but you must do one of two things. You may come down and live in my territories under my hand or, if you so prefer, you may go in to the British at Baghdad and join them against the Turks. I will give you letters of recommendation. But if you like neither the one course nor the other, see, I am your enemy and I will fight you where I find you in my path.' See, the proverb says: 'If you promise, fulfil, and if you threaten, fail not to perform; for him who promises and fulfils not no one will trust, and him who threatens and performs not no one will fear.' I have sent forth the order already to the tribes to muster here at Riyadh in the middle of *Sha'ban*, when Turki will lead them out to begin foraying with the crescent of *Ramdhan*; and, moreover, I have summoned a great gathering of the *Ikhwan* for a few days hence, when I will explain matters to them and work them up to a great enthusiasm; please God, there will be a great muster with happy results. A day or two ago Shaikh 'Abdullah, the *Qadhi*, was discussing the question of the Sharif with me and urged action in that direction, but I said to him: 'Be patient awhile and the Sharif will overreach himself.'" The *Ikhwan* gathering took place the day before my departure for the south in the 'Ataiqiyya garden in the southern part of the oasis, where, far from the bustle and mundane cares of the capital, the *Wahhabi* monarch had a heart-to-heart talk with the most fanatical elements of his people and paved the way for the coming *Jihad* or holy war. The previous evening, while I sat discussing matters with him on the palace roof, I heard the musical strains of a preacher's voice intoning passages from the *Quran* and relevant portions of the *Commentaries* to a great assembly of the faithful, over which Ibn Sa'ud had left his eldest son to preside on the roof of the public audience-chamber. How strange it seemed to me that faith should thus be made the handmaid of policy, that the embers of fanaticism should be fanned into flame in a secular cause. "What," I asked my host on this occasion, "is the real attitude of the *Ikhwan* towards your alliance with the British?" "It is not true," he replied, "that they are hostile to you, for according to our creed you are *Ahl Kitab* and not *Mushrikin* or infidels, against whom alone is the hatred of the *Wahhabis* directed. But there are many among my people, chiefly among the townsfolk, who, having travelled or been educated abroad, sympathise with the Turks as the representatives of *Islam*, and are therefore hostile towards the British, but they get short shrift here, and quite recently I have punished two men of that sort for giving expression to their views."

On the morrow of his marriage I met Qusaibi at Shilhub's public reception room—a large chamber on the ground floor of a house in a street leading towards the south-east gate, where coffee is served at the expense of the state to the many visitors, which his duties as treasurer compel him to see and entertain. "Well, how do you like her?" I asked of Qusaibi, "is she beautiful as they said, and are you satisfied?" "Fair," he replied, "middling, about ten annas in the rupee [1] and not more; but you people do better to choose your wives after seeing them. With us

[1] An Indian idiom picked up at Bombay.

many a man only finds out on his wedding night that he has been deceived." With little to boast of himself in the matter of looks he deemed himself something of a Don Juan, and it was clear that he was a little disappointed with the choice which Ibn Sa'ud had made for him to console him for his lonely state at Riyadh. In his arduous task of keeping the royal exchequer in reasonable order, Shilhub had the assistance of a clerk with a smattering of *Hindi* sufficient to enable him to spell out figures and words in bills received from Bombay, but the account books, which they produced for my amusement, scarcely constituted monuments to their joint efficiency. Shilhub told me he had six sons ranging between infancy and fourteen years.

One evening, while I was sitting with Ibn Sa'ud on the roof under a cloudless sky, I made bold, on the strength of the erratic movements of my aneroid, to prophesy a rough night. "God knows," he replied, a little perturbed at my trespassing on dangerous ground, for among the *Wahhabis* it is forbidden to pry into certain secrets, knowledge of which, according to the story, God withheld from Muhammad himself lest perfect knowledge should raise him in man's estimation to divine rank. The hidden things are five in number—the sex of an unborn child, the hour of one's death, the events of the morrow, the country in which one will die, and the fall of rain; to no man is knowledge of these things given, and into them may no man pry. But I was justified in my prediction, for the night was excessively stormy and drove indoors those, like myself, who had ventured to sleep on the roof. Next morning, while I was sitting with 'Abdullah ibn 'Abdulrahman in the great audience-chamber, Ibn Sa'ud, happening to see me as he passed by, stopped to comment on the accuracy of my prophecy and to confess that he had lost his sleep by disregarding it; and afterwards I learned that the fulfilment of my seemingly groundless prediction was widely discussed during the day and well received. Needless to say, I was very careful to ascribe all the credit to my "little machine for weighing the atmosphere."

'Abdullah ibn 'Abdulrahman was the first member of the royal family to respond to his brother's publicly pronounced orders for my better entertainment. He apologised for receiving me in the public audience-chamber, as his own house, next door to his father's residence, happened to be undergoing repairs and expressed a hope that, when it was ready, he would be able to receive me in more fitting state. We resumed the discussions of literature and kindred subjects which had begun at the Shauki camp. According to his judgment the greatest of the modern poets of Najd is one Sulaiman ibn Sahman, a native of Riyadh, whose collected works had recently been sent to Bombay to be printed; one of his poems, mostly of a religious turn, is a refutation of the claim of the Turks to be real *Muslims*. He told me that many old manuscripts of poetry and religious works were still to be found in the libraries of his father and of many of the *'Ulama* of the capital in spite of the depredations, which had resulted during the *Rashidite* occupation in the transference of the royal library of Ibn Sa'ud's ancestors to Hail. On my hinting that I should be very glad to purchase any manuscripts that might be available, he hastened to assure me that such a project would not be feasible, the sale of religious books being considered improper, while the traffic in ordinary works was but slight in Riyadh and elsewhere in Najd. 'Abdullah was as much at home in the discussion of the chase, of war and of *Badawin* life in general as in that of literature. In the Dahana, he told me, the commonest species of gazelle is the *Rim*, of whitish colour and somewhat larger than the ordinary gazelle of the plains —*Dhabi*, as they call them, or *'Idmi*.

On the same day after the midday prayer Ibrahim conducted me to the house of Sa'ud ibn 'Abdulrahman, Ibn Sa'ud's hermit brother, whom I had already met casually on two occasions during my walks abroad. He was effusively gracious in his reception of me and covered me with confusion by so resolutely insisting on my taking the first cup of coffee that I had to yield in spite of my fixed rule of refusing to be served before the senior member present of the royal family. This being my first visit to Sa'ud, conversation was largely of a formal character, but I found him unexpectedly discursive on many matters and far more intelligent than his reputation had led me to expect. His old father, he told me, had led a life of almost complete seclusion for about seventeen years, issuing forth from his house but once a week to attend the Friday prayer in the Great Mosque. On these occasions it is Shaikh ʿAbdullah, the *Wahhabi* high priest, who fills the rôle of *Imam*, Ibn Saʿud standing directly behind him in the centre of the front row with his father on his right hand, while other members of the royal family occupy unobtrusive positions in the rear or in the midst of the congregation, which comprises all male members of the population of Riyadh from six years of age upwards. Junaifi told me that on one occasion he counted thirty rows of worshippers in the body of the mosque and ten on the roofs of the two *Liwans*, each row, according to his estimation, containing 300 persons. These figures would give Riyadh a total male population above the age of six of 12,000 persons, but are deserving of no serious attention in view of the fact that the length of the mosque is only 75 paces—sufficient perhaps to hold 120 to 150 persons in a row, but not more. If we accept the larger of these figures the male population of mosque-going age would be about 6000 persons, to which are to be added the male infant population and the women and girls. It always seemed to me that 20,000 was a generous estimate of the total population of the capital, which is in all probability somewhere in the neighbourhood of 18,000.

Saʿud discoursed at length about the days of his family's exile, during which his father had spent about two years at Bahrain and Qatar before removing to Kuwait, where for six years he and his rapidly increasing family enjoyed the hospitality of Muhammad ibn Subah until the latter's murder by his own brother, the famous *Shaikh* Mubarak, under whose protection the royal house of Najd throve exceedingly in preparation for the *coup d'état*, which again placed it on the throne of Riyadh. I was somewhat surprised to find Tami in Saʿud's parlour when I arrived and still more so to find him in his most flippant vein, punctuating the proceedings by anecdotes, I know not whence obtained, of cannibal tribes and other strange peoples. He told us also that he had recently heard that the Chinese workmen at Basra had murdered a British officer and been giving much trouble in other directions—idle tales manufactured probably in the bazars of Kuwait, where a persistent little band of pro-Turk propagandists was ever engaged during these days of war in conceiving schemes to the disadvantage of the Allies and particularly of the British, whose blockade measures were at this juncture the theme of the most extraordinary insinuations. I have already referred to the unfounded rumour [1] of our troubles and defeats at this period in Palestine, but that was mild in comparison with the anti-British propaganda, which followed the news of the blockade trouble at Kuwait to Riyadh and caused Ibn Sa'ud no little anxiety regarding the real state of affairs in Europe—for, like his people and not his people alone, he was always somewhat sceptical of news that had filtered through our censorship, and he was too wise to reject news received from other sources without careful sifting. "Doubtless," ran one such communication received by Ibn Sa'ud from an anonymous correspondent at Kuwait, "'Abdullah Nafisi has informed you of the blockade measures directed against the people of Najd; in truth it is a bad business and harmful to the people, but your judgment is best. Nowadays the papers are full of news and people come to us from Damascus, Baghdad and Basra. In short, they tell of a large increase of troops in Palestine, mostly German and Austrian. Also they say that Ibn Laila [2] has returned to Syria, where he was well received by the Turks, and loaded with gifts, including rifles, guns and other things—but of course this has already reached you. Papers from Egypt tell of the increased tension of the war in France, of the plight of Italy and of the peace with Russia; also the American President has propounded seventeen conditions of peace, of which some have been accepted and others rejected. The same papers and others from Syria say that the fighting in France is in the neighbourhood of Paris and Rome, and that the French have moved their capital to another place in their territory about seventy miles from Paris on the Mediterranean coast. Again, we hear that reinforcements for Syria number nearly a

[1] *Vide* p. 302 *supra*.

[2] This man was Ibn Rashid's political agent with the Turks.

million men and that the Turks have advanced and cut off the retreat of the British in Jerusalem, and that the Sharif's son, Faisal, has been defeated near Karak and the Balqa. The Sharifial troops fled and all the prisoners were slain, and the Turks have advanced against the English, as it seems, and are near Yafa and Ghazza. As regards the defeat of the Sharif's son, they say that 300 of the Huwaitat were slain. . . . These bits of news we have taken from the papers and partly from the reports of people from Damascus, Baghdad and other places ; also the British have suffered a defeat in the neighbourhood of Baghdad. We have seen indications of all this in the newspapers forwarded herewith for your perusal. Peace be to you."

The following day, being Friday, I was left to myself until after the midday prayer, when Ibrahim fetched me away to visit Shilhub, in whose parlour I found Qusaibi and Hamdani already forgathered. It was very hot and stuffy and our faces were soon streaming with perspiration —my seat being of course in the most honourable position as near as possible to a blazing fire. My companions, exhausted by their devotions, eagerly tackled the good fare of dates and milk set before them, but I did not feel equal to eating in such an atmosphere. The coffee was the best of its kind, the real product of the Yaman, which in the assemblies of Riyadh is reserved for distinguished guests and visitors from the south, who would feel insulted at being offered Indian coffee, considered sufficiently good for the common herd. My weather prophecy came in for some discussion. " In such matters," said my host, " you are *abkhas*—you know better than we do, but our creed is sceptical—*mustankir*—in things, which are the province of God alone." " How then," I replied, " do you set limits to the seasons ? You say that the *Saif* season lasts forty days and is preceded by the *Rabi'* and succeeded by the *Qaidh* ; how can you say that, when God may alter their order as He pleases ? We do but weigh the atmosphere with instruments and can tell of coming rain or drought by that means according to the same science, which you use in another form." My endeavour was ever to disarm the prejudices of the strange people, among whom I lived, and to appear to them as one like themselves seeking the light which cometh of knowledge; and I never missed an opportunity of attributing the beginnings of our Western science to the Arabs themselves or of claiming for my instruments direct descent from those used by the astronomers and other learned men of Baghdad in the days when the *Khalifa's* court was one of the centres of the civilised world. On one occasion I was much flattered by the appearance at my door of a messenger sent expressly by the *Imam* 'Abdulrahman to enquire whether the sun was eclipsed or not. It was a dull day and the sun showed but dimly through a thick haze of dust, but I felt it incumbent on me to make the most of the occasion. Before the breathless envoy I turned over the pages of my *Nautical Almanac* and, having announced that no eclipse was recorded for that day in our books of science, I issued forth sextant in hand to examine the sun itself and confirmed the accuracy of our books of science by actual observation. The messenger sped away with the good tidings—for an eclipse is considered an untoward sign by the *Wahhabis* and involves much prayerful invocation of God's mercy—and my finding was accepted as conclusive. On a later occasion my skill in these matters—derived from the *Nautical Almanac*—was strikingly vindicated before a sceptical public, but that story must be reserved for another occasion.

The same evening Qusaibi entertained me and a few friends at the house of his newly wedded wife, whence we passed on to visit Muhammad ibn 'Abdulrahman, Ibn Sa'ud's eldest brother, whose house faces the east wall of the palace across the central square. On the outer door I saw inscribed the words *Bait Khalid*, signifying that the building was the residence of the mother of Muhammad's eldest son, named Khalid. Knocking at the door we entered without ceremony and turned from the passage into an oblong hall of more than ordinary dimensions. Its roof was supported by a central row of pillars and its plastered walls were profusely decorated with drawings of many kinds—for the most part concentric circles in red and blue paint, wheels and baskets or pots containing what appeared to be intended for growing plants or shrubs;

more elaborate panels showed unskilful attempts to represent mosques and minarets grouped together in lines without any arrangement or perspective, but I was particularly struck by two ambitious representations of ships in full sail, one of them gaily beflagged. The absence of any representations of living creatures was a noticeable feature of the decorative scheme, which was completed by the painting of the plaster-covered pillars with red, white and blue spirals reaching from floor to ceiling. The room was furnished as others of its kind with cushions and carpets, but the coffee-hearth was larger than any I saw at Riyadh, and in it stood nine coffee-pots, one of which was certainly the largest I have ever seen.

Curiously unlike his elder brother in face and figure, Muhammad takes no part, or at any rate no active part, in the politics or administration of the country and leads to a great extent the retired life of a country gentleman, living now in his gardens in the southern part of the oasis—the 'Ataiqiyya garden, I think, belongs to him—now on an estate he had then recently acquired in the neighbourhood of Dhruma and only seldom amid the bustle and turmoil of the capital. I found him somewhat taciturn and abrupt in his manner and had to do most of the talking myself, but once I attempted to draw him out of his silence by relapsing into silence myself. "What do you think of the Sharif?" he suddenly blurted out, and, without waiting for a reply, he expressed his own opinion with decisive terseness: "*Mukhabbal*—crazy—there is no good in him." He went on to tell me of the pilgrimage of the year before, when he had led 17,000—so he said—*Najdis* through the gates of Mecca, of which, however, he had seen but little, as, with the exception of a formal visit to the Sharif and the prescribed excursions to the spots, where the various rites of the pilgrimage took place, he had seldom left his own apartments. Nevertheless, he was anxious to perform a second pilgrimage as soon as Ibn Sa'ud would permit him to do so—if possible by sea in company with his father, who would now never be able to stand the fatigues of the long land journey. I promised that his wish would receive the consideration of the British authorities whenever he might desire to carry it out.

Such were the cadets of the house of ʻAbdulrahman, widely dissimilar characters, but each with a personality of his own—the yeoman, the hermit and the man of letters, with each of whom I would fain have cultivated closer personal relations than it was possible to do in the atmosphere of suspicion and restraint that pervaded the life of the *Wahhabi* capital. Apart from Ibn Saʻud's own dominating personality and the social inquisition, which exercised a restraining influence on liberty of association with an infidel—factors sufficient in themselves to impose on the leaders of society a certain circumspectness in their relations and conversation with me—I always felt at every turn the presence of a skeleton in the cupboard—the skeleton of the nightmare history of the royal line. Neither Ibn Saʻud nor the members of his family could ever forget the past which might repeat itself at any moment in the future. Amid the uncertainties of Arab politics and prejudices Ibn Saʻud alone—a single human life—stood between order and chaos. He stood there not as of right but by reason of the virtue that was in him, and he never forgot that his throne was set in the crater of a volcano amid all the paraphernalia of combustion. His task was to control the very forces, the failure to control which had wrecked his predecessors, and on his success or failure depends not only his own throne, but the future of the whole country. In these circumstances he has earned the reputation of striking quick and hard at the root of every potential trouble, and it is not unnatural that his brothers—by the accident of birth the potential centres of disturbance—shudder at the very thought of incurring his suspicion or displeasure and, for the peace of their own minds, have surrendered much of the liberty of thought and conduct, which is the outstanding characteristic of Arab society. They told me—and I regret deeply that I never had the privilege of meeting him —that Saʻd, the victim of his own folly and treachery in the campaign against the ʻAjman, was the very twin in character and to some extent in appearance of Ibn Saʻud ; and the love that united them was as the love of Saul and Jonathan.

While, however, political considerations militated to some extent against my free intercourse with the brothers of Ibn Sa'ud, there was no such bar to the development of friendly relations with one, who was like myself an honoured guest at the *Wahhabi* court and who was always treated by his host with a degree of consideration, which seemed to me to mark him out, in the event of certain developments in Central Arabia, as the future Viceroy of Jabal Shammar. This was Faisal ibn Rashid, a man of middle age and medium stature with a cheerful countenance slightly inclined to cunning and easy courtly manners, reminiscent, if one may judge by hearsay, of Haïl society in general, as his soft voice and wonderfully clear enunciation were of the speech of Jabal Shammar, which, almost classical in its purity, is distinguished by the frequent use of the *Tanwin*, nearly obsolete elsewhere, and by the complete absence of the asperity, which marks the diction of the full-throated denizens of 'Aridh, and of the characteristic lisp, which gives an air of preciosity to the speech of the Mutair. Tami, who accompanied me on my visit to Faisal, was always held up to me as a model of Shammar diction and of the natural eloquence which distinguishes that tribe among its fellows; his poetic compositions and ready flow of words in ordinary conversation always seemed to me deserving of the highest praise for the beauty of his utterance.

Faisal received me with the greatest cordiality and entertained me over his coffee cups—he insisted on my drinking before him—with anecdotes from the bloody history of the Rashid dynasty. In the days of the great *Wahhabi* domination over all Arabia, Haïl and the Shammar country acknowledged the sway of Sa'ud the Great and his successors, and were administered by an *Amir* appointed from Riyadh from among the senior members of the premier section of the Shammar—the 'Ali branch of the Ja'far subsection of the 'Abda. As time went on and the *Wahhabi* power suffered a temporary eclipse at the hands of the Turks, the local authority at Haïl, nominally subject now to the Turks and now to the Sa'ud dynasty as these alternated in the ascendancy, became in practice largely independent of exterior control, and, so far as the obscure details of Arabian history may be reconstructed, it would seem that during the third decade of the eighteenth century, when Turki ibn Sa'ud recovered the throne of his ancestors from the usurping Turks, the house of 'Ali was virtually independent at Haïl. Its title to rule in Jabal Shammar was, however, ever in dispute with a rival branch of the same subsection, the Rashid, whose senior representative, 'Abdullah ibn Rashid, took service under Turki, the nominal liege-lord of Haïl, and in due course found himself in a position to turn the tables on his cousins and rivals. Being asked by Turki to name his own reward for a signal act of service to the *Wahhabi* cause, he demanded the *Amirate* of his native city for himself and his heirs to the exclusion of the house of 'Ali for ever. The petition was granted and 'Abdullah was duly installed as Viceroy of Hail under the suzerainty of Turki, but in course of time, encouraged by the long warfare between the Turks and the *Wahhabi* rulers and the precariousness of the latter's tenure at Riyadh, he threw off all semblance of dependence and founded the royal house of Jabal Shammar, which under the surname of Ibn Rashid, has ruled Haïl without interruption since that time and for a period extended its sway over the greater part of the *Wahhabi* dominions. 'Abdullah was gathered to his fathers in the fulness of time, leaving a sufficiency of sons to ensure the succession to the throne he had created in the direct line of descent from himself; but he left also a brother, 'Ubaid, himself an unsuccessful aspirant to royal honours and the founder of a line of pretenders, whose ambitions have helped to drench Haïl with royal blood. Between 'Abdullah and his great-grandson, Sa'ud, who now rules at Haïl,[1] no fewer than eight sovereigns have sat on the throne, and of them all have died a violent death except one—the greatest of them all—Muhammad ibn Rashid, one of the greatest men that Arabia has ever produced. It was in his time that Doughty visited Haïl, and to those who would know something of the history of Northern Central Arabia up to that date and

[1] Sa'ud has maintained the reputation of his house by being assassinated recently (about April, 1920) at the age of about twenty-one, by 'Abdullah ibn Mit'ab, himself a youth in his teens, and a cousin of his victim.

would understand how the third son of ʿAbdullah—whose "bird-like looks are like the looks of one survived out of much disease of the world—and what likelihood was there formerly that he should ever be the Emir?"—came to occupy the throne of Haïl, I can offer no better counsel than to read the pregnant pages, in which he tells the story that was told him of the *Tragedies in the House of Ibn Rashid*.[1] Suffice it to say here that ʿAbdullah was succeeded by his eldest son, Talal, who died by his own hand rather than face the prospect of slow exhaustion by an incurable disease and was succeeded by his second brother Mitʿab. Two years later the sons of Talal, Bandar and Badr, conspired to slay their uncle, and, the deed being successfully accomplished by the shooting of the monarch as he sat in public assembly, Bandar, then a lad of nineteen, ascended the throne. He might have ruled in peace to the end of his natural life had he not by folly and unreasoning suspicion driven his surviving uncle, Muhammad, the third son of ʿAbdullah, to cut it short by the assassin's knife. Thus came Muhammad to sit on a throne never designed for his occupation, and "never was the government, they say, in more sufficient handling." His reign was long and prosperous and, himself denied offspring by an unkind fate, he left on his death in 1890 to his brother Mitʿab's son, ʿAbdulʿaziz, a vast, well-ordered empire, which embraced the whole of Central Arabia even to Wadi Dawasir in the south. ʿAbdulʿaziz was not a man of the same calibre as his predecessor, but his namesake and eventual conqueror was yet but a child in exile, and Najd had yet a decade to wait for its deliverance from a foreign yoke. In 1901 ʿAbdulʿaziz ibn Saʿud wrested Riyadh from the usurper, and during the next few years extended his sway slowly but surely over the territories of his ancestors until in 1906 the rival forces arrayed themselves for a final ordeal by battle over against the palm-groves of Raudhat al Muhanna in the Qasim. The troops of ʿAbdulʿaziz ibn Rashid were routed, the prince himself was slain and, when the news was brought by fleeing horsemen to Haïl, his young sons, Mitʿab,

[1] C. M. D. vol. ii. pp. 13 *et seq.* W. S. Blunt also visited Haïl about the same time (1879).

Mish'al and Muhammad, were seized and put to death by Sultan ibn Hamud, who ascended the vacant throne, the first of the house of 'Ubaid to do so. The murderer was himself murdered and succeeded by his younger brother, Sa'ud, who in his turn but two years later was laid low by assassins conspiring under the direction of Hamud ibn Subhan[1] to restore the throne to the direct line of 'Abdullah, whose sole survivor, Sa'ud, the son of 'Abdul'aziz and the present ruler of Haïl, was then but a child. Hamud, who was the brother of the child's mother and the husband of his elder sister, assumed the direction of affairs as regent on behalf of his *protégé*, and was succeeded in that post on his death by a cousin, Zamil ibn Subhan, who was murdered with other members of the family in 1914.

Such in brief is the story of the Rashid dynasty. Faisal, who told it to me, was one of the many sons of Hamud ibn 'Ubaid and, therefore, the brother of the homicide rulers, Sultan and Sa'ud,[2] younger than the former and older than the latter. On their assassination by the avengers of the tragedy of 1906 he and the remnants of the 'Ubaid line, including his first cousin and half-brother, Dhari ibn Fahad, saved their lives by flight. Faisal and Dhari, sons of the same mother by different fathers, themselves half-brothers, spent the first years of their exile at Jauf before settling at Riyadh, whence Dhari had betaken himself in the year preceding my visit to Mecca, there to live, as he was then doing, under the protection of the Sharif. Faisal, the senior surviving representative of the house of 'Ubaid, appeared to be very content to live a life of ease and luxury at the court of Ibn Sa'ud, until such time as circumstances might raise him to the not-altogether-to-be-envied position of ruler of Haïl. His memory goes back to the days of Muhammad, when as a boy he met Huber on his travels ; and he remembers too, more recently, seeing Messrs. Butler and Aylmer during the year he sojourned at Jauf. He had visited at various times Mecca, Basra, Khamisiyya and Samawa, but had never been beyond the limits of Arabia nor ever seen the sea. His only son at this time was a boy called Hamud. Of Dhari I know little or nothing except that he regards

[1] *Vide* p. 249 *supra*. [2] All three were by different mothers.

himself vaguely as the Sharif's nominee for the *Amirate* of Haïl should that post ever be, as he hopes, in his gift.

Among the company assembled in Faisal's parlour I made the acquaintance of an attractive youth of eighteen, Faisal al Jabar, who with his elder brother, Sultan, the two being the last suvivors of a collateral branch of the house of Rashid known as Al Jabar, appears to have come to Riyadh with his father and other members of the family at about the same time as Faisal and Dhari and for the same reasons. He did not take a prominent part in the conversation, but, as he rose to leave the assembly, he stopped before me to beg me to come on afterwards to drink coffee at his house—an invitation which, needless to say, I gladly accepted, and in response to which I shortly afterwards made my way to the Jabar mansion. I was there very cordially welcomed both by Faisal and Sultan, a pleasing young man of about twenty-three, and entertained with coffee and much talk, the conversation turning largely on the battle of Jarrab,[1] in which both had taken part, Faisal being badly wounded, while their father and elder brother, ʿAbdulrahman, had been killed. The whole family had served with Ibn Saʿud's cavalry which had carried the day against the mounted troops of Ibn Rashid, only to find that the latter's infantry, assisted by the treacherous desertion of the ʿAjman contingent at a critical moment in the battle, had routed Ibn Saʿud's infantry and captured his camp and stores. It was on this occasion that Captain Shakespear, the British representative with Ibn Saʿud, lost his life, largely, said Faisal, because he had insisted on going right up to the infantry line in spite of all warnings of the danger he incurred by so doing. But Faisal was not an eye-witness of the occurrence, and I was fortunately able to procure for the satisfaction of Shakespear's family somewhat fuller and more circumstantial details of the manner in which that very gallant officer came by his death—an irreparable loss to his country and to his great friend, Ibn Saʿud,—from the lips of one who was actually with him at the time, Husain, a master gunner in the *Wahhabi* forces. "When Ibn Sa'ud raised his standard," so ran his story of the events

[1] January, 1915.

of January, 1915, " to go forth against Ibn Rashid, we had but one gun of which I was in charge. We arrived in the vicinity of Jarrab, and the army was divided into two sections, Ibn Sa'ud in person leading out the whole of the cavalry to seek out the enemy who was reported to be near at hand, while the infantry, leaving the camels and baggage in the camp, marched out on a different course along the *Sha'ib*. With my one gun I accompanied the latter and with me was Skaishpeer "—such is the common pronunciation of a name held in high honour in Arabia—" who had been begged by Ibn Sa'ud the night before to betake himself to Zilfi, seeing that the issue of the morrow's battle was so uncertain, but had resolutely declined to do so and insisted on accompanying us. Of a sudden our scouts found the enemy advancing towards us and I immediately dragged my one gun to a commanding position whence to open fire. Without delay I began firing while Skaishpeer stood up on a little eminence watching the enemy through his glasses and telling me where to aim. I shouted at him not to expose himself and begged him to take off his *topi*—for he was dressed not as us but in his British uniform—but he heeded me not and went on telling me where to shoot. Before long he was struck in the thigh by a rifle-bullet, but, unable as he was to move, he went on with his work directing my fire until the opposing forces met at close quarters. Then I stopped firing and the two of us sat down to watch the battle. In a short while I noticed that our force was being pushed back. 'Come,' I said to him, 'it is finished; let us escape by the *Sha'ib*'; and with that I detached the removable parts of the gun and, burying them in the sand, started off in the direction I had indicated; he called out something about going in a different direction, but I waited not for our people were running for their lives." Well in the van of the rout Husain, looking back, saw the enemy camelry charging down upon Shakespear, who, wounded as he was, stood up to receive them and fell fighting; he saw no more. Meanwhile Ibn Sa'ud's cavalry had driven the enemy cavalry before them, but the 'Ajman, seeing how it fared with the infantry, deserted to pillage the camp and the battle was lost; Ibn Sa'ud claimed a victory by reason of his cavalry success, but the honours clearly rested with the enemy, who was, however, not in a strong enough position to court a further trial and retired with the booty of the plundered camp. "Two months later," said Husain, "I went back to recover the buried parts of the gun and found the battlefield strewn with the corpses of friend and foe, left as they had fallen, and among them I saw Skaishpeer *chinna inqatil ams*—as though he had been killed but yesterday; by his side lay a *Shammari*, and close by a camel, and, but a little way off, one of the *Badu* of our side. *Wallah!* they say that no less than 3000 men fell in that battle." This estimate of losses was, of course, greatly exaggerated, and it is probable that the total casualties on both sides did not exceed 300, but, judged by its results, the battle of Jarrab was one of the decisive battles of the Arabian theatre of war, and the death of Shakespear, followed as it was by the abandonment of all attempts to use Ibn Saʿud for the furtherance of our campaign against the Turks, put an end once and for all to the hopes of Arab co-operation in the war, which were not to be revived until eighteen months had elapsed, and were then revived in a different quarter with such remarkable results. It was left to Lawrence and the army of the Hijaz to accomplish what in other circumstances—with a little better luck, and a little more imagination on the part of the authorities responsible for the conduct of the Mesopotamian campaign—might have been accomplished by Ibn Saʿud and Shakespear. Under the star-spangled vault of the Arabian sky he lies as he fell on the field of Jarrab—a true friend of the Arabs as every Arab knows in Central Arabia—and some day, perchance, if a scheme recently initiated by his family proves to be practicable, the memory of his sacrifice may be perpetuated on the scene of his last endeavour by the simplest and best of monuments, a well in Desert Arabia—*ἄριστον μὲν ὕδωρ*.

END OF VOL. I

Printed in Great Britain by R. & R. CLARK, LIMITED, *Edinburgh*.